Accommodating National Identity

New Approaches in International and Domestic Law

Accommodating National Identity

New Approaches in International and Domestic Law

Edited by
Stephen Tierney

KLUWER LAW INTERNATIONAL
THE HAGUE – LONDON – BOSTON

Published by:
Kluwer law International
P.O. Box 85889, 2508 CN The Hague, The Netherlands
sales@kli.wkap.nl
http://www.kluwerlaw.com

Sold and Distributed in North, Central and South America by:
Kluwer Law International
675 Massachusetts Avenue, Cambridge, MA 02139, U.S.A

Sold and Distributed in all other countries by:
Kluwer Law International
Distribution Centre, P.O. Box 322, 3300 AH Dordrecht, The Netherlands

Library of Congress Cataloging-in-Publication Data is available

Printed on acid-free paper

ISBN 90 411 1400 9
© 2000 Kluwer Law International

Kluwer Law International incorporates the publishing programmes
of Graham & Trotman Ltd, Kluwer Law and Taxation Publishers
and Martinus Nijhoff Publishers

Printed and bound in Great Britain by Antony Rowe Limited.

Contents

National Identity:
the Territorial Question in International and Domestic Law

Concluding Remarks
Javaid Rehman

——

Introduction

Stephen Tierney

The origins of nationalism, the most enduring political phenomenon of the modern era, are often traced to the revolutionary upheavals of the eighteenth century, particularly in France. Although expressions of nationalism may have appeared sporadically in medieval Europe,[1] there is general agreement that its star rose "bright and clear in late eighteenth-century France and America."[2] In the two hundred years since, nationalism has fallen prey to a range of political movements which in turn have imbued the term with a variety of meanings both positive and negative. The contrast between the nationalism of the liberation movements of colonised Africa and the nationalism of Nazi Germany is a trite example, but it is one which goes some way to highlight the extremities encompassed by the schizophrenic nature of nationalism as an ideology, or, more appropriately, as a range of ideologies. The contrasting connotations which are variously attributed to nationalism have often been expressed as the dichotomy between romantic nationalism and civic nationalism: the former a reactionary, exclusivist cult of an ethnic (and typically majority) group, the latter a progressive, liberal and inclusive vision of a shared national identity based upon common political values and largely blind to biological differences such as race, colour and ethnicity. The incidence of nationalist movements which embody either model in a 'pure' form may be uncommon, but using these caricatures as the end-points on a scale may be helpful in the task of identifying which national movements most closely approximate to one or other tradition.

The fact that nationalism became the declared ideology of widely differing political movements has served only to intensify disagreement amongst those who seek to understand why and how nationalism developed. For many, nationalism is simply a modernist construct which emerged to fill the political vacuums which followed in the wake of the political revolutions of America and France and the macro-economic revolution of industrialisation, upheavals which required the establishment of a strong nation-state for their consolidation. Taking the industrial revolution as an example, the economies of scale resulting from the development of industrial capitalism made it imperative to build stronger political units within which processes such as, urbanisation; division of labour; the legal facilitation of capital growth; and the provision of expanded market places could be fostered. An ideology was in turn

---

[1]   Seton-Watson 1977: 6-8.
[2]   Smith 1998: 1 (see also p.17). Montserrat Guibernau also identifies nationalism as "an ideology closely related to the rise of the nation-state and bound up with ideas about popular sovereignty and democracy brought about by the French and American Revolutions." Guibernau 1996: 3.

Stephen Tierney (ed.), *Accommodating National Identity: New Approaches in International and Domestic Law, 1–10*
© 2000 *Kluwer Law International. Printed in Great Britain.*

required to build loyalty to these new political units and the ideology of state loyalty, the essential device in the inculcation of a new patriotism, was nationalism.[3] For others, who have been termed by Anthony Smith perennialists and primordialists,[4] the roots of nationalism lie in the ancient attachments of peoples. There are significant differences of approach between and amongst perennialists and primordialists but typically this tradition holds that nations are a natural and potent focus of human loyalty and that, accordingly, nationalist movements simply act as the expression of these ingrained identities rather than as the catalyst for their generation. These identities in turn originate from biological[5] or cultural[6] factors (or combinations of both[7]) and are not, as many classical modernists assert, materially determined constructs of the industrial age.

Anthony Smith eschews the polarised visions of both classical modernism and perennialism/primordialism. In an elaborately worked theory of nationalism he accepts that the material conditions of modernity played a dramatic role in the shaping of contemporary national identities but, like the perennialists, he also suggests that central to a fuller understanding of national identity is an appreciation of the resilience of older attachments which have endured in the process of identity formation within ethnic groups (or 'ethnies' as he would have it): 'we need to grasp the flawed nature of modernist theories such as Gellner's which, for all their perceptive originality, fail to account for the historical depth and spatial reach of the ties that underpin modern nations because they have no theory of ethnicity and its relationship to modern nationalism.'[8] For Smith the historical dynamics of national identity are more complex than the grand narratives of either the modernist or primordialist/ perennialist accounts would suggest. For him the origins and development of national identity are located in a complicated fusion of modernist ideology and ancient ethnic and social ties, and in order to understand this complexity we must turn to 'an historical sociology of nations and nationalism.'[9] The outcome of such a study leaves Smith assured of the pre-eminent importance of the nation as a focus of identity: 'To date, we cannot discern a serious rival to the nation for the affections and loyalties of most human beings.'[10]

The intensity of the debate on the development of both nationalism and national identity belies the fact that it is a debate which has in many ways been played out only relatively recently. It is perhaps surprising that, despite the grip which it has

---

[3]   Ernest Gellner offers the classic account which views the development of nations and nationalism as the by-product of the modern, industrial era. (Gellner 1964). Gellner's theory has since been substantially modified but retains at its core a strongly functionalist vision of nationhood (Gellner 1983). Following the publication of Gellner's seminal work *Thought and Change* there have appeared numerous constructivist analyses of nations and nationalism which together have been classified as the 'classical modernist' school (Smith 1998: 11-16).

[4]   Smith 1998: ch.7.

[5]   van den Berghe 1978.

[6]   Geertz 1973.

[7]   For a discussion of 'primordial and perennial' theories of nationalism see Smith 1998: ch.7.

[8]   Smith 1998: 46.

[9]   Smith 1998: 190. To trace the development of Smith's theory see, *inter alia*, Smith: 1971 (2nd ed., 1983); 1986; 1991; 1995.

[10]   Smith 1998: 195.

had over the passing 'ages'[11] of the post-enlightenment period, nationalism developed as a subject of rigorous study by social scientists only in this century and more specifically in the post-war period.[12] Since then, however, its importance to the development of the modern world has been scrutinised at length, with nationalism being elevated on occasion to dizzying heights of importance. Tom Nairn, for example, mirrors the prioritisation which Smith has accredited to nationalism as the pre-eminent topic of humanistic and social scientific study. In his most recent work he suggests that "the true subject of modern philosophy might be, not industrialisation... but its immensely complex and variegated aftershock - nationalism."[13]

It is difficult to contest that nationalism and national identity as topics of study deserve this level of prioritisation when in the post-modern era nationalist political movements continue to mount real-world challenges to the existing state system of international relations with ever more complex agendas and ever more vociferous claims. The exponential growth of literature on nationalism in recent decades reflects a series of political developments since World War II each of which has been characterised by the emergence of nationalist movements of different types. Although in many ways diverse, these movements share in common demands for greater accommodation of the multifarious national or ethnic identities which lie at their root.

It is possible to identify at least three periods since the end of the Second World War where the political rhetoric of nationalism has been used as the rallying call of radically different political processes in advancing arguments for the realignment of political and constitutional structures. First came the decolonisation process of the 1950s and 1960s when the subjugated peoples of Africa and Asia sought to replace European empires with new 'nations'. Secondly, in the late 1960s it was the turn of disaffected minorities in the industrialised countries of the Western world who would turn to nationalism: in the multi-national or multi-ethnic states of the UK, Canada and Spain amongst others, groups such as the Scots, the Welsh, Quebecois, Basques and Catalans voiced demands for greater accommodation of their distinctive identities.[14] Thirdly, the collapse of bureaucratic socialism in Eastern Europe led to the emergence of nationalism both among minority groups in multi-national states and also within the majority populations themselves. This cocktail was to prove particularly dangerous given the often conflicting political goals of minority and majority groups within one state. Disenfranchised minorities sought a realignment of state borders, either through secession or irredentism, while majority groups became the target of nationalist politicians who urged consolidation of the state and the prioritisation of the dominant ethnic group. This prioritisation would often be at

---

[11] Hobsbawm 1962; 1975; 1987; 1994. See also Hobsbawm 1990.
[12] In addition to those works otherwise cited in this introductory chapter, seminal treatments of the issues of nations and nationalism include: Brass 1991; Breuilly 1993; Deutsch 1966; Eriksen 1993; Kedourie 1960; Seton-Watson 1965.
[13] Nairn 1997: 1, and see also p.17.
[14] Attempts to explain the development of these 'neo-nationalist' movements have been made by Nairn 1977 and Hechter 1975.

the expense of minorities and this chauvinistic dynamic often resulted in 'romantic' nationalism of the most crudely exclusivist type. The internecine wars in the former Yugoslavia and the Russian conflict in Chechnya represent this phenomenon to differing degrees.

Bloody conflicts of this kind have served to re-focus attention on nationalism and national identity as scholars examine the diverse upsurges in nationalist sentiment since 1945 and attempt to determine how, if at all, they are linked through the national rights claims they commonly assert. Interest and analysis has been generated not only from those scholars seeking to understand the origins, nature and resilience of national identity and nationalism as social phenomenon and ideology respectively, but also from political and moral philosophers who grapple with the normative issues raised by nationalist demands.[15]

These writers are moving the debate from an empirical attempt to understand the phenomenon of nations and nationalism to an ethical discussion of how the political demands nationalism generates ought to be received.[16] On one level descriptive and prescriptive accounts of nationalism cannot be discretely compartmentalised. For example, whether a particular model of nationalism accords more with the romantic than the civic model or *vice versa* will necessarily impact upon the moral legitimacy of its political aspirations. Nonetheless, in asking how nationalism and national identity ought to be accommodated it may be possible, to some extent, to set aside intractable debates on how national identities developed. In considering the political claims of national groups one can simply accept as a social reality that such groups exist (if for no other reason than that a group presents itself as a national group and advances political claims) and that, therefore, they ought to have the right to political accommodation on the same self-determining terms as any other group. To accord such recognition to a national group one might ask first, does a group exist (whether that group be the product of perennial/primordial attachment, voluntary association, social construction or a complex fusion of processes)? Secondly, does the group possess an internal decision-making mechanism which in turn can be tested for its legitimacy against a range of democratic models? And thirdly, through that decision-making mechanism, does the group advance political claims which can be assessed by measuring them against competing interests and rights?

Inevitably the debate on the morality of nationalist claims has been conducted largely on rights-based lines and has resulted in a range of arguments on the moral necessity of self-determination for such groups: for example, there are those who advocate a 'pure' liberal right of secession;[17] others advance justifications for a restricted liberal right of secession, also from a liberal perspective;[18] a number of writers concentrate instead on wider treatments of the issue of self-determination;[19] while the issue has also, inevitably, caught the imagination of communitarian

---

[15] For example, Beran 1984 and 1987; Buchanan 1991; Gauthier 1994; Philpott 1995; Wellman 1995; de-Shalit 1996; Moore 1997.

[16] McKim and McMahon 1997.

[17] Beran 1984; McGee 1992.

[18] Buchanan 1991.

[19] Philpott 1995; de-Shalit 1996; Moore 1997.

writers.[20] The problem which a number of writers identify is in attempting to reconcile *prima facie* justifications for self-determination (whether as secession or otherwise) with rival rights and interests, be they strategic (the interest of the international community in stability); pragmatic (the interests of existing states in their continued economic well-being); or more clearly normative (*inter alia*, the interests of majority populations not to have their state destabilised; the interests of internal minority groups within the would-be self-determining unit and the individual rights of those who may suffer within a seceding group which is likely to be illiberal or reactionary).[21]

In this context the theoretical debate over the morality of self-determination and secession has largely been situated within the broader tension of the individual/group rights debate. Liberals, in attempting to take seriously either self-determination or group rights in general, must decide what level of priority they ought to accord these rights claims in the face of conflicting individual rights: in other words how they as liberals can accommodate collective rights claims when that accommodation may, directly or indirectly, threaten to undermine rights cherished within the liberal project. The traditional liberal's attachment to methodological individualism may be over-exaggerated and unfairly caricatured by critics,[22] but it remains true that the liberal rights framework does, except perhaps at the margins ventured to by the likes of Kymlicka,[23] accord lexical and normative precedence to the individual, over the group, as rights-bearer. This makes the task of the liberal who seeks to accommodate group rights especially difficult and in this task he may strain the methodological and normative underpinnings of the liberal project to breaking-point.

The attention which nationalism and national identity have received from social scientists and moral philosophers begs the question why the debates generated by the search for the sociological roots and normative implications of national identity have generally not featured in discussions on the law of self-determination. This is all the more surprising when it is considered that the political agenda of nationalist movements usually centres around demands either for enhanced recognition under international law or for accommodation of the group's distinctiveness through amended domestic constitutional structures. In particular, it is the term self-determination, a phrase pregnant with legal meaning, which encapsulates many collective claims to greater political and constitutional accommodation of ethnic and national difference. It was self-determination which became the mantra of the nationalist politician in each of the three post-1945 upsurges in nationalist sentiment, and in large part the reason for this was the term's legal significance. Now recognised by international law as a 'right of all peoples',[24] self-determination has become the pre-eminent device with which national and ethnic groups seek, through international law, to legitimise their political claims.

---

[20] Addis 1992.
[21] Kymlicka 1995 (*The Rights of Minority Cultures*).
[22] Buchanan 1989.
[23] Kymlicka 1995 (*Multicultural citizenship*).
[24] International Covenant on Civil and Political Rights, Article 1; International Covenant on Economic, Social and Cultural Rights, Article 1.

6

Stephen Tierney

The proliferation of ever more diverse self-determination claims has served to heighten the difficulties lawyers face in attempting to concretise the meaning of a term which has been politicised and distorted perhaps more than any other international legal right or principle. Certainly there is no shortage of references to self-determination in international legal instruments since 1945, beginning most notably with the UN Charter itself,[25] but still international law has difficulty in responding coherently to conflicts resulting from, or in, nationalist claims. The collapse of Yugoslavia; the war in Kosovo; and the conflict in Chechnya highlight the debilitating effect of this incoherence. Despite both its appearance in numerous international legal instruments, and the fact that it is widely accorded the rarefied status of jus cogens,[26] the scope of application of self-determination remains very unclear and the development of its meaning has been, since the end of the Second World War, riddled with inconsistencies, both in terms of the internal contradictions of the international instruments in which it has been situated, and also in respect of state practice.

The lack of clarity which surrounds self-determination as a legal right has encouraged the view that its content is essentially political, that it constitutes merely a general commitment to democratic ideals which does not lend itself to detailed legal application.[27] Differences of opinion persist on the subject fuelled by the fact that different instruments point in varying, and at times conflicting, directions as to the meaning, status and scope of the principle, all of which add to the general contention and confusion surrounding it. This problem is expressed by Deborah Cass by borrowing H.L.A. Hart's distinction between the 'core' meaning of a legal concept and its 'penumbra of uncertainty'. "The point has been reached" she writes, "where.... the "penumbra of uncertainty" surrounding the concept of self-determination is so pronounced that it obscures the term's "core of settled meaning."[28]

The central role played by the term self-determination in the formulation of nationalist demands requires that any holistic treatment of nationalism must take seriously this legal dimension. At the same time the confusion surrounding self-determination suggests that those with an interest in developing the meaning of self-determination as a legal right should inform themselves first, of the work being done by social scientists in their attempt to locate the origins of national identity, and secondly, of the efforts of theorists to engage with the moral issues arising from the rights claims of ethnic or national groups. In the context of ever-recurring nationalist crises, it seems detrimental to prospects of their successful resolution that engagement by lawyers with the empirical and ethical studies of national identity and nationalism has hitherto been negligible. The trend within the legal academy has been to address the issue of self-determination by detailed forensic analysis of

---

[25] Articles 1 and 55.
[26] Cassese 1995: 133-140.
[27] Eisner 1992: 413.
[28] "Current international law theory regarding self-determination is in a state of uncertainty and confusion. It is inconsistent within itself, and it does not accord with state practice." Cass 1992: 21-22. See also 22-23.

the international legal instruments which make reference to it. The preference for textual analysis over an interdisciplinary search for the substance and validity of nationalist claims has left a significant gap between, on the one hand, the work of social scientists and philosophers who grapple with the empirical and normative manifestations of national identity, and, on the other hand, international lawyers who address the 'right of all peoples to self-determination' simply in terms of the internal structures of the conventions and declarations in which the right appears.[29]

The enormous complexity of ongoing nationalist disputes would seem to demand a more sophisticated engagement by lawyers with the political and moral justifications which are inextricably linked in most nationalist claims to better legal recognition. Such an interdisciplinary approach may provide important instruction both for those searching for a more coherent application of the international law of self-determination, and for those who seek to resolve nationalist disputes within the domestic constitutional arrangements of a particular nation-state. Attempting to find a proper accommodation of ethnic and national group claims therefore challenges the imagination of the law and of those who shape and practise it to take nationalist aspirations seriously whilst at the same time understanding and giving appropriate weight through often complex balancing exercises to interests which compete with nationalist agendas. The purpose of this book is to attempt to assess the extent to which law, at both international and municipal levels, is actively engaging with these difficulties and is capable of responding to the challenges they present.

The idea for this collection of essays emerged from a conference entitled 'Accommodating National Identity: New Approaches in International and Domestic Law', which was held in London, in November, 1998. In particular, the intention was to combine case studies from both international law and the constitutional systems of multinational states with a view to examining the degree to which a process of cross-fertilisation is taking place between the two levels of legal order and whether each might offer lessons to the other.

The issue of nationalism presents challenges not simply for international law and international relations. It also raises complex political and legal issues for the operation of the domestic bodies politic of states containing a national minority or minorities. Accordingly, this volume brings together international lawyers with their perspectives on how the international community has coped with contemporary cases of nationalist crisis, in particular those resulting from the collapse of Yugoslavia (McGoldrick; Tierney), and ongoing issues of minority nationalism in Asia (Ali) and Eastern Europe (Bowring; Pogany); and constitutional lawyers from states which are attempting to facilitate the political expression of national identity through developments in federalism, devolution, and the protection of minority rights (Oliver; Munro; Thompson).

It is hoped that this combined approach will provide mutually beneficial insights into how lawyers from different fields address the complex issue of using legal mechanisms to accommodate or control the political aspirations associated with national identity in four key areas: the internationalisation of constitutional structures;

---

[29] This point is made by Bill Bowring in his chapter.

the construction of new constitutions; the protection of minority rights both domestically and internationally; and in the complex relationship between national identity and territory at both international and domestic levels. In particular, the aim is to highlight the increased level of interaction between international and constitutional legal norms in these areas. This process is evidenced, for example, in the rights claims advanced by both the Gypsy/Roma peoples of Eastern and Central Europe (Pogany) and by ethnic minorities in Pakistan (Ali). These claims are made against both the constitutional structures of the states concerned and the supranational regime of minority rights protection which exists at international law.

Another manifestation of this development is to be found in the new and forward-looking constitutional models which embrace international legal norms within developing domestic structures, for example, the recently established or currently emerging constitutional systems in Bosnia and Herzegovina (McGoldrick); Northern Ireland (Thompson)[30] and Nepal (Subedi). The ongoing search for a solution to the especially difficult Western Saharan situation also serves to highlight the complex range of competing interests and claims which can challenge legal mechanisms as they attempt to resolve seemingly intractable nationalist issues (Castellino).

The process by which norms can be transferred between international and domestic legal systems was recently and dramatically enhanced by the imaginative approach of the Canadian Supreme Court, which, in its decision last year in the Secession Reference,[31] attempted to inter-weave the international legal right of self-determination with principles of Canadian constitutional law in formulating its judgment on the complex legal status of Quebec (Oliver). The ramifications of this judgment for other systems undergoing constitutional reconstruction, for example Scotland (Munro) and Bosnia and Herzegovina (McGoldrick) remain to be seen. Similarly, the prospect of domestic courts taking greater cognisance of the work of international tribunals in this field, such as the Arbitration Commission's opinions on recognition of the former Yugoslav Republics[32] and the ICJ's decision in the Western Sahara case (Castellino), are enhanced by the Canadian approach.[33]

Whatever its sociological origins, national identity has survived the competing ideological and material pressures of international socialism and transnational capitalism to remain a talismanic focus for identity as the world enters a new century. National and ethnic identities which were for so long viewed as reactionary forces standing in the way of progressive internationalism, are now enjoying a renaissance in terms of political acceptability, and are gaining stature as the legitimate voices of dispossessed sub-state groups struggling to be heard in an increasingly interdependent world.

---

[30] It should be noted that the complex arrangements for the devolved governance of Northern Ireland agreed upon in the Belfast Agreement of 10 April 1998 and described in detail by Brian Thompson in his chapter were suspended by the UK Secretary of State for Northern Ireland, Peter Mandelson on 11 February 2000 in light of an impasse over the issue of decommissioning of paramilitary arms. The institutions of government were, however, revived on 30 May, 2000.

[31] *Reference re Secession of Quebec* [1998] 2 S.C.R. 217.

[32] Conference on Yugoslavia Arbitration Commission: Opinions on Questions Arising from the Dissolution of Yugoslavia, (1992) 31 ILM 1488.

[33] The Western Sahara case has already been given prominent consideration by the Australian High Court in its consideration of the land claims of aboriginals, Mabo and others v Queensland (No. 2) (1992) 175 CLR 1 F.C. 92/014.

It seems that law, both domestic and international, has until recently been slow to respond to these shifting political realities. This collection seeks to explore to what extent we are witnessing within legal mechanisms a flexible re-engagement with, and accommodation of, the aspirations of national and ethnic groups. In this respect, the essays collected here tend to suggest that a heightened level of fluidity in the interaction and exchange of normative standards now exists in the relationship between international and domestic law, as both systems confront the challenge which national identity continues to constitute. If this process does indeed mark a renewed preparedness on the part of legal systems to expand imaginatively to meet the ever-evolving challenges which nations and nationalism continue to posit, the stage is set for an ongoing process of development in this complex and troubled area.

Stephen Tierney

REFERENCES

Addis, A. (1992). Individualism, communitarianism, and the rights of ethnic minorities, *Notre Dame Law Review*, 67: 615-76

Beran, H. (1984). A Liberal Theory of Secession, *Political Studies* 32: 21-31

Beran, H. (1987). *The Consent Theory of Political Obligation*, London: Croom Helm Publishers

Brass, P. (1991). *Ethnicity and Nationalism: theory and comparison*, London: Sage

Breuilly, J. (1993). 2nd ed., *Nationalism and the State*, Manchester: Manchester University Press

Buchanan, A. (1991). *Secession: The Morality of Political Divorce from Fort Sumter to Lithuania and Quebec*, Boulder, Col.: Westview Press

Buchanan, A. (1989). Assessing the Communitarian Critique of Liberalism, *Ethics* 852

Cass, D. Z. (1992). Re-thinking Self-Determination: A Critical Analysis of International Law Theories, *Syracuse Journal of International Law and Commerce* 18: 21-40

Cassese, A. (1995). *Self Determination of Peoples A Legal Appraisal.* Cambridge: University Press

de-Shalit, A. (1996). National Self-Determination: Political, not Cultural, *Political Studies* 44: 906-920

Deutsch, K (1966). 2nd ed., *Nationalism and Social Communication*, New York: MIT Press

Eisner, M. (1992). A procedural model for the resolution of secessionist disputes, *Harvard International Law Journal* 33: 407-425

Eriksen, T. (1993). *Ethnicity and Nationalism: anthropological perspectives*, London: Pluto Press

Gauthier, D. (1994). Breaking Up: An Essay on Secession, *Canadian Journal of Philosophy* 24: 357-72

Geertz, C. (1973). *The Interpretation of Cultures*, London: Fontana

Gellner, E. (1964). *Thought and Change*, London: Weidenfeld and Nicolson

Gellner, E.(1983) *Nations and Nationalism*, Oxford: Blackwell

Guibernau, M. (1996). *Nationalisms: The Nation-State and Nationalism in the Twentieth Century*, Cambridge: Polity Press

Hechter, M. (1975). *Internal Colonialism: The Celtic Fringe in British National Development, 1536-1966*, London: Routledge

Hobsbawm, E. J. (1962). *The age of revolution : Europe, 1789-1848*, London: Sphere

Hobsbawm, E. J. (1975). *The age of capital, 1848-1875*, London: Weidenfeld and Nicolson

Hobsbawm, E. J. (1987). *The age of empire 1875-1914*, London: Weidenfeld and Nicolson

Hobsbawm, E. J. (1994). Age of extremes : the short twentieth century, 1914-1991, London: Michael Joseph.

Hobsbawm, E. J. (1990) *Nations and Nationalism since 1780*, Cambridge: Cambridge University Press

Kedourie, E. (1960). *Nationalism*, London: Hutchinson

Kymlicka W. (ed.) (1995). *The Rights of Minority Cultures*, Oxford: Oxford University Press

Kymlicka W. (1995) *Multicultural citizenship : a liberal theory of minority rights*, Oxford: Clarendon Press

McGee, R.W. (1992). A Third Liberal Theory of Secession, *The Liverpool Law Review* XIV: 45.

McKim, R. and McMahon, J. (1997). *The Morality of Nationalism*, Oxford: Oxford University Press

Moore, M. (1997). On National Self-Determination, *Political Studies* 45: 900-13

Nairn, T. (1977). *The Break-up of Britain: Crisis and Neo-Nationalism*, London: New Left Books

Nairn, T. (1997). *Faces of Nationalism: Janus Revisited*, London: Verso

Philpott, D. (1995). In Defense of Self-Determination, *Ethics* 105: 352-385

Seton-Watson, H. (1965), *Nationalism, Old and New*, Sydney: Sydney University Press

Seton-Watson, H. (1977) *Nations and States*, London: Methuen

Smith, A. D. (1971, 2nd ed., 1983). *Theories of Nationalism*, London: Duckworth

Smith, A. D. (1986). *The Ethnic Origins of Nations*, Oxford: Blackwell

Smith, A. D. (1991). *National Identity*, Harmondsworth, Penguin

Smith, A. D. (1995). *Nations and Nationalism in a Global Era*, Cambridge: Polity Press

Smith, A. D. (1998). *Nationalism and Modernism*, London: Routledge

Thornberry, P. (1992). *International Law and the Rights of Minorities*. Oxford: Clarendon Press)

van den Berghe, P. (1978). 'Race and Ethnicity: a sociobiological perspective', *Ethnic and Racial Studies*, 401

Wellman, C. H., (1995). A Defense of Secession and Political Self-Determination, *Philosophy and Public Affairs* 24: 142-171

National Identity and the Internationalisation of Constitutional Structures

The Tale of Yugoslavia:
Lessons for Accommodating National Identity
in National and International Law

Dominic McGoldrick

INTRODUCTION

This essay examines the constitutional and international law aspects of accommodating national identity in the historical process from Yugoslavia to Bosnia. It takes a broad approach to 'national identity',[1] which thus includes identity on geographical, ethnic, political, racial, religious or other bases, and a broad compass of accommodation techniques. Section I considers how constitutions and international law are used to accommodate national identity or identities. Sections II–IV briefly trace the history of Yugoslavia, and give an account of the conflicts in Yugoslavia and its dissolution respectively. Broad strategies to deal with crises are outlined in section V. In section VI consideration is given to the whole range of international legal responses to the conflict in Yugoslavia, which were deployed in the pursuit of accommodating national identity. These included economic measures, decisions on recognition, responses from the OSCE, International Human Rights Bodies, and the International Court of Justice, the establishment of the International Criminal Tribunal for the Former Yugoslavia, military measures and the contribution of Non-Governmental Organizations. Section VII outlines the range of proposals that were considered in and around *The International Conference on the Former Yugoslavia.* Section VIII analyses in detail the Dayton Peace Agreement of November 1995, which included a Constitution of Bosnia and Herzegovina and an Agreement on Human Rights. Particular attention is given to the 'internationalising' of the Constitution of Bosnia in terms of its making, its terms and its implementation. Section IX contains an assessment of the implementation and of the significance of the Dayton Agreement three years on. Finally, section X provides an overall assessment of the international responses and section XI considers future strategies for accommodating national identity.

---

* Professor of Public International Law, Liverpool Law School, University of Liverpool, Fulbright Distinguished Scholar and Human Rights Fellow, Harvard Law School (2000)
1 See Horowitz 1985; Moynihan 1993; Smith 1991.

Stephen Tierney (ed.), Accommodating National Identity: New Approaches in International and Domestic Law, 13–64
© 2000 *Kluwer Law International. Printed in Great Britain.*
First published in the International Journal on Minority and Group Rights, Volume 6 No. 1/2 1999.
The article has been revised for this publication.

I. Accommodating national identity in national law and international law

In classical terms Constitutions are expressions of orders and values. They constitute a defining point of reference for the State, its people or peoples and its citizens. A Constitution may formally locate sovereignty.[2] It is often a reflection, faithful or otherwise, of 'national identity' and of the national obsession with that concept. One of the first necessities of a new state is to adopt or approve its Constitution by some internal legitimising process. New Constitutions are also often associated with new beginnings either in a positive sense of looking to the future or in a rejection of past order and values. Examples would be the German Basic Law of 1948,[3] the new Constitutions in Central and Eastern Europe and the former Soviet Republics after 1989[4] and the interim and final South African constitutions.[5] Those examples generally fit with the classical use of constitutions in terms of new orders and new values. Their language, terms, structure, inclusions and exclusions can all bear degrees of significance. In addition, the last decade has witnessed a clear trend for Constitutions to explicitly address the relationship between municipal law and international law. Moreover, within that relationship the status of international law has been raised both in formal normative terms[6] and also in its use in the interpretation of Constitutions or legislative acts.[7] As part of that higher status for international law generally, has been a higher status for international human rights law. Part of the rationale for this has been to secure some international protection against changes that are destructive of national identity.

When national Constitutions are adopted it has necessarily and consciously been as the product of an 'indigenous' process. That process may not have been democratic. Indeed, it may not have been participatory in anything but the most perfunctory sense. It may have had to be politically acceptable to other powers, but it has at least been indigenous rather than being imposed by outsiders.[8] Such imposition would seem unnatural, impertinent and inconsistent with even the narrowest notions of self-determination. It would create immediate problems of legitimacy, belonging and ownership – all of which can be important psychological concepts for the individuals, groups, minorities, and politicians who live in the relevant state.[9] From one perspective it would be a failure to recognise and respect 'national identity'. Ironically, from another perspective, the very rationale of outside imposition would

[2] See, for example, the Thai Constitution of 1997.
[3] It is interesting to note that, strictly speaking, the Basic Law of 1948 was intended as a provisional instrument until a Constitution adopted by a free decision of the German people came into force, see Article 146 Basic Law.
[4] See Pogany (ed.) 1995.
[5] See van Wyk, et al (eds.) 1996.
[6] See Stein 1994; Vereshchetin 1996.
[7] A good example is Article 35 of the South African Constitution, see Dugard 1997.
[8] In the decolonisation context there was often agreement on an interim constitution and provisions for the determination of a final constitution.
[9] It is notable that many contemporary Security Council resolutions dealing with conflicts have specifically stated that the people or populations of the area concerned must decide the eventual settlement of the future.

be to ensure recognition and respect for national or minority traditions. The historical examples of imposed constitutional protections have generally been part of the settlement of conflicts by Great Powers. The minorities regimes and guarantees in the inter-war period represent outstanding examples of these although it must be immediately noted that they normally added constitutional protections. They did not impose whole Constitutions. The orthodox explanations for their 'failure' include their outside imposition, their claimed lack of legitimacy, their discriminatory application to limited numbers of States, their weak enforcement mechanisms at both national and international levels, and their alleged inconsistency with evolving norms which focused more on universal and individualistic human rights protection.[10]

In a broad historical sense then the evolution outside of Bosnia of a post-conflict Bosnian 'Constitution' is a relatively unusual event.[11] The new constitution has also to be put into the narrower historical context of the constitutional evolution of Yugoslavia. Devising a Constitution in the mid 1990s represents a different historical epoch from the inter-war period or even in the immediate aftermath to World War Two and thus necessarily has something to say about the present state of international law and international society.[12] Whether we are past,[13] beyond, or having to tier notions of sovereignty[14] may be open to debate. However, it has clearly had to become a much more complex and sophisticated concept[15] to accommodate the stringent demands of international human rights law,[16] international environment law[17] and the emerging international civil society with its greater emphasis on democracy and, arguably, multiculturalism.[18] Although scholars may differ in degree it would appear to be incontestable that the millenarian era, if not the end of history, does at least represent a significant historical discontinuity with the past.[19]

Concepts of 'nationalism', 'national identity', and 'ethnicity' of course, are not new in any sense.[20] They have vigorously forced their way back to the forefront of international legal and political discourse.[21] How do we identify it, cope with it, manage it, deal with it, and give expression to it? Is it a good thing or a bad thing? Should we be for it or against it? On what criteria does an answer depend? While the

---

[10] It is not necessary in the context of this essay to consider the validity of each of these explanations but it is of interest to note that contemporary retrospectives return to that period seeking to learn lessons from it. See Berman 1993; Mertus 1999 and Mertus 1998.

[11] Cf. Cyprus offers a partial analogy. See Grant 1998. 'It remains an open question whether a new basic norm of a legal system, in the form of a Constitution, can be imposed externally', Cox 1998, 630.

[12] In the same way that the Statute of the International Criminal Court (July 1998) says something about such matters.

[13] See MacCormick 1993.

[14] See (1994) *ASIL Proceedings*, pp.51-87, 88th Annual Meeting.

[15] See Lyons and Mastanduno 1995; Schruer 1993.

[16] See Reisman 1990.

[17] See McGoldrick 1996a; International Court of Justice, *Advisory Opinion on Nuclear Weapons (General Assembly Request)*, ICJ Reps. 1996, prs.27-33.

[18] See Kymlicka 1995a. It has been argued that we are now in the era of a clash of civilizations, see Huntingdon 1993.

[19] See Fukuyama 1992; Marks 1997.

[20] See footnote 1 above. There is a massive contemporary literature on ethnicity and ethnic conflicts.

[21] See Bogdanor 1995; Dunay 1995.

concepts are not new we are now analysing them in our own time and space – the post-modern era. We also analyse with newer post-ontological tools, which recognise the importance of language, deconstruction, narratives, identity, difference, exclusion, inclusion and relativism.[22] Within those tools lie different views on the importance of history, historical characteristics and the search for ethical reconstruction.[23] The post World War Two stress on individualistic human rights protection has arguably been retreating or is at least being more balanced in terms of minority and group rights.[24] This is reflected in the adoption of an increased number of international texts including the UN Declaration on the Rights of Minorities (1992),[25] the Council of Europe Framework Convention on Minorities (1995),[26] and the Draft Universal Declaration of the Rights of Indigenous Peoples.[27]

The concept of 'autonomy' has also emerged with increasing presence in national constitutional arrangements as a technique for accommodating national identity.[28] Discussion of autonomy now extends to consideration of the degree to which it is giving rise to rights in international law as distinct from constitutional law. While the relationship between international and constitutional law is significant in the context of national identity, it can be crucially important to distinguish constitutional rights and obligations from international law rights and obligations.[29]

II. A Brief History of Yugoslavia

The 'Kingdom of the Serbs, the Croats and the Slovenes' was one of the artificial creations of the post First World War settlement.[30] Its name was changed to Yugoslavia in 1929.[31] As a state it was something of an enigma. Its history, geography, and politics left it at the mercy of scholars of all disciplines. It was all things to all men and all women. It was linked to the USSR but then split from it. Yugoslavia was a member of the League of Nations and of the United Nations. It was a participating state in the OSCE process and a leading member of the Non-Aligned Movement.[32]

Yugoslavia was described as communist as well as socialist. It was an alternative political model – a bridge between East and West, between capitalism and communism: self-management and market socialism. A new kind of democracy

---

[22]   See Wijeyeratne 1996. It is also interesting to note the efforts of the European Court of Justice to see the EC Treaty as a 'Constitution', with the legitimacy and superior legal and political value and political obedience from its subjects that that implies. See Ward 1995.

[23]   See Derrida 1990; Ward 1996.

[24]   See Kymlicka 1995b; Ramaga 1993; Thornberry 1996; the OSCE Charter of Paris (1990) was an important watershed in positive thinking about minority rights.

[25]   GA Resn 47/135 (18 December 1992).

[26]   The Convention will enter into force in 1999.

[27]   See Scott 1996.

[28]   See Dinstein 1981; Hannum 1990; Hannum & Lillich 1981; Lapidoth 1997; Suski 1997; Steiner 1991.

[29]   It can also be important to distinguish between constitutional rights and duties, for example concerning Quebec, see Oliver 1999, and political commitments, for example, in the context of Scotland, see Munro 1999.

[30]   Laderer 1967.

[31]   For a very valuable source of information see Trifunovska 1994.

[32]   See Rubenstein 1970.

was apparently being constructed. The 'national question' was 'accommodated' and 'contained' within the concept of a single, multi-ethnic state. Multicultural coexistence and equality were encouraged and supported by the State while the partisan advocacy of national or ethnic interests was considered and treated an anti-socialist.

The reality, of course, was rather different.[33] Constitutional crises were regular.[34] There were three major constitutional revisions in 1946, 1963 and 1974. Each had an impact on 'national identity' either by fostering it, recognizing it or both.[35] Some of the constitutional complexity can be realized from the fact that, for example, as of 1974 there was a federal constitution, a constitution for each of the six Republics (one of which was Bosnia)[36] and a constitution for each of the two 'autonomous provinces' of Kosovo[37] and Vojvodina.[38] Each constitution was used to express relative differences in power and status among different groups. Constitutional changes were used to effect direct or indirect changes in status between 'nation', 'nationality' (usually understood to mean minorities), 'minority', 'Others'[39] or no recognition at all.[40] Constitutional status reflected power, legal rights and symbolism. Each of these has an important bearing on identity and self-perception. Their effects were strongly felt in crucial areas like language use and education.

Theoretically decentralized powers were in fact highly centralized and oppressive. The Communist Party was dominant. An authoritarian leader, Tito, dispensed enormous power through a complex set of institutional structures.[41] The Army gradually increased its role in society.[42] Human rights were routinely suppressed. Economic disparities between the various republics and autonomous regions were keenly felt. Any political, legal, social, or economic analysis tends to lead to the conclusion that the only enigma was that Yugoslavia continued to exist at all for the length of time that it did. The things that divided the state seem overwhelming by comparison with the things that united it.

This brief historical, social, and political background to Yugoslavia is important to an understanding, if not an explanation, of events in that state since 1989. However, it must not be overstated. The world is full of states with divisions and contradictions which, whilst not exactly the same, are just as intense. Yet they continue to exist as states in the international law system. Indeed, once the international law requirements of statehood are satisfied, then international law has not much concerned itself with the internal politics and dynamics of states except to the extent that they are internationalised, for example, as concerns human rights.

---

[33] A famous description was of Yugoslavia as 'eight one party states'.
[34] See Irwin 1984.
[35] See Mertus 1999; Paunovic 1993.
[36] See Malcolm 1994; Pinson (ed.) 1996.
[37] Kosovo's autonomous status was effectively ended by a series of Serbian legislative acts in 1990 and 1991. Nonetheless, there effectively developed in Kosovo a whole set of parallel governmental and civic institutions. See Malcolm (2000).
[38] Its Constitution was ended in 1989.
[39] Interestingly, the concept of 'Others' also appears in operating procedures of the new Northern Ireland Assembly under the Belfast Agreement on Northern Ireland (1998), see Gilbert 1998.
[40] See Varady 1997.
[41] See West 1994.
[42] See Gow 1992.

III. The Conflicts in Yugoslavia

The conflicts in the Former Yugoslavia generally, and in Bosnia specifically,[43] have widely been regarded as litmus tests of the post cold-war security and legal orders.[44] International organizations and many states faced substantial criticism for their failures of policy and organization in response to ethnic nationalism.[45] The responses of the international community and of international law were widely condemned as inadequate.[46]

Before considering in turn the variety of international legal responses, we must put the argument that the timing of the Yugoslavia crisis was bad. 1989 had seen the fall of the Berlin Wall and the end of the Cold War. Germany was back at the centre of Europe. The European Community was in the throes of transition into a European Union with a Common Foreign and Security Policy to replace European Political Co-operation.[47] The Conference (now Organization) on Security and Co-operation in Europe (OSCE) was developing new institutions, procedures, and mechanisms.[48] NATO was struggling to find a new mission and a new identity for itself. Finally, 1990–1 saw the Gulf War with Iraq. This diverted substantial political, diplomatic, and military resources away from Yugoslavia. The 'bad timing' argument is valid to the extent that the international community would handle a similar crisis differently now.[49]

IV. The Dissolution of Yugoslavia

From the end of the 1980s onwards there were a succession of crises in Yugoslavia. They included acute constitutional disagreements of high intensity,[50] the series of Declarations on Independence, various separate and overlapping armed conflicts, and horrific violations of human rights law and humanitarian law.[51] What has often been lost in the kaleidoscopic confusion is how consistent the theme of constitutional aspects was. As noted above (Part II) constitutional crises and revisions in Yugoslavia had been regular. Although there were undoubtedly political and social forces at work, the immediate cause of what became known as the Yugoslav crisis were constitutional disagreements between the Yugoslav Republics from the late 1980s onwards.

---

[43] See Burg 1997; Rogel 1998.
[44] See Akhavan and Howse (eds.) 1995; Denitch 1997; Duncan 1994; Dyker & Vejvoda 1996; Glenny 1996; Lukic 1996; Owen 1995a; Owen 1995b; Ramet 1995; Silber & Little 1996; Thompson 1992; Woodward 1995.
[45] Orentlichter 1998.
[46] See Bethlehem & Weller (eds.) (1997); Higgins 1993; McGoldrick 1996b; Weller 1992.
[47] The eventual outcome was the Maastricht Treaty on European Union (1992).
[48] See McGoldrick 1993.
[49] See sect.XI, 1 below.
[50] Dimitrijevic 1995. The 1974 Constitution and the Constitutional Process as a Factor in the Collapse of Yugoslavia, pp.45-74, in Akhavan and Howse (eds.) 1995.
[51] See Biserko 1993; Kandic 1993; Pajic & Hampson 1993; Helsinki Watch 1992.

V. STRATEGIES FOR THE INTERNATIONAL COMMUNITY

A. *Strategies*

The first strategy must be *preventive*, namely to stop Yugoslav crises ever happening. Such crisis-prevention is an ongoing strategy. When it works it may never even be publicly acknowledged. Important elements of crisis-prevention are the principles laid down by the international community concerning how it will respond e.g. to claims of self-determination and statehood. When will such claims be supported and how (see section VI, D below)?

The second strategic response, which became *de rigueur* in the 1990s, is *crisis management*. There is an element of irony in this. If a situation can be managed it is probably not a crisis. If it is a crisis then you cannot manage it. A critical element of crisis management in Yugoslavia was to stop the conflict spilling over into neighbouring states and thus lighting some kind of Balkan tinderbox. In this the international community was successful, and this must be acknowledged as important. To help defuse the crisis in Macedonia, the Security Council approved the Secretary-General's recommendation that a United Nations peacekeeping operation – a preventive deployment – be established in Macedonia. An infantry battalion consisting of some 700 armed troops, with logistic support, military observers, and United Nations civilian police performed this task.

Finally, *resolving* the crisis. The traditional international law view has been that the best persons to resolve an internal, civil crisis are those involved. An agreement by them is more likely to be kept than one imposed from outside. International law does not legitimate internal struggles, but nor does it inhibit them. There should not be outside intervention to determine the political outcome.[52] International law will accommodate the eventual outcome, usually by the process of recognition. This 'neutral' attitude on international law to civil conflicts is not based on a passive or uncaring attitude but on a policy basis. A policy favouring intervention would require that one of the parties is supported and the other(s) opposed. Choosing sides is a dangerous gamble and the conduct of the warring parties usually reflects degrees of responsibility rather than innocence. In Yugoslavia the standard diplomatic formulation became that it was the Serbs (without necessarily distinguishing between the Bosnian Serbs and the Serbian Serbs) who were 'primarily responsible', but it was recognized that there was appalling conduct by all of the parties. Moreover, different states may appreciate the facts differently or have their own political and historical allegiances. Thus intervention on one side can result in intervention on the other and the process of escalation has begun. After years of high-level bloodshed the interveners may decide that they should both move out and leave the warring parties to resolve their conflict. This is what happened with Afghanistan. Translated into Yugoslavian terms, the *realpolitik* analysis was that any intervention by Western

---

[52] For example, UN peacekeeping 'was in no way intended to prejudice the terms of a political settlement', SC Resn. 743, pr.10.

European states on behalf of the Bosnian Muslim government raised the possibility that Russia might have supported the Serbian side.[53]

B. *Pressure to Intervene*

The Yugoslav crises witnessed pressures to adopt a more interventionist approach. The pressure came from a number of sources. The much fabled 'world community' played a role. The Yugoslav conflict became probably the most publicised conflict in the history of humanity and inhumanity. Satellites, video-links, and the massive amount of data on the Internet, especially on Bosnet, created a well-informed international public opinion. This is sometimes referred to as the 'CNN Effect'. The information gap between political élites and their populaces has been substantially closed. How could states stand by in the face of such atrocities?

Secondly, pressure came from the parties to the conflict. They used and abused the national and international media.[54] The whole of the conflict was characterized by lies, deceit, deception, and broken promises.[55] For example, there was embarrassing evidence that the Bosnian Muslims attracted shelling on their own people to generate adverse international publicity for the Serbs. The Bosnian Serbs pushed the United Nations Protection Force (UNPROFOR) and NATO to the limit in the hope that it might engender a supportive response from Serbia or possibly even Russia. One of the reasons that the final peace agreement was concluded at a remote US airbase in Dayton was that the parties were bored into agreement and had no press gallery to play to.

Thirdly, pressure came from national Parliaments, in particular the US Congress, the German Bundestag, the Russian Parliament, and the European Parliament. It is important for international lawyers not to be dismissive of such views. There was strong pressure on states to support a 'democratically elected' Bosnian Muslim government, committed to a pluralist and multi-ethnic state. States and international organizations were accused of complicity in genocide,[56] mass rape,[57] and ethnic cleansing.[58] Fourthly, criticism came from Muslim states that rightly asked whether the response would have been the same if the victims had been predominantly Christian.[59]

---

[53] Much of the Russian criticism of the Yugoslavia crisis was that it felt that it was not consulted appropriately.
[54] See Hampson 1992.
[55] See Owen 1995a.
[56] See Gutman 1993; Cushman & Mestrovic (eds.) 1996.
[57] See Chinkin 1994.
[58] See Petrovic 1994; Vullaimy 1998; Salzman 1998. Over half of the population of Bosnia does not reside where it did in 1991.
[59] Lord Owen's response was that this charge had no substance. As for comparisons with the international community's response to the invasion of Kuwait, he said that the situation in the former Yugoslavia was different, "politically, military and geographically", S/ 25015, pr.19.

VI. The Responses of the International Community

Given these pressures we must consider how states and international organizations engaged in the crisis.

A. Political and Diplomatic Responses

More resources of this kind were put into the crisis than any comparable crisis. Initially many of the resources came from Europe because of the perception that it was a 'European problem'.[60] Quite why alleged genocide, mass rape, and ethnic cleansing are European problems was never explained. What was more accurately conveyed by this perception was the hope that Western Europe could deal with the crisis without the assistance of the United States. In fact, Europe responded very quickly. The EC Conference on Yugoslavia (EC-COY) was established in September 1990. The EC Troika was actively used. Successions of Special Representatives were appointed: Lord Carrington, Lord Owen, and Carl Bildt.[61]

B. The International Conference on the Former Yugoslavia.[62]

In 1992 the EC Conference was replaced by the ICFY.[63] This was one of the most important responses of the international community. It built on the work done by the EC's Conference on Yugoslavia but the wider participation served to give it a greater legitimacy.[64] The major joint actors within it were the UN and the EC, but other international organizations, for example, the OSCE and the Organization of Islamic Countries (OIC), also participated. Its membership included representatives of a troika of the EC, a troika of the OSCE, the five permanent members of the SC, a representative for the OIC and two representatives of neighbouring states. Its successive co-chairmen represented the public face of the ICFY. The wide-ranging activities of the ICFY included active preventive diplomacy, peace-making, peace-keeping, and a potential peace enforcement component, which was never in fact exercised. More specifically its activities included consultation, inquiry, monitoring, co-ordination with international institutions, providing information and briefings to governments and international institutions, media appearances, humanitarian issues in association with the UNHCR and the ICRC, extensive diplomatic activities at sub-national, national and international levels, obtaining cease-fires, proposals for

---

[60] In the fall of 1992 during the worst of the ethnic cleansing, concentration camps, mass deportations and mass rape, the UN Secretary-General caused controversy when he described the situation as a 'rich man's war' suggesting that it was racist to make such a fuss about these events in Europe when so many worse things were happening in the Third World.

[61] Bildt later became the High Representative under the Dayton Peace Agreement.

[62] This account is largely based on the series of Reports to the Security Council from the UN Secretary-General on the International Conference on the Former Yugoslavia: See S/24795, 11 November 1992; S/25015, 24 December 1992; S/25221, 2 February 1993; S/25248, 8 February 1993; S/25403, 12 March 1993; S/25479, 26 March 1993; S/25490, 30 March 1993; S/25708, 30 April 1993; S/26066, 8 July 1993; S26233, 3 August 1993.

[63] See S/24795, 11 November 1992, prs.1-2.

[64] Cf. Betts 1994.

constitutional reform, peace initiatives and proposals, obtaining agreement on the deployment of observers, issuing public statements and appeals, assessing compliance with agreements, securing undertakings from the parties, co-operation and consultation with the two successive Special Rapporteur of the Commission of Human Rights, informal contact groups on human rights and humanitarian issues.

The Steering Committee which managed the operational work of the Conference was co-chaired by the representative of the Secretary-General of the United Nations, Mr. Cyrus Vance and a representative of the Presidency of the European Community, Lord Owen. It was organized to remain in being until a final settlement of the problems of the former Yugoslavia was been reached. Much of the crucial work of the ICFY was done in six Working Groups.[65] The Working Group on Bosnia-Herzegovina came to dominate its activities. The other groups were on Humanitarian Issues,[66] Ethnic and National Communities and Minorities,[67] Succession Issues,[68] Economic Issues, and Confidence and Security-building and Verification Measures.[69]

An Arbitration Commission – the Badinter Commission, supported the ICFY.[70] This was originally established under the EC-COY. It provided a serious of Opinions on key issues of recognition, self-determination,[71] and succession.[72] The original members of the Commission were drawn from constitutional court judges rather than international lawyers because it was originally envisaged that it would be advising on constitutional issues and matters of economic succession. Later members drew on public international law expertise.

The ICFY also provided a focus for important political support on the establishment of an International Criminal Tribunal for Yugoslavia, maintenance of the arms embargo (where it provided a counterweight to the national Parliaments), the various peace plans and in particular the Vance-Owen Peace

---

[65] The WGs adopted a pattern of flexible representation for relevant countries rather than fixed membership.

[66] Its task was to promote humanitarian relief in all its aspects, including refugees, and assess the effectiveness of the humanitarian assistance operation. Interference with humanitarian provision and the controlled release of detainees became a regular staple of political and military strategy of all of the parties. There was clear evidence of the deliberate targeting of humanitarian personnel and aid convoys. The UNHCR condemned the practice of ethnic cleansing but on occasions was effectively faced with the choice of assisting those being cleansed or leaving them to face greater hardship or even death.

[67] See S/25795, prs.82-92; S/25490, prs.9-20. This Working Group was charged with recommending initiatives for resolving ethnic questions in the former Yugoslavia. It did important work on the situations in Kosovo (large Albanian population), Vojvodina (largely Hungarian population which was heavily affected by the resettlement of Serb refugees and an overproportional and disproportionate draft of Hungarians into the Yugoslav army) and Macedonia.

[68] See S/25015, 24 December 1992; prs.93-9; S/25490, prs.21-30. This WG sought to resolve succession issues arising from the emergence of new states in the territory of the former Yugoslavia. A number of the opinions from the Badinter Commission were concerned with issues of succession. See Opinions 11-13. As of May 2000 negotiations were still continuing.

[69] See S/25015, 24 December 1992; prs.100-9; S/25490, prs.31-2. The London Conference document on confidence, security-building and verification (LC/Cl 1) was the basis for consideration of longer-term confidence- and security-building measures.

[70] See Craven 1995; Terrett 1998.

[71] See Pellet 1992.

[72] See 31 *ILM* (1992) 1488-1526; 32 *ILM* (1993) 1586-98.

Plan. The ICFY also developed a strong relationship with the Security Council. The adoption of various Security Council Resolutions was closely linked to the ICFY process. At various times reports from the ICFY requested that Security Council resolutions be adopted or delayed so that they could operate as a diplomatic threat in the negotiations.

C. Economic Measures

Extensive UN and EC sanctions regimes were established by around 20 resolutions.[73] International sanctions are now legally very highly developed and sophisticated and have been tested in both UK law and under EC law. A UN Security Council Sanctions Committee exercised tight control and there were a number of EC Monitoring Missions. Although sanctions are necessarily a blunt instrument there is strong evidence that over time they had an increasing effect on Serbia by causing great damage to its economy. On the positive side, massive humanitarian assistance was provided to Yugoslavia both during and after the conflict.[74]

D. The Recognition Decisions[75]

1. The Decisions
On 15–16 December 1991 at an extraordinary European Political Co-operation ministerial meeting in Brussels the EC adopted a 'Declaration on Yugoslavia' and a 'Declaration on the "Guidelines on the Recognition of New States in Eastern Europe and in the Soviet Union"'.[76] On the basis of these Guidelines it would recognise those new states which applied for it and which satisfied certain criteria. These included respect for the provisions of the UN Charter, the Helsinki Final Act, and the Charter of Paris; guarantees for the rights of ethnic and national groups and minorities; respect for the inviolability of all frontiers; acceptance of all relevant commitments on disarmament and nuclear non-proliferation, security, and regional stability; and a commitment to settle by agreement, including where appropriate by recourse to arbitration, all questions concerning state succession and regional disputes. The criteria do not appear to be additional or replacement conditions of statehood, but rather they go to the exercise of the political decision to recognise. Entities that were the result of aggression would not be recognised and account would be taken of the effect of recognition on neighbouring states.

The injection of principles of human rights law and security into that political decision is commendable in itself. Advice on the satisfaction of the criteria was to be provided by the Badinter Commission. Recognition was to take place on 15 January 1992. The Commission advised that Slovenia and Macedonia satisfied the

---

[73] See in particular SC Resns 713, 724, 727, 743 757, 760 787, 820, 843.
[74] See Boutros Boutros-Ghali (1995). *Confronting New Challenges Annual Report on the Work of the UN Organization 1995* (New York), prs.896-929; Mercier 1995.
[75] See Rich 1993, 36-65 and additional comment and documentation on 66-91; Warbrick 1992; 1993 and 1997.
[76] See 31 *ILM* (1992) 1485.

criteria.[77] Slovenia was recognised, but not Macedonia because of Greek objections to emblems on its flag and the use of the name 'Macedonia' which it took as implying territorial claims over part of Greece. It took a long time for Greek objections to be satisfied. Greece regarded the matter as of vital national interest and its support for the Treaty on European Union was needed. The Commission advised that Croatia should not be recognised because it lacked constitutional guarantees of minority rights.[78] However, the EC states recognised it anyway. They were under great pressure from Germany to recognise Slovenia and Croatia in particular. Part of the motivation lay in guilt over the establishment of a puppet state in Croatia in World War II. Historic guilt is not necessarily a good basis of recognition policy. Germany persuaded the then other eleven EC members to go along with its policy despite many of them having substantial reservations. Presumably the Member States considered it better for the EC to act together even if it was a bad decision. Notwithstanding the EC Guidelines and the agreed date, Germany decided to recognise Croatia and Slovenia in December 1991. When Croatia was recognised, between a third and a quarter of its territory was not under its control.

As for Bosnia-Herzegovina the Commission expressed the view that its people had not clearly expressed a desire of independence.[79] A referendum was held but the Bosnian Serbs refused to take part. Over 60 per cent of the population voted for independence. Bosnia was then recognised on 6 April 1992 in the midst of major, armed conflict on its territory.

The greatest defect of the recognition policy pursued was that it operated in the absence of an overall agreement for Yugoslavia. If none of the former Republics had been recognised in the absence of such an agreement, then the carrot of recognition would have been an important element of pressure to moderate behaviour and to reach agreements respecting minority rights. The practical effect on the recognition policy was to try to predetermine the outcome of the military and political crisis. Conflict could continue in the Former Yugoslavia but the end result would be six new states. Claims to statehood by units within the former Republics would not be accepted even if they were militarily successful. So claims to statehood by the Krajina region of Croatia were not accepted, nor those of Kosovo in Serbia, or of the Republika Srpska in Bosnia.

There must be substantial doubts whether Bosnia ever satisfied the traditional criteria for statehood. If that is correct then the basic premise of Security Council and EC action was wrong all along. It may have been done with the best of intentions of stabilising the situation but it paved the road to hell as states were warned that it would.[80] UK Ministers at the time argued that the recognition decisions were not really that crucial or important.[81] This is not convincing. Recognition of statehood is often crucial to the operation of international law rules. Once recognised Bosnia

---

[77] See 31 *ILM* (1992) 1512 and 1507 respectively.
[78] See 31 *ILM* (1992) 1503 and later comments at 1505.
[79] See 31 *ILM* (1992) 1501.
[80] See Owen, 1995a: 29.
[81] See *Central and Eastern Europe*, Report of the Foreign Affairs Committee, House of Commons, 21-I and II (1991-92) and the Government Response in Cm 1969 (1992).

could seek OSCE and UN membership, which it duly did. Its borders were internationally protected by Article 2(4) of the UN Charter. The analogy with the Gulf conflict (1990–91) was thus closer.[82] Why was Bosnia not defended from direct and indirect armed attacks from Serbia and Montenegro when Kuwait was so defended? Bosnia had the inherent right to self-defence under Article 51 of the Charter. All forces and armies of Croatia and of Serbia and Montenegro that were operating in Bosnia were legally required to withdraw.[83] Any armed conflict between Croatia and Bosnia, and between Bosnia and Serbia and Montenegro must have the character of an 'international armed conflict' which is crucial for the applicability of rules of international humanitarian law.[84] Notwithstanding that they had recognised Bosnia, many states continued to refer to it as a civil war situation without clearly explaining the basis of this.

2. Borders
Article 2(4) of the UN Charter is concerned with the protection of international or internationalised borders. The Helsinki Final Act (1975) reflected the same principle with the addition that borders could be changed by consent. In the Yugoslav crisis a new twist was added. Both NATO and the OSCE asserted that there would be no recognition of any change of borders, external or internal, brought about by the use of force. If that is a new assertion of an international law rule then it is indeed a radical development. The question would be raised about which party was using force to change an internal border. If the political authorities within a Republic declare independence and station their forces on the internal border, can the state authorities use force to prevent this? It is submitted that it is more likely that the statements on internal borders got mixed up with decisions on recognition of the internal republics.[85]

3. Does the Recognition Policy have Implications for Self-Determination?
Self-determination has been one of the most controversial and revolutionary socio-political concepts of the twentieth century. Before its dissolution the right of self-determination rested in the people of Yugoslavia as a whole. The Republics had no right to secede on the basis of an international right of self-determination.[86] To hold otherwise would reverse long-standing UN and state practice against secession.[87] International law is not a suicide club. Self-determination has been much more conservatively applied in international legal practice than some of the theorists and human rights advocates would have us believe. Thus, self-determination remains first and foremost a territorial concept to which a human rights mantle is added,

---

[82] See Owen 1995a.
[83] This was reflected in a number of SC resolutions.
[84] Questions of the applicable international law in various armed conflicts are particularly difficult because there was at various times overlapping international and non-international armed conflict. See the important decision of the Appeals Chamber of the International Criminal Tribunal for the Former Yugoslavia, *Prosecutor v. Tadic*, 35 *ILM* (1996) 32 especially at prs. 71-145.
[85] See *Opinion No. 3* of the Badinter Commission, 31 *ILM* (1992) 1499. See Shaw 1997.
[86] See Cassese 1995: 269. On self-determination under Yugoslav law see Iglar 1992.
[87] See Doehring 1995.

rather than a human rights concept.[88] However, the recognition policy effectively made a new self-determination unit out of each of the Republics. It effectively said that they could secede. Territorial units within the Republics such as Kosovo[89] or Krajina could not secede though. The most likely explanation of all of this is that the process in Yugoslavia took place without reference to the principle of external self-determination.[90] Under the Dayton peace agreement there were to be two 'Entities' within Bosnia but there is only one state. Neither 'Entity' has the right to secede.

There is no doubt that international law could develop clear international criteria for secession or autonomy.[91] It has not done so to date.[92] Moreover, the political reality is that the parties fighting in Yugoslavia were seeking statehood.[93] Statehood remains the golden chalice from which all wish to drink.

E. The OSCE Response

In political terms the Helsinki Follow-Up Conference (1992) was dominated by the deteriorating situation in Yugoslavia. This raised a number of problems for the OSCE.[94] It had always been a state-to-state process founded on the principle of consensus decision-making. The application of OSCE commitments to internal conflicts or civil wars raised some difficult questions as to the application of a number of fundamental OSCE principles: the inviolability of frontiers, self-determination, non-intervention, and the human dimension.[95] The recognition of the various republics of the State of Yugoslavia as states in their own right and the admission of a number of them to the OSCE,[96] made the relevance of OSCE commitments unarguable. As concerned the situation in Bosnia, the general view at the Helsinki Conference was that primary responsibility lay with Serbia.[97] The obvious problem was how to deal with the situation in Yugoslavia on the basis of consensus. Unless

---

[88] Cf. Higgins 1994: ch.7.

[89] See Phillips 1996; *Kosovo Disappearances in Times of Armed Conflict*, (1998). SPOTLIGHT Report No.27. Belgrade: Humanitarian Law Center; SC Resn 1160 (1998) imposing an arms embargo on the Federal Republic of Yugoslavia, Press Release SC/6496, 3868th meeting, 31 March 1998. The resolution stated that the principles for a solution to the problem should be based on the territorial integrity of FRY. It expressed support for an 'enhanced status for Kosovo which would include a substantially greater degree of autonomy and meaningful self-administration'. See also SC resns 1199 and 1203.

[90] See Koskenniemi 1994; Quane 1998; Tierney 1999; Tomuschat (ed.) 1993.

[91] See Hannum 1998.

[92] Cf. However, the approach of the Supreme Court of Canada in the Quebec secession case (1998) where it effectively treated the UN's Friendly Relations Declaration of 1975 as providing criteria by which to judge a claim for secession, *In the Matter of Section 53 Supreme Court Act, R.S.C., 1985, c.S-26 and In the Matter of a Reference by the Governor in Council concerning Certain Questions Relating to the Secession of Quebec from Canada, as set out in Order in Council P.C. 1996-1497, dated the 30th Day of September, 1996.* See Bayefsky 2000.

[93] So too is Kosovo. See p. 54 below.

[94] See Zaagman 1992; *Breakdown: War and Reconstruction in Yugoslavia* (1992). London: Institute of War and Peace Reporting.

[95] See Rosas 1992.

[96] Croatia, Slovenia (Mar. 1992), and Bosnia-Herzegovina (Apr. 1992) and FYROM.

[97] See the Declaration on Bosnia adopted by the CSO at the Helsinki 1992 Conference; Zimmermann 1995.

the consensus rule was altered, Yugoslavia would effectively have had a veto on any OSCE response or action. The OSCE Council of Ministers had signalled a crack in the consensus principle in its Prague Document on Further Development of OSCE Institutions and Structures. The section on the 'Human Dimension' was followed by a section headed 'Safeguarding Human Rights, Democracy and the Rule of Law'.[98] 'In order to develop further the OSCE's capability to safeguard human rights, democracy and the rule of law through peaceful means', the Council decided that 'appropriate action' could be taken by the Council or the Committee of Senior Officials (CSO), if necessary in the absence of the consent of the state concerned, in cases of 'clear, gross and uncorrected violations of relevant OSCE commitments'. The 'appropriate action' was to consist of 'political declarations and other political steps to apply outside the territory of the state concerned'. The decision was stated to be without prejudice to existing OSCE mechanisms. The 'relevant commitments' were not identified, but the understanding was that they were those relating to the human dimension of the OSCE, rather than to all OSCE commitments. The basis for taking action against Yugoslavia was 'clear, gross and uncorrected violations' of human dimension commitments. In such circumstances action could be taken on a consensus minus one (C-1) basis. Apparently on this basis action was taken against Yugoslavia in two stages. On 10 June 1992 the CSO decided that Yugoslavia be suspended from decisions relating to the crisis in Yugoslavia. On 8 July 1992 they were suspended by the CSO from participation in OSCE meetings. Therefore, Yugoslavia was unable to prevent a consensus forming. There is no reference in any of the OSCE documents to the possibility of suspension. The increasing institutional flexibility of the OSCE was becoming evident.

The questions of the statehood of Yugoslavia and the occupation of its seat were deliberately treated as separate. This was partly because the Badinter Commission under the European Community Conference on Yugoslavia had been asked to report on this question.[99] It reported in July 1992 that the Federal Republic of Yugoslavia 'appears to be a new state that cannot be considered the single successor to SFRY of Yugoslavia', and that its membership in international organizations 'must be discontinued'.[100] The decisions of the Badinter Committee were not binding on the EC,[101] nor, of course, on any one other state or organization. However, its approach was followed and the FRY (Serbia and Montenegro) was treated as a new state. It has never applied to become a new participating state in the OSCE. It maintains that it is a continuation of the Former Yugoslavia. Moreover, its recognition by the EC member states would be subject to recognition criteria, which includes commitments to OSCE principles.[102]

---

[98] 31 *ILM* (1992) 976 at 987; and in (1992) 13 *Human Rights Law Journal* 174-6.
[99] For the first three opinions of the Badinter Committee see (1992) 3 *EJIL* 182-5.
[100] At its 47th session the General Assembly of the UN effectively suspended Yugoslavia. See GA Res. 47/1 of 23 Sept. 1992. See Blum 1992; Szasz 1993. See also SC Resn. 777. FRY (Serbia and Montenegro) is still not a member of the UN, and there is uncertainty as to its status. It is recognized by a number of states, including all of the EU States. The real issue is as to its identity.
[101] As noted above, 24, they were ignored in substance concerning recognition of Croatia.
[102] See Warbrick 1992, 1993 and 1997.

The OSCE was also part of the London Conference on Yugoslavia,[103] sent a number of missions and joint missions to Yugoslavia, and was part of the ICFY. It had a very significant role in implementing the Dayton agreement, particularly in relation to elections (see below). The OSCE, as an institution, was assuming a permanent place in the architecture of European diplomacy,[104] alongside the European Community (now Union).

F. The Response of International Human Rights Bodies

A special session of the UN Human Rights Commission was held for the first time ever in 1992.[105] A Special Representative on Yugoslavia was appointed, Mr T. Mazowiecki. He submitted seventeen damning reports and a series of recommendations. When he resigned, Elizabeth Rehn replaced him. The damning reports continued. The Human Rights Committee under the International Covenant on Civil and Political Rights (1966) made requests for special reports under Article 40(1)(b) from the Republic of Croatia, the FRY (Serbia and Montenegro), and the Republic of Bosnia-Herzegovina.[106] It did so on the basis that 'all the peoples within the territory of the former Yugoslavia are entitled to the guarantees of the Covenant'. This guarantee appears to be automatic and not dependent on formal notification of succession by any new state or continuing state. Reports were submitted and were subject to a searching examination by the HRC in November 1992. The HRC adopted comments on each report containing important recommendations. The decisions of the HRC set an important precedent in terms of succession of obligations to human rights treaties.[107] What is less well known is that the initiative for the HRC's request came from the Co-Chairmen of the ICFY.

G. The Establishment of the International Criminal Tribunal for the Former Yugoslavia

The mere establishment of this Tribunal was significant for international law and the international community in its own right.[108] It gave legal effect to the many statements of states and international organizations that individuals who committed grave war crimes would be held personally responsible.[109] The Tribunal has publicly

---

[103] See the Documents Approved and Endorsed by the London Conference, LC/C1-12 Aug, 1992; 31 *ILM* (1992) 1527.

[104] See the agreement of 16 October 1998 between the FRY and the OSCE, which gave the OSCE a major observation role in Kosovo.

[105] See Weissbrodt 1993.

[106] See UN Doc CCPR/C/SR/1178/Add.1.

[107] The HRC affirmed the approach in a General Comment on 'Issues Relating to the Continuity of Obligations to the International Covenant on Civil and Political Rights', GC 26(61), 5 IHRR (1998), 301. See generally Mullerson 1993.

[108] See Akhavan 1993, 1996 and 1998; Symposium 1995; Greenwood 1994; Patel-King & A-M. La Rosa 1997. The experience of the ad-hoc tribunals was crucial to the agreement on a permanent international criminal court in July 1998. See McGoldrick 1999b.

[109] Various legal actions may also be possible at the national level, e.g. for war crimes or tortious acts against aliens. See *Kadic and Karadic*, Court of Appeal for the Second Circuit, US, 34 *ILM* (1995) 1592.

indicted ninety four individuals, mainly Serbs, but a number of Croats and Muslims. As of 16 May 2000, forty accused were involved in proceedings. Twenty seven accused were at large. In the *Tadic case* a challenge to the Security Council's jurisdiction to establish the Tribunal was rejected by the Tribunal's Appeal Chamber.[110] The 1999 budget was $94 million.

H. The International Court of Justice Response

In as much as the International Court of Justice can be said to have a 'world order role' it played its part by granting an interim measures order at the request of Bosnia against FRY (Serbia and Montenegro).[111] In July 1996 the Court ruled that it did have jurisdiction to hear the case on the basis of the Genocide Convention (1948).[112] In November 1993 Bosnia threatened to bring a case against the UK arguing that it was not meeting its responsibilities under the Genocide Convention.[113] It was persuaded not to do so.

I. Military Measures[114]

1. The Arms Embargo

One of the most legally and politically controversial of the military measures was the arms embargo imposed by Security Council Resolution 713 with the consent of the government of Yugoslavia. Paragraph 6 of that resolution stated that the embargo was for 'the purposes of establishing peace and stability in Yugoslavia'. Bosnia indirectly challenged the SC Resolution before the International Court of Justice.[115] The first argument is whether it applied to Bosnia at all, given that Bosnia did not exist as a state when it was imposed. The clear object and purpose of the Resolution would suggest that it continued to apply to Bosnia. Both the Security Council and the ICFY acted on that basis. Secondly, an argument could be made that there had been a substantial change of circumstances since the passing of the resolution. However, even if this is arguable, it is established Security Council practice that once the Security Council passes a resolution, it is for it to lift it. It should not be done unilaterally.[116] Thirdly, Bosnia argued that the Security Council resolution conflicted with its inherent right to self-defence under Article 51 of the UN Charter. In response it can be argued that the Security Council was not taking away Bosnia's right of self-defence, it was simply prohibiting other states from assisting it militarily. It is also important to remember that the resolution applied to the whole of Yugoslavia

---

[110] *Tadic Case*, Chamber of the International Tribunal for the Former Yugoslavia, 35 *ILM* (1996), 32. See comments in 45 *ICLQ* (1996), 691-701.
[111] Two applications were made. See [1993] ICJ Rep. 3 and 325. See comment by Gray 1997. FRY (Serbia and Montenegro) counterclaimed. Its claims were held admissible in December 1997. No decision on the merits is likely before 20z01.
[112] ICJ Reps. 1996, 595.
[113] See S/26806, S/26847, 26908.
[114] See Leurdijk 1994.
[115] See footnote 111 above.
[116] The US wanted to lift it but ultimately accepted that only the SC should do this.

and not just Bosnia. If the view is taken that Bosnia has the right to be able to secure the level of weaponry and armaments that would make its right of self-defence successful then this is a clear path to conflict escalation, the 'level killing-field' as the then UK Foreign Secretary graphically described it. It is submitted that the arms embargo was a defensible and rational decision for the Security Council to take and was not open to legal challenge.[117] The embargo was terminated in stages after the signing of the Dayton Peace Agreement (see below).[118]

2. *UNPROFOR, IFOR and SFOR*[119]

These were massive and costly peacekeeping and implementation forces respectively.[120]

3. *No-fly Zones*

These were established and extensively monitored.[121]

4. *Establishment of a Number of Safe Areas*[122]

Again the concept of these is a good one but only on certain conditions. First, there must be a clear legal mandate to use force to enforce and protect the areas and their inhabitants, and not just a mandate to use force to protect UN personnel and act in self-defence to the bombardment of safe areas. The absence of such a mandate leaves safe areas as a dangerous deception, which undermines the credibility of the UN when the areas are patently not safe.[123] Secondly, such areas must be demilitarised. It is not defensible to allow such areas to be used as safe havens for parties involved in the fighting.

5. *Access for Humanitarian Provision*

Security Council resolution 770, paragraph 2, provided for 'all necessary means' to ensure the delivery of humanitarian aid. The problem was a more practical one of the UN not wishing to use force to deliver aid.

J. Non-Governmental Organizations

These groups, from both inside and outside the Former Yugoslavia, have responded massively to the crisis in informing, publicising, and investigating events. These have contributed to the substantial pressure on states and international organizations to act.

---

[117] The view of the Co-Chairmen of the ICFY was that the lifting of the arms embargo would have widened and deepened the war in Bosnia and Herzegovina. It would have encouraged the delivery of more sophisticated and more destructive weapons to all the warring parties, and could also have led to the spread of the conflict throughout the Balkan region.

[118] See SC Resn 1021, in 35 *ILM* (1996) 257-8.

[119] See Wentz 1998. In 1998 there were approximately 34,000 ground troops.

[120] See in particular SC Resns 743, 758, 761, 762, 764, 769, 770, 776, 779, 786, 795, 802, 807, 815, 819, 842, 844, 847, 869, 871, 908, 913, 914, 941, 947, 958, on UNPROFOR; 1031 on IFOR. See generally de Rossanet 1996; Mayall (ed.) 1996.

[121] See SC Resn 816.

[122] See SC Resns 819, 824, 836 and 844.

[123] See Higgins 1995. Judge Higgins is very critical. Mixed mandate actions are 'doomed to failure' (458) and 'the technique of safe havens is not to be regarded as desirable' (460).

VII. THE EVOLUTION OF PROPOSALS FOR CONSTITUTIONS,
HUMAN RIGHTS AND MINORITY RIGHTS FOR BOSNIA

In retrospect it is astonishing to canvass the variety and depth of proposals relating to constitutional matters and human rights.[124] Various categorisations would be possible but for the sake of simplicity it is helpful to identify the major sets of distinct proposals, many of which drew on elements of each other. The following section thus traces the principal points of interest in the evolution of constitutional and human rights provisions. The Dayton Agreement is considered in particular detail in section VIII.

(1). The Carrington text on 'Treaty Provisions for the Convention' (October 1991).
The Carrington text was premised on keeping the SFRY together and so the obligations were directed at the Republics. Even at that early stage there was an extensive set of provisions on 'Human Rights and Rights of National or Ethnic Groups' which was referred to by the Badinter Arbitration Commission in its opinions.

(2). The Cutiliero 'Statement of Principles for new constitutional arrangements for Bosnia and Herzegovina' (March 1992).
The EC-COY's rounds of talks in 1992 on the Future Constitutional Arrangements for Bosnia and Herzegovina resulted in a "Statement of Principles for new constitutional arrangements for Bosnia and Herzegovina" which was tentatively agreed to on 18 March 1992. These were supplemented by some additional principles on human rights developed on 31 March. However, these tentative agreements were repudiated soon thereafter. Further talks produced no agreement. By the time of the Cutiliero principles, Bosnia was moving towards independence and so the principles were directed to 'Bosnia and Hercegovina and its constituent units'. The human rights to be covered were those in the Carrington Convention. There was to be a Mixed Commission on human rights and a monitoring mission, both of which would include members drawn from the EC.

(3). The ICFY's WG's three constitutional papers on Bosnia (September 1992).
The task of the ICFY's WG on Bosnia was to promote a cessation of hostilities and a constitutional settlement in Bosnia and Herzegovina. It picked up on the work of the EC-COY and largely focused on constitutional matters. Major items on the agenda were human rights protection and implementation systems and the distribution of responsibilities between the central government and constituent units.[125] The Co-Chairmen presented to the parties a paper on a possible constitutional structure for Bosnia and Herzegovina.[126] Major differences between the Bosnian parties were evident.[127] The Muslims wanted a centralised, unitary State, arranged into a number of regions possessing merely administrative functions. The Serbs wanted Bosnia to

---

[124] For texts see Szasz 1995a; 1995b; 1996.
[125] See S/24795, prs.46-72 (11 November 1992).
[126] *Ibid.*, Annex VII.
[127] S/24795, pr.34.

be divided into three independent States, respectively for the Muslim, Serb and Croat peoples, with each of these States having its own international legal personality. These States might form a loose confederation for the purpose of coordinating certain of their activities. The Croats supported a middle position. The basis for the consideration of this issue was the 'Statement of Principles adopted by the International Conference on the Former Yugoslavia' in London.[128] This condemned forced expulsions of populations, required the reversal of those which had already taken place, called for the inviolability of all borders and rejected all efforts to change borders by force.

Given that the final peace settlement for Bosnia divided it into two Entities (see section VIII below), it is interesting to note why the co-chairmen of the ICFY considered that Bosnia could not be divided in the way the Serbs wanted:

36. The population of Bosnia and Herzegovina is inextricably intermingled. Thus, there appears to be no viable way to create three territorially distinct States based on ethnic or confessional principles. Any plan to do so would involve incorporating a very large number of members of the other ethnic/ confessional groups, or consist of a number of separate enclaves of each ethnic/ confessional group. Such a plan could achieve homogeneity and coherent boundaries only by a process of enforced population transfer which has already been condemned by the International Conference on the Former Yugoslavia as well as by the General Assembly (resolution 46/242, preamble and para. 6) and the Security Council (resolutions 771 (1992) and 779 (1992)). Consequently, the Co-Chairmen deemed it necessary to reject any model based on three separate, ethnic/confessional based States. Furthermore, a confederation formed of three such States would be inherently unstable, for at least two would surely forge immediate and stronger connections with neighbouring States of the former Yugoslavia than they would with the other two units of Bosnia and Herzegovina...

37. The Co-Chairmen also recognised, however, that a centralised state would not be accepted by at least two of the principal ethnic/confessional groups in Bosnia and Herzegovina, since it would not protect their interests in the wake of the bloody civil strife that now sunders the country.

38. Consequently, the Co-Chairmen believe that the only viable and stable solution that does not acquiesce in already accomplished ethnic cleansing, and in further internationally unacceptable practices, appears to be the establishment of the decentralised State. This would mean a State in which many of its principal functions, especially those directly affecting persons, would be carried out by a number of autonomous provinces. The central government, in turn, would have only those minimal responsibilities that are necessary for a state to function as such, and to carry out its responsibilities as

---

[128] (LC/C2 (FINAL); partial text also in Szasz 1995a: 268.

a member of the international community. The proposed decentralisation also appears to reflect the wish of all the parties...There were also differences on the number of "provinces" into which Bosnia and Herzegovina might be arranged...[129]

There were also differences between the parties as to the degree of constitutional recognition that should be given to the three major "constituent peoples" or ethnic/confessional groups, namely the Muslims, the Serbs and the Croats, and also to a category of "others". The Serbs and the Croats considered that predominant roles should be given to the "constituent peoples". This approach reflected a continuation of the importance of such designations in Yugoslav constitutional development. The Muslims wanted no such overt recognition, although they accepted that political processes would continue to be characterised by religious and ethnic factors.

As noted, all of the parties preferred a considerably decentralised State, with only minimal responsibilities entrusted to the central authorities. Only a single citizenship was to exist in the country. A person could hold dual citizenship but not 'provincial citizenship'. The central government would only have the power to tax for limited purposes. Some governmental functions could be centralised but not carried out by the central government, but rather by independent authorities administered by representatives of all the provinces. Most governmental functions would be carried out at the provincial, or local level, for example, the policing, educational and cultural activities, the licensing of trades, professions and business and the provision of health, social care, and insurance. A classic separation of power structure was envisaged for the central government with legislative, executive and judicial branches.[130] Bosnia was to observe the 'highest internationally accepted standards of human rights'. The provisions covered both substantive rights and domestic and international procedural arrangements. The human rights of individuals and groups were to be written into the Constitution, which would also require that Bosnia become a party to a series of listed treaties which would be 'immediately applicable' as law. The former Yugoslavia had been a party to most of the UN treaties in question so only the filing of a notice of succession with the Secretary-General would be necessary.[131] International monitoring or other supervision by the bodies created by certain of these treaties was to be allowed. As to the treaties originating with the Council of Europe, Bosnia and Herzegovina would only become eligible to become a party when it became a member of the Council. Among a number of transitional international control measures were a Human Rights Court and a number of Ombudsmen. Military forces were to be entirely under the control of the central government and were to have exclusive possession of military power in Bosnia.

These broad themes were reflected in the ICFY's WG's three constitutional papers on Bosnia (September 1992) and the Vance Owen Plan (1993) and its precursor. It was also evident by this time that great political pressure was going to have to be put

---

[129] S/24795.
[130] S/24795, prs.51-62.
[131] Cf. the view of the HRC that automatic succession takes place, section VI, F above.

on the three parties to reach an agreement. The co-chairmen were expressing concern that the Bosnian Government was increasingly becoming representative only of the Muslim population. They sought to encourage the Bosnian Muslims and Bosnian Croats to work in a more representative Presidency. There was also growing recognition that the authorities in Belgrade had such political, economic and military control over the Bosnian Serbs that they were crucial to achieving a settlement. This made it important to maintain the sanctions against Serbia.

(4) The Vance Owen Plan (1993) and its precursor.
One of the central and well-publicised peace initiatives to emerge from the discussions in the ICFY was the Vance-Owen Plan (VOPP) of January 1993. It emerged after months of tortuous negotiations on the framework and principles and on a map put forward by the co-chairmen.[132] The VOPP was a complicated and wide-ranging agreement, which came tantalizingly close to success. Its constitutional framework provided, *inter alia*, that,

(1) Bosnia and Herzegovina shall be a decentralized State; the Constitution shall recognise three constituent peoples, as well as a group of others, with most governmental functions carried out by its provinces.
(2) The provinces shall not have any international legal personality and may not enter into agreements with foreign States or with international organizations.
(3) Full freedom of movement shall be allowed throughout Bosnia and Herzegovina, to be ensured in part by the maintenance of internationally controlled throughways.
(4) All matters of vital concern to any of the constituent peoples shall be regulated in the Constitution, which as to these points may be amended only by consensus of these constituent peoples; ordinary governmental business is not to be veto-able by any group.
(5) The provinces and the central Government shall have democratically elected legislatures and democratically chosen chief executives and an independent judiciary. The Presidency shall be composed of three elected representatives of each of the three constituent peoples. The initial elections are to be United Nations/European Community/Conference on Security and Cooperation in Europe supervised.
(6) A Constitutional Court, with a member from each group and a majority of non-Bosnian members initially appointed by the International Conference on the Former Yugoslavia, shall resolve disputes between the central Government and any province, and among organs of the former.
(7) Bosnia and Herzegovina is to be progressively demilitarised under United Nations/European Community supervision.

---

[132] See S/25050 (12 January 1993); S/25403 (12 January 1993); S/25100 (23 January 1993); S/25221 (2 February 1993); S/25248 (8 February 1993); S/25479 (26 March 1993); S/25490 (30 March 1993); S/25708 (30 April 1993); S/26066 (8 July 1993).

(8) *The highest level of internationally recognised human rights shall be provided for in the Constitution, which shall also provide for the implementation through both domestic and international mechanisms* (emphasis added).[133]

(9) A number of international monitoring or control devices shall be provided for in the Constitution, to remain in place at least until the three constituent peoples by consensus agree to dispense with them.

The Vance-Owen Peace Plan was a complex set of agreements that included constitutional principles, a military agreement, a provisional provincial map and an agreement on interim arrangements. The Co-Chairmen estimated that a United Nations force of 15,000 to 25,000 would be required to implement the plan and accepted that it would be difficult to implement. As expected, all of the parties had some initial objections to the VOPP, but by the end of March 1993, ten out of the twelve signatures required for the conclusion of the VOPP plan had been obtained. Progress appeared to be promising. However, throughout the negotiations there was a fundamental difference on the issue of the legitimacy of the State of Bosnia and Herzegovina. The Muslim Government side insisted that since Bosnia and Herzegovina was an independent, sovereign State recognised as such by the United Nations, the existing constitutional order, government and governmental institutions should all be preserved and endorsed in any peace settlement by all the parties. The Bosnian Serb view was that a civil war was raging because of the circumstances surrounding the creation of Bosnia. For them the independent State of Bosnia had never existed and did not exist. They were being forced by the international community to live within Bosnia against their wishes. They therefore wished to retain as much of "Republika Srpska" as possible and to restrict the functions of the central governmental institutions of Bosnia to a minimum. Effectively it wanted Bosnia to be divided into what would effectively be three separate states. Signature of the peace plan was completed on 2 May when Mr. Karadzic signed the provisional provincial map and the agreement on interim arrangements. However, the decision of the Bosnian Serb Assembly meeting at Pale (5 May) to put the issue to a referendum annulled Mr. Karadzic's signature almost immediately (15 and 16 May), despite President Milosevic and Prime Minister Mitsotakis intervening in favour of it. Immediately after the Assembly meeting, the Federal Republic of Yugoslavia (Serbia and Montenegro) announced that it was cutting off all but humanitarian supplies to the Bosnian Serbs. The referendum rejected the VOPP. In May 1993 armed conflict resumed between the Croats and Muslims in central Bosnia.

Why did the VOPP not succeed? It was initially supported by the EC and by the Security Council but was ultimately dropped because of US opposition.[134] In the face of that opposition the EC was not willing to pursue the plan alone. It was thus forced to wait until the US became more engaged in the diplomatic efforts and

---

[133] There was also an agreement on interim arrangements which included, *inter alia*, provisions on human rights protection and the reversal of ethnic cleansing, see S/25479, Annex I.

[134] See Owen 1995a: chs.3-4. Owen is clearly bitter that the US failed to support it and the UK were duplicitous with him.

developed its own alternative plan which it would then support diplomatically and, if accepted by the parties, militarily. The central element of US opposition was that the VOPP appeared to reward ethnic cleansing by the Serbs who were regarded as the aggressors. It is thus ironic that many elements of the VOPP survived into the final Peace Agreement and that the eventual peace plan promoted by the US actually gave the Serbs greater territory than the VOPP.

(5) The Owen-Stoltenberg or Invincible [135] Plan (September 1993).
Within a few months came the Owen-Stoltenberg or *Invincible* Plan (September 1993).[136] This contained a Constitutional Agreement on the Union of Bosnia and Herzegovina. This provided for minimal centralised functions for a 'Union of the Republics of Bosnia and Herzegovina' composed of three Constituent Republics and encompassing three constituent peoples: the Muslims, Serbs and Croats, as well as a group of other peoples. All governmental functions and powers, except those assigned by the Constitutional Agreement to the Union or to any of its institutions, were to be those of the Constituent Republics. It was possible to have citizenship of the Union, of the Republics and dual citizenship, that is, citizenship of another State such as Croatia or Serbia.

In addition to a specific section in the constitutional agreement on human rights and fundamental freedoms (sect.V), there were extensive provisions in the annexes on a human rights court, human rights instruments to be incorporated into the constitutional agreement, and Ombudsmen (there were to be four – one from each recognised group: Muslims, Serbs, Croats and Others). All citizens had the rights to settle in any part of the territory of the Union, to have restored to them any property of which they were deprived in the course of ethnic cleansing and to be compensated for any property which could not be restored to them. There was also a side agreement on agreed arrangements concerning the constitutional agreement. This dealt, *inter alia*, with police matters, refugees, reversal of ethnic cleansing and an international human rights monitoring mission. The *Invincible* plan failed because the percentage of territory for the Muslim Republic did not meet the minimum demanded by the government of Bosnia and Herzegovina.

(6) Confederation proposals; The Constitution of the Federation of Bosnia and Herzegovina (March 1994).
In June 1993 proposals emerged from the Bosnian Croats and the Bosnian Serbs based on a confederation of three constituent republics. The constitutional principles already agreed upon as part of the Vance-Owen Peace Plan were the basis for this document. Under the proposals Bosnia and Herzegovina was to be a Confederation. The Constitution would recognize three constituent peoples, as well as a group of others, with most governmental functions carried out by its provinces. The Republics were not to enter into agreements with foreign States or with international organizations if it could damage the interests of other Republics. Other constitutional

---

[135] The *Invincible* was a British aircraft carrier.
[136] See S/26233, S/26337, S/26395, S/26486; Szasz 1995a: 243-4; Owen 1995a.

principles dealt with freedom of movement, matters of vital concern to any of the constituent peoples and their Republics, democratically elected legislatures for the Republics, an independent judiciary, a Constitutional Court, the progressive demilitarisation of Bosnia, the highest level of internationally recognised human rights to be provided for in the Constitution, which should also provide for the ensuring of implementation through both domestic and international mechanisms, and a number of international monitoring or control devices to be provided for in the Constitution.[137]

Although these specific proposals were not agreed, because of failure to agree on the map, detailed negotiations continued between the Bosnian Muslims (Bosniacs)[138] and the Bosnian Croats joined by the Government of Croatia. Significantly, the United States sponsored the negotiations. The outcome was reflected by two agreements of 18 March 1994. The first was a Preliminary Agreement Concerning the Establishment of a Confederation between Bosnia and Herzegovina and Croatia.[139] The establishment of the Confederation was not to change the international identity or legal personality of Croatia or of the Federation.[140] The Federation was to provide a negotiating counterweight to the Serbs.

The second and more important agreement was the proposed 'Constitution of the Federation of Bosnia and Herzegovina' which entered into force on 30 March 1994.[141] The Federation was to be composed of cantons, the boundaries of which were to demarcated.[142] Decisions on the status of territories with a majority Serb population were to be made in the course of peace negotiations. Section II of the Constitution contained provisions on Human Rights and Fundamental Freedoms. In addition to a specific list of rights, a series of international human rights instruments were to be applied throughout the territory.[143] There were provisions on the right of refugees and displaced persons to return home, the restoration of property of which persons were deprived in the course of ethnic cleansing, the permissibility of dual citizenship, cooperation with international human rights monitoring mechanisms and the appointment and functioning of Ombudsmen.[144] Further sections of the Constitution dealt in detail with the division of responsibilities between the federation government and the cantons, the structure of the federation government (including a constitutional court and a human rights court), the cantonal governments,

---

[137] S/26233, Appendix I, 3 August 1993.

[138] It is interesting to consider the use of this term. Szasz explains that it was used by the Muslims 'to emphasize their allegedly non-ethnic, non-religious character', 1995b: 371. By contrast Pajic 1998: 136, questions the name as impractical and etymologically inconsistent and implicitly eliminated the traditional label 'Bosnian' which was free of any national or political connotations.

[139] See 33 *ILM* (1994), 605. Annexes provided for respective rights of transit. The agreement was to remain in force for 99 years unless otherwise agreed.

[140] *Ibid.*, art.3.

[141] 33 *ILM* (1994), 740 and 781.

[142] One problem is that 'the Cantons have no historical basis and must themselves be constructed as a first step in achieving the Federation', Szasz 1995b: 373.

[143] 33 *ILM* (1994), 780.

[144] See also the Regulations of the Bosnia Herzegovina Ombudsmen on the method of executing their functions and on their internal organization, reproduced in Szasz 1995a: 304-310.

municipality governments, international relations,[145] amendments,[146] approval, entry into force and transitional arrangements.

As well as representing an important accommodation between the Bosnian Muslims and the Croats, the Federation in time became an integral part of the Dayton Agreement and so part of Bosnia's constitutional structure and legal order.

VIII. THE DAYTON AGREEMENT, INCLUDING A CONSTITUTION OF BOSNIA AND HERZEGOVINA AND AN AGREEMENT ON HUMAN RIGHTS (NOVEMBER 1995)

The Dayton Agreement, the 'General Framework Agreement for Peace in Bosnia and Herzegovina' (GFA) was initialled on 21 November 1995 and officially signed in Paris in 1996.[147] It represented the outcome of twenty-one days of 'Proximity Peace Talks' held at Wright-Patterson Air Force Base in Dayton, Ohio. Although officially under the auspices of the five-member Contact Group the U.S. dominated the negotiations.[148] It is a complex and fascinating series of agreements and undertakings which draw heavily on the five initiatives considered above. It contains sophisticated constitutional arrangements and its structure and content raise some interesting questions of international law and organization.

On 10 November 1995 an Agreement was reached on implementing the Federation of Bosnia and Herzegovina, with attached agreed principles for the interim statute for the city of Mostar.[149] The general principle of the Federation Agreement was that the Government of the Republic should retain only those functions that enabled it to act as the government of the internationally recognised state of Bosnia. All other functions were to be transferred to the Government of the Federation. The aim was a 'complete functional separation of competencies'.[150] Inclusive lists of the responsibilities of the Federation and Republic respectively were set out. Every two weeks there were to be joint reports on the implementation of the Agreement to the witnesses (US, FRG, Spain (for EU), EU Administrator for Mostar. Also on 10 November an Agreement was reached on the region of Eastern Slavonia, Baranja and Western Sirmium.[151]

These two agreements helped pave the way for the 'General Framework Agreement for Peace in Bosnia and Herzegovina' to which is annexed a series of

---

[145] International law is directly incorporated and has primacy in cases of incompatibility, section VII, article 3.

[146] No amendment can eliminate or diminish any of the rights in section II A of the Constitution.

[147] Cm 3154 (1996); 35 *ILM* (1996) 75-183. See SC Resns 1031 and 1035 in 35 *ILM* (1996) 251-6, SC Resns 1023 and 1037 in 35 *ILM* (1996) 188-92 and SC Resns 1021 and 1022 on sanctions in 35 *ILM* (1996) 257-60. It is not unknown for historic treaties to have been agreed in one place but be signed or known as the treaty of another place.

[148] Among the elements of US pressure on Bosnia was that NATO would not be its air force, on Croatia that it would face economic sanctions, and on Serbia that it would not gain international acceptance.

[149] 35 *ILM* (1996), 170.

[150] *Ibid.*, sect.II, A, 2.

[151] 35 *ILM* (1996), 184. This provided for the establishment of a transitional administration supported by a UN peacekeeping force with military and civilian components. See SC Resns 1023 (1995) and 1037 (1996).

other agreements. In addition to various side letters,[152] and a 'Concluding Statement by the Participants on the Bosnia Proximity Peace Talks',[153] there was an 'Agreement on Initialling the General Framework Agreement'.

It is broadly possible to divide the agreement into the military part – the general framework agreement and Annexes 1A and 1B, and the non-military part – Annexes 2-11. We consider the two parts in turn. The aim is to provide a general outline of the structure of the peace agreement and identify the significant aspects from international and constitutional law perspectives in terms of standards, principles and institutional organization.

1. The Military Aspects of the Agreement
The agreement begins with the 'General Framework Agreement for Peace in Bosnia and Herzegovina' (GFA). The 'Parties' to the agreement are the Republic of Bosnia and Herzegovina (to be known in the future simply as Bosnia Herzegovina), the Republic of Croatia and the Federal Republic of Yugoslavia. The agreement appears to be an inter-governmental agreement between three states. The agreement notes an earlier agreement of 29th August 1995 under which the delegation of the FRY was authorised to sign, on behalf of Republika Srpska (RS), the parts of the peace plan which concerned it.[154] Under that agreement the RS was obliged to implement any Agreement that was reached 'strictly and consequently'.

The GFA is short, containing only 11 articles. Under article I the parties shall conduct their relations in accordance with the principles set forth in the UN Charter, as well as the HFA and other OSCE documents. In particular, the parties agreed to fully respect each others sovereign equality, to settle their disputes by peaceful means, to refrain from any action, by threat or use of force or otherwise, against the territorial integrity or other political independence of Bosnia or any other State.[155] Under article II the parties endorsed the military aspects of the agreement and aspects of regional stabilisation and undertake to fully respect and promote the fulfilment of the commitment made in Annexes 1–A and 1–B.

Article III notes the arrangements concerning the boundary demarcation between the two 'Entities', the Federation of BH and RS (see at 2 below). Article IV welcomes the elections programme in Annex 3 and Articles V and VI welcome the constitutional arrangements in Annex 4 and the various other agreements in Annexes 5–9. Article VII is important in recognising that the observance of Human Rights and the protection of refugees and displaced persons are of vital importance in achieving a lasting peace. It referred the provisions on human rights set forth in Chapter 1 of

---

[152] 35 *ILM* (1996), 153.

[153] 35 *ILM* (1996), 168.

[154] The US would not deal directly with the Bosnian Serbs because of their repeatedly broken promises. Szasz states that the delegation was induced by a combination of military and political threats and promises from the US. Another reason for this was that some of the major military and civilian leaders of RS were under indictment before the ICTY.

[155] The language of 'threat or use of force' is taken directly from Article 2(4) of the UN Charter. The reference to 'or otherwise' would seem to have an even broader effect than the Charter. It might for example catch certain economic or diplomatic pressure that would otherwise be outside the scope of article 2 (4) of the UN Charter.

Annex 6 and the provisions concerning refugees and displaced persons in Chapter 1 of the Annex 7. Article VIII welcomed other aspects of the civilian implementation as set forth in Annexes 10 and 11. Under Article IX the parties agreed to fully cooperate with all entities involved in the implementation of the peace settlement or which were otherwise authorised by the UN Security Council, pursuant to the obligation of all parties to cooperate in the investigation and prosecution of war crimes and other violations of international humanitarian law. Under Article X the FRY and the Republic of Bosnia Herzegovina recognised each other as sovereign independent states within their international borders. Further aspects of mutual recognition were to be subject to subsequent discussions. Mutual recognition as independent states was an important issue in the negotiations. Croatia and Federal Republic of Yugoslavia (Serbia/ Montenegro) recognised each other in 1996, as did Macedonia and Federal Republic of Yugoslavia (Serbia /Montenegro).[156]

Annex 1A contained the detailed 'Agreement on the Military Aspects of the Peace Settlement'. This was an agreement between the Republic of BH, the Federation of BH and the RS. Article I provided for a force to be sent on behalf of the international community to assist in the implementation of the territorial and other military related provisions of the peace agreement. The UN SC was invited to adopt a resolution authorizing member states or regional organisations and arrangements to establish a multinational military implementation force (IFOR). IFOR could be composed of ground, air and maritime units from NATO and non-NATO nations. It was to be deployed to Bosnia to help ensure compliance with the provisions of the Agreement.[157] There was to be a transfer of authority from the UNPROFOR Commander to the IFOR Commander. The NATO force was to operate under the authority and subject to the direction and political control of the North Atlantic Council (NAC) through the NATO chain of command. This clearly put NATO in the lead in terms of direction and political control. Agreements between NATO and non-NATO states were foreseen in Article II(c). Article I (2) set out the purpose of the general obligations in article I. These were to establish a durable cessation of hostilities, to provide for the support and authorisation of the IFOR and in particular to authorise the IFOR to take such actions as required, including the use of necessary force, to ensure compliance with the annex, and to ensure its own protection; and to establish lasting security and arms control measures as outlined in Annex 1B. In relation to the purpose of establishing a durable cessation of hostilities, neither Entity was to threaten or use force against the other Entity. Under no circumstances should any armed forces or either Entity enter into or stay within the territory of the other Entity without the consent of the government of the latter and of the Presidency of Bosnia. The effect was to provide for two separate armed forces in the Federation of BH and in RS.

SC authority for IFOR was given in Resolutions 1031 (1995) and 1035 (1995).[158] It was important that IFOR had the authority to use the 'necessary force' to ensure

---

[156] More generally on FRY see footnote 100 above.
[157] A substantial number of non-NATO states contributed to IFOR, including the Russian Federation.
[158] 35 *ILM* (1996), 235, 251.

compliance with the Annex. This was reminiscent of the wording of SC Resolution 678 concerning the second Gulf War. It was also important that the force could be used not only to ensure its own protection, which it was argued that some of the Security Council resolutions have been limited to, but also 'to ensure compliance with this annex'. There was clearly a very wide authorisation for the use of force.

Each party was to ensure that all personnel and organisations with military capability 'under its control or within territory under its control', including armed civilian groups, national guards, army reserves, military police and the Ministry of Internal Affairs Special Police, complied with the annex. This was important because much difficulty has arisen in terms of whether particular personnel were under the control of particular political authorities.

Article VI provided for the deployment of the IFOR. The SC was invited to 'authorise member states or regional organizations and arrangements to establish the IFOR acting under chapter VII of the UN Charter'. IFOR was to have extensive rights related to the monitoring and implementation of the peace agreement. The IFOR Commander shall have the authority, without interference or permission of any party, to do all that the Commander judged necessary and proper, including the use of military force, to protect the IFOR and to carry out its responsibilities. IFOR had extensive rights of observation, monitoring and inspection.

Article VIII provided for the establishment of a Joint Military Commission (JMC). This was not to include any persons 'who are now or who come under indictment by the International Tribunal for the Former Yugoslavia'. Article IX dealt with prisoner exchanges.[159] Each party was obliged to comply with any order or requests of the International Tribunal for the arrest, detention, surrender of or access to persons who would otherwise be released and transferred, but who are accused of violations within the jurisdiction of the Tribunal. Each party was obliged to detain persons reasonably suspected of such violations for a period of time sufficient to permit appropriate consultation with tribunal authorities. Under Article XII the IFOR Commander was the final authority in theatre regarding the interpretation of the agreement in the military aspects of the peace settlement.

Annex 1B contained the Agreement on Regional Stabilisation. The Republic of BH, the Republic of Croatia, FRY and the Federation of BH, and the Republika Srpska signed this. The parties accepted that there was a need for progressive measures for reasonable stability and regional arms control in order to create a stable peace in the region. Various forms of co-operation and confidence and security building measures were agreed. The CSBM's in Bosnia were to be determined by negotiations under the auspices of the OSCE drawing upon the 1994 Vienna document on negotiations on CSBM's of the OSCE and the objective is to reach an initial set of measures within forty five days. Detailed provisions addressed the issues of importing arms, establishing a stable military balance via an armaments agreement. The OSCE thus had an important role in assisting the parties to reach agreement on a regional balance.

---

[159] The ICRC had an important role in relation to the release of prisoners.

2. The Agreement on the Inter-Entity Boundary Line (IEBL) and related issues
This was an agreement between the Republic of BH, the Federation of BH and the Republika Srpska. The boundary between the Federation of BH and the RS was to be delineated in accordance with a map and could only be adjusted by mutual consent. The boundary largely followed the final frontlines of the conflict and reflected a 51%/49% split. Earlier in 1995 Serb forces had been in control of 70% of the territory. The inter-Entity boundary thus comes close to being an inter-ethnic boundary and is thus open to the criticism that it implicitly legitimises military gains made on the back of ethnic cleansing, extensive war crimes and crimes against humanity.[160] There was to be freedom of movement throughout Bosnia and so neither Entity was to establish controls at the boundary between the Entities.[161]

Article V provided for arbitration to take place for the Brcko area. What was so astonishing about this was simply that the parties could not reach agreement even on a precise definition of their dispute and so they just referred it to arbitration. The arbitration decision was to be final and binding and implemented by the parties without delay. As for the applicable law for the arbitration there was no guidance beyond the provision that the 'arbitrators shall apply relevant legal and equitable principles'. Would those be principles of international law or Yugoslav law? It was provided that unless there was agreement otherwise the administration of the Brcko area will continue without change. This was fortunate because in the first award of the arbitrator no final decision was reached because the institutions of the Federation had not developed enough and the RS had shown almost total disregard to its Dayton obligations in the Brcko area.[162] Instead an innovative award made provision for interim multi-ethnic administration under international supervision and directed towards the development of representative democratic local government. RS obstruction continued and the Final Award in 1999 provided for a new multi-ethnic governmental structure under the sovereignty of BH.

Finally, under article VI, for the areas transferring from one Entity to another in accordance with the demarcation of the inter-Entity boundary line, there should be a transitional period for the orderly transfer. The transition was to be completed within 45 days after the transfer of authority to the IFOR Commander.

3. The Agreement on Elections
Annex 3 provided that the parties should ensure that 'conditions exist for the organization of free and fair elections, in particular a politically neutral environment'. The parties requested the OSCE to adopt, put in place and supervise an elections programme for Bosnia. The elections were to take place six months after the entry into force of the agreement or, if the OSCE determined that a delay was necessary, no later than nine months after the entry into force of the agreement. The OSCE has extensive experience in election monitoring. It is organized through the Office for Democratic Institutions and Human Rights (formerly the Office for

---

[160] See Pajic 1998: 126.
[161] Freedom of movement has been assisted by military bridges, of which there were fifty seven as of November 1998.
[162] See *Arbitral Tribunal for Dispute over Inter-Entity Boundary in Brcko Area*, n.172 below.

Free Elections). In terms of the substantive rules governing the elections the parties agreed to fully comply with paragraphs 7 and 8 of the OSCE Copenhagen Document. This is an interesting use of substantive standards developed within the OSCE.

4. The Constitution of Bosnia: The evolution outside of Bosnia of a post-conflict Bosnian 'Constitution'

Annex 4 sets out a Constitution for Bosnia that entered into force upon signature of the GFA as a constitutional act superseding the Constitution of the Republic of Bosnia and Herzegovina.[163] The preamble recognised the Bosniacs, Croats, and Serbs as 'constituent peoples' (along with Others). Article I of the agreement provided that the 'Republic of BH', henceforth to be officially known simply as 'Bosnia Herzegovina', was to continue its legal existence under international law as a state, with its internal structure modified as provided in the peace agreement and with its present internationally recognised borders. It was to remain a member state of the UN and could maintain or apply for membership in organizations within the UN system and other international organisations. This was crucial in terms of international law in that Bosnia Herzegovina continued as a state. It, and only it, was a state and it was not a new state but a continuation of the Republic of Bosnia Herzegovina.[164] The Federation of BH and the RS are not states. They are entities within Bosnia (article I (3)). There is a citizenship of Bosnia to be regulated by the Parliamentary Assembly. Alongside this there is a citizenship of each Entity that is to be regulated by each Entity. However, all citizens of either Entity are automatically citizens of Bosnia. No one shall be deprived of Bosnian or Entity citizenship arbitrarily or so as to leave him or her stateless. In international law terms the important citizenship will be that of Bosnia. Citizens of Bosnia can hold the citizenship of another state (for example, Croatia or Serbia) provided there is a bilateral agreement approved by the Parliamentary Assembly between Bosnia and the state concerned. This is a more restrictive provision on dual citizenship than many of the earlier constitutional texts.

Article II of the Constitution dealt with Human Rights and Fundamental Freedoms. Article II (2) provided that the rights and freedoms set forth in the European Convention on Human Rights (ECHR) and its Protocols shall apply directly in Bosnia. They have priority over all other law. It is interesting that all of the protocols, presumably on substantive rights, apply and secondly that they apply directly. Therefore, they can be relied upon by individuals before national courts and tribunals. Those rights are also supreme over 'all other law'. Bosnia and all courts, agencies, governmental agencies, and instrumentalities operated by or within Entities, shall apply and conform to the human rights provisions in Article II(2). The human rights are to be enjoyed by all persons within the territory of Bosnia. Enjoyment of the rights and freedoms provided for in Article II or in the fifteen international agreements

---

[163] This was important in terms of the argument about the continuity of the state. The Republic of BH, the Federation and the RS approved of the Constitution in three separate declarations.

[164] It has thus continued its membership in international organizations like the UN and OSCE.

or sets of agreements in Annex I[165] to the Constitution are to be secured to all persons in Bosnia without discrimination on a series of grounds. The grounds are taken from Article 14 ECHR. The end result is a much wider non-discrimination clause than article 14 ECHR because the non-discrimination also extends to all of the accompanying international agreements.

Article II(5) dealt with refugees and displaced persons. They have the right freely to return to their homes of origin. Property is to be restored to them in accordance with Annex 7 to the GFA. Any commitments or statements made relating to the property of refugees and displaced persons, which was made under duress, are null and void. Under article II (7) Bosnia shall remain or become a party to the series of international agreements listed in Annex I to the Constitution. Article II(8) provided for cooperation by all competent authorities in Bosnia with any international human rights monitoring mechanisms or supervisory bodies under any of the instruments in Annex I, and with the ICTY.

Article III dealt with the responsibilities of and relations between the institutions of Bosnia and the Entities. The Entities have the right to establish 'special parallel relationships with neighbouring states consistent with the sovereignty and territorial integrity of Bosnia'. Each Entity may enter into agreements with states and international organizations with the consent of the Parliamentary Assembly. The relationships between the new Entities and the neighbouring states, in particular Serbia and Croatia, were important political points of difference. It also meant that RS's aim to either be a separate independent state or be a part of Serbia has not been achieved, at least in law. It may well be that very close relationships develop between RS and the FRY as well as between the Federation and Croatia.[166] The Constitution is structured upwards from the Entities. In this sense, all government functions and powers, which are not expressly assigned by the Constitution to the institutions of Bosnia, remain with the Entities. Article III(3)(b) provided that, 'The general principles of international law shall be an integral part of the law of Bosnia and Herzegovina and the Entities'.[167]

Article IV makes detailed provisions for a Parliamentary Assembly (PA) consisting of a House of Peoples and House of Representatives. Sub paragraph (e) makes provision for the situation where a proposed decision of the PA is declared to be destructive of a 'vital interest' of the Bosniac, Croat, or Serb people by a majority of the relevant delegates to the PA. Before such a proposed decision could be approved it needs to have acquired a majority in the House of Peoples of the representatives of the relevant group. Article V made provision for a Presidency of Bosnia to consist of three members, one Bosniac and one Croat, each directly elected from the territory

---

[165] These include the Conventions on Genocide, the Geneva Conventions and Protocols on international humanitarian law, the International Conventions on the Elimination of all Forms of Racial Discrimination and Discrimination against Women, the two International Covenants on Human Rights and the two Optional Protocols to the International Covenant on Civil and Political Rights, the 1992 European Charter for Regional or Minority Languages and the 1994 Framework Convention for the Protection of National Minorities.

[166] See the Special Agreement referred to in section IX, 4 below.

[167] This is consistent with the trend noted in section I above.

of the Federation, and one Serb directly elected from the territory of RS. There are detailed provisions on elections, procedures, powers, and the establishment of the Council of Ministers. The establishment of the Standing Committee on Military Matters was to co-ordinate the activities of the armed forces in Bosnia.

Article VI provided for the establishment of a Constitutional Court composed of nine members. Four are selected by the House of Representatives of the Federation, and two by the Assembly of the RS. The President of the European Court of Human Rights selects the other three members after consultation with the Presidency. The judges selected by the latter were not to be citizens of Bosnia or of any neighbouring state. The Court has exclusive jurisdiction to decide any dispute arising under the Constitution between the entities or between Bosnia and an Entity or Entities, or between institutions of Bosnia. It is specifically provided that included in this jurisdiction are the questions of whether an Entity's decision to establish a special parallel relationship with a neighbouring state is consistent with the Constitution, and whether any provision of an Entity's constitution or law is consistent with the constitution of Bosnia. The Court has appellate jurisdiction over constitutional issues from any court in Bosnia. It also has jurisdiction over issues referred by any court in Bosnia concerning whether a law, on whose validity the decision of that court depends, is compatible with the Constitution, with the ECHR and its Protocols, or with the laws of Bosnia, or concerning the existence of or the scope of a general rule of public international law pertinent to the Court's decision. The decisions of the Court are final and binding.

Under article IX (1) 'no person who is serving a sentence imposed by the ICTY, and no person who is under indictment by the Tribunal and who has failed to comply with an order to appear before the Tribunal, may stand as a candidate or hold any appointive, elective or other public office in the territory of Bosnia and Herzegovina'. This was an important provision relating to suspected war criminals and some individuals have ultimately had to stand down from public office.

The Constitution can be amended by a decision of the PA including a two-thirds majority of those present and voting in the House of Representatives. However, no amendment to the Constitution can eliminate or diminish any of the rights or freedoms referred to in Article 2 of the Constitution or the paragraph which entrenches those rights. Annex II to the Constitution provided for certain transitional arrangements concerning public officers, law, and various other matters. The Entities were to amend their respective constitutions to ensure conformity with the Constitution within a period of three months from entry into force of the Constitution.

5. The Agreement on Human Rights
Annex 6 contained an extensive agreement on human rights. The parties were to secure to all persons within their jurisdiction the highest level of internationally recognised human rights and fundamental freedoms, including the rights of freedoms provided for the ECHR and its protocols and the series of other international agreements listed in an appendix.[168] Chapter Two of the Annex provides of the

---

[168] The list is the same as that appended to the Constitution with the addition of the ECHR and its protocols.

establishment of the Commission on Human Rights (Commission). It was to consist of two parts – the Office of the Ombudsman[169] and the Human Rights Chamber. Each of them can consider alleged or apparent violations of human rights in the ECHR and its protocols or any alleged or apparent discrimination on any ground, with an illustrative list, arising in the enjoyment in the rights and freedoms provided for in the international agreements listed in the appendix. All persons have a right to submit to the Commission and to other human rights bodies applications concerning alleged violations of human rights, in accordance with the procedures of this annex and such bodies. The Human Rights Ombudsman was to be appointed for a non-renewable term of five years by the Chairman in Office of the OSCE, after consultation with the parties.[170] The Ombudsman can investigate on his or her own initiative or in response to an allegation by any Party or person, non-governmental organization or group of individuals claiming to be a victim of a violation by any Party or acting on behalf of alleged victims who are deceased or missing, alleged or apparent violations of human rights within the scope of paragraph 2 of Article II. The language here is largely drawn from Article 25 ECHR. There are provisions for the Ombudsman to have access to, and to examine, all official documents.

The Human Rights Chamber is composed of 14 members, a majority of whom (8) were to be appointed by the Committee of Ministers of the Council of Europe, after consultation with the parties. The Chamber can receive referrals from the Ombudsman on behalf of applicants or directly from a party, person, NGO, or group of individuals claiming to be the victim of a violation. The Chamber can decide which applications to accept and in what priority to address them. In doing so the Commission shall take account of a series of criteria which are largely taken from the admissibility conditions which apply under the ECHR. However, it is specifically directed to endeavour to accept and give priority to allegations of specially severe or systematic violations and those founded on alleged discrimination on prohibited grounds. A friendly settlement is expressly stated to be permissible provided that it is on the basis of respect for the rights and freedoms in the agreement. This parallels the practice under the ECHR. The hearings in the chambers are to be in public except for exceptional circumstances in accordance with rules made by the Chamber. A panel of the Chamber can refer a case to the plenary Chamber for review. Otherwise, however, the decisions of a Chamber are final and binding. The Chamber's decision shall address whether there is a breach by a party of its obligations under the agreement and what steps it should take to remedy the breach. This can include an order to cease and desist, monetary relief for both pecuniary and non-pecuniary injuries and provisional measures. The parties must fully implement decisions of the Chamber.[171]

Article 8 deals with organizations concerned with human rights. The activities of non-governmental organizations and international organizations are to be promoted and encouraged. The parties are to allow full and effective access to NGOs for the

---

[169] Interestingly the institution of an Ombudsman had not been present in Yugoslavia, Szasz 1995a: 253. Most of the cases concern housing.

[170] Initially the person was not to be a citizen of Bosnia or of a neighbouring state, see article XIV.

[171] For the rules of procedure and decisions of the Chamber see http://www.ohr/hr.htm 5 IHRR (1998) 452. Simor 1997. Compliance has since improved.

purposes of investigating and monitoring human rights conditions in Bosnia and are to refrain from hindering or impeding them in the exercise of these functions. Under paragraph 4 'All competent authorities in Bosnia shall co-operate with and provide unrestricted access to the organizations established in this agreement; any international human rights monitoring mechanisms established for Bosnia, the supervisory bodies established by any of the international agreements listed in the Appendix to the Annex, the International Tribunal for the Former Yugoslavia; and any other organization authorised by the UN Security Council with a mandate concerning Human Rights or Humanitarian law'. This is an extensive acceptance of international supervision and monitoring. The sixteen agreements in the Appendix include the ECHR and the first Optional Protocol to the ICCPR.

6. Agreement on Refugees and Displaced Persons
Annex 7 contained extensive details on the steps to be taken for refugees and displaced persons. The UNHCR was given a leading role. Under Article VI, any returning refugee or displaced person charged with a crime, other than a serious violation of international humanitarian law as defined in the Statute of the International Tribunal for the former Yugoslavia since January 1, 1991 or a common crime unrelated to the conflict, was to enjoy an amnesty upon return. It is interesting that such an amnesty measure is specifically included in the agreement at this stage rather than at a later stage. Chapter Two provides for the establishment of an independent Commission for Displaced Persons Refugees. Its mandate includes receiving and deciding upon any claims for real property in Bosnia where the property has not voluntarily been sold or otherwise transferred since 1 April 1992 and where the claimant does not now enjoy possession of that property. The claims may be for return of the property or for just compensation in lieu of return.[171a] There are some detailed provisions governing its procedures and powers.

7. Other Agreements
Annex 8 was an agreement on the Commission to preserve national monuments. The destruction of national monuments was a significant feature of the conflict in the Former Yugoslavia. Annex 9 contained an Agreement on the Establishment of Bosnian Public Corporations. In practical terms these are enormously important for the reconstruction and internal functioning of Bosnia.

Annex 10 was the Agreement on Civilian Implementation of the Peace Settlement. This paralleled the military side of the peace agreement. The parties recognised the wide range of activities that would be required for implementing the civilian aspects of the peace agreement. Partly in view of that they requested the designation of a High Representative to provide assistance and coordination.[172] The mandate and methods of co-ordination and liaison are set out in Article II. An extensive number of international bodies and states have been involved in the civilian implementation

---

[171a] van Houtte 1999.
[172] The first High Representative was Karl Bildt. Wolfgang Petritsch now holds the office. See http://www.ohr.int for comprehensive information including regular reports to the UN and quarterly human rights reports.

side of the agreement. Hence, co-ordination has been crucial. Under Article V the High Representative was the final authority in theatre regarding interpretation of the agreement on the civilian implementation of the peace settlement.

Finally, Annex 11 dealt with the very important matter of the International Police Task Force (IPTF) with an extensive range of functions.

IX. AN ASSESSMENT OF THE IMPLEMENTATION OF THE DAYTON AGREEMENT: THREE YEARS ON

1. The role of institutions and agencies

Given the range and complexity of the Dayton Agreement it will come as no surprise that any assessment of its implementation will be complex. In an address to NATO's North Atlantic Council in October 1998 the High Representative stated that, ' Bosnia was not at war but it was also not at peace with itself'.[173] That would seem to be an accurate reflection. A range of major international actors has been extensively involved in a continuing role in supporting the implementation of the agreement. These include the OSCE,[174] ICRC, UNHCR, Office of the High Commissioner for Human Rights, NATO, EU,[175] ECHO[176] and UN.[177] In addition to preventing a resumption of hostilities, SFOR supported the various activities of UNHCR, OSCE, OHR, UN mission in Bosnia, and the continued efforts against persons indicted for war crimes[178] and the process of exhumations.[179] It has also supported the rebuilding of the infrastructure of Bosnia including bridges, highways, roads (important in terms of freedom of movement) and schools. SFOR has been assisted by the establishment of a Multinational Specialised Unit (MSU) in May 1998, which was intended to fill any gap between the mandates of SFOR and the ITPF. It was particularly useful for riot control and civil unrest. The roles played by national and international NGOs and the development of civil society has also been very significant.

The first elections to the post Dayton institutions were held in September 1996. The OSCE view was that they were carried out in a technically correct manner, with discipline and without incident but that there was a negative political climate.[180]

---

[173] See also North Atlantic Council. Statement on Bosnia and Herzegovina, 8 December 1998; Bass 1998.
[174] The OSCE has a Military Mission known as Regional Stabilisation. See generally the OSCE website on Bosnia, http://www.oscebih.org
[175] The EU granted 1bn ECU in humanitarian aid and 1bn ECU for reconstruction, refugees and technical assistance to Bosnia for 1996-99. In November 1998 the Commission proposed another ECU 60 million. In 1997 the EU spent ECU 10 million on de-mining activities.
[176] As of November 1998, ECHO had rehabilitated approximately 2,800 houses in Bosnia.
[177] The current Special Representative of the UN Secretary-General is Jiri Dientsbier.
[178] SFOR's mandate only extended to it being authorised to detain such persons when encountered in the course of its activities. There is a studied ambiguity about how creatively this can be used and interpreted but it is noticeable that more detentions are occurring (19 as of 17 May 2000).
[179] There were a number of violations of the 'Rules of the Road Agreement' on the arrest and detention of alleged war criminals under which the ICTY was to be informed and conduct a review before any arrest took place. The agreement got its name from an incident in which two Serbian military personnel were arrested after taking a wrong turning in a road.
[180] Only a small share of the refugees and displaced persons crossed over the inter-Entity boundary line to vote. Not surprisingly there was a great deal of misinformation and real or perceived pressure related to registration for voting and voting was mixed with senses of duty and obligation to take part in the democratic processes.

Thus the Dayton conditions for free; fair and democratic elections had not been satisfied.[181] Important municipal elections were held in September 1997 after a delay due to manipulation of the voter registration process. For the general elections in December 1998, 5900 candidates for all electoral levels were approved. Media guidelines were adopted for those elections. The OSCE's role has included adjudicating on who are the authorised persons to submit lists of candidates for elections and issuing arbitration awards concerning election issues. It established a Media Experts Commission, a Provisional Election Commission, and an Election Appeals Sub-Commission. By mid-2000, there have been six major elections since the Dayton Agreement. Participation in the elections was at a high level and in 1998 there was an increase in the number of women elected. The OSCE has held conferences on the role of the international community in the development of a democratic and multi-ethnic political environment in Bosnia. The OSCE is planning for the gradual transition of the electoral process to national control. A draft election law of October 1999 has not been adopted.

The Office of the High Representative (OHR) has had an important role which includes coordination of the civilian organizations and agencies in Bosnia. In some circumstances the High Representative has been obliged to impose State level laws, for example, on privatisation and on citizenship. He has also exercised powers to remove more than twenty persons from office for serious and persistent obstruction of GFA, to impose key laws, and to extend deadlines to claim socially-owned property. The role of UN IPTF in support of local policing authorities has included the vetting of police officers. Obstructionism and failure to cooperate by the government of Republika Srpska have hindered the Human Rights Chamber.[182]

2. *The Right to Return*

Progress on the right to return has been mixed.[183] As of November 1998, the UNHCR put a figure of 535,000 for returns of refugees and displaced persons to Bosnia or to their homes. 53,000 were registered minority returns. For 1998, one-third was to RS and two-thirds were to the Federation. It not only required confidence in the safety and security of the environment, it also required physical rebuilding of homes and communities.[184] As of November 1998 the UNHCR had recognised 14 open cities and spent over $60 million on them.[185] The UNHCR policy is to direct funding to open cities. 3000 Bosnian Croats had returned to Travnik. Among the problems have been illegal and corrupt property transactions and illegal demolitions of buildings

---

[181] See Bantekas 1998.

[182] For example, by cancelling the venue for hearings, failing to appoint a government agent.

[183] See Cox 1998: 631, who comments that, 'The competing goals of the intervention are likely to continue to cause problems. If the Entities were to become multi-ethnic, the constitutional structure would become obsolete. More realistically, if ethnic separation continues into the future, the extensive provision of the right to return in the Constitution will become a dead letter, slipping quietly off both domestic and international political agendas'.

[184] 'We need to send people back to live, not to occupy a house', Elizabeth Rehn, the then Special Representative of the Secretary-General, November 1998, New York.

[185] It had also derecognised the city of Vogosca because of its negative approach to property and right to return issues.

belonging to displaced persons and refugees, for example, in the municipality of Bugojno. This matter was the subject of a special investigation by the Federation Ombudsman and the OSCE. Estimated returns in 1999 were 80–90,000.

In November 1998 USAID and the EU suspended projects in Sarajevo, the capital of Bosnia and located in Federation territory, worth approximately $20 million because of the non co-operation of local authorities on minority returns, for example, by refusing to release housing and not dealing with problems of multiple occupancy. At that time the UNHCR estimate of minority returns to Sarajevo was 800 persons. A 'Sarajevo Declaration' on returns was adopted on 3 February 1998 and implementation was assessed against the target it set of 20,000 minority returnees.[186] As of September 1998, 2500 persons had returned. This was in the context of a major accommodation crisis in Sarajevo. In May 1998, the donors adopted the principle of conditionality to put further pressure on the Entity and local authorities. The vast proportion of the aid (over 95%) has gone to the Federation Entity because of the non co-operation of Republika Srpska. The economy of Republika Srpska has been devastated and there is massive unemployment.

3. General implementation of the civilian and constitutional aspects of the Dayton Peace Agreement

Although it has undoubtedly been militarily successful in ending the conflict in Bosnia,[187] implementation of the civilian and constitutional aspects of the Dayton Peace Agreement has been very difficult.[188] There have been substantial problems at all levels. These have included the non-co-operative attitudes of political parties within Bosnia; problems in getting election results implemented; minimal communications; lack of political and administrative cooperation; obstacles to freedom of movement; political obstructionism;[189] internal power struggles in the Entities; non co-operation with the ICTY; frequent violent incidents and general criminality in a culture of impunity;[190] divisive political propaganda transmitted to Bosnia from neighbouring States and from within; the continued pressure from Bosnian Serbs for a Union of the whole Serb people;[191] nationalist activities by Bosnian Croat and Serb political parties especially on television and on radio; attacks and explosions on privately owned property and on churches; intimidation of the media; arbitrary arrests of journalists

---

[186] A 'Banja Luka Declaration' was also adopted but this stressed political cooperation rather than setting targets.

[187] There has also been extensive work on developing military cooperation in Bosnia, codes of conduct, civil defence, and democratic control over armed forces. The long-term hope is that Bosnia could participate in NATO's Partnership for Peace programme.

[188] The scope of the implementation difficulties was realised at the time, see 'Peace Implementation Conference for the Bosnian General Framework Agreement: Conclusions of the London Meeting', 35 *ILM* (1996), 223; S/1995/1029/Annex. On PIC see http://www.ohr/pic.htm

[189] For example, in the municipality of Gornji Vakuf parallel administrations continued to operate and councillors and officials on both sides obstructed all efforts to create municipal structures.

[190] A number of international organizations complained about inadequate responses to such matters, for example, suspended sentences for persons found guilty of physical attacks resulting in death of Slavko Subotic, an elderly Serb returning from a graveyard visit to his wife. There is an unconfirmed report that the Prosecutor appealed the sentence.

[191] This was the aim, for example, of the Serb Radical Party. The High Representative took the view that this was contrary to the Dayton Peace Agreement and to the Constitution of Bosnia.

and failure of the police to recognise internationally accepted standards relating to journalists' freedom of movement; the failure of local authorities and local police to ensure freedom of movement and to provide a safe and secure environment for refugees;[192] massive customs fraud, parallel customs structures and a failure to adopt a customs code that recognises the whole of Bosnia as a common customs area; attempts to impose taxes and cumbersome procedures on goods crossing the inter-ethnic boundary line; limited progress and cooperation on common institutions;[193] massive and organized fraud; and not even the beginnings of arms control negotiations. It was intended that part of the proceeds from privatisation be used to pay compensation for claims arising from the conflict. However, massively inflated claims for soldiers' pay have been a major obstacle to progress on this issue. Leading Bosnian Serbs, Mr Karadzic and General Mladic, have been indicted by the ICTY but have remained at liberty. Trafficking of women for forced prostitution is a major human rights problem in BH.

4. Positive Developments

There have also been more positive elements and some degrees of cooperation. Two Commissions for Missing Persons from the Federation of Bosnia-Herzegovina worked together with RS police and forensic experts on exhumations of a mass grave in Modrica. At the end of 1998 over 20 mass graves had been found containing the remains of over 230 persons. In 1998 the three Commissions on Missing Persons in Bosnia had worked on 250 sites and found some 1700 bodies. In November 1998 a Framework Agreement on Special Relations between Croatia and the Federation was signed. The first Inter-Entity Painting Exhibition was held in November 1998. OSCE essay and poster competitions were held for children. Telephone cards promoting multi-ethnic tolerance were produced in both Entities. The Democratisation Department of the OSCE held a number of seminars and conferences. An Independent Media Commission was inaugurated in June 1998. In 1998 there was agreement on the restructuring of RTV BiH necessary to establish genuine free, public service broadcasting. Proper laws and a regulatory structure for the media were recognised as priorities. A Free Election Radio Network was established. OSCE also provided assistance in kind, for example, printing posters, for political parties committed to a multi-ethnic, pluralist Bosnia. By the end of 1998, there were around 24 inter-Entity bus lines. In November 1998 an ethnically diverse Bosnian parent-teachers association was formed. A common licence plate project was a great success in improving freedom of movement. There is a common currency and a new flag. Tuzla international airport has been opened and there has been progress in establishing normal civilian air traffic in Sarajevo and Mostar.

Joint meetings of constitutional judges from the three constitutional courts were held.[194] A UN Judicial Assistance programme was inaugurated in 1998. In November 1998 an important agreement was signed between the two Entity Ministries of the

---

[192] In 1998 there were over 70 security incidents in Stolac alone.

[193] The EC's PHARE programme now provides consultants to some of the common institutions.

[194] One of these was a seminar on the interpretation and implementation of international investment treaties.

Interior dealing with drug control, terrorism, corruption, protection of the peace and security of voters. There has been a partial delegation of authority over airspace to national control. Joint de-mining operation between the armies of the Federation and the RS have taken place. Consideration is even being given to the idea of a Bosnian Truth and Reconciliation Commission.

5. Economic Aspects

The Contact Group has continued to meet to provide support for and assessment of implementation. By the end of 1998 it premised the continued support from the international community on a united and multi-ethnic Bosnia. It also made it clear that Bosnia had to plan on the basis of a reduction in international assistance and so had to make the transition to a sustainable market economy *via* private sector development, privatisation, modern payment systems and functioning capital markets and banking institutions.[195] There has been a Consultative Task Force dedicated to foreign direct investment in which the EU has played a leading role.[196] Among the other priority areas recommended by the Contact Group were increasing the momentum of the return of refugees, providing a safe environment through the rule of law including judicial reform and the further establishment and democratisation of a multi-ethnic police, developing and reinforcing central institutions, adoption of a permanent election law, media reform and education issues. In October 1998 the Paris Club agreed to write down 67% of Bosnia's debts and extend repayment to a term of over 30 years. However, as early as the end of 1998, the international community expressed concern at the emerging of a culture of dependency in Bosnia. Following the Dayton Peace Implementation Council Ministerial meeting, held between 15th–16th December 1998, in Madrid, over 300 million Euros have been pledged. A trade agreement with the EU came into force on 1 January 2000.

6. The broader significance of the Dayton Agreement

In formal terms the complex range of agreements is impressive. It is a veritable legal and political framework for the rebuilding of a country. What is perhaps most remarkable about the agreement is the extent and the degree to which the internal functioning of Bosnia is internationalised.[197] There is an extensive range of human rights and domestic (Constitutional Court, Ombudsman and a Human Rights Chamber) and international mechanisms to protect them. The direct application, with priority status, of the rights in the European Convention on Human Rights and its Protocols could prove to be a powerful tool. This is supported by the other fifteen international human rights instruments, which bring with them various degrees of established international jurisprudence on their meaning and interpretation. Bosnia remained or became a party to a substantial list of international human rights agreements.[198] This

---

[195] For a broad analysis of contemporary developments on economic order see McGoldrick 1999a.

[196] In April 1997 the EU adopted a Regional policy Approach towards South-Eastern Europe. This covers conditions for aid, trade etc.

[197] See Pajic 1998: 126, who argues that Bosnia is implicitly under the 'protectorate of the international community'; Mertus 1998.

[198] See Szasz 1996.

includes the ECHR and the First Optional Protocol to the International Covenant on Civil and Political Rights, which thus provides for two international individual petition systems. This firmly locates Bosnia within a predominantly individualistic human rights discourse in the hope that it will act as a check on nationalism. There is little or no acknowledgement for minority rights in any collective sense.[199] The argument can be made that this represents a partial turning back of the history of constitutional and social evolution under which group rights and territorial bases have been dominant but ultimately to invidious effect. In one sense the Dayton Agreement represented the 'end of history' for Bosnia.[200] A new democratic vision is set out which had to be disconnected from its political and historical legacy.[201] It remains an open question as to whether one of the lessons to be drawn from Yugoslavia is more questioning of the value of group or collective rights, at least to the extent that a rights system should be on an individualistic basis with minority rights grafted on rather than the other way around. Only time and the operation of human rights institutions will tell whether this human rights vision can credibly be given effect in a state composed of two ethnically based 'Entities' and which is heavily decentralised.[202]

X. Assessing the international responses

It is submitted that, given the totality of the responses considered in sections VI–IX above, the international community clearly made massive efforts to end the conflict and alleviate the suffering. Tens of thousands of lives were saved. The financial costs have run into billions of dollars, and reconstruction costs are adding many more. Almost every known diplomatic and economic strategy has been employed and many military ones. Personal responsibility for war crimes has at least some possibility of effective enforcement. The ultimate criticism is that states and the international community were not willing to resolve the crisis militarily in favour of the Bosnian Muslim government. This basic policy restraint remained throughout the crisis. The most the international community would do was to pressure Serbia to sever its military and economic links with the Bosnian Serbs.[203] Nor would states act on the basis of any doctrine of humanitarian intervention notwithstanding the precedent of the safe havens in Iraq.[204] There seems little possibility that the Security

---

[199] See Mertus 1999: 268. The 1994 Framework Convention for the Protection of National Minorities is a limited instrument. The European Charter for Regional and Minority Languages is more detailed. See Gilbert 1996. Earlier lists had included more extensive provisions on minorities such as the 1992 UN Declaration on Minorities and the 1990 Copenhagen Document of the OSCE.

[200] See footnote 19 above.

[201] Note the comments of Varady 1997: 11, 'The purpose of minority rights is to neutralize, rather than reflect and emphasize, changes in the status of a territory'; 'It seems that the only civilized solution is to allow "difference in equality": to have equal citizens while simultaneously protecting the right of particular groups to preserve their identity, language and culture', p.39.

[202] Cf. Pajic 1998: 135-6, who argues that the agreement does not favour the protection of individual rights because it is preoccupied with the rights of ethnic groups. For a valuable comparative study see Davis and others 1996.

[203] See e.g. SC Resns. 943 and 970.

[204] See the statement of Aust 1992. Arguably the doctrine was a legal basis for military intervention in Kosovo. See Tsagourias (1999).

Council would authorise intervention on that basis. While these remain the governing international policy constraints then the best hope is that the massive range of international pressure and responses that can be brought to bear on international crises will normally have effect sooner than they did in the Former Yugoslavia. At the very least the range of responses considered in this essay has made it clear that to describe the response of the international community and of international law to the crisis as 'neutral'[205] is, in reality, substantially misleading. It was heavily and directly involved at almost all levels short of militarily determining the outcome of the conflict.

XI. Future Strategies for Accommodating National Identity

1. Bad Timing?

To return to the 'Bad Timing Argument' (see section III above). If the Yugoslavia crisis happened now is the international community better equipped to deal with it? The analogy with the response to the crisis in Kosovo in 1998–99 gives some hope. There was a quick and clear EU position[206] and an early military threat from NATO[207] backed to at least some degree by the SC.[208] The political message was clearer – you can deal with terrorists but you can't commit massive human rights violations. The necessary solution was also spelt out. It was to be a political agreement giving greater autonomy to Kosovo. The result was withdrawal of thousands of Serbian police and security forces, return of many displaced persons, and improvement of the humanitarian situation. NATO established a general framework with the OSCE to coordinate air and ground surveillance and verification missions in support of UN SC resolutions. When this failed massive military force was used by NATO.

There has also been institutional evolution among the key international actors. NATO has evolved a New Strategic Concept and increased to 19 members in 1999 with the additions of the Czech Republic, Hungary, and Poland. It adopted a revised Strategic Concept in April 1999 in which its role in crisis management and non-proliferation will feature prominently and its out-of area role will be more explicit. There is a clear political commitment to develop the European Security and Defence Identity within the Alliance. NATO's Partnership for Peace (PfP) programme has steadily expanded and the total partnership extends to 27 states. There is closer NATO-Russia cooperation evidenced by the NATO-Russia Founding Act and the Permanent Joint Council NATO (1997). NATO and Russia disagreed as to the proper means to resolve the Kosovo crisis but the PJC worked through the crisis. NATO-Ukraine relations are also good. Ukrainian forces participated in both IFOR and SFOR. The EU has also evolved *via* the Treaty of Maastricht and did so again on entry into force of the Treaty of Amsterdam in 1999. In the latter it has adopted the St.Petersburg humanitarian and rescue tasks, peacekeeping tasks, and tasks of combat

---

[205] See section V above.

[206] See 'Declaration by European Union on a Comprehensive Approach to Kosovo', 27 October 1998, Doc.12278/98 (Presse 355).

[207] See the agreement of 15 October 1998 between FRY and NATO based on the relevant SC resolutions; Statement on Kosovo, North Atlantic Council, 8 December 1998.

[208] See SC Resolutions 1160, 1199 and 1203. Report of High Commissioner for Human Rights on the Situation of Human Rights in Kosovo (31 May 1999); essay by Tierney in this collection.

forces in crisis management. It is gradually developing a more substantial Common Foreign and Security Policy and a more distinct European Defence Identity.[209] The OSCE has assumed a major role in the institutional architecture of Europe. For example, it was given a leading role in the agreement on Kosovo.

2. Techniques and Mechanisms

This chapter has illustrated the diversity and sophistication of the available techniques and mechanisms for accommodating national identity. The international community currently has significantly more political will than in the past to deal with issues of national identity. In the world of *realpolitik* though, it must be recognised that active US involvement can be crucial both materially and psychologically.[210]

3. Multiculturalism

The fundamental issue remains whether there is a genuine attachment of the international community to the rhetoric of stable, civilised, multicultural coexistence. Will rampant nationalism produce more and more ethnically pure societies, if only in myth?[211] How much could the eventual hope of membership of the EU exercise a restraining influence? Will the international community in general, and the U.S. in particular, be willing to countenance the perpetual military implementation of the Dayton Agreement?[212] Is the Dayton Agreement best seen as creating an opportunity for the two entities to work together? If they are ultimately unwilling to do so, then should the *de facto* partition of Bosnia be made *de jure*? Should the primary focus be on security or on integration? There is some evidence that partition is being openly discussed by Muslim politicians even if that means a return to conflict.[213]

4. The balance between individual and minority rights

How does the contemporary balance lie between individual and minority rights? Do we need a return to more individualistic universalism or more treaty-based detail on minority rights and a constructive fostering of identity?

5. Autonomy

Does the chameleon concept of autonomy offer some hope in its various forms – self-representation, territorial or personal, cultural autonomy?[214] The OSCE has offered some encouragement in this direction.[215] Can the concept of positive

---

[209] See McGoldrick 1997.

[210] See Boyd 1998; Rose 1998. This phenomenon is also clearly evident in the accommodation of the national identity of the Palestinians in the context of the Middle East Peace Process.

[211] See Varady 1997; Mertus 1999b.

[212] See Rose 1998, who notes that some see the Agreement as providing an opportunity for the training and equipping programme for the Muslims in preparation for a resumed conflict.

[213] See Boyd 1998. See p. 42 above on Brcko.

[214] Illustrated, for example, in the 1992 Constitutional Act on Human Rights and Freedoms of National and Ethnic Communities or Majorities in the Republic of Croatia. Such autonomy could conceivably have persuaded the Serb population to remain in the Krajina region.

[215] See, e.g. report of the CSCE Meeting of Experts on National Minorities, 31 *ILM* (1992), 1692 at 1698; see Eide 1993, who argues that any decentralization in territorial terms should be coupled with genuine pluralist democratic governance.

discrimination to correct the natural consequences of the majority ethnic group be viewed in a more favourable light than it has historically attracted?

6. Greater internationalisation of rights protection?
Is greater internationalisation of rights protection on the Dayton model before armed conflict occurs the way forward? This would include national and international monitoring and guaranteed access to international tribunals.

7. Decreasing Relevance of the State?
As the roles of regional, international and transnational actors become more relevant so, in some senses, do the roles of the State become less relevant.[216] Thus Mertus comments that,

> The Dayton accord reflects an understanding that in today's Europe, nation-state boundaries have become more fluid and less relevant for the purpose of fashioning guarantees for regional and international security and minority rights. International and local élites influence regional and international law and policy on the treatment of minority groups. This process in turn influences the identity of national groups and the range of acceptable solutions to their problems.[217]

8. Experimentation
The complexities of accommodating national identity necessarily call for a political willingness to experiment with solutions and to depart to some extent from foundational assumptions. The 1990s witnessed some remarkable developments in conflict resolution in Germany, the USSR, Central and Eastern Europe, Namibia, Cambodia, South Africa and Northern Ireland that again offer hope, guidance and inspiration.

9. Relevance of law
It is probably sensible to end on a note of caution. Many lawyers tend to the view that problems can ultimately be resolved by legal solutions. It is undoubtedly true that law and lawyers can have major roles to play. It must be stressed though that accommodating national identity is often concerned with the most powerful and destructive of social and political forces, rather than with legal ones.

* I am grateful to Stephen Cooper for his technical assistance in the preparation of this article

---

[216] The Belfast Agreement on Northern Ireland can be analysed in similar terms, see Gilbert 1998; Thompson 1999.
[217] Mertus 1999a: 278.

REFERENCES

Akhavan, P. (1993). Punishing War Crimes in the Former Yugoslavia: A Critical Juncture for the New World Order, *HRQ* 15: 262–89

Akhavan, P. & Howse, R. (eds.) (1995). *Yugoslavia: The Former and the Future: Reflections From Scholars in the Region*, Washington: Brookings Institution

Akhavan, P. (1996). The Yugoslav Tribunal at a Crossroads: The Dayton Peace Agreement and Beyond, *HRQ* 18: 259–85

Akhavan, P. (1998). Justice in the Hague, Peace in the Former Yugoslavia? A Commentary on the United Nations War Crimes Tribunal, *HRQ* 20: 737–816

Aust, T. (1992). 63 *BYIL* 827–8

Bantekas, I. (1998). Internationally Organized Elections and Communications: The Reality for Bosnia's Failed Repatriation, *Int.J.Refugee Law* 10: 199–204

Bass, W. (1998). The Triage of Dayton, *Foreign Affairs* 77(5): 95–108

Bayefsky, A.F. (2000). *Self-determination in international law: Quebec and lessons learned*. The Hague: Kluwer.

Berman, N. (1993). "But the Alternative is Despair": European Nationalism and the Modernist Renewal of International Law, *Harvard Law Review* 106: 1792–1903

Bethlehem, D. & Weller, M. (eds.) (1997). *The Yugoslavia Crisis in International Law, Part I*, Cambridge: Cambridge Univ. Press

Betts, R.K. (1994). Delusions of Impartiality: the United Nations and Intervention, *Foreign Affairs* 73(6): 20–33

Biserko, S. (1993). *Yugoslavia: Collapse, War, Crimes*. Belgrade: Centre for Anti-War Action

Blum, Y.Z. (1992). UN Membership of the New Yugoslavia: Continuity or Break, *AJIL* 86: 830–3

Bogdanor, V. (1995). Overcoming the Twentieth Century: Democracy and Nationalism, 1–15, in Pogany, I., (ed.) (1995). *Human Rights in Eastern Europe*, Aldershot: Edward Elgar

Boutros Boutros-Ghali (1995). *Confronting New Challenges – Annual Report on the Work of the UN Organization 1995*, New York

Boyd, C.G. (1998). Making Bosnia Work, *Foreign Affairs* 77(1): 42–55

Burg, B. (1997). *Ethnic Conflict and International Intervention: Crisis in Bosnia-Herzegovina, 1990–93*. New York: M E Sharpe

Cassese, A. (1995). *Self-Determination – A Legal Reappraisal*, Cambridge: Cambridge Univ. Press

Chinkin, C. (1994). Rape and Sexual Abuse of Women in International Law, *EJIL* 5: 326–41

Cox, M. (1998). The Right to Return Home: International Intervention and Ethnic Cleansing in Bosnia and Herzegovina, *ICLQ* 47: 599–631

Craven, M. (1995). The EC Arbitration Commission on Yugoslavia, *British Yearbook of International Law* 66: 333–413

Cushman, T. & Mestrovic, S.G. (eds.) (1996). *This Time We Knew: Western Responses to Genocide in Bosnia*. New York: New York Univ. Press

Davis, D., Chaskalson, M. & de Waal, J., (1996). Democracy and Constitutionalism: the Role of Constitutional Interpretation, 1–130, in: van Wyk, D., Dugard, J., De

Villiers, B. & Davis, D., (eds.) (1996). *Rights and Constitutionalism – The New South African Legal Order*. Oxford: Clarendon Press

Denitch, B. (1997). *Ethnic Nationalism – The Tragic Death of Yugoslavia*. Minneapolis/ London: Minnesota Press

Derrida, J. (1990). The Force of Law: "The Mystical Foundation of Authority", *Cardozo L.R.* 11: 920–1045

Dimitrijevic, V. (1995). The 1974 Constitution and the Constitutional Process as a Factor in the Collapse of Yugoslavia, pp.45–74, in: Akhavan, P. & Howse, R. (eds.) (1995). *Yugoslavia: The Former and the Future: Reflections From Scholars in the Region*, Washington: Brookings Institution

Dinstein, Y. (ed.) (1981). *Models of Autonomy*. New Brunswick, N.J.: Transaction Books

Doehring, K. (1995). Self-Determination, pp.56–72, in: B. Simma (ed.) 1994. *A Commentary on the UN Charter*, Oxford: OUP

Dugard, J. (1997). International Law and the South African Constitution, *EJIL* 8: 77–92

Dunay, P. (1995). Nationalism and Ethnic Conflicts in Eastern Europe: Imposed, Induced or (Simply) Re-emerged, 17–45, in Pogany, I., (ed.) (1995). *Human Rights in Eastern Europe*. Aldershot: Edward Elgar

Duncan, W.R. (1994). *Ethnic Nationalism and Regional Conflict: the Former Soviet Union and Yugoslavia*. Boulder: Westview

Dyker, D.A. & Vejvoda, I. (eds.) (1996). *Yugoslavia and After: A Study in Fragmentation and Despair*. London: Longman

Eide, A. (1993). In Search of Constructive Alternatives to Secession, 139–77, in: Tomuschat, C. (ed.) (1993). *The Modern Law of Self-Determination*. Nijhoff, Dordrecht

Fukuyama, F. (1992). *The End of History and the Last Man,* Harmondsworth: Penguin

Glenny, M. (1996). *The Fall of Yugoslavia: The Third Balkan War*, 3rd edn. Harmondsworth: Penguin

Gow, J., (1992). *Legitimacy and the Military: the Yugoslav Crisis*, London

Gilbert, G. (1996). The Council of Europe and Minority Rights, *HRQ* 18: 160–189

Gilbert, G. (1998). The Northern Ireland Peace Agreement, Minority Rights and Self-Determination, *ICLQ* 47: 943–50

Grant, T.D. (1998). Internationally Guaranteed Constitutive Order: Cyprus and Bosnia as Predicates for a New Nontraditional Actor in the Society of States. Typescript, University of Cambridge

Gray, C. (1997). Application of the Convention on the Prevention and Punishment of the Crime of Genocide, *ICLQ* 46: 688–93

Greenwood, C. (1994). The Prosecution of War Crimes in the Former Yugoslavia, *Bracton LJ* 26: 13–22

Gutman, R. (1993). *A Witness to Genocide*. New York: Macmillan

Hampson, F. (1992). *Incitement and the Media: Responsibility of and for the Media in the Conflicts in the Former Yugoslavia*, Essex: Essex University

Hannum, H. & Lillich, R.B. (1981). The Concept of Autonomy in International Law, *AJIL* 74: 858–89

Hannum, H. (ed.) (1990). *Autonomy, Sovereignty and Self-Determination: The Accommodation of Conflicting Rights*. Philadelphia: Univ. of Philadelphia Press

Hannum, H. (1998). The Specter of Secession, *Foreign Affairs* 77: 13–18

Helsinki Watch (1992). *War Crimes in Bosnia*, New York: Helsinki Watch

Higgins, R. (1993). The New United Nations and the Former Yugoslavia, *Int. Affairs* 69: 465–483

Higgins, R. (1994). *Problems and Process*, Oxford: OUP

Higgins, R. (1995). Peace and Security. Achievements and Failures, *EJIL* 6: 445–60

Horowitz, D.L. (1985). *Ethnic Groups in Conflict*. Berkeley: Univ. of California Press

Huntingdon, S. (1993). The Clash of Civilizations? *Foreign Affairs* 72(3): 22–49

Iglar, R. (1992). The Constitutional Crisis in Yugoslavia and the International Law of Self-Determination: Slovenia's and Croatia's Right to Secede, *Boston College International and Comparative Law Review* 25: 213–39

Irwin, Z.T. (1984). Yugoslavia and Ethnonationalists, pp.72–105, in: F.L. Shiels, *Ethnic Separatism and World Politics*. Lanham/ London: Univ. Press of America

Kandic, N. (1993). *Spotlight on Human Rights Violations in Times of Armed Conflict*. Belgrade: Humanitarian Law Centre

Koskenniemi, M. (1994). National Self-Determination Today: Problems of Law and Practice, *ICLQ* 43: 241–69

Kymlicka, W. (1995a). *Multicultural Citizenship: A Liberal Theory of Minority Rights*. Oxford: OUP

Kymlicka, W. (1995b). *The Rights of Minority Cultures*. Oxford: OUP

Laderer, I.J. (1967). *Yugoslavia at the Paris Peace Conference: A Study in Frontier-Making*. New Haven: Yale Univ. Press

Leurdijk, D. (1994). *The United Nations and NATO in the Former Yugoslavia*, Netherlands Atlantic Commission in Co-operation With the Netherlands Institute of International Relations: 'Clingendael'

Lapidoth, R. (1997). *Autonomy – Flexible Solutions to Ethnic Conflicts*, Washington: U.S. Institute of Peace Press

Lukic, R. (1996). *Europe From the Balkans to the Urals: the Disintegration of Yugoslavia and the Soviet Union*, Oxford: OUP

Lyons, G.M. & Mastanduno, M. (1995). *Beyond Westphalia? State Sovereignty and International Intervention*, Baltimore: John Hopkins University Press

MacCormick, N. (1993). Beyond the Sovereign State, *Modern Law Review* 56: 1–18

Malcolm, N. (1994). *Bosnia – A Short History*, London: Macmillan

Malcolm, N. (2000). *Kosovo: A Short History*, New York: New York Univ. Press.

Marks, S. (1997). The End of History? Reflections on some International Legal Theses, *EJIL* 8: 449–77

Mayall, J. (ed.) (1996). *The New Interventionism, 1994: United Nations Experience in Cambodia, Former Yugoslavia, and Somalia*, Cambridge: Cambridge Univ. Press

McGoldrick, D. (1993). From "Process" to "Institution" – The Development of the CSCE, pp.135–82, in: B.S. Jackson and D. McGoldrick (eds.) *Legal Visions of the New Europe*. London: Graham and Trotman

McGoldrick, D. (1996a). Sustainable Development and Human Rights – An Integrated Conception, *ICLQ* 45: 796–818

McGoldrick, D. (1996b). Yugoslavia: The Responses of the International Community and of International Law, *Current Legal Problems* 49(II): 376–94

McGoldrick, D. (1997). *International Relations Law of the European Union*, London: Longmans

McGoldrick, D. (1999a). From the New International Economic Order to the Agenda for Development, pp.197–232, in: McEldowney, J. (ed.) *National and International Perspectives on Privatization*. London: British Institute for International and Comparative Law

McGoldrick, D. (1999b). The Permanent ICC, *Criminal Law Rev.*: 627–55.

Mercier, M. (1995). *Crimes Without Punishment: Humanitarian Action in Former Yugoslavia*. London: Pluto

Mertus, J. (1998). Prospects for National Minorities under the Dayton Accords – Lessons from History: The Inter-War Minorities Schemes and the "Yugoslav Nations", *Brooklyn J.Int.L.* 23: 793–832

Mertus, J., (1999). The Dayton Peace Accords: Lessons From the Past and for the Future, pp.261–83, in: P. Cumper & S. Wheatley (eds.) *Minority Rights in the 'New' Europe*, The Hague: Kluwer

Mertus, J., (1999b). *Kosovo*. Berkeley: Univ of California Press

Moynihan, D.P. (1993). *Pandemonium: Ethnicity in International Politics*. Oxford: OUP

Mullerson, R. (1993). The Continuity and Succession of States, by Reference to the Former USSR and Yugoslavia, *ICLQ* 42: 473–93

Munro, C. (1999). The Scotland Bill: Devolution within the United Kingdom, *Int. J. on Minority and Group Rights* 6: 97–119

Oliver, P. (1999). Federalism at its Limits: the Decision of the Supreme Court of Canada on Quebec's Status in Constitutional and International Law, *Int. J. on Minority and Group Rights* 6: 65–95

Orentlichter, D. (1998). International Responses to Ethno-Separatist Claims, *Yale JIL* 23: 1–78

Owen, D. (1995a). *Balkan Odyssey*. London: Gollancz

Owen, D. (1995b). The Limits of Enforcement, *Netherlands International Law Review* XLII: 249–58

Pajic, Z. & Hampson, F. (1993). *Violation of Fundamental Human Rights in the Former Yugoslavia*, London: David Davies Institute

Pajic, Z. (1998). A Critical Appraisal of Human Rights Provisions of the Dayton Constitution of Bosnia and Herzegovina, *HRQ* 20: 125–38

Patel-King, F. & La Rosa, A-M (1997). ICTY– Current Survey: the Jurisprudence of the Yugoslavia Tribunal 1994–96, *EJIL* 8:123–79

Paunovic, M. (1993). Nationalities and Minorities in the Yugoslav Federation and in Serbia, in: J. Packer & K. Myntti (eds.) *The Protection of Ethnic and Linguistic Minorities in Europe*, Turku/Abo: Abo Akademi Univ. Press

Pellet, A. (1992). The Opinions of the Badinter Arbitration Committee: A Second Breath of Life for Self-Determination of Peoples, *EJIL* 3: 178–85

Petrovic, D. (1994). Ethnic Cleansing – An Attempt at Methodology, *EJIL* 5: 342–59

Phillips, D.L. (1996). Comprehensive Peace in the Balkans: The Kosovo Question, *HRQ* 18: 821–32

Pinson, M. (ed.) (1996). *The Muslims of Bosnia-Herzegovina: Their Historic Development from the Middle Ages to the Dissolution of Yugoslavia*, 2nd edn. Harvard: Harvard Univ. Press

Pogany, I., (ed.) (1995). *Human Rights in Eastern Europe*. Aldershot: Edward Elgar

Quane, H. (1998). The UN and the Evolving Right to Self-Determination, *ICLQ* 47: 537–72

Ramaga, P.V. (1993). The Group Concepts in Minority Protection, *HRQ* 15: 575–88

Ramet, S.P. (1995). *Beyond Yugoslavia: Politics, Economics and Culture in a Shattered Community*. Boulder: Westview

Reisman, M. (1990). Sovereignty and Human Rights in Contemporary International Law, *AJIL* 84: 866–76

Rich, R. (1993). Recognition of States: Recent European Practice, *EJIL* 4: 36–65 and 66–91

Rogel, C. (1998). *The Breakup of Yugoslavia and the War in Bosnia*. Westport: Greenwood Press

Rosas, A. (1992). Internal Conflicts and the CSCE Process, *Helsinki Monitor* 3/2: 5–9

Rose, G. (1998). The Exit Strategy, *Foreign Affairs* 77(1): 56–67

de Rossanet, B. (1996). *Peacemaking and Peacekeeping in Yugoslavia*. The Hague: Kluwer

Rubenstein, A.Z. (1970). *Yugoslavia and the Non-Aligned World*. New Jersey: Princeton

Salzman, T.A. (1998). Rape Camps as a Means of Ethnic Cleansing: Religious, Cultural and Ethical Responses to Rape Victims in the Former Yugoslavia, *HRQ* 20: 348–78

Schruer, C. (1993). The Waning of the Sovereign State, *EJIL* 4: 447–71

Scott, C. (1996). Indigenous Self-Determination and Decolonisation of the International Imagination: A Plea, *HRQ* 18: 814–820

Shaw, M.N. (1997). Peoples, Territorialism and Boundaries, *EJIL* 8: 478–507

Silber, L. & Little, A. (1996). *The Death of Yugoslavia*, 2nd edn. London: Penguin

Simor, J. (1997). Tackling human rights abuses in Bosnia and Herzegovina: the Convention is up to it, are its institutions? *European Human Rights Law Review* 6: 644–662

Smith, A. (1991). *National Identity*. London: Penguin.

Stein, E. (1994). International Law in Internal Law: Toward Internationalization of Central-Eastern European Constitutions?, *AJIL* 88: 427–50

Steiner, H.J. (1991). Ideals and Counter-Ideals in the Struggle for Autonomy Regimes for Minorities, *Notre Dame Law Review* 66: 1539–60

Suski (ed.) (1997). *Autonomy: Applications, Implications*. The Hague: Nijhoff

Symposium (1995). A Critical Study of the International Tribunal for the Former Yugoslavia, *Criminal Law Forum* 6

Szasz, P.C. (1993). The Fragmentation of Yugoslavia, *Proc. ASIL* 88: 33–9

Szasz, P.C. (1995a). Protecting Human and Minority Rights in Bosnia: A Documentary Survey of International Proposals, *California Western International Law Journal* 25: 237–310

Szasz, P.C. (1995b). The Quest for a Bosnian Constitution: Legal Aspects of Constitutional Proposals Relating to Bosnia, *Fordham Int.L.J.* 19: 363–407

Szasz, P.C. (1996). The Protection of Human Rights Through the Dayton/Paris Peace Agreement on Bosnia, *AJIL* 90: 301–16

Terrett, S.T. (1998). The Dissolution of Yugoslavia and the Badinter Arbitration Commission, Typescript, Ph.D. thesis, University of Liverpool

Thompson, B. (1999). Transcending Territory: Towards the Construction of an Agreed Northern Ireland?, *Int. J. Minority and Group Rights* 6: 235–266

Thompson, M. (1992). *A Paper House – The Ending of Yugoslavia.* London: Vintage

Thornberry, P. (1996). Minority Rights, *Collected Courses of the Academy of European Law*, Vol. VI, Book 2, 326–390

Tierney, S. (1999). In a State of Flux: Self-Determination and the Collapse of Yugoslavia, *Int. J. on Minority and Group Rights* 6: 197–233

Tomuschat, C. (ed.) (1993). *The Modern Law of Self-Determination.* Nijhoff, Dordrecht

Trifunovska, S. (1994). *Yugoslavia Through Documents – From Its Creation to its Dissolution.* Dordrecht: Kluwer

Tsagourias, N.K. (1999). *Jurisprudence of International Law – The Humanitarian Dimension.* Manchester: MUP

Van Houtte, H. (1999). Mass Property Claim Resolution in a Post-War Society: the Commission for Real Property Claims in Bosnia and Herzegovina, *ICLQ* 4: 625

van Wyk, D., Dugard, J., De Villiers, B. & Davis, D., (eds.) (1996). *Rights and Constitutionalism – The New South African Legal Order.* Oxford: Clarendon Press

Varady, T. (1997). Minorities, Majorities, Law, and Ethnicity: Reflections on the Yugoslavia Case, *HRQ* 19:10–54

Vereshchetin, V.S. (1996). New Constitutions and the Old Problem of the Relationship Between International Law and National Law, *EJIL* 7: 29–41

Vulliamy, E. (1998). Bosnia: The Crime of Appeasement, *International Affairs* 74 (1): 73–92

Warbrick, C. (1992). Recognition of States, *ICLQ* 41: 473–82

Warbrick, C. (1993). *ICLQ* 42: 433–42

Warbrick, C. (1997). Recognition of States: Recent European Practice, 9–43, in: M. Evans (ed.), Aspects of Statehood and Institutionalism in Contemporary Europe, Aldershot: Dartmouth

Ward, I. (1995). Identity and Difference: The European Union and Postmodernism, pp.15–28, in: J. Shaw and G. More (eds.), *New Legal Dynamics of the European Union.* Oxford: OUP

Ward, I. (1996). *A Critical Introduction to European Law*, London: Butterworths

Weissbrodt, D. and others, (1993). The 44th session ... and the Special Session of the Commission on Human Rights on the Situation in the Former Yugoslavia, *HRQ* 15: 410–58

Weller, M. (1992). The International Response to the Dissolution of the Socialist Federal Republic of Yugoslavia, *AJIL* 86: 569–607

Wentz, L. (ed.) (1998). *Lessons From Bosnia: The IFOR Experience*, National Defence Press: Virginia

West, R. (1994). *Tito – And The Rise and Fall of Yugoslavia*, London: Sinclair-Stevenson

Woodward, S.L. (1995). *Balkan Tragedy – Chaos and Dissolution After the Cold War*. Washington DC: Brookings Institution

Wijeyeratne, R. De Silva. (1996). Ambivalence, Contingency and the Failure of Exclusion: the Ontological Schema of the 1972 Constitution of the Republic of Sri Lanka, *Journal of Social and Legal Studies* 5(3): 365–81

Zaagman, R. (1992). The CSCE and the Yugoslav Crisis, *Helsinki Monitor* 3/1: 43–50

Zimmermann, W. (1995). The Last Ambassador, *Foreign Affairs* 74(2): 2–20

Canada's Two Solitudes: Constitutional and International Law in *Reference re Secession of Quebec*[1]

Peter Oliver*

INTRODUCTION

The French community in what is now the Canadian federation predates all but the aboriginal settlement. For this reason alone, the story of accommodating national identity in Canada is long, rich and complex. It is difficult to summarise in a short space. The political and legal history of Canada and Quebec includes examples of constitutional planning on a grand scale (colonies, legislatures, union and federation) alongside more haphazard, but no less important, developments of a more evolutionary nature (notably the various arrangements regarding the civil law system, the language of courts and legislatures, religious education, the wording of oaths, *etc.*). At the family and community level, it is of course important to remember that traditional dichotomies were and are being constantly broken down, even if they remain pronounced at the societal level: French-aboriginal inter-marriage was common in the early years of settlement; after the British 'Conquest', English, Scottish and, especially, Irish Catholics regularly married into French-Canadian Catholic families; and today family connections cross over many religions, languages, races and cultures, especially in Quebec's largest and most cosmopolitan city, Montreal. However, concepts such as 'the nation /*la nation*' and 'a people/*un peuple*' have long been discussed in Quebec (and to a lesser extent in Canada). The linking of these concepts to principles of international law is only a recent phenomenon. They are emotionally charged, not surprisingly, and even the Supreme Court of Canada has chosen to tread gingerly through this sort of territory.

Canada's recent years of constitutional turmoil indicate that the North American model north of the 49th parallel is not perhaps ideal. Sympathetic observers might nonetheless agree that Canada's greater national and multicultural aspirations have always been more difficult to achieve. Consequently, failure for Canada (though failure is difficult to define) would deprive other nations of a long-standing example of the attempt to accommodate difference. Canadians themselves are constantly trying

*   Senior Lecturer, School of Law, King's College, London
[1]   This article was written with financial assistance from the Canadian High Commission's Faculty Research Programme.

Stephen Tierney (ed.), Accommodating National Identity: New Approaches in International and Domestic Law, 65–88
© 2000 *Kluwer Law International. Printed in Great Britain.*
First published in the International Journal on Minority and Group Rights, Volume 6 No. 1/2 1999.

to draw lessons from their past. The Supreme Court of Canada has recently, and remarkably, discovered legal principles in that same past. This article explores some of these lessons and principles in historical perspective.

A number of themes will emerge from this account. First, there is the assertion that national accommodation is unlikely to be achieved on the basis of strict or formal equality. A French language and culture which is surrounded and threatened by the overwhelming English fact in North America requires special treatment to have any hope of achieving real equality. Secondly, political leaders who promote the necessary measures for accommodation must understand and be able to articulate the reasons for what might appear to some as unfair preference, otherwise backlash may defeat the endeavour. Thirdly, continuity and recognition guaranteed to one national group should not be denied to smaller groups within: the removal of the 'imperial' aspects of power at one level should not be simply replaced by a smaller version of the same. Finally, even if such admittedly controversial themes are accepted, the practical task of drafting and re-drafting legal and constitutional arrangements is immensely difficult. Whatever the flaws in legal method in the *Secession Reference*, the Supreme Court of Canada's emphasis on negotiation in good faith is immensely important on its own.

FROM BILINGUALISM AND BICULTURALISM TO SEPARATISM AND SECESSION: PIERRE TRUDEAU AND RENÉ LÉVESQUE

The current wave of Quebec separatism began in earnest in the late 1950s and 1960s. This was a period of decolonisation world-wide and of broadly based civil rights movements in North America. Some in Canada's only predominantly French-speaking province identified with the liberating and activist spirit of the times. The most extreme nationalist group, the *Front de libération du Quebec*, took part of its name and inspiration from the Algerian anti-colonial activists. The writer and polemicist Pierre Vallières published a book called *Les nègres blancs d'Amérique*, or *The White Niggers of America* as it was eventually translated, explicitly linking the experiences of Afro-Americans and French-Canadians (Vallières 1968; 1991).

The 1950s ended with the death of Quebec Premier Maurice Duplessis who had dominated, and many would say stultified, the province's development during his almost uninterrupted term of power beginning in the mid-1930s. Much like his contemporaries, Franco in Spain and de Valera in Ireland, Duplessis created a formidable political force through a strategic alliance of conservatives, nationalists, the Roman Catholic Church hierarchy and all those committed to suppressing communism and other 'subversive' forces. While Duplessis masterfully played his nationalist cards in numerous negotiations with the Canadian federal government, grass roots nationalist movements were given little or no opportunity to develop. Most of those with any civil libertarian spirit found themselves united against Duplessis' repressive brand of politics.

Included amongst the anti-Duplessis activists were René Lévesque, a journalist, and Pierre Trudeau, a Université de Montréal law professor. The next four decades of Quebec-Canada relations were to be influenced (if not dominated) by these two powerful personalities. Soon after Duplessis' death in 1959 the province of Quebec elected a Liberal government committed to such a radical reversal of the Duplessis programme that its new direction came to be known as *La révolution tranquille*, or Quiet Revolution. René Lévesque became the powerful and popular Minister of Natural Resources in the new provincial Liberal government. By 1968, impatient with the pace and direction of change, Lévesque broke away from the provincial Liberal party and formed the separatist *Parti québécois*, the very party which has twice asked Quebecers to vote by referendum in favour of sovereignty (or sovereignty-association), and which currently governs the province under the premiership of Premier Lucien Bouchard.[2]

Pierre Trudeau on the other hand took the federal political line. In 1964, then leader of the federal Liberal party, Lester Pearson, convinced three prominent francophone Quebecers to run for political office and join his government. The three, Pierre Trudeau, Gérard Pelletier and Jean Marchand, known collectively at the time as the 'Three Wise Men', made their mark immediately. It was Trudeau who took the lead, however, rapidly becoming Minister of Justice and, in 1968, leader of the federal Liberal party. As Prime Minister for most of the next two decades he promoted the rights of French Canadians across the country through such measures as the *Official Languages Act* and, most significantly (for English and French Canadians alike), the *Charter of Rights and Freedoms*. Trudeau's right hand man and Minister of Justice during the negotiations over the *Charter of Rights and Freedoms*, Jean Chrétien, is the present Prime Minister of Canada.

René Lévesque and Pierre Trudeau had strong, divergent views about the place of Quebec in Canada. To a great extent it is the practical elaboration or realisation of these approaches over almost four decades which has culminated in the *Secession Reference*, recently decided by the Supreme Court of Canada. Both had a profound, highly personal sense of what was necessary to allow the French language and culture to thrive. The two approaches could be summarised, roughly speaking, as follows.

Trudeau's greatest fear was that Quebec would return to the inward-nationalism and authoritarianism of the Duplessis era. Consistent with his own urbane, individualistic and internationalist outlook Trudeau wanted to ensure that francophone Quebecers had opportunity beyond the boundaries of their province, and, accordingly, that francophone Canadians across the country felt properly represented at the federal level of government. Picking up on recommendations by the Bilingualism and Biculturalism Commission which reported in the early 1970s, Trudeau's Liberal government transformed the linguistic landscape of the country. In a country where, despite a French-speaking population of almost one-third, the language of business

---

[2]   Bouchard's *Parti québécois* government was recently re-elected for another term, obtaining virtually the identical number of seats in the National Assembly as it had had before the election. Bouchard had been hoping for the sort of resounding electoral victory that would have provided a mandate to hold another referendum on separation; however it was not forthcoming.

and administration had been predominantly English, the *Official Languages Act* ensured, for example, bilingual packaging on consumer products, bilingual services at federal offices across the country, and, perhaps most significant, bilingual positions throughout the federal civil service. Just as important as providing services and opportunity across the country for French Canadians was the task of ensuring that the tyranny which had limited so many rights in Duplessis' Quebec did not reproduce itself in Quebec or elsewhere. Trudeau's writings well prior to his political career had emphasised the importance of an entrenched bill of rights (Trudeau 1968). This goal was achieved with the passage of the *Canada Act 1982* which contained the *Charter of Rights and Freedoms* (together with a new domestic amending formula). It also provided further protection for the official languages, by extending language of education guarantees, for example, and by entrenching existing provisions regarding the use of the English and French language.

Trudeau's admirable goals were achieved at some cost. The initial sense of goodwill and pride regarding the expansion of bilingualism and biculturalism across the country provided only part of the story. Federal politicians discovered later to their surprise that aboriginal and non-English/non-French multicultural groups harboured some resentment regarding the preferential treatment shown to French Canadians. Furthermore, in small towns across the country, grand ideals sometimes understandably gave way to more practical concerns. For example, in areas where relatively well-paid, pensionable federal civil service positions were highly sought after, a bilingualism requirement often resulted in the best jobs going to francophones (whose proficiency in English often exceeded others' ability in French). The fact that many of the Trudeau reforms were viewed as insufficient at best or irrelevant at worst by some Quebecers was lost on much of the rest of the country. Perceived gains for French Canada were seen as gains for Quebec, thereby running down most of any pre-existing willingness to go the extra mile for Quebec.

There is no doubt that many French Canadians, inside and outside of Quebec, benefited from Trudeau's reforms. But for the many who did not venture beyond the province's borders, or for whom the reforms were in any event insufficient, a sense of grievance remained. To this grievance was added the insult that the Trudeau government and the nine (predominantly) English provinces had amended the Canadian Constitution in 1982, adding a *Charter of Rights and Freedoms* and a new domestic amending formula, without obtaining the consent of the province of Quebec. Using Supreme Court of Canada reference cases as his permission and eventual justification, Trudeau chose to emphasise legality over a clear deficit of legitimacy, at least insofar as Quebec was concerned.[3] When the federal Parliament passed the resolution which was eventually to become the *Canada Act 1982*, both the *Parti québécois* government and the provincial Liberal Opposition voted in favour of a resolution opposing the measure. The flags of the Quebec National Assembly flew at half-mast on that day.

---

[3]   In the *Senate Reference (Reference re Authority of Parliament in Relation to the Upper 3 House* [1980] 2 S.C.R. 54) the Supreme Court of Canada indicated that fundamental constitutional change had to be accomplished via the United Kingdom Parliament, the body which had originally enacted

Where Trudeau's approach was national, even international, in perspective, René Lévesque's was focused on Quebec and on francophone Quebecers. It was not that Lévesque was naturally narrow or provincial in his outlook; on the contrary, he had made his name as an international reporter for Radio-Canada. Even while he passed legislation giving prominence to the French language in Quebec, he spoke of his admiration for those who spoke many languages and understood many cultures. Although the nuances of the man were ignored by many Quebec voters, it was clear that Lévesque reached a part of the French Quebecers' psyche that Trudeau overlooked. Many francophone Quebecers would not want to take their opportunities in a predominantly English country, continent and world until they felt secure and confident in their own home: *maître chez nous*, or masters in our own home, as the provincial Liberal slogan of the 1960s had put it. Even the Federally inspired Bilingualism and Biculturism Commission had recognised this need, although the insight was not as clearly articulated as one might have liked. André Laurendeau, co-chair of the Commission and anti-Duplessis activist of even longer standing than Trudeau, drew the commissioners' attention to the fact that a strong French Canadian language and culture in Canada required a strong Quebec. Unfortunately, Laurendeau died before the final Report had been drafted (see Oliver 1993).

If a strong French Canada required a strong Quebec, or to put it another way, if Quebec was not a province like all the rest, then it would have to acquire a special status. Whereas Trudeau's more pragmatic predecessor, Lester Pearson, had allowed Quebec special administrative powers in areas such as immigration, taxation and pension provision (Simeon 1972), Trudeau mistrusted what he saw as Quebec's power-grabbing strategies, preferring to benefit French, English, aboriginal and multicultural Canadians directly and equally (at least in the strict sense of equality). In a context where successive Quebec governments moved from an early strategy of seeking changes to the federal institutions and increased constitutional powers for all provinces, to one of seeking special status for Quebec, Trudeau's recalcitrant position made confrontation inevitable. And whereas in 1968 it had been the nominally federalist *Union nationale* party which had demanded special status on behalf of Quebec, before long it was the avowedly separatist *Parti québécois* which spoke for the province, elected to office for the first time in 1976.

The new *Parti québécois* government was committed to a plan of sovereignty-association, a new option for Quebec which was eventually described, as part of the preparation for the first Quebec referendum on separation, in a publication entitled *Quebec-Canada: A New Deal* (Quebec 1979). Essentially what was envisioned was

---

Canada's key constitutional texts. In the *Patriation Reference (Reference re Amendment of the Constitution of Canada* [1981] 1 S.C.R. 753) the Court declared that, as a matter of convention, such fundamental constitutional change required the consent of a substantial number of Canada's ten provinces. When, in the autumn of 1981, the Trudeau government negotiated a constitutional package with support from all provinces except Quebec, it was assumed that Quebec's approval need not be part of this 'substantial number', and this was ultimately confirmed by the Supreme Court of Canada in the *Quebec Veto Reference (Reference re Objection to a Resolution to Amend the Constitution of Canada* [1982] 2 S.C.R. 793). In any event, the *Patriation Reference* had confirmed that, as a matter of law, the United Kingdom Parliament's powers vis-à-vis Canada were undiminished. (For further discussion of the 1981–1982 process, see Oliver 1994).

sovereign legislative jurisdiction for Quebec in a context of continuing economic association with Canada. It was difficult for many Canadians outside Quebec to understand how the imposition of official bilingualism at a national level could be met with dissatisfaction and rejection in Quebec. Nonetheless, the leaders of the federal Liberal government, principally Trudeau and his ally, Jean Chrétien, spoke out at pro-federalist referendum rallies in 1980 and promised constitutional changes to improve Quebec's position in Confederation. The vote in the May 1980 referendum was roughly 40 per cent for and 60 per cent against the mandate to negotiate the brand of sovereignty-association that the Quebec government had sought. Two years later, following federal-provincial negotiations which included a re-elected *Parti québécois* still committed to leaving Canada and less than committed to improving the Canadian constitution, the *Canada Act 1982* was passed, Quebec all the while objecting (see Rémillard 1984; Romanow, Whyte & Leeson 1984; Sheppard & Valpy 1982).

It could be said that Trudeau's accent on Canada-wide provision of French-language rights, together with his over-emphasis on legality and a narrow sense of the rule of law in constitutional reform, resulted in an undercurrent of resentment outside of Quebec without any significant level of increased satisfaction from francophone Quebecers. Many Quebecers continued to vote for the *Parti québécois* and harboured a sense of grievance over what they referred to disparagingly, even after 1982, as *le Canada Bill*. Whereas Lévesque's emphasis on increased constitutional powers for Quebec and effective legislation on language in the schools, workplaces, restaurants and stores of Quebec earned him wide support from French Quebecers, these same policies, together with his party's cynical tactics in constitutional negotiations and apparent lack of interest in the reform of the institutions of the Canadian Confederation, resulted in a loss of trust both inside Quebec's non-francophone minority communities and outside the province's borders where non-francophones and francophones felt, respectively, offended or abandoned.

By 1982, the moment of greatest constitutional change in Canadian history since the country's founding in 1867, Quebec and the rest of Canada were as riven as they had ever been. 'Two solitudes', the expression drawn from a popular novel published by an anglophone Quebecer in the 1960s, seemed to apply more accurately than ever to the relationship between the two official language communities and between Quebec and Canada (Maclennan 1993). What too many forgot was that the French-English partnership had strong, deep roots in Canadian history and that much of the country's past had involved the working out of appropriate relations between these two language communities. In fact, the letter by Rainer Maria Rilke from which the novel's title had been taken expressed more optimism than its most memorable two words conveyed: 'Love consists in this, that two solitudes protect and touch and greet each other.'

THE CONSTITUTIONAL POSITION IN HISTORICAL PERSPECTIVE:
FROM CANADA TO QUEBEC AND BACK

In order to speak of the early history of the French fact in Canada it is necessary to reappropriate the term 'Canada', the (aboriginal) word used by French settlers to describe their new home. From the time of the first established settlement in the early 1600s, Canada and New France as a whole were ruled over by the French Crown and governed by French law. The 'Conquest', as it is still referred to in Canadian history, does not refer to the successive victories over and eventual subordination of the aboriginal population, but to the victory of the British armies at Quebec and Montreal in 1760, signalling the end of the Seven Years War, and the end of French colonial rule in North America.[4]

The fact of conquest meant, under British Imperial law, that the Crown was entitled to rule over the newly subjugated territory by means of the royal prerogative. Accordingly, the *Proclamation of 1763* set out the territory called Quebec and provided for its governance. An elected assembly, typical of other British colonies, was promised, but in the meantime a Governor appointed by the Crown would rule. Governor Murray, the first appointee, ordered that English law would govern all civil and criminal matters coming before the courts of the colony. The preexisting French law was effectively abrogated.

At least two circumstances altered this harsh treatment of the French settlers. First, the local population tended to ignore the new courts set up by their British governors, preferring to resolve legal disputes using laws familiar to them, with the help of local notaries or priests. Secondly, the anti-British intentions of the nearby Thirteen Colonies accentuated the need to ensure the loyalty of the majority French inhabitants of Quebec. Accordingly, the British Parliament enacted the *Quebec Act* of 1774 which not only expanded the territory of Quebec to a vast extent, such that it virtually encircled the Thirteen Colonies, but also specified terms which were more favourable to the French settlers. The *Quebec Act* renewed the guarantees of religious freedom, 'within the bounds of English law' and, by rewording the oath of allegiance in a way that was more acceptable to their religious convictions, made it possible for Catholic Canadians to hold government positions. The 1774 *Act* retained English criminal law but reinstated French civil law over 'property and civil rights', without excluding the right of British settlers holding property and entering into legal relations using English law. It stopped short of establishing a Legislative Assembly, constituting in its place a Legislative Council consisting of 17–23 members chosen by the King or his representative. The overall scheme was successful in that it corresponded more closely to the day-to-day realities of the colony and, perhaps even more important at the time, it secured the loyalty of the French settlers.

Even if the French inhabitants were somewhat appeased, the British settlers in Quebec were dismayed by the continuing absence of a Legislative Assembly. After all, Virginia had had an elected assembly since 1619. When United Empire Loyalists fleeing the radical new republic being created to the south swelled the numbers of British settlers, the pressure to establish elected institutions became irresistible. By the *Constitution Act* of 1791 the Imperial Parliament reformed the political institutions of the colony in dramatic fashion. First, the existing colony of Quebec was divided into two parts: Upper Canada and Lower Canada. Upper Canada, which made up

---

[4]   With the exception of the relatively insignificant fishing islands in the Gulf of St. Lawrence, St. Pierre and Miquelon, which are still today governed from France.

the southern part of what is now the province of Ontario, had a large majority of English-speaking settlers, whereas Lower Canada, the southern part of modern-day Quebec, had a large majority of French settlers. Secondly, in each colony, legislative power was shared between an elected Legislative Assembly and an appointed Legislative Council. In Lower Canada, the elective principle ensured a French-speaking majority in the Assembly, but the practice of appointment to the Council always guaranteed control by an English majority. In any event, there was no question at this time of the English executive being responsible to the Legislature – that battle would come later. Finally, Imperial power retained its priority by means of rules and powers which remained the markers of colonial rule well into the twentieth century: the doctrine of repugnancy and the powers of reservation and disallowance.

In Lower Canada, the French members of the Assembly who formed the majority in that elected body had a great deal to learn regarding British parliamentary practice. There were also practical matters such as the language of deliberations that had to be resolved. Compromises were necessary almost from the day of first meeting. For example, the practice developed whereby criminal laws were presented in English and then translated into French, while civil law matters were presented in French and afterwards translated into English. In both Upper and Lower Canada, but with added linguistic piquancy in the latter colony, great resentment developed over the ability of the appointed Legislative Council to overrule the elected Assembly's wishes. Furthermore, as already noted, the appointed Executive of these colonies was in no way responsible to the elected representatives, but allied instead to the similarly appointed Council.

Dissatisfaction in Upper and Lower Canada came to a head in the late 1830s with rebellions in each colony, in each case calling for responsible government. The Lower Canadian rebels, *les Patriotes*, and their leader, Louis-Joseph Papineau, remain heroes in present-day nationalist and separatist Quebec. The rebellions failed but the level of dissatisfaction and disorder prompted the British authorities to suspend the *Constitution Act* of 1791 and to request from one of the Empire's most eminent officials an investigation into the problems in the Canadian colonies.

The Durham Report conceded some of the rebel's arguments. Lord Durham agreed that the British Crown should before long consent to responsible government in its Canadian colonies. However, on the national question, his response was brutal. Durham concluded that the perpetuation of a French nation together with corresponding representative institutions was impossible. French-Canadians should retain their religion and their civil law, but they should be ruled by an English-Canadian majority and English-Canadian institutions. As the constitutional historian W.P.M. Kennedy has written, Durham's proposal was 'not merely a legislative union (of Lower and Upper Canada). It was a fusion. The French-Canadians were to be absorbed, amalgamated, absolutely united' (Kennedy 1931: 174).

The *Act of Union* of 1840 brought about the legislative union of the two Canadas. As of February 1841 Upper and Lower Canada (now designated, respectively, Canada West and Canada East) formed a single colony named Canada. The constitutional structure was as before – a Legislative Assembly and a Legislative Council whose separate consents were necessary to adopt laws in the colony – but now serving only one province, Canada. The *Act of Union* did not change the two legal systems, leaving French law as the basis of private law in Canada East. Most notable in these new arrangements were the other provisions which worked to the disadvantage of French Canadians. Despite the greater population of Canada East as compared to Canada West, the new Act provided for equal representation in the Canadian Legislative Assembly: 42 members each from Canada East and Canada West. Furthermore, the Act made clear, for the first time since the Conquest, that English was the only official language for public documents, acts and proceedings. These last provisions were short-lived, however. As of the first meetings of the new Canadian Legislature, its enactments were published in English and French, even though the English version remained the only official one. By 1848, constant lobbying of Westminster paid off. The British Parliament repealed the provisions of the *Act of Union* which made English the official language, and in 1849, the Governor General made the Speech from the Throne in both English and French (Kennedy 1931: 257).

Despite Durham's original unifying vision, the abiding dualism on the linguistic front was reproduced elsewhere in the Canadian legal and political system. Equality of representation from Canada East and Canada West meant in theory that the English could dominate. However, the political reality was that successful governing required majority support from each region. This in turn required dual representation in the executive and a virtual co-prime-ministership, the most famous of these being the Baldwin-Lafontaine administration which governed from 1847–1851. Far from submerging the French-Canadian identity, the *Act of Union* and its aftermath re-affirmed the central position of French-Canadian law, language and leaders in the Canadian constitutional system.

As Peter Hogg, the eminent Canadian constitutional writer, has said, the Confederation of the colonies of British North America[5] was driven by political developments in the largest colony, Canada (Hogg 1997: 2–10). Furthermore, the federal plan was driven forward by a powerful coalition of English-and French-Canadian politicians, most notably John A. Macdonald and Georges-Etienne Cartier. By the 1860s, the population of Canada West had outstripped that of Canada East, making the equal representation in the Legislative Assembly inequitable, and a free-standing Upper Canadian polity more desirable. The French population of Canada East and its leaders were attracted by the idea of a separate provincial Legislature which could not only protect but even promote French language, culture, education and private law. The *British North America Act, 1867* (renamed the *Constitution Act, 1867* in 1982) established the constitutional arrangements which still govern the relationship between the political entities which make up the Canadian Confederation. Most significantly, it (re)created the province of Quebec.

Although the crucial events of 1867 are regularly referred to as the Confederation of the Canadian provinces, the term is potentially misleading. Whereas a 'confederation' usually describes a loose association of states to which the central

---

[5]   Canada, Nova Scotia and New Brunswick initially, followed soon after by Prince Edward Island, Manitoba and British Columbia. Alberta and Saskatchewan were to join at the turn of the century, Newfoundland in 1949.

government is subordinate, the Canadian Confederation is more accurately described as a federal system. Sections 91 and 92 of the *Constitution Act, 1867* divided up legislative responsibilities between the federal (or central) Parliament and the provincial legislatures. In large measure to please Quebec, the provincial powers include 'property and civil rights in the province' and, most importantly as it turned out, 'generally all matters of a merely local and private nature in the Province', a sort of local peace, order and good government power. A separate provision, section 93, made clear that the provinces, but especially Quebec, had jurisdiction to make laws in relation to education, subject to various elaborate rules to protect denominational schooling. Section 98 of the *Constitution Act, 1867* provided that 'the Judges of the Courts of Quebec shall be selected from the Bar of that Province'. Finally, section 133 required that 'either the English or French Language may be used by any Person in the Debates of the Houses of the Parliament of Canada and of the Houses of the Legislature of Quebec', that 'both those Languages shall be used in the respective Records and Journals of those Houses', and that 'either of those Languages may be used by any Person or in any Pleading or Process in or issuing from any Court of Canada established under this Act, and in or from all or any of the Courts of Quebec'. As these examples indicate, the *Constitution Act, 1867* set up provisions which accommodate the special circumstances of Quebec, both in terms of its French majority (language, culture and legal system) but also its English minority. Aboriginal issues were largely ignored at this stage, as they had been, for the most part, since the *Royal Proclamation* of 1763.

The next century of legal development has naturally seen much development in terms of the interpretation and application of these and other constitutional provisions. This is not the place to summarise them. Several points stand out, however. Some have already been mentioned. For example, Quebec has over time negotiated separate and distinct administrative arrangements in the spheres of taxation, pensions and immigration. Developments in official bilingualism have already been noted. The *Official Languages Act* remains one of the most powerful manifestations of a two-nation conception of Canadian constitutional law and politics. Section 101 of the *Constitution Act, 1867* empowers the federal Parliament to set up 'Courts for the better Administration of the Laws of Canada'. It was under this power that the Supreme Court of Canada was established early on in Confederation. The *Supreme Court Act* now makes clear that three of the nine judges of that Court must come from the Bar of the Province of Quebec.

Alongside these legal developments there have been important political developments many of which have acquired the status of constitutional conventions. Andrew Heard notes, for example, that Prime Ministers regularly ensure that the Cabinet includes at least one minister from each province, and Quebec's representation regularly exceeds that number. Conservative Prime Minister Joe Clark, for example, felt obliged to appoint three Quebec senators to his Cabinet when it became clear that he had insufficient Quebec MPs (Heard 1991: 108).

One of the most important alleged conventions in Canadian history came to be abandoned or denied, depending on one's perspective, in the fraught context of 1981–1982. For the fifty or so years preceding, Canadian political leaders had tried to reach agreement on a domestic amending formula (see Oliver 1994). The *Constitution Act, 1867* had not contained such a provision on the assumption that the United Kingdom Parliament would amend the relevant legislation as and when such changes were required. In all the various phases of negotiations regarding a domestic amending formula, Quebec had consistently claimed a right of veto over fundamental constitutional change (McWhinney 1979; Pelletier 1996: 17; Hurley 1996: 23; Hogg 1997: 4–4). Initially, this demand had been merged into a claim by all provinces to a principle of unanimous consent to constitutional amendments. When this highly rigid proposal came to be abandoned (and with it the compact (or contractual) theory of Confederation that underpinned it (see Rogers 1931; Black 1975), Quebec persevered in claiming a veto, but now on the basis that Quebec was a province 'not like others'.[6] Furthermore, Quebec had twice used this alleged veto to block patriation[7] packages which had been approved by the Federal government and all other provincial governments. In 1965 Premier Lesage of Quebec withdrew his support from the Fulton-Favreau formula (based essentially on a unanimity principle in amendment), and in 1971 Premier Robert Bourassa backed out of the Victoria Charter (which had itself included a veto for Ontario, Quebec and the two other regions, Eastern and Western). In both instances, the other provinces and the Federal government had chosen not to proceed absent Quebec's consent. It was therefore surprising to many Quebecers to learn in the 1982 *Quebec Veto Reference* that, in the opinion of the Supreme Court of Canada, Quebec had never even had a conventional right to a veto over constitutional change. Those who defended this conclusion typically argued, first, that the other parties had never clearly articulated their agreement to such a convention, and, secondly, that the separatist *Parti québécois* government under René Lévesque had effectively abandoned the province's claim by agreeing in 1981 to an eight-province constitutional amendment proposal which did not contain any veto. Lévesque and his colleagues, and those who sympathised with them, claimed in turn that they had only done so (1) in response to the extreme provocation of the Trudeau government in seeking to amend the Constitution unilaterally by proceeding to the United Kingdom Parliament over the objections of eight out of ten provinces, including Quebec, and (2) that the veto had only been 'abandoned' in exchange for a valuable right to opt out of proposed amendments with compensation. Critics of the *Parti québécois* strategy observed that opting out with compensation might suffice for amendments regarding legislative powers – environmental matters, for example – but it would be of no use if the other provinces and the federal government decided to alter the central institutions without Quebec's consent: opting out would be of no use then.

It was in this context that Quebec and the rest of Canada had their most dramatic falling out. From an English Canadian perspective, the province of Quebec and French Canadians generally had been given much already, and any failure to achieve other political objectives had simply been scuppered by the *Parti québécois*

[6] '*Le Québec n'est pas une province comme les autres.*' (See Quebec 1956: 182)
[7] 'Patriation' refers to the process by which the remaining levers controlling the amendment of Canada's constitution were transferred fully into Canadian control. Patriation was finally achieved with the passage of the *Canada Act 1982* (UK).

negotiators cynical and ineffective strategies. Through the eyes of many Quebecers, the province had been ganged up on by an unsympathetic alliance of the other, predominantly anglophone, provinces, the Trudeau-led federal government, and a compliant (federally appointed) Supreme Court of Canada. The result was a *Charter of Rights and Freedoms* which entrenched a Trudeau vision of individual rights and inadequate language guarantees, together with a constitutional amending formula stopping short of a Quebec veto and offering only a watered-down scheme of opting out (compensation being limited only to educational and cultural matters).[8]

Vast amounts of commentary have been written on the years which followed the patriation of the Canadian constitution in 1982 (see, e.g., Hogg 1997: 4–7; Hurley 1996: 99; Pelletier 1996: 17). There is really no possibility of adequately summarising these events in this short essay. For the purposes of the *Secession Reference* we need to know that the rest of Canada attempted in two major rounds of constitutional negotiations to put things right, in both instances at the initiative of the Conservative administration of Prime Minister Brian Mulroney.

The first of these, the 1987 Meech Lake Constitutional Accord (Canada 1987), had originated as an overt and formal attempt to address Quebec's concerns. A reincarnated Liberal leader Robert Bourassa,[9] Prime Minister of Quebec as of 1985, set Quebec's demands by building on the policy of his *Parti québécois* predecessors. Most importantly, he called for (1) recognition of Quebec as a distinct society, (2) a greater role for Quebec in immigration, (3) a provincial role in appointments to the Supreme Court of Canada, and (4) the return of Quebec's traditional veto over constitutional amendments. The 1987 Accord essentially met these demands. However, although all parties had indicated their initial approval to the deal, and eight out of ten provinces together with the federal Parliament passed resolutions adopting the Meech Lake slate of amendments, the project lapsed in 1990 for lack of two provinces' assent. Far worse, despite the relatively small margin of failure, the Meech Lake process had been a public relations disaster. Far from bringing Quebec closer into the Canadian fold, it alienated many Canadians both inside and outside Quebec.[10] For most Quebecers, Meech Lake was a further sign of rejection. To make matters worse, a significant number of Canadians began to articulate the view, none too subtly in many cases, that Quebec had been treated more than well enough, and that if Quebec was distinct then distinctiveness existed elsewhere in Canada as well. Aboriginal Canadians presented by far the most convincing claim both to historic neglect and enduring distinctiveness. Much of this disquiet was channelled through the two dissenting provinces, but political leaders across the country realised post-Meech that such views would have to be taken seriously. And

---

[8] See sections 39 and 40 of the *Constitution Act, 1982*.

[9] Bourassa had been Prime Minister of Quebec during the early 1970s, had negotiated and ultimately withdrawn from the Victoria constitutional accord (referred to above), and had eventually been defeated, in 1976, by René Lévesque's first *Parti québécois* administration.

[10] Alongside the mishandling of the Meech Lake Accord at the federal level, the Quebec government hardly helped matters. When the Supreme Court of Canada declared sections of provincial language legislation invalid as violations of freedom of expression, Quebec responded by overriding the *Charter of Rights and Freedoms* using s. 33 of the *Constitution Act, 1982*. See *Ford v. Quebec* [1988] 2 S.C.R. 712.

not only would political leaders have to take heed, but they would have to be seen to be listening, learning and responding accordingly (Hurley 1996: 151).

Consequently, the new round of constitutional discussions, which began in 1990, was weighed down with virtually unmanageable expectation. What had begun in pre-Meech Lake days as the Quebec Round had now become the Canada Round, with all provinces submitting wish lists for constitutional change: an elected and more representative Senate and aboriginal self-government, for example, on top of Quebec's own unchanged demands. The perceived public relations mistakes with Meech meant that hours of public consultations had to be held, making Canada one of the very few countries in the world where high matters of constitutional law and policy had become matters of everyday conversation. In a further significant break with past practice, the political leaders agreed that the new slate of proposals should be submitted to a consultative, non-binding national referendum, or plebiscite, eventually held on October 26, 1992. The proposal was soundly and relatively mercifully defeated. Fifty-four per cent of the population voted against the 'Charlottetown Accord' (Canada 1992), as it had come to be known, and majorities in six out of ten provinces, including Quebec, voted against the deal (Hurley 1996: 114).

Majority popular opinion in Quebec had moved from hurt and anger in 1982 to solace and hope in 1987, devastating insult in 1990, and cynicism, resignation and new secessionist resolve post-1992. Recognition of Quebec as a distinct society had seemed a small concession, especially when set out only in the unenforceable paragraphs of a constitutional preamble, but rejection of that small concession and growing understanding of its legal ineffectiveness made the whole project seem increasingly futile. Jacques Parizeau, leader of the newly elected *Parti québécois* government, exploited this emotionally charged terrain to the full as of 1994. Parizeau's party had promised to hold a referendum on Quebec's sovereignty if elected, and measures were immediately put in place to allow that to happen. It is those measures which prompted the litigation which eventually led to the *Secession Reference*, so it is to that affair that we now turn.

THE SECESSION REFERENCE –
REFERENDUM AND REPLY

The story begins with a draft Bill entitled *An Act respecting the sovereignty of Quebec*[11] which was presented to the Quebec National Assembly in December of 1994. The Bill was also distributed to every home in the province. It basically set out the steps by which the government proposed moving towards Quebec sovereignty: (1) publication of the draft Bill; (2) a period of public information and consultation within Quebec; (3) adoption of the Bill by the National Assembly; (4) approval of the new Act in a province-wide referendum; (5) discussion with the rest of Canada on transitional arrangements; (6) drafting of a new Quebec

---

[11] Quebec, National Assembly, 1st Sess., 35th Leg, 6 December 1994.

constitution, and (7) accession to sovereignty. The tone of the Bill was captured by its first provision. Article 1 stated baldly 'Quebec is a sovereign country'. In the original scheme, the Bill was to have come into force one year after a pro-sovereignty verdict in a referendum. However, following discussions between the sovereigntist parties in Quebec in the summer of 1995, the Bill was changed so as to require formal negotiations aimed at establishing a new economic and political partnership with Canada. If, one year after the referendum, these negotiations had still proved unsuccessful, only then could the National Assembly proclaim Quebec's sovereignty. An appropriately amended Bill was presented to the National Assembly in September 1995.[12]

While some in the province were participating in the information and consultation process contemplated by the draft Bill, others formulated a strategy to oppose it. In August 1995, a Quebec City lawyer named Guy Bertrand began proceedings in the Quebec Superior Court challenging the constitutionality of the draft Bill, especially its open contemplation of sovereignty. When the Quebec government sought to block this litigation, the Superior Court defended Bertrand's right to proceed. Mr Justice Lesage noted that '[i]t is manifest, if not expressly stated, that the Quebec government has no intention of resorting to the amending formula in the Constitution to accomplish the secession of Quebec ... The actions taken by the Government of Quebec in view of the secession of Quebec are a repudiation of the Constitution of Canada'.[13] Following this interlocutory decision, the Quebec government announced that it would no longer participate in the case.

The next stage was a referendum to be held on October 30, 1995, almost exactly three years after the nation-wide referendum regarding the Charlottetown Accord. Whereas 1992 had produced a clear-cut result, October 1995 could not have been closer. Those who watched television as the results came in saw a victory for the pro-sovereignty forces in the vast Quebec countryside disappear as the results from densely populated metropolitan, cosmopolitan Montreal emerged. The final result was 49.2 per cent 'Yes' and 50.8 per cent 'No'. In the wake of the failed referendum initiative Jacques Parizeau resigned and was replaced by Lucien Bouchard, the present Prime Minister of Quebec.

Given the *Parti québécois* government's unwavering intention to bring about a successful referendum result and eventual sovereignty, Guy Bertrand saw fit to amend his proceedings and use legal means to block the government's strategy permanently. The Quebec government sought once again to have Bertrand's action dismissed; however, this time the Attorney General of Canada also intervened. Mr Justice Pidgeon, like his colleague Mr Justice Lesage, ruled that Bertrand's case should be heard on the merits.[14] Subsequent to this interlocutory decision, in September of 1996, the Quebec government once again announced that it would no longer participate in the case.

---

[12] Bill 1, An Act respecting the Future of Quebec, Quebec, National Assembly, 1st Sess, 35th Leg, 7 September 1995.
[13] *Bertrand v. Quebec* (1995), 127 D.L.R. (4th) 408, 428. Lesage J. stopped short of issuing an injunction prohibiting the holding of a referendum on the sovereignty issue.
[14] *Bertrand v. Bégin* (1996), 138 D.L.R. (4th) 481.

On September 26, 1996, the federal Minister of Justice, Allan Rock, announced that the Canadian government would send a reference case[15] to the Supreme Court of Canada on the legality of the Quebec government's secession plans. The questions were as follows:

'Under the Constitution of Canada, can the National Assembly, legislature or government of Quebec effect the secession of Quebec from Canada unilaterally?

Does international law give the National Assembly, legislature or government of Quebec the right to effect the secession of Quebec from Canada unilaterally? In this regard, is there a right to self-determination under international law that would give the National Assembly, legislature or government of Quebec the right to effect the secession of Quebec from Canada unilaterally?

In the event of conflict between domestic and international law on the right of the National Assembly, legislature or government of Quebec to effect the secession of Quebec from Canada unilaterally, which would take precedence in Canada?'

Intervenors in the case included other provinces and territories, aboriginal organisations, Guy Bertrand and Roopnarine Singh (who had initiated a similar action to Bertrand's), political parties and concerned citizens. With no official representation for the province of Quebec, the Supreme Court saw fit to appoint an *amicus curiae*, Mr André Joli-Coeur. In addition to hearing from the federal Minister of Justice, the intervenors and the *amicus*, the Court also questioned a small number of experts, notably in the field of international law.

The Supreme Court of Canada's decision in this case, hereinafter referred to as the *Secession Reference*,[16] is undoubtedly one of the most important in the Court's history. Using the Court's own words, the case deals with 'momentous questions that go to the heart of our system of constitutional government' (148). The judgment contains both abstract legal reasoning and astute political advice. Beginning with the Court's conclusions, the case seems relatively straightforward. The answer to the first question, regarding the existence of a unilateral right to secede in domestic law, was 'No'. Given that the same answer applied to such a right as might have existed in international law, the Court saw no need to answer the third question.

The first question will be dealt with first. The broad approach to constitutional law taken by the Court will be fairly familiar to lawyers in the United Kingdom.

---

[15] A reference is a procedure by which the government of Canada (or the government of a province) refers important legal or factual questions to the Supreme Court of Canada (or the Court of Appeal, in the case of a provincial reference). The Court issues an advisory opinion in the form of a judgment. There have been 75 federal references since 1892, some of which have already been cited, below (i.e. the *Upper House, Patriation,* and *Quebec Veto* references).

[16] *Reference re Secession of Quebec* [1998] 2 S.C.R. 217. Subsequent references are to the relevant paragraph numbers in the case. The case can also be found on the internet at http://www.lexum.umontreal.ca/CSC-Scc/en/pub/1998/vol2/html/1998scr2_0217.html

Whereas it was widely assumed after 1982 (see, *e.g.,* Hogg 1985: 6) that the 'Constitution of Canada' had been exhaustively defined by the *Constitution Act, 1982,*[17] the Court in the *Secession Reference* stresses that these constitutional texts are 'not exhaustive' (32). Quoting from the *Patriation Reference,* which pre-dated the *Constitution Act, 1982,* the Court reiterated that the Constitution of Canada includes 'the global system of rules and principles which govern the exercise of constitutional authority in the whole and in every part of the Canadian state'.[18]

Given the unprecedented nature of the issues in the *Secession Reference* the emphasis in this case was on principles rather than on constitutional rules. The Court derived such principles from 'an understanding of the constitutional text itself, the historical context, and previous judicial interpretations of constitutional meaning (32), and on the basis of these sources four 'fundamental and organizing principles' emerged: federalism; democracy; constitutionalism and the rule of law; and respect for minorities. It is these principles which do much of the work in the *Secession Reference* reasoning, essentially by repeated emphasis on the fact that one principle cannot be preferred to any other.

One of the difficulties in reading the *Secession Reference* is in determining whether the Court is referring to legal or political rights and obligations, and whether even legal rights and obligations always produce clear legal consequences. The first marker of this difficulty is thrown down early in the judgment:

> 'Underlying constitutional principles may in certain circumstances give rise to substantive legal obligations (have "full force", as we described it in the *Patriation Reference* ..., p. 845) which constitute substantive limitations on government action. These principles may give rise to very abstract and general obligations, or they may be more specific and precise in nature. The principles are not merely descriptive, but are also invested with a powerful normative force, and are binding upon both courts and governments' (54).

It is not clear in the case whether the sense of bindingness or normative force refers to the law or conventions of the constitution, although more will be said on that point later. However, having looked through all the relevant references in the case, the safest conclusion seems to be that (a) the Court is referring to a legal obligation which it is in the process of declaring, but that it does so on the understanding that (b) the detailed elaboration (and enforcement) of this legal obligation may have to be left entirely to the political sphere.

The first principle discussed by the Court is federalism. The overlap between federalism and the other designated principles is emphasised in various ways. For example, federalism assists the recognition and flourishing of minority language

---

[17] See subsection 52 of the Constitution Act, 1982:
52.(2) The Constitution of Canada includes
(a) the Canada Act, 1982, including this Act;
(b) the Acts and orders referred to in the schedule; and
(c) amendment to any Act or order referred to in paragraph (a) or (b).
[18] *Patriation Reference,* p. 874 (paragraph 32 in the *Secession Reference*).

and culture. It also facilitates democratic participation by distributing power to the government which is most able and suited to achieving the objectives of particular communities. The orderly arrangement of such a system in turn requires a division of power governed by law. Drawing on historical context, the Court observes that without the federal concept, none of the British North American colonies would have consented to union in 1867.

The Court then turns to the democratic principle, noting that this principle is said to justify the right to unilateral secession reflecting as it does the sovereignty of the people of Quebec voting in a referendum. The Court acknowledges that the democratic principle is commonly understood as being based on majority rule, but it is at pains to connect this principle to other equally important concepts. In a federal system, for example, no one majority has priority over others. Furthermore, 'democracy cannot in any real sense exist without the rule of law' (66), defined essentially as a framework within which the variously defined 'sovereign' democratic wills can operate.

The Supreme Court of Canada could have stated that the rule of law excludes the possibility of secession entirely, but it opted instead to emphasise the importance of 'a continuous process of discussion' (68). It is at this stage that the broad outlines of the Court's political compromise begin to appear:

'The *Constitution Act, 1982* gives expression to this [democratic] principle, by conferring a right to initiate constitutional change on each participant in Confederation. In our view, the existence of this right imposes a corresponding duty on the participants in Confederation to engage in constitutional discussion in order to acknowledge and address democratic expressions of a desire for change in other provinces. This duty is inherent in the democratic principle which is a fundamental predicate of our system of governance'(69).

The Court then moves on to discuss the principles of 'constitutionalism and the rule of law', and here the principles of federalism and democracy are pulled together into a tighter bundle. The rule of law is defined as embracing three key elements: (1) the idea that 'the law is supreme over the acts of both government and private persons'; (2) quoting from the 1985 *Manitoba Reference*,[19] that 'the rule of law requires the creation and maintenance of an actual order of positive laws which preserves and embodies the more general principle of normative order'; and (3) quoting from the *Provincial Judges Reference*,[20] that 'the exercise of all public power must find its ultimate source in a legal rule' (71). The related concept of 'constitutionalism' is defined as 'the principle [that] requires that all government action comply with the Constitution' (72). It is these principles that explain why constitutional rules are entrenched beyond the reach of simple majority rule. The detailed explanation of entrenchment leads back to some of the other constitutional principles identified earlier and to some new but no less important ones: an added safeguard for fundamental human rights and individual freedoms; the protection of

---

[19] *Reference re Manitoba Language Rights* (1985) 1 S.C.R. 721.
[20] *Reference re Remuneration of Judges* (1997) 3 S.C.R. 3.

vulnerable minority groups through the provision of representative institutions and collective rights as a bulwark against majority pressure; and the division of political powers which keeps such a system in balance. In order to protect these and other key constitutional principles, constitutionalism and the rule of law require that majority democratic rule does not always mean a simple majority. On the contrary, 'enhanced' majorities ensure substantial consensus and offer greater protection to minority interests.

The Court discusses the principle of protection of minorities more briefly having already emphasised it sufficiently under other headings. Essentially the idea is that constitutional texts (*e.g.*, s. 93 of the *Constitution Act, 1867*, the *Charter of Rights and Freedoms*, s. 35 of the *Constitution Act, 1982* dealing with aboriginal rights), historical context and numerous constitutional cases make clear that Canada has had a long tradition of respecting minorities, and that accordingly this principle deserves independent protection alongside the other three.

In a section entitled 'The Operation of the Constitutional Principles in the Secession Context' all the broader 'principled' considerations are pulled together into a more precise ruling on the requirements of domestic law regarding secession. First, the Court makes clear that, in legal terms, secession of a province must require an amendment to the constitution, and that this in turn requires negotiation. As noted earlier, the Court could have taken the view that secession is an entirely extra-legal or illegal act. But clearly the Court saw its role as encouraging negotiation rather than confrontation – political, military or other. Secondly, drawing in part on the democratic principle identified earlier (as well as the discussion of enhanced majorities), the Court states that considerable weight must be given to the expression by a 'clear majority' of the people of Quebec of their will to secede, 'clear' being taken to refer both to the clarity of the referendum question and to the level of support (87). Thirdly, if the government of Quebec then used its power to initiate a constitutional amendment calling for secession, the 'clear' repudiation of the existing order and 'clear' expression of a desire to pursue secession would give rise to a 'reciprocal obligation' on all parties to Confederation to negotiate constitutional changes. What seems important here is that it is the legitimacy of the Quebec initiative which generates the 'reciprocal obligation'. Initiation of a secession amendment not preceded by the type of 'clear majority' identified earlier would impose no obligation to negotiate at all.

So here we can see the principles at work: democracy provides legitimacy but not legality; federalism dictates that the expression of one 'sovereign' popular will is not enough; and constitutionalism and the rule of law together with the protection of minorities dictate that the popular vote must produce a clear result both in its terms and in its numbers. But once these conditions have been met, the combination of the legitimacy already described and the legality of the constitutional procedures allowing a province to initiate an amendment thereby generate a reciprocal obligation on the other parties to negotiate.

What is the content of this obligation to negotiate? The Court is reluctant to say. What is clear is that there is no legal obligation on the other parties to accede to another province's secession amendment. However, it is equally clearly wrong to conclude that a clear expression of self-determination by the people of Quebec imposes no obligation at all on the other parties. To conclude otherwise would effectively subordinate the democratic principle to the other principles, rather than allowing it to play a full part. Or viewed otherwise, it would amount to preferring one majority view to another, a possibility which the Court refuses to accept. This would seem to rule out the potential effectiveness of a federal strategy involving a nation-wide anti-secession referendum. Once again, the Court pulls the parties back to the negotiating table. It emphasises the fact that if secession were to become inevitable, there would be a vast array of details to iron out through negotiation given the 'high level of integration in economic, political and social institutions' which has occurred over the past 131 years of Confederation (98): (quoting the oral arguments of the Attorney General of Saskatchewan) 'the threads of a thousand acts of accommodation are the fabric of a nation' (96).

The Court acknowledges that between the unacceptable extremes of Quebec dictating acceptance of its secession amendment and the rest of Canada refusing to negotiate there are still many possibilities. Quebec would not be entitled to successfully negotiate secession, nor would there be any guarantee that impasse could be avoided. However, beyond this point the Court is unwilling to speculate. Instead, it returns to the subtle balance of legal and political factors with which it began this part of the Reference. Averting to the *Patriation Reference* discussion of the law and conventions of the Constitution, the Court reiterates that the former 'generally speaking' is enforced by the courts while 'other constitutional rules, such as the conventions of the Constitution' carry only political sanctions (98). It adds, however, that 'it is also the case ... that judicial intervention, even in relation to the *law* of the Constitution, is subject to the court's appreciation of its proper role in the constitutional scheme (98). The Court's role is limited[21] to the 'identification of the relevant aspects of the Constitution in the broadest sense', here, the right, and corresponding duty, to negotiate secession (100). Beyond that, however – *i.e.,* the clarity of the question, the size of the requisite majority, the good faith of the negotiations – it would be up to political actors to judge and act. Imagining, for example, that there might be a dispute as to whether one party was defending its position strongly and legitimately, or unreasonably taking positions which ignored the legitimate interests of others, the Court would have no role to play, such matters being deemed to defy legal analysis. Clearly the identification of legal rules 'in their broadest sense' does not determine the subsequent justiciability of the many divisive issues which would be likely to arise. But the Court is at pains to stress that 'the non-justiciability of political issues that lack a legal component does not deprive the surrounding constitutional framework of its binding status, nor does this mean that constitutional obligations could be breached without incurring serious legal repercussions' (102).

---

[21] This sort of limitation based on the Court's perception of justiciability can be compared to the House of Lords present approach to judicial review of the Crown prerogative. It is prepared to state as a matter of law that the prerogative includes the power to declare war, for example; however, it declines the ability to review the exercise of such highly politicised powers. See *Council of Civil Service Unions v. Minister of State for Civil Service* (1985) A.C. 374 (especially *per* Lord Roskill, *ibid.* 418).

The Court was clearly reluctant to leave the negotiation of secession entirely to the political process. Had it done so Quebec would have been left with nothing more than the democratic legitimacy of its claim and an increased sense of grievance at its inequitable treatment by Canadian lawmakers. The Court was aware, however, that in setting out a legal obligation to negotiate it risked wading too deeply into political waters. This seems to explain the mixing of law and convention, legal and political. The breach of a convention, such as the convention requiring substantial provincial consent to amendments pre-1982, can have legal consequences followed by political consequences.[22] Similarly, the breach of the legal obligation to negotiate can have political consequences followed only later by legal consequences.[23] In part this is due to the Supreme Court of Canada's own ambiguous role as constitutional reference court, but in the context of the right to negotiate it is also a consequence of the interrelationship between domestic law and international law. Essentially the Supreme Court of Canada seems to be engaging in the practice of dishing out political home truths. The Court is reminding the political actors that if secession ever comes to be an issue, Canadian affairs will be watched as closely from abroad, in France for example, as in Canada and Quebec, and accordingly issues of legitimacy may come to determine one sort of legality. The Court refuses to accept that a principle of effectiveness can give Quebec a legal right to secession, but the judges clearly do not ignore the fact that, as S.A. de Smith said, 'successful revolution begets its own legality' (de Smith 1968: 96).

The Court's treatment of Question 2, a right to secession in international law, is far less detailed. The Court begins by noting that 'international law contains neither a right of unilateral secession nor the explicit denial of such a right' (112). It notes, however, that the denial of the right is to some extent 'implicit in the exceptional circumstances required for secession to be permitted under the right of a people to self-determination', and it is these circumstances which form the greatest part of the Court's analysis (112).

The Court begins by stating that 'the existence of the right of a people to self-determination is now so widely recognised in international conventions that the principle has acquired status beyond "convention" and is considered a general

---

[22] For example, in the *Patriation Reference*, *op. cit.*, the Supreme Court of Canada stated that although there was no legal requirement of provincial consent to fundamental constitutional reform, the conventions of the constitution required 'substantial provincial consent'. Although a Supreme Court of Canada reference on an issue of constitutional convention was not strictly speaking binding, the federal government of the time treated it as though it was. Substantial provincial consent was achieved through negotiation, and this in turn resulted in the enactment of the *Canada Act 1982*. The failure of Quebec to ratify the *Canada Act 1982* has had ongoing political consequences which lead eventually, and some would say inevitably, to the *Secession Reference*.

[23] For example, the failure of the federal government to negotiate with Quebec after a clear referendum result would have dramatic political consequences, and might lead to a unilateral declaration of independence capable of achieving its own (revolutionary) legality. This would undoubtedly have legal consequences for Canada, notably in relation to its amending formula. Section 41 of the *Constitution Act, 1982* requires unanimous provincial consent to certain amendments, including amendment of the amending formula. If Quebec unilaterally seceded section 41 would become impossible to operate, unless, perhaps, the Supreme Court of Canada ruled that unanimity no longer required Quebec.

principle of international law' (114). The right is illustrated by references to Articles 1 and 55 of the *Charter of the United Nations*, Article 1 of the *International Covenant on Civil and Political Rights*, Article 1 of the *International Covenant on Economic, Social and Cultural Rights*, the *Declaration on Principles of International Law Concerning Friendly Relations and Co-operation Among States in Accordance with the Charter of the United Nations*, the *Declaration on the Occasion of the Fiftieth Anniversary of the United Nations* and the *Helsinki Final Act*. The Court should then have paid roughly equal attention to the questions (1) whether the population of the province of Quebec represents a 'people', and (2) whether such a people qualifies for the right of self-determination. However, the Court was inclined to avoid the prickly issues associated with question (1). Merely listing these issues made clear that they embraced some of the intractable questions which had preoccupied and bedevilled Canadian political and legal experts at least since Meech Lake (as well as some brand new ones), and that where possible they should be left unanswered:

> 'While much of the Quebec population certainly shares many of the characteristics (such as common language and culture) that would be considered in determining whether a specific group is a "people", as do other groups within Quebec and/or Canada, it is not necessary to explore this legal characterization to resolve Question 2 appropriately. Similarly, it is not necessary for the Court to determine whether, should a Quebec people exist within the definition of public international law, such a people encompasses the entirety of the provincial population or just a portion thereof. Nor is it necessary to examine the position of the aboriginal population within Quebec (125).'

After stating that 'the precise meaning of the term "people" remains somewhat uncertain', the Court indicates that it is unnecessary to make any determination for the moment given that Quebec's present circumstances do not ground a right to unilateral secession.

With regard to the right to self-determination, the Court notes that international law places great importance on the territorial integrity of nation states, and that, accordingly, a right to '*external* self-determination' such as Quebec might claim was limited to 'the most extreme cases', and even then only under carefully defined circumstances (126).

After reviewing the relevant sources, those circumstances are identified and dealt with as follows. First, there is 'the right of colonial peoples to exercise their right to self-determination by breaking away from the "imperial" power' (132). Although this right is now undisputed, the Court views it as 'irrelevant to the Reference'. Secondly, and equally undisputed, there is 'a right to external self-determination … where a people is subject to an alien subjugation, domination or exploitation outside the colonial context' (133). Given that even the *amicus curiae* had conceded that 'the Quebec people is manifestly not … an oppressed people' (135) it was unlikely the Court would come to a different conclusion. Thirdly, the Court notes that a number of commentators have asserted a right to self-determination, as a last resort, 'when a people is blocked from the meaningful exercise of its right to self-determination internally' (134). Regardless of whether this third proposition reflected an international law standard, the 'current Quebec context' could not be said to meet the threshold (135). In something of a public relations exercise the Court then lists examples of the extent to which Quebec and Quebecers are integrated and well-represented in the Canadian polity.

Having disposed of the grounds on which a right to self-determination could be said to exist in international law, the Court then returns briefly to the issue of whether international law could adapt so as to recognise the political and/or factual reality of a separate Quebec. Given the wording of the *Reference* questions, it was possible for the Court to respond by saying that even if such recognition of successful secession does occur, as undoubtedly it does, it could not be said that the process was legal at all times. The Court seems here to be deliberately avoiding the issue of conflicting perspectives. Clearly from the view of Canadian courts a unilateral declaration of independence could only subsequently be recognised as legal. However, from the perspective of Quebec judges who may have sworn an oath to uphold a new Quebec constitution, the legality may be deemed to flow from the first moment.

Rather than provide currency to the sort of ideas which could be said to undermine the constitutional principles – democracy, federalism, constitutionalism and the rule of law, protection of minorities – the Supreme Court of Canada prefers to return to the political home truths referred to earlier. If international law can contribute to the process of securing secession, the process of recognition is itself guided by legal norms. And 'one of the legal norms which may be recognised by states in granting or withholding recognition of emergent states is the legitimacy of the process by which the *de facto* secession is, or was, being pursued' (142). According to this and previously expressed lines of reasoning, both Quebec and Canada would be legally bound and politically well advised to bargain in good faith if secession emerged as a constitutional amendment proposal following a clear verdict from the people of Quebec.

CONCLUSION

Whether by post-Meech, post-Charlottetown constitutional reform, or by negotiated or unilateral secession, Canadians will not be able to avoid the issues which form the subject of this book. Prospects for pro-Canadian constitutional change would seem to require, on the one hand, that the rest of Canada accept that the objective of substantive equality must often be achieved through the appearance of inequality or preferential treatment; and, on the other hand, that Quebec accept that recognition of its continuity, consent, mutuality and diversity (Tully: 1995) require that it in turn recognises the minorities within its boundaries: aboriginal, anglophone and other. Two solitudes reaching out and embracing each other. Alternatively, Quebec and Canada may travel down a route which leads to the sort of half-way house that member states of the European Union have reached (having, admittedly, travelled from the opposite direction). If that is to occur then the Supreme Court of Canada has sensibly directed the parties to obtain proper mandates and then to negotiate in good faith.

SOURCES CONSULTED

Black, E.R. (1975). *Divided Loyalties*. Montreal: McGill/Queen's Press.

Canada (1987). *Strengthening the Canadian Federation: The Constitution Amendment, 1987*. Ottawa: Supply and Services.

Canada (1992). *Consensus Report on the Constitution: Draft Legal Text*.

de Smith (1968). Constitutional Lawyers in Revolutionary Situations. *University of Western Ontario Law Review* 7: 93.

Heard, A. (1991). *Canadian Constitutional Conventions*. Toronto: Oxford University Press.

Hogg, P. (1985). *Constitutional Law of Canada*. 2nd ed. Toronto: Carswell.

Hogg, P. (1997). *Constitutional Law of Canada*. 4th ed. Toronto: Carswell.

Hurley, J.R. (1996). *Amending Canada's Constitution*. Ottawa: Canada Communication Group.

Kennedy, W.P.M. (1931). *The Constitution of Canada*. Toronto: Oxford University Press.

Maclennan, H. (1993). *Two Solitudes*. Toronto: General Publishing.

McWhinney, E. (1979). *Quebec and the Constitution, 1960–1978*. Toronto: University of Toronto Press.

Morin, J.-Y. & Woehrling, J. (1994). *Les constitutions du Canada et du Québec du régime français à nos jours*. 2nd ed. Montreal: Thémis.

Oliver, M. (1993). The Impact of the Royal Commission on Bilingualism and Biculturalism on Constitutional Thought and Practice in Canada, *International Journal of Canadian Studies* 7–8: 315.

Oliver, P. (1994). The 1982 Patriation of the Constitution of Canada: Reflections on Continuity and Change, *Revue juridique Thémis* 28: 875.

Pelletier, B. (1996). *La modification constitutionnelle au Canada*. Toronto: Carswell.

Quebec (1956). *Report of the Royal Commission of Inquiry on Constitutional Problems*. Quebec: Éditeur officiel.

Quebec (Executive Council) (1979). *Quebec-Canada: A New Deal*. Quebec: Éditeur officiel.

Rémillard, G. (1984). L'historique du rapatriement, *Cahiers du droit* 23: 1.

Rogers, N. (1931). The Compact Theory of Confederation, *Canadian Bar Review* 9: 400.

Romanow, R., Whyte, J. & Leeson, H. (1984). *Canada ... Notwithstanding: The Making of the Canadian Constitution 1976–1982*. Toronto: Carswell.

Sheppard, R. & Valpy, M. (1982). *The National Deal: The Fight for a Canadian Constitution*. Toronto: Macmillan.

Simeon, R. (1972). *Federal Provincial Diplomacy*. Toronto: University of Toronto Press.

Trudeau, P. (1968). *Federalism and the French Canadians*. Toronto: Macmillan.

Tully, J. (1995). *Strange Multiplicity: Constitutionalism in an Age of Diversity*. Cambridge: Cambridge University Press.

Vallières, P. (1968). *Les nègres blancs d'Amérique*. Montréal: Parti pris.

Vallières, P. (1991). *White Niggers of America*. Toronto: Macmillan.

The Road Back to Hell[1]:
the international response to the crisis in Kosovo

Stephen Tierney*

I. INTRODUCTION

On March 24, 1999 NATO began a sustained bombing campaign against the Federal Republic of Yugoslavia following the collapse of the talks process at Rambouillet in France. The Rambouillet process was the culmination of a series of diplomatic initiatives aimed at reaching a long-term solution to the conflict which had raged for over a year. It was particularly significant because it constituted an elaborate attempt by important international actors to accommodate Kosovan aspirations for self government by the construction of a detailed blueprint of autonomy for Kosovo.

The legality of NATO's military intervention has been subjected to considerable scrutiny given the absence of Security Council authorisation under Chapter VII of the UN Charter.[2] In attempting to assess the legal justification for intervention, this chapter will examine the course of political events from March 1998 until the commencement of NATO air-strikes and, in particular, it will address the attempts made by the international community to broker a political settlement to the nationalist crisis in Kosovo in the face of the worsening security and humanitarian situation on the ground. If NATO's action is seen as legally permissible (on the basis, for example, of humanitarian concerns and the argument that it was tacitly endorsed by the Security Council) this will hold profound implications for international law and in particular for the doctrine of state sovereignty. It could also have wide ramifications for the principle of self-determination. Intervention in Kosovo followed directly from the collapse of the Rambouillet process thereby creating a temporal, and seemingly causal, nexus between the use force by the major Western powers and the refusal by Belgrade to accede to demands for the exercise of internal self-determination by Kosovo.

---

*   The author, Faculty of Law, The University of Edinburgh, is grateful to the European Social Science Information Research Facility which enabled research for this chapter to be carried out at the European University Institute in Florence in the course of 1999.
[1]   In April 1998 US Secretary of State Madeleine Albright described the emerging crisis in Kosovo in the following terms: "The result could be a full-fledged civil war, putting at risk the peace in Bosnia and spreading conflict like an infectious disease to neighbouring states...this escalating violence is the road back to hell." US News On-line World Report April 13 1998.
[2]   Cassese 1999; Simma 1999.

Stephen Tierney (ed.), Accommodating National Identity: New Approaches in International and Domestic Law, 89–130
© 2000 *Kluwer Law International. Printed in Great Britain.*
First published in the International Journal on Minority and Group Rights, Volume 6 No. 1/2 1999.
The article has been revised for this publication.

This chapter will conclude that NATO's intervention in Kosovo may herald the emergence of a new norm of international law, namely a right of limited international intervention, even absent Security Council authorisation, where egregious human rights violations are being perpetrated by a state and where the Security Council has failed to act. NATO's actions also raise the question of how far the international community is prepared to go in pressurising states, which deny autonomy to an ethnic or national minority, into permitting the effective exercise of the right to internal self-determination by the group concerned.

2. Kosovo: background to crisis

A. *The constitutional status of Kosovo*

The background to the conflict in Kosovo is one of protracted political and constitutional struggle contextualised within the now tragically familiar Balkan cocktail of ethnic division and historical grievance.[3] If one institutional starting point for the crisis of 1998-9 can be identified it is the dismantling of the political autonomy Kosovo, an Autonomous Province of the Republic of Serbia, enjoyed under the Constitution of the Socialist Federal Republic of Yugoslavia (SFRY) of 1974. Both the Republic of Serbia and the SFRY[4] between 1989 and 1992 embarked upon a process of constitutional centralisation which terminated Kosovan autonomy and which in turn led to the emergence of a strong separatist movement within Kosovo.[5] Under the 1974 Constitution Kosovo acquired the status of an autonomous province within Serbia and enjoyed political control over many areas of internal administration. However, crucially Kosovars did not constitute a 'nation' in terms of the Constitution which described the State as 'having the form of a state community of voluntarily united nations and their Socialist Republics, and of the Socialist Autonomous provinces of Vojvodina and Kosovo'.[6]

The reference to 'nations' in the Constitution is important due to the connection between 'nations' and 'their Socialist Republics'. 'Nations' in the SFRY were peoples

---

[3]   For a history of Kosovo see: Elsie (ed.) 1997; Vickers 1998, and Veremis and Kofos (ed.) 1998. Useful discussions of Serbian nationalism, and in particular of the relevance of Kosovo to Serbs, include Cerovic 1993–4, and Mertus 1993–4.

[4]   Since the dissolution of the SFRY (below footnotes 9 and 13), the state comprising the Republics of Serbia and Montenegro is most commonly referred to as the Federal Republic of Yugoslavia. For the remainder of this article this term, abbreviated to 'the FRY', will be used. On the question of nomenclature and in particular toponyms, the 1974 Federal Constitution referred to 'Kosovo'. Kosovo, however, is generally known to Serbs as Kosovo-Metohija. As with so many of the internecine conflicts in the Balkans, place names carry great political significance. Metohija is a Greek word which indicates part of a district which was Orthodox Church property. Kofos 1998: 48. For Kosovo Albanians, the preferred term is Kosova, an Albanian name which describes it as an ethnically Albanian land, (Kofos: 48). Throughout the crisis the name Kosovo was used by most members of the international community including the United Nations Security Council, and this term will be used by the author.

[5]   Surroi 1999. (Veton Surroi is a prominent Kosovo Albanian politician who was a senior negotiator in the talks between Kosovo representatives and Belgrade authorities in May 1998. See for example, *Kosovo Albanians Encouraged by Clinton Meeting,* Reuters, June 1, 1998).

[6]   Constitution of the Socialist Federal Republic of Yugoslavia, 1974, Art. 1.

having 'their own' republics, and a republic was defined by the 'nation' which formed the majority of its population (Serbs, Croats, Slovenians, Macedonians and Montenegrins). They were distinguished under the Constitution from 'nationalities' namely minority groups within the SFRY, whose ethnic group formed the majority population of neighbouring states such as Hungary and Albania. This distinction is crucial, since, with the status of 'nation' came the constitutional right of self-determination.[7]

The acquisition of statehood by Slovenia, Croatia, Bosnia and Herzegovina and Macedonia, and in particular the process by which that statehood was recognised by the Member States of the European Community (EC), gave additional importance to the connection within the SFRY Constitution between 'nations' and republican status. Two Declarations issued by the EC on December 16, 1992 established that the EC would recognise as independent states those republics (but only republics) which applied for recognition provided they satisfied certain criteria.[8] The Guidelines on Recognition set out criteria which were intended to guide Member States in the recognition of new states and an Arbitration Commission was established, which gave opinions on whether or not applicant republics had satisfied these criteria.[9] Statehood was not an option for non-republican entities including Autonomous Provinces,[10] a rule resented by separatist Kosovo Albanians who felt that the technical distinction between Republic and Autonomous Province in the SFRY Constitution was being used to deny Kosovo its legitimate right to self-determination.[11] This sense of grievance was exacerbated by the opinion of the Arbitration Commission that the SFRY was in a state of dissolution[12] and by the fact that the FRY is still not recognised by many states including the Member States of the European Union (EU) and the USA, a state of limbo which fostered Kosovo Albanian claims that the legal status of Kosovo awaited a final settlement.[13]

Returning to the 1974 Constitution, the absence of republican status was compensated for by two factors. As members of a 'nationality' Albanians in Kosovo and elsewhere in the SFRY were protected by extensive rights guarantees which also applied equally to Yugoslavia's 'nations'. Nationalities for example enjoyed

---

[7]   Constitution of the Socialist Federal Republic of Yugoslavia, 1974, Basic Principles.

[8]   European Community: Declaration on Yugoslavia, 31 International Legal Materials 1485–86 (1992), and Declaration on the "Guidelines on the Recognition of New States in Eastern Europe and the Soviet Union", 31 International Legal Materials 1486–87 (1992). Commentaries include, Warbrick 1992, 1993; Rich 1993; Craven 1995; McGoldrick 1996; Tierney 1999.

[9]   The EC finally recognised Slovenia and Croatia on January 15 and Bosnia and Herzegovina on April 7, 1992. All three new states joined the UN on May 22, 1992 the date on which recognition was extended to them by the USA. The states were admitted as follows: Bosnia and Herzegovina by SC Res. 752 (May 15, 1992); Croatia by SC Res. 753 (May 18, 1992); and Slovenia by SC Res. 754 (May 18, 1992). Macedonia was only recognised by the EC after it was admitted to the UN in April 1993 as the Former Yugoslav Republic of Macedonia, SC Res. 817 (Apr. 7, 1993).

[10] The Arbitration Commission applied the principle of *uti possidetis juris* to the internal republican boundaries of the SFRY thereby denying the possibility of recognition for entities other than republics. This excluded not only the Autonomous Provinces of Kosovo and Vojvodina from seeking statehood but also minorities within republics such as Bosnian Serbs.

[11] See Vickers 1998: 250–272 and Kofos 1998: 76–79.

[12] Arbitration Commission, Opinion No.1, 31 International Legal Materials 1494 at 1497 (1992).

[13] Surroi 1999: 162 and 168.

comprehensive language rights; discrimination on grounds of nationality, race, and language was outlawed; and incitement to racial hatred and intolerance were proscribed as unconstitutional. Secondly, Kosovo, as an Autonomous Province of Serbia, enjoyed substantial executive, legislative and judicial autonomy; it possessed its own constitution, and had legislative jurisdiction which extended to defence and even foreign affairs. Although not a full republic, Kosovo also held a seat in the Federal Parliament of the SFRY together with a seat on the Constitutional Court and on the Presidency.[14]

B. Serbian centralisation and the development of Kosovo Albanian separatism

In spite of the autonomy it enjoyed under the 1974 Constitution, Kosovo was and is constitutionally part of the Republic of Serbia and in 1989 constitutional changes approved by the Parliament of Serbia extensively centralised many important areas previously devolved to Kosovo, a process which was eventually entrenched in the Constitution of the Republic of Serbia adopted in 1990 which substantially reduced the powers of Kosovo as an Autonomous Province.[15] In addition, a new federal Constitution was promulgated in 1992 which also served to entrench Kosovo's emasculated status within the federation. Crucially, both constitutions outlawed secession from Serbia and the FRY respectively,[16] thereby combining to preclude the possibility of Kosovo gaining either independent statehood or the status of a republic within the FRY but independent of Serbia.

A defining moment came on July 2, 1990 with a political declaration by the Parliament of Kosovo which declared the Autonomous Province to be a republic of the Yugoslavia Federation.[17] Shortly thereafter the parliament and government of Kosovo were dissolved by the Republic of Serbia which in turn led a number of deputies from the Kosovo provincial parliament to issue a declaration of independence resulting in the proclamation of the Constitution of the Republic of Kosovo in September 1990 shortly before the adoption of Serbia's new Constitution. In September 1991 an unofficial referendum was held in Kosovo to validate this effective declaration of independence,[18] and backed by a positive result in the referendum, the Kosovo Albanian leadership pressed on with its quest for independence holding presidential and parliamentary elections for the 'Republic of Kosova' on May 24, 1992 which

---

[14] See, Rehn 1996.

[15] Kofos 1998: 55. As the Special Rapporteur of the Commission on Human Rights notes: 'Under its [i.e. the 1990 Constitution's] provisions the "autonomous provinces" retained some authority over the provincial budget, cultural matters, education, health care, use of languages and other matters, but the authority was thenceforth to be exercised only in accordance with decisions made by the Republic. In fact, the new Constitution gave the Republic the right directly to execute its decisions if the provinces failed to do so.' Rehn 1996: Chapter II(c).

[16] Constitution of the Republic of Serbia, 1990, Art. 44(2); Constitution of the Socialist Federal Republic of Yugoslavia, 1974, Art. 42(1).

[17] Surroi 1998: 150.

[18] The referendum was conducted between 26 and 30 September 1991 and was largely clandestine. Of 1,051,357 eligible voters, 87% participated and 99.87% voted for an independent Republic of Kosovo. See, International Crisis Group 1998: 12; Vickers 1998: 251–2; Rehn 1996: Chapter II(c), who also confirms that over 90% of those taking part opted for independence.

resulted in the election of Dr Ibrahim Rugova, the leader of the Democratic League of Kosova (LDK) as President.[19] This attempt by Kosovo Albanians to implement their unilateral declaration of independence led firstly to a boycott by most Kosovo Albanians of both Serbian and FRY elections, and secondly to the establishment of institutions by the self-styled Republic which now operated a separate system of public administration running parallel to the Serbian system, in a very elaborate process of civil disobedience.[20] Following these developments, relations between Kosovo and both Serbian and Federal authorities in Belgrade effectively broke down leading ultimately to the armed conflict which prompted international intervention.

3. THE DEVELOPING CRISIS AND THE INTERNATIONAL REACTION

A. The framework of international co-operation

The Kosovo crisis began to develop a serious military dimension with the emergence of the Kosovo Liberation Army (KLA) which, dissatisfied with the campaign of peaceful civil disobedience led by Rugova and other moderate Kosovo Albanians, by September 1997 had begun an armed campaign seeking independence for Kosovo.[21] Matters intensified considerably however, in February and March of 1998 when the FRY/Serbian authorities launched a campaign against the KLA which resulted in widespread fighting in the province and reports of attacks on civilians.[22]

The escalating military crisis from March 1998 was to present a challenge to the capacity of the international community to respond to it in a principled and consistent way. The response was led by a Contact Group of the main power blocks of the USA, Russia and the EU (represented by the UK, France, Germany and Italy),[23] for all of whom the emerging crisis was an unwelcome reminder of the aftermath of the SFRY's collapse from 1991-2 and the mistakes of hesitancy and confusion which characterised the international response to the Bosnian war in particular.[24]

---

[19] His party is reported to have polled 76.4% of the vote in the unofficial election. International Crisis Group 1998: 12.

[20] Vickers 1998: 251–264 and Kofos 1998: 72–76. This government attempted to function abroad, see International Crisis Group 1998: 15, but its real influence has been perceived to be marginal, Kofos 1998: 73.

[21] This movement is generally recognised to have begun life in 1995 but other armed resistance groups existed in Kosovo from at least 1993, Vickers 1998: 278–9.

[22] *Serbs leave trail of death in Kosovo*, The Guardian (London), Mar. 6, 1998. Throughout the crisis there were varying reports of the extent to which government security forces in Kosovo were composed of either Serbian police and/or the Yugoslav armed forces. In light of this confusion they will generally be described here as 'the security forces', the term generally used by the UN Security Council, e.g. SC Res. 1199 (Sept. 23, 1998) para. 4(a).

[23] An initial meeting of the Foreign Ministers of Contact Group states was held in London. Office of the High Representative, Statement of the London Contact Group Meeting, March 9, 1998 (hereafter, Contact Group Statement 1998).

[24] Articles which have chronicled the international response to the collapse of the FRY include: Weller 1992; Stojanovic 1995–6; McGoldrick 1996; and Gray 1997. In early March 1998 British Foreign Secretary Robin Cook stated: "We are showing a degree of urgency in Kosovo which was unfortunately not present when the Bosnian crisis broke out in 1991". The Guardian (London), Mar. 4, 1998.

The Contact Group's response to the developing situation in Kosovo contained certain imperatives which are relevant to the justifications which would be claimed by NATO for the air strikes which began in March 1999.[25] In particular, it is clear that the removal of Kosovan autonomy by Belgrade was a considerable concern for the Contact Group and that the Group was insistent from the beginning that a long term solution to the crisis would require a resolution of the self-determination claim which the Kosovo Albanians were advancing, but that this claim must be addressed within the context of respect for the FRY's territorial integrity.

The first notable feature of the international approach was the consistent attempt to co-ordinate the positions taken by different organisations, in particular the Contact Group; the UN Security Council; the Organisation for Security and Co-operation in Europe (OSCE); the EU, and NATO. An example of this was the effort undertaken by the Contact Group to secure Security Council backing for its initiatives. As early as March 1998 the Contact Group requested the Security Council to impose an arms embargo on the FRY which was eventually secured through Security Council Resolution 1160 (1998).[26] Another example is the way in which the Contact Group referred frequently to Security Council Resolutions 1160 (1998), 1199 (1998)[27] and 1203 (1998)[28] in both framing its efforts to resolve the crisis and in claiming legitimacy for its role as mediator.[29]

A second aspect of the international response was the way in which international organisations, particularly the Contact Group, endeavoured to force the pace by pro-active initiatives intended to secure a political settlement and guarantee greater autonomy for Kosovo whilst also securing the territorial integrity of the FRY.[30] After the initiative of March 1998, attempts to secure a diplomatic settlement continued through the summer, leading to agreements in October 1998 which in the end were not fully implemented, and concluding in the elaborate Rambouillet process which also collapsed with no agreement being reached between the parties. Again NATO claimed that the failure of this initiative was the latest in a catalogue of examples of Belgrade intransigence, which together highlighted the significant diplomatic efforts which had been undertaken by the international community to resolve the conflict before military force was resorted to.

Thirdly, the international response from the beginning was driven not only by the goal of achieving a political settlement but also by an attempt to mitigate the worsening human rights situation on the ground, a factor which was used to support the claim that NATO's intervention was largely inspired by humanitarian

---

[25] The merits of NATO's claim to legal justification for its actions will be discussed in the concluding section of the chapter.

[26] SC Res. 1160 (Mar. 31, 1998). This embargo was called for in the Contact Group Statement 1998.

[27] *supra* footnote 22.

[28] SC Res. 1203 (Oct. 24, 1998).

[29] Both the arms embargo and the relevant Resolutions will be discussed below.

[30] These began with the Contact Group Statement of March 9, 1998 which set out a list of proposals including a new mission by Felipe Gonzalez as the Personal Representative of the OSCE Chairman-in-Office. Other initiatives such as the process of shuttle diplomacy undertaken by US Ambassador to Macedonia, Christopher Hill in the Summer of 1998, and the Rambouillet process of February 1999, will be discussed below.

considerations. Such a claim requires, *inter alia*, evidence of even-handedness in the treatment of combatants. In this respect both the Contact Group and the Security Council can claim to have repeatedly condemned violence by the KLA as well as the FRY government.[31]

Finally, the Contact Group was concerned with the possibility of escalation of the crisis beyond the borders of Serbia. This was a real and a significant fear particularly as refugee flows into Albania intensified following the offensive by Serbian and FRY security forces in August 1998. This concern was also expressed by other actors including the Secretary-General of the UN[32] and, often pursuant to his reports, by the Security Council itself, which went as far as to declare in Resolutions 1199 (1998) and 1203 (1998) that the situation represented a threat to peace and security under Chapter VII of the UN Charter.[33]

B. The Contact Group and attempts at mediation

The initial strategy pursued by the Contact Group in the Spring of 1998 was to pressurise the FRY into accepting international mediation as a way of reaching accommodation on the question of autonomy with the moderate Kosovan leadership led by Rugova.[34] The plan was for mediation to take place through former Spanish Prime Minister Felipe Gonzalez who, in an effort to co-ordinate policy, was nominated not only by the Contact Group but also by the OSCE[35] and the European Union. However, this plan met with firm resistance from the FRY government,[36] which had remained consistently hostile throughout the crisis to external interference in what it considered to be an issue of internal security.[37] To reinforce its opposition to

---

[31] For example, the Contact Group in March 1998 stated: "We wholly condemn terrorist actions by the Kosovo Liberation Army or any other group or individual." Contact Group Statement 1998: para. 3. Similarly the Security Council Resolution of March 31, 1998 "condemn[ed] the use of excessive force by Serbian police forces against civilians and peaceful demonstrators in Kosovo, as well as all acts of terrorism by the Kosovo Liberation Army or any other group or individual and all external support for terrorist activity in Kosovo, including finance, arms and training". SC Res. 1160 *supra* footnote 26, Preamble. This position was maintained in Resolution 1199(1998) which condemned "all acts of violence by any party, as well as terrorism in pursuit of political goals by any group or individual, and all external support for such activities in Kosovo." SC Res. 1199 *supra* footnote 22, Preamble, a phrase repeated in SC Res. 1203 *supra* footnote 28, Preamble.

[32] In July 1998, the Secretary-General reported to the Security Council as follows: "I am increasingly concerned that, unless hostilities in Kosovo are stopped, tensions could spill across borders and destabilise the entire region. Kosovo therefore becomes a key issue for the overall stability of the Balkan region." UN Doc. S/1998/608, July 2, 1998 at para. 13.

[33] SC Res. 1199 *supra* footnote 22, Preamble, and SC Res. 1203 *supra* footnote 28, Preamble.

[34] The Group also made clear that it disapproved of Belgrade's security crackdown in Kosovo: "We are dismayed that in the period since September [1997], rather than taking steps to reduce tensions or to enter without preconditions into dialogue toward a political solution, the Belgrade authorities have applied repressive measures in Kosovo." Contact Group Statement 1998: para. 2.

[35] See UN Doc. S/1998/608, July 2, 1998 *supra* footnote 32.

[36] *Milosevic rejects mediation, defies sanctions*, Reuters, May 8, 1998.

[37] In this early period the FRY's resistance was maintained despite considerable pressure from the US which was the major player in the eyes of both Belgrade and Pristina. In May, lengthy talks took place between President Milosevic and US envoy Richard Holbrooke, *US sends peace broker Holbrooke to Yugoslavia*, Reuters, May 9, 1998; *US envoy Holbrooke starts Kosovo mission*, Reuters May 10, 1998. For a discussion of FRY intransigence on the question of international mediation see Kofos 1998: 83.

mediation Belgrade staged a referendum on April 23, 1998 which asked the Serbian people for their views on international mediation resulting in a message of overwhelming hostility to the idea thereby creating a mandate for Belgrade's resistance to Contact Group pressure.[38] The question of mediation was by this point the clear stumbling block to talks as Rugova, who was already perceived as too conciliatory by many Kosovo Albanians, came under strong domestic pressure not to accept talks without international involvement.[39] Although a compromise of sorts was reached and talks began on May 15[40] without mediation but with the possibility of US involvement at some stage, before long the entire process collapsed. As was to occur on a number of occasions in the next twelve months, attempts to reach a political settlement were rendered obsolete by events on the ground. Talks scheduled for May 29 were cancelled and subsequently the Kosovo Albanians suspended the negotiations scheduled for June 5.[41] Up until the agreements brokered by Richard Holbrooke and signed on October 15 and 16, 1998[42] all attempts to revive the process failed.[43] These early days of international involvement highlight the difficulty which any international group faces in pressurising for an autonomy settlement when the state in question can demonstrate strong popular opposition to any such accommodation. It also highlights the practical difficulty, which had arisen in 1992 over the question of recognition for Bosnia-Herzegovina, of attempting to foster a long-term solution to the sovereignty dispute when the more urgent question is the escalating military crisis on the ground.

---

[38]   *Serbs vote on Kosovo amid fears of violence,* Reuters, April 23, 1998. According to the Serbian Referendum Commission almost 95% voted against intervention – *Serbs vote 'No' to West in Kosovo,* Reuters, April 23, 1998.

[39]   Hard-liners had already split from Rugova's party, the LDK, and he was being pressurised against compromise by the KLA. *Holbrooke bid to broker Kosovo meeting,* Reuters, May 12, 1998.

[40]   *US coaxes Kosovo enemies to talks,* Reuters, May 13, 1998, and, *Belgrade, Kosovo to continue talks,* Reuters, May 15, 1998. Talks first took place between Slobodan Milosevic and Ibrahim Rugova on May 15 in the course of which they agreed that weekly meetings should thereafter take place between negotiating teams. These talks between Kosovo Albanian leaders and Belgrade negotiators began on 22 May 1998, and it was reported that the FRY negotiating team guaranteed to the Kosovo side the possibility of an American background presence – *Serbs and Albanians hold first Kosovo talks,* Reuters, May 22, 1998. It is not quite clear what role the US intended to play, although President Clinton indicated that the US intended "serious involvement" in the talks – *Kosovo Albanians Encouraged by Clinton Meeting,* Reuters, June 1, 1998. The Government of Albania was particularly sceptical of the FRY's goodwill in these talks – *Kosovo talks a sham – Albanian leader,* Reuters, May 25, 1998.

[41]   Fighting intensified in the lead up to the talks planned for June 5 with reports of villages being "purged" of KLA fighters, and of security forces forcing people from towns. *US Officials Fear Ethnic Cleansing in Kosovo,* Reuters, June 3, 1998. This resulted in increased refugee flows to Albania, all of which made a resumption of talks very difficult. *Albania Cries for Help for Refugees from Kosovo,* Reuters, June 4, 1998. The Western powers clearly laid the blame for the upsurge in violence at Belgrade's door and European foreign ministers meeting in Palermo called upon Milosevic directly to, in the words of British Foreign Secretary Robin Cook, "halt the killing now" – *Ministers Warn Milosevic to Stop Killing Now,* Reuters, June 4, 1998.

[42]   The 'October Agreements' discussed below.

[43]   For example on June 18, 1998 Yugoslavia offered a resumption in talks, but did not offer international mediation or a troop pull-out, which were requirements of the Contact Group: *Serbia: Talks yes, but no go-between,* Reuters, June 18, 1998.

C. Background to sanctions

The intensifying military dimension of the conflict led to the imposition of sanctions. As of March 1998 an 'outer wall' of sanctions against the FRY remained in place as a consequence of the war in Bosnia and Herzegovina.[44] In the face of Belgrade's intransigence on talks, the Contact Group hardened its position and began the process of imposing fresh sanctions. In the course of its meeting on March 9 it announced: "In the light of the deplorable violence in Kosovo, we feel compelled to take steps to demonstrate to the authorities in Belgrade that they cannot defy international standards without facing severe consequences."[45] The Contact Group reiterated its position by setting out a series of goals which remained fairly constant demands for the following twelve months, and which were to be largely endorsed by the Security Council in its subsequent resolutions. First, the Contact Group requested access for a mission to Kosovo to be undertaken by the United Nations High Commissioner for Human Rights. The opportunity for the international community to monitor the human rights position in Kosovo was a consistent demand of the Contact Group and it was also to form an important element of the October Agreements. Secondly, the Group urged the Office of the Prosecutor of the International Criminal Tribunal for the Former Yugoslavia (ICTY) to begin gathering information related to the violence in Kosovo that may fall within its jurisdiction. The Group was clearly of the view that the jurisdiction of the ICTY which applied to the territory of the former Yugoslavia extended to cover Kosovo.[46] In addition, on March 9, given the already grave situation, the Contact Group proposed the imposition of sanctions, in particular a comprehensive arms embargo against the FRY, including Kosovo.[47]

---

[44] This outer-wall of sanctions was largely financial and cut the FRY off from foreign credit and membership of the International Monetary Fund.

[45] Contact Group Statement 1998: para. 6.

[46] The Contact Group's demand was subsequently supported by the Security Council which urged: "the Office of the Prosecutor of the International Tribunal... to begin gathering information related to the violence in Kosovo that may fall within its jurisdiction, and notes that the authorities of the Federal Republic of Yugoslavia have an obligation to co-operate with the Tribunal ..." SC Res. 1160 *supra* footnote 26, para. 17. The chief prosecutor of the ICTY on July 7, 1998 communicated to the Contact Group her view that the situation in Kosovo represented an armed conflict within the terms of the mandate of the Tribunal. The significance of the crisis being deemed an "armed conflict" is that it thereby invoked the jurisdiction of the ICTY, which is mandated to prosecute *inter alia* crimes against humanity and violations of the laws or customs of war in the territory of the former Yugoslavia. Statute of the ICTY Article 1, SC Res. 827 (May 25, 1993). Notably, in the course of her subsequent investigations into alleged war crimes in Kosovo, the chief prosecutor, on May 27, 1999, announced her intention to indict President Milosevic and other leading figures (Milan Milutinovic, the President of Serbia; Nikola Sainovic, Deputy Prime Minister of the FRY; Dragoljub Ojdanic, Chief of Staff of the Yugoslav Army; Vlajko Stojiljkovic, Minister of Internal Affairs of Serbia) for war crimes. *Milosevic and Others*, ICTY Case No.: IT–99–37.

[47] Contact Group Statement 1998: para. 9.

D. Sanctions in action: more carrot than stick

From March 1998 the international community adopted the strategy of using sanctions against the FRY as both incentive and deterrent in their attempt to encourage a political settlement on autonomy for Kosovo.[48] After its March statement the Contact Group steadily strengthened sanctions. Initially in April, as tension mounted in Kosovo in the face of a continuing absence of any dialogue, came a freeze on FRY assets held abroad.[49] At this stage however, the Contact Group's incentive/deterrent approach to sanctions was evident. On the one hand the Group confirmed that the freeze would be lifted immediately if Belgrade took the necessary steps, as outlined by the Group, to engage in political dialogue with the Kosovo Albanian leadership. At the same time however, the Group made clear that failure to engage in dialogue would result in further sanctions aimed at halting new investment in the FRY.[50]

In the end negotiations had not begun by May 9, 1998 and on that date the Contact Group indicated that it would impose the investment ban on the FRY.[51] However, the Contact Group's eagerness to reward the FRY for taking positive steps led to an easing of sanctions less than two weeks later when talks began between Milosevic and Rugova. With the commencement of these negotiations, the Contact Group decided not to put the proposed ban on new investment into effect and undertook to consider later in May whether to continue with the freeze on the FRY funds held abroad as well as with the other sanctions still in place.[52] This relaxation of sanctions would seem to have been implemented somewhat prematurely given the early collapse of the negotiations, but it can be cited as another indication of the Contact Group's attempts to accommodate Belgrade and to encourage the initiation of dialogue on the worsening military situation and on Kosovo's long-term status.

The imposition of sanctions is also noteworthy for the degree of co-operation among the Contact Group, the Security Council and the EU. On March 31, 1998 the

---

[48]   This approach was set out by the Contact Group at its meeting of 9 March as follows: "Unless the FRY takes steps to resolve the serious political and human rights issues in Kosovo, there is no prospect of any improvement in its international standing. On the other hand, concrete progress to resolve the serious political and human rights issues in Kosovo will improve the international position of the FRY and prospects for normalisation of its international relationships and full rehabilitation in international institutions." Id., para. 8. In this regard President Milosevic was given an ultimatum, "to take rapid and effective steps to stop the violence and engage in a commitment to find a political solution to the issue of Kosovo through dialogue." Treating Milosevic as personally responsible for the situation, the Contact Group made clear that he should within 10 days: "withdraw the special police units and cease action by the security forces affecting the civilian population; allow access to Kosovo for the ICRC and other humanitarian organisations as well as by representatives of the Contact Group and other Embassies; commit himself publicly to begin a process of dialogue... with the leadership of the Kosovar Albanian community and co-operate in a constructive manner with the Contact Group in the implementation of the actions specified in paragraph 6 [supra footnote 45]... which require action by the FRY government." Contact Group Statement 1998: para. 7.

[49]   This was imposed immediately on April 29, 1998. *Big powers back new sanctions on Yugoslavia*, Reuters, April 29, 1998.

[50]   Id. It should be noted that there was a general lack of enthusiasm for these measures from Russia, which indicated an underlying tension within the Contact Group which would eventually split the Group with the commencement of NATO's air-strikes in March 1999.

[51]   *West imposes sanctions on Yugoslavia*, Reuters, May 9, 1998. Once again Russia dissented from the decision.

[52]   *Serbian sanctions put on hold*, Reuters, May 19, 1998.

Security Council, in response to a recommendation by the Contact Group in its statement of March 9, adopted Resolution 1160 (1998) which imposed an arms embargo.[53] The construction of a web of sanctions also involved the European Union. In response to the failure to engage in constructive dialogue with the Kosovo Albanians, and in particular as a result of the FRY's rejection of international mediation, the European Commission, which had in any case already suspended the autonomous trade regime for the FRY, decided to continue with this suspension.

The EU also supported Security Council Resolution 1160 (1998) with its own arms embargo the imposition of which was announced by the Presidency on March 20 in a statement setting out the common position of the Union.[54] The EU, in light of the Contact Group's appeal of March 9, also introduced a ban on the supply of equipment that might be used for internal repression or terrorism and imposed a moratorium on export credit and a ban on visas for a list of Serbian officials identified as having clear security responsibilities in Kosovo.[55] Once again mirroring the Contact Group approach which had demanded that negotiations begin through the mediation of Felipe Gonzalez, the stated aim of the EU was "to maintain the pressure on the Belgrade authorities to launch a meaningful dialogue without preconditions."[56]

The speedy co-ordination of measures taken against Belgrade in March 1998 by the Contact Group, the Security Council of the UN and the EU displayed a high level of common purpose among different international actors which was lacking during the Bosnian crisis. Ensuing events, however, were to highlight Belgrade's preparedness to test fully the will of the international community to continue with its relatively tough approach. Despite the commencement of talks between Belgrade and Pristina at the end of May 1998, and the subsequent partial lifting of sanctions by early June, Belgrade's offensive in Kosovo intensified considerably in June leading to allegations that forced mass civilian displacement was taking place at the hands of the security forces.[57] As thousands of refugees arrived fatigued over the border into Albania, a pattern which was to repeat itself periodically in the following year, many tales were told of systematic attacks on towns and villages, the driving out of the civilian population by heavy shelling and the subsequent burning of buildings, a process which echoed the process of forced civilian displacement during the Bosnia war.[58]

The Contact Group was now faced with a situation in which it had relaxed sanctions against the FRY only to see the Kosovo Albanians suspend the talks scheduled for June 5 in the face of the advancement by Serbian/FRY forces on civilian population centres, a scenario which prompted Albania's Foreign Minister Pascal Milo to comment: "Unfortunately the Contact Group of countries has given Milosevic much

---

[53] See below footnote 64.
[54] Declaration by the Presidency on behalf of the European Union on the adoption of responsibilities in Kosovo. EU Doc. PESC/98/23, Brussels, March 20, 1998.
[55] Both of these steps were advocated by the Contact Group, Contact Group Statement 1998: para. 7(b) and (c).
[56] Declaration by the Presidency on behalf of the European Union, *supra* footnote 54.
[57] *US officials fear ethnic cleansing in Kosovo*, Reuters, June 3, 1998.
[58] There were also reports of atrocities and the random murder of civilians. See the report by Jonathan Steele, the first western journalist to gain access to western Kosovo following the commencement of the June offensive. The Guardian (London), June 8, 1998.

more carrot than stick."[59] It was widely suspected that Belgrade was in fact using the talks as a smoke-screen to continue its military campaign in Kosovo whilst at the same time benefiting from an easing of sanctions.

4. THE UN RESPONSE

The Security Council followed the Contact Group lead, not only by imposing an arms embargo but also in promoting mediation and in endorsing the October Agreements which were eventually brokered by the Group in the autumn of 1998. Before this, the Security Council passed two Resolutions[60] which had three main aims: the two short-term goals of conflict control and alleviation of the growing humanitarian crisis; and thirdly, the more ambitious objective of reaching a political resolution to the dispute. In this regard it walked the same tight-rope as the Contact Group in endorsing greater autonomy for Kosovo[61] while confirming the commitment of all Member States to the sovereignty and territorial integrity of the Federal Republic of Yugoslavia.[62] These aims were advanced in conjunction with a general condemnation of both excessive force by Serbian/FRY security forces against civilians and peaceful demonstrators in Kosovo, and acts of terrorism by the Kosovo Liberation Army.[63]

A. *The arms embargo of March 1998*

The UN Security Council, acting under Chapter VII of the UN Charter, responded to the Serbian offensive of February/March with an arms embargo.[64] Resolution 1160 (1998) of 31 March 1998[65] declared that, for the purposes of fostering peace and stability in Kosovo, all States would prevent the sale or supply to the Federal Republic of Yugoslavia, including Kosovo, of arms and related matériel of all types and would also prevent arming and training for terrorist activities there.[66] In addition it appointed a committee to monitor the effective implementation of the embargo.[67]

The Resolution also requested more information from the Secretary-General in the form of regular reports on the arms embargo and other issues.[68] Per paragraphs

---

[59] *Big powers plan Kosovo meeting next week,* Reuters, June 4, 1998.
[60] SC Res. 1160 *supra* footnote 26 and SC Res. 1199 *supra* footnote 22.
[61] It supported the Contact Group's attempts to secure a peaceful resolution of the conflict which would include an enhanced status for Kosovo, involving a substantially greater degree of autonomy and meaningful self-administration. SC Res. 1160 *supra* footnote 26, para. 5.
[62] Id.
[63] SC Res. 1160 *supra* footnote 26, Preamble.
[64] In doing so it noted with appreciation "the statements of the... the Contact Group... of 9 and 25 March 1998... including the proposal on a comprehensive arms embargo on the Federal Republic of Yugoslavia, including Kosovo." SC Res. 1160 *supra* footnote 26, Preamble.
[65] SC Res. 1160 *supra* footnote 26.
[66] Id., para. 8.
[67] Id., para. 9.
[68] These were to be delivered every 30 days, para. 14. The OSCE was also invited to keep the Secretary-General informed on the situation in Kosovo and on measures taken by it in this regard, para. 13. Furthermore, the Secretary-General was requested to include in his first report recommendations for the establishment of a comprehensive regime to monitor the implementation of the embargo.

9, 14 and 15 the Secretary-General duly reported to the Security Council with detailed recommendations for a comprehensive regime to monitor the prohibitions imposed by the Resolution.[69] The Secretary-General recommended the deployment of teams composed of qualified experts and the establishment of a fully equipped communications centre, but noted that the UN was unable within existing budgetary resources to establish and administer such a comprehensive regime.[70]

This admission is of considerable significance, signalling that the Secretary-General was reliant upon the co-operation and assistance of other international organisations. Specifically, the Secretary-General suggested that the OSCE with contributions and assistance from other regional organisations such as the EU, NATO and the Western European Union (WEU), would be in a position to carry out the requested functions effectively,[71] and concluded that he would explore with the OSCE and the other regional organisations, their readiness to participate in such a comprehensive monitoring regime.[72] NATO, the WEU and the OSCE agreed to help enforce the prohibitions contained in Resolution 1160 (1998).[73] The EU also did so, asking the European Community Monitoring Mission (ECMM) to report to the Secretary-General's Committee any relevant information on the movement of arms that should come into its possession as a result of its operations in Albania, Bosnia, Croatia, the FRY and Macedonia.[74] Generally, therefore, a network of co-operation built up involving the UN (through UNPREDEP[75]); the EU; NATO; the WEU; and the Danube Commission, which provided a framework for reporting on violations of 1160 (1998) to the Committee established pursuant to the resolution.[76] The Secretary-General's reports were, for the following year, to become one of the Security Council's main sources of information on the questions of the FRY's compliance with the arms embargo and with the other demands contained in the Resolution. NATO in March 1999 could again point to the assistance it gave the Secretary-General in his task of keeping the Security Council informed of the FRY's compliance or non-compliance with Resolution 1160 (1998) and subsequent Resolutions.

B. *The role of the Security Council*

Endorsing the Contact Group's efforts to reach a settlement, the Security Council called upon the authorities in Belgrade and the leadership of the Kosovar Albanian

---

[69]   The first report came in April, Report of the Secretary-General Prepared Pursuant to Security Council Resolution 1160 (1998). S/1998/361, April 30, 1998.
[70]   UN Doc. S/1998/361, April 30, 1998, para. 6.
[71]   Id., para. 7.
[72]   Id., para. 8.
[73]   UN Doc. S/1998/608, July 2, 1998, paras. 5–8 and Annexes I – IV.
[74]   Id., para. 8 and Annex IV.
[75]   See below footnote 121.
[76]   This was recognised by the Secretary-General in his August report. UN Doc. S/1998/712, August 5, 1998, para. 7. Accordingly he invited these organisations to forward "relevant information... concerning violations or allegations of violations of the prohibitions imposed by Security Council resolution 1160 (1998)" for consideration by the Committee (para. 8).

community "urgently to enter without preconditions into a meaningful dialogue on political status issues".[77] The urgency in the Security Council's message reflected the worsening situation on the ground as the Serbian offensive intensified in March 1998. The Security Council also connected the issue of sanctions to the broader issue of dispute resolution by adopting the Contact Group's carrot and stick approach. This is evident in paragraph 16 of the Resolution which replicates the demands which the Contact Group had made of the FRY and which also employed the combination of threat and enticement in which the Contact Group's requirements had been double-wrapped. The Security Council set out its intention to:

> "review the situation on the basis of the reports of the Secretary-General, which will take into account the assessments of, *inter alia*, the Contact Group, the OSCE and the European Union, and decides also to reconsider the prohibitions imposed by this Resolution, including action to terminate them, following receipt of the assessment of the Secretary-General that the Government of the Federal Republic of Yugoslavia... [is] co-operating in a constructive manner with the Contact Group".

The Secretary-General would judge this co-operation by assessing whether or not the FRY government had:

> "(a) begun a substantive dialogue in accordance with paragraph 4 above,[78] including the participation of an outside representative or representatives, unless any failure to do so is not because of the position of the Federal Republic of Yugoslavia or Serbian authorities;
>
> (b) withdrawn the special police units and ceased action by the security forces affecting the civilian population;
>
> (c) allowed access to Kosovo by humanitarian organisations as well as representatives of Contact Group and other embassies;
>
> (d) accepted a mission by the Personal Representative of the OSCE Chairman-in-Office for the Federal Republic of Yugoslavia that would include a new and specific mandate for addressing the problems in Kosovo, as well as the return of the OSCE long-term missions;
>
> (e) facilitated a mission to Kosovo by the United Nations High Commissioner for Human Rights".[79]

---

[77]   SC Res. 1160 *supra* footnote 26, para. 4.
[78]   Id.
[79]   Id., para. 16.

Reiterating that the FRY could either improve or weaken its international standing by the action it took, the Resolution confirmed that "concrete progress to resolve the serious political and human rights issues in Kosovo will improve the international position of the Federal Republic of Yugoslavia and prospects for normalisation of its international relationships and full participation in international institutions",[80] but that "failure to make constructive progress towards the peaceful resolution of the situation in Kosovo will lead to the consideration of additional measures".[81]

The Secretary-General's reports after March 1998 dealt with all areas of compliance, and not only the question of the arms embargo. As has been noted, the Secretary-General in his first report in April 1998 relied heavily on information from other sources.[82] He reprinted reports from the Presidency of the EU and the Chairman-in-Office of the OSCE and, having received no reply from the co-ordinator of the Contact Group, he also included a report from the Russian Federation. Unsurprisingly, the Russian report was considerably more enthusiastic about the extent of FRY compliance with Res. 1160 (1998) than those from the other two bodies. With regard to the commencement of dialogue required by paragraph 16(a), the EU noted the continuing failure to commence talks and identified the stumbling block as the disagreement over the involvement of a third party. The Republic of Serbia continued to refuse outside representation offering only the involvement of a representative of the FRY government, and furthermore insisted that a solution must be found within the Republic of Serbia which as far as the EU was concerned amounted to the establishment of a precondition[83] (which the Security Council had declared to be unacceptable in paragraph 4 of Resolution 1160 (1998)).

The EU was also sceptical of the FRY's compliance with other aspects of paragraph 16 although it did note that with regard to paragraph 16(c), neither EU embassies nor the relevant humanitarian organisations had recently reported any specific problems in obtaining access to parts of Kosovo.[84] With respect to 16(d) the FRY had not agreed that any mission by a Personal Representative of the EU and the OSCE Chairman-in-Office to discuss relations between the FRY and the EU/OSCE should include a new and specific mandate for addressing the problems in Kosovo.[85]

---

[80] Id., para. 18.
[81] Id., para. 19.
[82] He acknowledged, initially in a letter of April 9, 1998 to the President of the Security Council, that his Secretariat was not in a position to make an independent assessment of the situation on the ground. Therefore, his report of April 30 in assessing whether or not the Government of the FRY had complied in a constructive manner with the five conditions contained in para. 16 of the Resolution, relied upon information provided by the Contact Group, the OSCE and the EU.
[83] UN Doc. S/1998/361, Annex 1, paras. 2–4. The OSCE took the same view, (Annex II para. 4). The Russian Federation report, however, suggested that it was the leadership of the Kosovo Albanians which was setting forth preconditions by demanding the presence of international mediators and the conduct of negotiations solely with the representative of the President of the FRY (Annex III para. 8).
    To add legitimacy to its refusal of participation by an outside representative, it has been noted that Serbia held a referendum on April 23 one week before the Secretary-General's report to the Security Council. The referendum was criticised by the OSCE as being a diversionary tactic and having "a disruptive effect on an already inflamed situation" (statement of the OSCE Troika, April 8, 1998). UN Doc. S/1998/361, *supra* footnote 70 Annex II, para. 6.
[84] UN Doc. S/1998/361, Annex 1, para. 10.
[85] Id., para. 11.

The OSCE reported similar intransigence on the part of Belgrade. On March 27, 1998, the Chairman-in-Office visited the FRY where he met authorities in Belgrade, Pristina, and Podgorica (Montenegro). During his talks with President Milosevic in Belgrade, the latter confirmed that the FRY would not be ready to accept OSCE demands before taking back its seat in the Organisation. He indicated that Mr. Gonzalez, as Personal Representative to the Chairman-in Office, would be welcome on the condition that his mandate would be limited to the question of re-admittance of the FRY to the OSCE. In other words the FRY continued to reject any outside participation in a dialogue on Kosovo, and continued to impose preconditions on such talks.[86]

Finally, in respect of 16(e) of SC Resolution 1160 (1998) the EU noted that the FRY had not granted the requested visa to the United Nations High Commissioner for Human Rights Special Rapporteur on extra-judicial, summary or arbitrary executions, although visas were granted for visits by the Special Rapporteur on the Former Yugoslavia and three human rights officers.[87]

C. *May to September 1998: the conflict intensifies*

Throughout the spring and summer of 1998 the Security Council continued to receive the Secretary-General's reports pursuant to Res. 1160 (1998),[88] which described: mounting tension on the ground and continued fighting;[89] human rights abuses by both sides;[90] an increase in the number of internally displaced persons and, as of May, a significant flow of refugees to Albania.[91]

The Secretary-General identified the failed talks of May 1998 and the continued refusal of Belgrade to accept the participation of Felipe Gonzalez as problematic,[92] and he expressed his grave concern that in light of this failure, mounting violence in Kosovo might overwhelm political efforts to prevent further escalation of the crisis. His criticism, while focusing more on the FRY was fairly even-handed and directed at both sides: "I deplore the excessive use of force by the Serbian police in Kosovo and call upon all parties concerned to demonstrate restraint and commit themselves to a peaceful solution. The use of violence to suppress political dissent or in pursuit of political goals is inadmissible. Terrorist activities from whatever quarter contribute

---

[86]   Id., paras. 17–18.
[87]   Id., para. 12.
[88]   UN Doc. S/1998/470, June 4, 1998; UN Doc. S/1998/608, *supra* footnote 32; UN Doc. S/1998/712, *supra* footnote 76; UN Doc. S/1998/834, September 4, 1998. His reports continued up until the air-strikes of March 1999: UN Doc. S/1998/912, October 3, 1998; UN Doc. S/1998/1068, November 12, 1998; UN Doc. S/1998/1221, December 24, 1998; UN Doc. S/1999/99, January 30, 1999; UN Doc. S/1999/293, March 17, 1999.
[89]   e.g. UN Doc. S/1998/470, *supra* footnote 88, paras. 13–15.
[90]   Id., paras. 16–18.
[91]   UN Doc. S/1998/470, *supra* footnote 88, paras. 19–20. The situation regarding displaced persons and refugees was to deteriorate through the summer of 1998. UN Doc. S/1998/608, *supra* footnote 32, para. 10, and *Information on the Situation in Kosovo and on Measures taken by the Organisation for Security and Co-operation in Europe*, submitted pursuant to paragraphs 13 and 16 of SC Resolution 1160 (1998). See also UN Doc. S/1998/712, *supra* footnote 76, paras. 11–14.
[92]   UN Doc. S/1998/470, *supra* footnote 88, para. 36.

to the deadly spiral of violence that jeopardises stability in the region."[93] By July the tone of the Secretary-General had become even stronger. He was "appalled by the continued violence in Kosovo." His concern was increasingly with the broader security implications of a possible escalation in the crisis: "The parties concerned must demonstrate restraint and resume negotiations to find a peaceful solution to the conflict. I am increasingly concerned that, unless hostilities in Kosovo are stopped, tensions could spill across borders and destabilise the entire region. Kosovo therefore becomes a key issue for the overall stability of the Balkan region."[94]

The concern with escalation of the conflict and the endangerment to peace and security in the region was a preoccupation of the international community from the beginning of the crisis. As the situation deteriorated in the summer of 1998, and in light of the continuing failure on the part of the FRY to initiate talks, the Contact Group began to draw up a new peace plan and thereby commenced the process which would ultimately lead to the wide-ranging Rambouillet draft agreement.[95] A Contact Group statement of June 12, 1998 set out further demands,[96] which would later be repeated by the Security Council in Res. 1199 (1998),[97] and on July 9 the group had prepared an outline peace agreement based on a plan of autonomy for Kosovo.[98] Again this marks a further proactive attempt to force the hand of Belgrade. However, as had occurred in May, moves towards political dialogue were soon undone by events on the ground, and by the end of July fighting had intensified as a result of a massive Serbian/FRY offensive against the KLA which led ultimately to the collapse of this initiative.[99]

---

[93] Id., para. 46.
[94] UN Doc. S/1998/608, *supra* footnote 32, para. 13.
[95] *Major powers begin talks on Kosovo crisis,* Reuters, July 8, 1998. The Interim Agreement for Peace and Self-Government, negotiated at Rambouillet, France in February 1999 was the final detailed plan for an overall settlement on the issues of security and autonomy for Kosovo. It was eventually signed by the Kosovo Albanian delegation. See, Weller 1999. It was the rejection of the Interim Agreement by the FRY which finally triggered the air-strikes of March 23.
[96] A British Foreign Office spokesman announced the demand by Contact Group ministers of an immediate cessation of all action by the security forces against civilians, unimpeded access for international monitors and humanitarian organisations to Kosovo, the right of refugees to return to their homes and rapid progress towards a dialogue with the Kosovo Albanian leadership. Contact Group Statement, June 12, 1998. *Russia opposes NATO force against Serbia,* Reuters, June 12, 1998.
[97] SC Res. 1199 *supra* footnote 22, para. 4.
[98] The plan, although detailing self rule for Kosovo, ruled out independence as an option for Kosovo. *Serbian parties hail Kosovo plan, US warns of war,* Reuters, July 9, 1999. Notably both sides initially reacted positively to the plan.
[99] This led to a growing pessimism among the Contact Group powers. *Despair in West as prospects for peace diminish,* Reuters, July 28, 1998; *Kosovo faces all-out war as Serb tanks shell rebels,* Daily Telegraph (London), July 27, 1998. On July 23, the OSCE reported that it had failed to persuade the FRY government to allow a permanent OSCE diplomatic mission to return to Kosovo or to accept the mediation of Felipe Gonzalez without a restoration of Yugoslavia's full membership of the OSCE. *Milosevic refuses permanent OSCE mission,* Reuters, July 23, 1998. By August 5, Reuters reported that the West was growing increasingly frustrated and that again NATO was drawing up contingency plans. *West warns Milosevic on Kosovo,* Reuters, August 6, 1998. On August 6, the Albanian parliament appealed to the international community to intervene militarily in Kosovo, *Albania urges Western military action in Kosovo,* Reuters, August 6, 1998.

D. Security Council Resolution 1199 (1998)

The Secretary-General's report to the Security Council of September 4 catalogued the worsening situation from July to August resulting from the ongoing offensive against the KLA, which was the most intensive to date. The Security Council responded again with a second Resolution, which now adopted much stronger language than Security Council Resolution 1160 (1998) in demanding that all parties cease hostilities.[100] As such it affirmed that the deterioration of the situation in Kosovo constituted a threat to peace and security in the region.[101] It also called upon the authorities in the FRY and the Kosovo Albanian leadership to enter immediately into a meaningful dialogue without preconditions and with international involvement, and to a clear timetable, leading to an end to the crisis and to a negotiated political solution to the issue of Kosovo,[102] and demanded that the authorities of the FRY and the Kosovo Albanian leadership take immediate steps to improve the humanitarian situation and to avert an impending humanitarian catastrophe.[103]

The Secretary-General in his September report also noted considerable human rights concerns,[104] concluding in strong terms: 'I am alarmed by the lack of progress towards a political settlement in Kosovo and by the further loss of life, displacement of civilian population (sic) and destruction of property resulting from the ongoing conflict. It is essential that negotiations get under way so as to break the cycle of disproportionate use of force by the Serbian forces and acts of violence by the Kosovo Albanian paramilitary units by promoting a political resolution of the conflict.'[105]

The prospect of new talks had further diminished from the already unpromising position which had prevailed in the Spring of 1998. The Secretary-General's report in August followed the collapse of the Contact Group's July initiative to broker a settlement, and included a report from the OSCE which highlighted that the Republic of Serbia continued to maintain the precondition that dialogue should be conducted within the framework of both Serbia and the FRY and that the territorial integrity of the FRY should first be guaranteed.[106] The difficulties in commencing negotiations

---

[100] SC Res. 1199 *supra* footnote 22, para. 1.

[101] SC Res. 1199 *supra* footnote 22, Preamble.

[102] SC Res. 1199 *supra* footnote 22, para. 3. The Security Council's language was by the October 24, 1998 to become even more imperative in Resolution 1203 (1998) which stressed the 'urgent' need for such dialogue. SC Res. 1203 *supra* footnote 28, para. 5.

[103] SC Res. 1199 *supra* footnote 22, para. 2. This dramatic language was first used by the Secretary-General. His report of September 4, 1998 related the tale of heavy fighting from mid-July into August. It also focused on the ensuing humanitarian concerns and, in particular, upon the displacement of over 230,000 civilians including, according to UNHCR, up to 50,000 forced into the woods and mountains. UN Doc. S/1998/834, *supra* footnote 88, paras. 7–8. Accordingly, the report warned that "the approaching winter... could transform what is currently a humanitarian crisis into a humanitarian catastrophe." (para. 11).

[104] Based upon information from the Office of the United Nations High Commissioner for Human Rights he noted, in particular, reports of arbitrary arrests, torture, ill-treatment and deaths in custody, as well as abductions by the KLA. UN Doc. S/1998/834, *supra* footnote 88, paras. 15–17.

[105] UN Doc. S/1998/834, *supra* footnote 88, para. 28.

[106] *Information on the situation in Kosovo and on measures taken by the Organisation for Security and Co-operation in Europe, submitted pursuant to paragraphs 13 and 16 of Security Council Resolution 1160 (1998)*, UN Doc. S/1998/712, *supra* footnote 76, Annex I, para. 12.

were also heightened by the fact that over the summer the Kosovo Albanian position had radicalised with the KLA gaining influence following the considerable territorial gains it had made prior to the Serbian/FRY backlash from July to August. Now the Kosovo Albanians had themselves set preconditions for a resumption of the dialogue, namely withdrawal from Kosovo of the Serb special forces, a cessation of the operations aimed against the Albanian civilian population and inclusion of Kosovo's independence as an agenda item for the negotiations. The KLA was also demanding that the political parties should accept its existence and importance.[107]

Resolution 1199 (1998), clearly took on board the tone of the Secretary-General's criticism which by September was increasingly directed towards the FRY on account of the excessive use of force and levels of human rights abuse which were being reported.[108] The Resolution focused upon three issues surrounding talks, namely: preconditions, international involvement and a clear timetable, all of which represented impediments imposed largely by Serbia and the FRY.[109]

Resolution 1199 (1998) also laid much of the blame for the violence at Belgrade's door. It expressed grave concern 'at the recent intense fighting in Kosovo and in particular the excessive and indiscriminate use of force by Serbian security forces and the Yugoslav Army which have resulted in numerous civilian casualties and, according to the estimate of the Secretary-General, the displacement of over 230,000 persons from their homes'.[110] It also expressed deep concern at the flow of refugees into northern Albania, Bosnia and Herzegovina and other European countries and at the increasing numbers of displaced persons within Kosovo.

Resolution 1199 (1998), and Resolution 1203 (1998) passed almost one month later,[111] displayed a growing frustration within the Security Council at the worsening situation and an increasing sense of urgency in its calls for a resolution to the crisis. In even stronger tones than 1199 (1998), Resolution 1203 (1998) confirmed that the Security Council was 'deeply alarmed and concerned at the continuing grave humanitarian situation throughout Kosovo and the impending humanitarian catastrophe'.[112] Accordingly, it demanded immediate action from the authorities of

---

[107] The KLA had not been represented at talks to date by any of the parties but, the Secretary-General reported, the KLA did not recognise the leadership of Ibrahim Rugova and would not accept the possibility of declaring a cease-fire should the talks resume without the KLA being accepted as one of the negotiating parties. UN Doc. S/1998/712, *supra* footnote 76, Annex I (paras. 13–14).

[108] The Secretary-General made reference to atrocities in his October report: 'There are concerns that the disproportionate use of force and actions of the security forces are designed to terrorise and subjugate the population, a collective punishment to teach them that the price of supporting the Kosovo Albanian paramilitary units is too high and will be even higher in future.' UN Doc. S/1998/912, *supra* footnote 88, para. 7. He also stated that he was 'outraged by reports of mass killings of civilians in Kosovo, which recall the atrocities committed in Bosnia and Herzegovina.' (para. 9).

[109] SC Res. 1199 *supra* footnote 22, para. 3.

[110] SC Res. 1199 *supra* footnote 22, Preamble. The reference to the Secretary-General's report is to UN Doc. S/1998/834, *supra* footnote 88, para. 7.

[111] SC Res. 1203 *supra* footnote 28. This Resolution was passed following the October Agreements and will be discussed in this context below.

[112] SC Res. 1203 *supra* footnote 28, para. 11. This followed the Secretary-General's report of 3 October which reported no improvement in the overall humanitarian problem. UN Doc. S/1998/912, *supra* footnote 88, paras. 11–25, although freedom of movement for humanitarian agencies such as the UNHCR and the ICRC had improved.

the FRY and the Kosovo Albanian leadership to co-operate with international efforts to improve the humanitarian situation and to avert this potential disaster.[113] This was tempered by an insistence that "the Kosovo Albanian leadership condemn all terrorist action, and... that all elements in the Kosovo Albanian community should pursue their goals by peaceful means only".[114] The Security Council's criticism and the force of its demands in both Resolutions do centre, however, on the FRY. For example, Res. 1199 (1998) sets out detailed demands of the FRY to implement immediately the following concrete measures towards achieving a political solution to the situation in Kosovo (measures originally contained in the Contact Group statement of June 12, 1998[115]):

'(a) cease all action by the security forces affecting the civilian population and order the withdrawal of security units used for civilian repression;
(b) enable effective and continuous international monitoring in Kosovo by the European Community Monitoring Mission and diplomatic missions accredited to the Federal Republic of Yugoslavia, including access and complete freedom of movement of such monitors to, from and within Kosovo unimpeded by government authorities, and expeditious issuance of appropriate travel documents to international personnel contributing to the monitoring;
(c) facilitate, in agreement with the UNHCR and the International Committee of the Red Cross (ICRC), the safe return of refugees and displaced persons to their homes and allow free and unimpeded access for humanitarian organisations and supplies to Kosovo;
(d) make rapid progress to a clear timetable, in the dialogue referred to in paragraph 3 with the Kosovo Albanian community called for in resolution 1160 (1998), with the aim of agreeing confidence-building measures and finding a political solution to the problems of Kosovo...'

Resolution 1199 (1998) marks a clear shift in the attitude of the Security Council from the position adopted in Resolution 1160 (1998). The demand for a clear timetable for talks largely repeats the terms of 1160 (1998), but the call for a cessation of security force action is more forceful, with its reference to "civilian repression". Similarly a more detailed demand on international monitoring is made, together with a new requirement that the return home of refugees and displaced persons be facilitated. These demands clearly highlight very grave human rights and humanitarian concerns. That they were expressed in a resolution which also confirmed that the situation represented a threat to peace and security in terms of Chapter VII of the UN Charter provided a context of some urgency. Certainly a more forceful approach was now adopted by the Contact Group and by NATO as the crisis moved into its third phase with a threat of force by NATO in the lead up to the October

---

[113] SC Res. 1203 *supra* footnote 28, para. 11.
[114] SC Res. 1203 *supra* footnote 28, para. 6. This is coupled in Res. 1203 with a demand that such actions cease immediately (para. 10).
[115] *supra* footnote 96.

Agreements. It was the concern expressed in Resolution 1199 (1998) over human rights abuses, the escalating humanitarian "catastrophe" and the threat to peace and security which would also be advanced as purported justification for this threat to use force and ultimately for the unilateral NATO action in the spring of 1999.

5. 'A THREAT TO INTERNATIONAL PEACE AND SECURITY': THE ROLE OF NATO THROUGHOUT THE CRISIS

A. Events leading to the simulated air-strikes of June 1998

The degree of involvement by the international community in mediating a solution to any particular internal conflict has often been contingent upon the risk it poses to international peace, and it is clear that the violence in Kosovo which had by October 1998 claimed hundreds of lives and left hundreds of thousands displaced, was capturing international attention largely because of the possibility of escalation of the conflict.

A major preoccupation of the Contact Group from spring 1998 was the threat that the dispute might spread beyond the FRY's borders,[116] with the immediate fear being that Albania would become involved. In May Albania put its armed forces on alert along the border with Kosovo and warned of the possibility of an all out war,[117] and as the conflict escalated through the Spring and Summer so too did tension between the FRY and Albania, particularly as a result of FRY suspicions that Albania was lending implicit or even explicit support to the KLA.[118] Fear also existed of escalation beyond Albania involving Macedonia and perhaps even Greece and other states.[119]

---

[116] The Contact Group in a statement on April 29 warned of this danger – Statement of the Contact Group, Rome, April 29, 1998. US envoy Richard Holbrooke also warned that the conflict could become 'a wide conflagration' in the south-east Balkans. *US envoy Holbrooke starts Kosovo mission,* Reuters, May 10, 1998.

[117] *Albania warns of war as Kosovo fighting rages,* Reuters, May 4, 1998. On June 3 Albania also warned that it might change its position which had hitherto not supported independence for Kosovo. *Albania Adopts Tougher Tone on Kosovo Crisis,* Reuters, June 3, 1998.

[118] The FRY accused Albania of providing the KLA with men, training and weapons and suspected there were bases where the KLA was receiving military training. *Yugoslav Army in border clash with Albanians,* Reuters, April 23, 1998. On June 22 Albanian Prime Minister Fatos Nano, declared that his country was 'on the eve of war' with Yugoslavia. *Albania says on eve of war with Yugoslavia,* Reuters, June 22, 1998. See also, *The View From Tirana: The Albanian Dimension Of The Kosovo Crisis,* International Crisis Group Report, July 10, 1998, p.6.

[119] The International Crisis Group described the danger thus: 'In the event of ethnic fighting in Kosovo, the conflict will be more difficult to isolate than in Bosnia. Albania may yet decide that it has no option but to intervene, and the ethnic Albanians in Macedonia may seize the opportunity to assert their own independence. If Macedonia appears on the verge of disintegration, both Bulgaria and Greece may pursue their own territorial claims against Skopje. The permutations are endless and potentially very destabilising.' International Crisis Group Report, March 10, 1998. The spectre of Bosnia at this time weighed considerably on the minds of Contact Group leaders. On May 6 President Clinton announced that he was not ruling out any options 'because we don't want another Bosnia to happen'. *US, Italy say troops an option in Italy,* Reuters, May 6, 1998. See also, *Blair says Kosovo will not turn out like Bosnia,* Reuters, June 5, 1998, and the warning given by Greek defence minister Akis Tsohatzopoulos that, 'Kosovo can turn into a crisis worse than Bosnia', *Holbrooke says big divides remain on Kosovo,* Reuters, May 11, 1998.

The threat of involvement of other individual states was always over-shadowed by the possibility of military intervention in Kosovo by NATO should the efforts of the Contact Group to secure a negotiated peace fail. At the end of May 1998, for example, NATO announced measures it intended to take aimed at fostering a peaceful solution with the initial purpose being to stop the conflict from spreading and to promote talks.[120] These measures divided into immediate steps and also forward plans which could be implemented at a later date.

Immediately NATO called for an extension of the mandate for the United Nations Preventive Deployment Force (UNPREDEP) present in Macedonia.[121] This appeal was endorsed by the Secretary-General in his June report pursuant to Res. 1160 (1998), in which he concluded that the UNPREDEP mandate due to expire on August 31, 1998 ought to be extended.[122] However, he was also of the view that within its current strength, UNPREDEP would not be able to sustain intensive monitoring and reporting on activities at the borders.[123] On July 21, 1998, the Security Council adopted Resolution 1186 (1998), by which it decided to authorise an increase in the troop strength of UNPREDEP to 1,050 and to extend its current mandate for a period of six months until February 28, 1999 as had been requested by the Secretary-General. It was also vested with the task of monitoring the border areas and reporting to the Secretary-General on illicit arms flows and other activities prohibited under Resolution 1160 (1998).[124]

The forward plans put in place by NATO included providing NATO-commissioned military advice on helping to monitor the Albanian and Macedonian borders as well as considering NATO preventive deployments to help achieve a peaceful solution and strengthen security. NATO members also ordered the Organisation to consider the political, legal and, as necessary, military implications of further deterrent measures, if the situation so required.[125] Although these plans were phrased in general terms without explicit reference to military action, crucially by the end of May NATO indicated that no option was excluded although, consistently, direct reference to intervention was avoided.[126]

---

[120] *NATO plots course in case of Kosovo flare-up,* Reuters, May 28, 1998.

[121] There was already a NATO force of some 800 in Macedonia and NATO now favoured an increase to at least 1,500 troops. *NATO plots course in case of Kosovo flare-up,* Reuters, May 28, 1998, *NATO plans Kosovo firebreak, other options open,* Reuters, May 28, 1998.

[122] UN Doc. S/1998/470, (June 4, 1998), para. 10.

[123] Id.

[124] SC Res. 1186 (July 21, 1998).

[125] It is notable that the Secretary-General confirmed these developments without criticism. UN Doc. S/1998/470, *supra* footnote 122, paras. 26–7. Options for preventive deployment in Albania as mooted by NATO included increasing the number of troops in the region from 7,000 to a figure perhaps over 20,000.

[126] *NATO Warns on Kosovo: No Option is Excluded,* Reuters, May 29, 1998, *NATO Plans Firebreak, other options open,* Reuters, May 28, 1998. Germany's Foreign Minister Klaus Kinkel said: "Escalation and spill-over must be stopped at any price...if there is no political solution then we must study further steps, among them military intervention." *NATO Warns on Kosovo: No Option is Excluded,* Reuters, May 29, 1998. At the same time plans intensified to shore up Albania's border. *Peace Partners Back NATO on Kosovo firebreak,* Reuters, June 1, 1998, and *Ministers Warn Milosevic to Stop Killing,* Reuters, June 4, 1998.

This hardening in the West's position came as the conflict worsened in late May 1998. By now a week long exercise by the Serbian and FRY security forces had resulted in reports of scores of casualties, and led to the abortion of the peace talks which began at this time.[127] From June 5 NATO started to send messages that it was ready for a show of force.[128] This tough approach was partly a response to the perceived snub Belgrade had delivered to the lifting of sanctions and partly a pre-emptive effort to prevent the development of 'another Bosnia' as refugees poured out of Kosovo in early June in ever greater numbers, amid harrowing scenes and in the wake of shelling and burning of villages by security forces.[129]

The first clear indication that NATO was prepared to intervene with or without Security Council authorisation came in June 1998 when, without explicit UN backing, it launched an operation involving simulated bombing raids[130] declaring that the intervention mission would be based on "the relevant legal basis" but with no specific reference to Chapter VII of the UN Charter.[131] This initial show of force highlighted tensions within the Contact Group. The June 1998 action led to demands from Russia that any intervention must secure prior authorisation from the Security Council and during this period it seemed that the UN Security Council might be asked for a Chapter VII mandate to authorise the use of outside force,[132] perhaps authorising "all necessary measures",[133] and Russia at this time indicated that it would not oppose force if it had Security Council approval.[134]

There were however confused signals emanating from certain members of the Contact Group throughout the summer of 1998. Germany for example, as was noted above, initially took a tough position on the issue and frequently floated the idea of intervention with or without Security Council approval,[135] yet before long the tone had become far more moderate.[136] The US however has consistently maintained

---

[127] *Kosovo talks postponed*, Reuters, May 27, 1998; and *Albanians refuse talks until Serbs end attacks*, Reuters, June 5, 1998.

[128] *US ready to punish Serbia*, Reuters, June 6, 1998, and *World preparing to intervene in Kosovo?* Reuters, June 7, 1998.

[129] For example, the UNHCR estimated 800 refugees in 24 hours from June 4–5, and about 10,000 in the preceding few days, *UN: Kosovo refugee flow into Albania slows*, Reuters, June 5, 1998.

[130] *NATO approves 'simulated' Kosovo action*, Reuters, June 11, 1998.

[131] The exercise, NATO declared, had the "aim of demonstrating NATO's capability to project power rapidly into the region." *NATO told to draw up plans to halt Kosovo violence*, Reuters, June 11, 1998. The FRY opposed this as an invasion of its sovereign territory. *NATO To Send Yugoslavia Warning*, Reuters, June 11, 1998.

[132] *UN to mull authorising military action for Kosovo*, Reuters, June 6, 1998.

[133] *World preparing to intervene in Kosovo?* Reuters, June 7, 1998.

[134] *Pressure builds on Serbia over Kosovo*, Reuters, June 8, 1998.

[135] Klaus Kinkel, further to his comments at the end of May *supra* footnote 126, pressed for the deployment of troops on the Albanian border and then went further stating: "Milosevic should know that once NATO troops are stationed there, if it then should come to an absolutely chaotic situation, ways must be sought of intervening in Kosovo itself ." *Big Powers to meet on Kosovo as deaths rise*, Reuters, June 5, 1998.

[136] Indeed Kinkel seemed to back down from his earlier position as early as June 12 when he declared the German government's position to be: "Any kind of intervention in Kosovo whatsoever, including by NATO, would not be possible without a mandate from the Security Council." *Contact Group divisions show through over Kosovo*, Reuters, June 13, 1998. Also on August 4 he was quoted as saying that there should be no outside military strikes against Serbian/FRY forces without UN backing. *Reports: Mass graves discovered in Kosovo*, Reuters, August 5, 1998.

that authority for intervention existed,[137] and that while a Security Council mandate was desirable it was not imperative for legitimate intervention.[138] In light of this hardening in attitude, embodied in the simulated air raids in June and the apparent resolve by most members of the Contact Group and of NATO to intervene in light of further failure by the FRY to comply with the demands of the Contact Group and of Security Council Resolution 1160 (1998), it is perhaps surprising that these threats were not in the end acted upon as the events of the summer of 1998 unfolded. Indeed it was not until the full consequences of the August fighting had become clear that NATO took the next step of issuing activation orders in October 1998 which would lead in the short term to the October Agreements and in the longer term to the air-strikes of 1999.

B. The Agreements of October 1998

The path to the October Agreements was a bloody one in which by late Summer 1998 the earlier resolve of the Contact Group and NATO either weakened or was replaced by a more ambivalent attitude towards the nature of the struggle and its possible strategic implications, particularly as the military tables, prior to the FRY offensive of July-August, seemed to be turning in favour of the KLA. The FRY/ Serbian offensive of July-August came as a result of intense fighting in June and

---

[137] By October NATO was also of the view that it had Security Council authority to act. Acting US Ambassador to the UN Peter Burleigh following the 13–0 vote in favour of UN SC Resolution 1203, said that NATO retained the authority to use force if necessary to enforce compliance with UN SC Resolutions 1160 and 1199. "The NATO allies," Burleigh said, "in agreeing on October 13 to the use of force, made clear that they had the authority and the means to resolve this issue. We retain that authority." Information from US Government electronic mailing list, KOSOVO@INFO.USIA.GOV, 24 October 1999.

[138] *US says UN mandate on Kosovo "not imperative"*, Reuters, June 1, 1998. US Defence Secretary William Cohen suggested that the justification would be collective self defence: "We believe under the UN Charter itself that nations are certainly permitted to engage in self defence and even collective defence." Madeleine Albright also referred to Article 51 of the UN Charter as justification for the action. *Contact Group divisions show through over Kosovo*, Reuters, June 13, 1998. This justification will be examined below. See also *NATO draws up plans for strikes on Kosovo*, Reuters June 11, 1998. France as well as Germany, however, expressed the view that UN Security Council approval was required. *Contact Group divisions show through over Kosovo*, Reuters, June 13, 1998. On June 19 Russia warned of a new Cold War if there was intervention without a Resolution, *NATO could spark new Cold War over Kosovo – Russia*, Reuters, June 19, 1998, and accordingly, the US and other members of the Contact Group made considerable diplomatic efforts to keep Russia on board, *European ministers seek Kosovo diplomacy*, Reuters, June 20, 1998.

Despite the uncertain legal position, at a meeting on June 8 the EU had called for NATO to accelerate its evaluation of its military options. Also a spokesman for the UN Secretary-General noted on June 5: "The Secretary-General is deeply disturbed by the latest reports of an intensifying campaign against the unarmed civilian population in Kosovo. He reiterates in the strongest possible terms his condemnation of the atrocities committed by Serbian military and para-military forces. They must not be allowed to repeat the campaign of ethnic cleansing and indiscriminate attacks on civilians that characterised the war in Bosnia. If the world has learned anything from that dark chapter in history, it is that this kind of aggression must be confronted immediately and with determination. The Secretary-General is encouraged by the North Atlantic Treaty Organisation(NATO)'s resolve to prevent a further escalation of the fighting and reiterates his call for a negotiated settlement that will facilitate a peaceful and democratic future for the people of Kosovo." UN Press Release SG/SM/6583, June 5, 1998.

July by which time the KLA had made considerable advances. The security forces responded by launching operations on a number of fronts to open three important roads which the separatists had earlier captured.[139] In political terms the ground had also shifted with more pronounced splits in the Kosovo Albanian leadership resulting in radical elements gaining influence at the expense of the more conciliatory approach of Rugova.[140]

Although on August 6 NATO and the US Defence Department announced a series of planned military exercises in Albania,[141] and declared that further violence would trigger intervention, no action pursuant to the June ultimatum was in fact taken in response to the FRY/Serbian offensive nor was there even a repeat of the Contact Group's threats. The NATO flyover of June was not repeated and there was little if any discussion of a UN Resolution to authorise intervention as there had been two months earlier.[142] This apparent climb-down in the Contact Group's rhetoric provoked allegations that due to fears that further destabilisation would result from excessive KLA gains and in particular from the boost this was providing to the more radically separatist elements within the Kosovan leadership, a green light was being shown to Belgrade in tacit acceptance of the new offensive. There is evidence that the Contact Group did not entirely oppose the Serbian offensive, for example a statement issued by the US asserted that "each nation has the right to control its highways."[143] This ambivalent approach was also reflected in the words of the Secretary-General in his October report where he confirmed that: "the authorities of the Federal Republic of Yugoslavia have the inherent right, as well as the duty, to maintain public order and security and to respond to violent acts of provocation." Conscious, however, that the Serbian offensive had led to the 'impending humanitarian catastrophe' to which the Security Council had otherwise referred,[144] the Secretary-General attempted to qualify his remarks by stating: "[h]owever, this can in no way justify the systematic terror inflicted on civilians these past few days and weeks."[145] The attempt to, on the one hand, accept the legitimacy of the FRY's

---

[139] *Despair in West as prospects for peace diminish*, Sydney Morning Herald, July 28, 1998, *Kosovo faces all-out war as Serb tanks shell rebels,* Daily Telegraph (London), July 27, 1998.

[140] The Economist, August 8, 1998.

[141] *West warns Milosevic on Kosovo,* Reuters, August 6, 1998. This was to be a show of force and a sign the West could move quickly.

[142] *West silent as Serb offensive tightens grip,* Irish Times, August 6, 1998.

[143] According to one commentator the FRY offensive was "quietly condoned by western governments," because it was anticipated that "the Albanian side could be brow-beaten into co-operation with western mediation efforts if it was exposed to a taste of Serbia's wrath." The Economist, August 8, 1998. The divisions among the Kosovo Albanians were noted and described by the Contact Group in information given to the Secretary-General, and annexed to his October report. UN Doc. S/1998/912, *supra* footnote 88, Annex.

NATO it seemed had now reviewed its plans following KLA successes and in light of the international community's desire not to encourage the drive towards Kosovo's independence. This arguably encouraged the FRY to pursue a strategy of gaining as much territory as possible before entering talks, a policy pursued ruthlessly in March-April 1999. By the end of July, the Sydney Herald wrote: "the diminishing prospects of NATO intervention now appear to be a significant factor in the decision by the Serb authorities to launch a major offensive against the KLA." *Despair in West as prospects for peace diminish, supra* footnote 139.

[144] SC Res. 1199 *supra* footnote 22, para. 2.

[145] S/1998/912, *supra* footnote 88, para. 29.

repression of the KLA while, on the other, calling for a halt to attacks on civilians proved to be a difficult balancing act to maintain, and in this state of confusion the massive FRY offensive continued into August 1998.

The reaction of prominent NATO members, particularly the USA, in passively accepting the August offensive perhaps goes some way to weaken arguments that the NATO intervention of 1999 was justified for the joint goals of protecting human rights, preventing a humanitarian catastrophe, and alleviating the threat to peace and security. On this basis intervention could have taken place in the Summer of 1998, but the right of the FRY to protect its own territorial integrity was implicitly accepted as a significant counterweight to these concerns.

In the end the Belgrade backlash of August proved to be so brutal, resulting in such a massive displacement of civilians, that the attitude of the Contact Group and NATO hardened once more and this time there did seem to be a stronger sense of finality in the threats directed at Belgrade. It would appear that the scale of the humanitarian crisis[146] which resulted from the massive Serbian campaign and which so alarmed the Security Council had not been envisaged when the right of the FRY to reopen its roads was acknowledged. From September 1998 therefore, it is possible to trace the development of the Contact Group and NATO strategy to tie the FRY down to a lasting agreement which culminated ultimately in the Rambouillet Accords and the final ultimatum which accompanied it. One day after the passage of Res. 1199 (1998), on September 24, NATO's North Atlantic Council (NAC) issued a general ultimatum to Belgrade to the effect that it was prepared to act if the FRY did not *inter alia* withdraw its troops from Kosovo to pre-conflict levels.[147] This was backed up by a more specific ultimatum when on October 13 the NAC voted to activate NATO forces and authorise its supreme commander to commence air-strikes following a ninety-six hour delay. This was done by way of "activation orders" for military action (ACTORDS) issued by the NAC.[148] Air-strikes would take place after the four day period (which was later extended to fourteen days[149]) if Belgrade did not comply with UN demands contained in Resolutions 1160 (1998) and 1199 (1998). NATO claimed legal justification for these ACTORDS based upon the following factors: the FRY's failure to comply with these Resolutions; the ongoing humanitarian catastrophe; the fact that a Security Council resolution providing for clear enforcement action in the foreseeable future was unlikely, and on the basis that the deteriorating situation constituted a serious threat to peace and security in the region per SC Res. 1199 (1998).[150]

---

[146] SC Res. 1199 *supra* footnote 22.

[147] This was announced in the UK House of Lords by the Parliamentary Under-Secretary of State, Foreign and Commonwealth Office (Baroness Symons of Vernham Dean) HL Debs., October 5, 1998, col. WA68.

[148] See Statement by the NATO Secretary-General following the Decision on the ACTORD, October 13, 1998.

[149] The deadline for execution of these orders was ultimately extended to October 27 by which time Belgrade had signed a series of agreements and withdrawn some troops although not to pre-conflict levels as had been agreed. The Times (London), October 22, 1998.

[150] On October 9, 1998 NATO Secretary-General Javier Solana wrote a letter addressed to the permanent representatives to the North Atlantic Council, arguing that action by it would be legally justified on humanitarian grounds for the following reasons:

In the intervening period between the initial ultimatum and the firmer approach taken on October 13 the UN Secretary-General had issued his latest report to the Security Council on October 3 in which he confirmed that the FRY had not changed its position on allowing the return of the OSCE long-term missions, nor on accepting the mission of Felipe Gonzalez.[151] The details of his report which seemed to influence the Contact Group and NATO particularly however, were those concerning the declining security situation, which was being exacerbated by the worsening humanitarian problem. The Secretary-General reported that the intense fighting since his last report had begun to wind down towards the end of September,[152] but that the humanitarian situation had worsened:

"The desperate situation of the civilian population remains the most disturbing aspect of the hostilities in Kosovo. I am particularly concerned that civilians increasingly have become the main target in the conflict. Fighting in Kosovo has resulted in a mass displacement of civilian populations, the extensive destruction of villages and means of livelihood and the deep trauma and despair of displaced populations... There are concerns that the disproportionate use of force and actions of the security forces are designed to terrorise and subjugate the population, a collective punishment to teach them that the price of supporting the Kosovo Albanian paramilitary units is too high and will be even higher in future."

Early signs of the mass civilian displacement which would reach unprecedented levels in the Spring of 1999 were evident:

"The tactics include shelling, detentions and threats to life, and finally short-notice demands to leave or face the consequences... The level of destruction points clearly to an indiscriminate and disproportionate use of force against civilian populations. As of mid-September, an estimated 6,000 to 7,000 buildings in 269 villages had been severely damaged or destroyed by shelling and deliberate burning in the Serb forces' main areas of operations."[153]

"The FRY has not yet complied with the urgent demands of the International Community, despite UN SC Resolution 1160 of 31 March 1998 followed by UN SC Resolution 1199 of 23 September 1998, both acting under Chapter VII of the UN Charter.
• The very stringent report of the Secretary-General of the United Nations pursuant to both resolutions warned inter alia of the danger of a humanitarian disaster in Kosovo.
• The continuation of a humanitarian catastrophe, because no concrete measures towards a peaceful solution of the crisis have been taken by the FRY.
• The fact that another UN SC Resolution containing a clear enforcement action with regard to Kosovo cannot be expected in the foreseeable future.
• The deterioration of the situation in Kosovo and its magnitude constitute a serious threat to peace and security in the region as explicitly referred to in the UN SC Resolution 1199.
On the basis of this discussion, I conclude that the Allies believe that in the particular circumstances with respect to the present crisis in Kosovo as described in UN SC Resolution 1199, there are legitimate grounds for the Alliance to threaten, and if necessary, to use force." Cited by Simma 1999: 7.
[151] UN Doc. S/1998/912, *supra* footnote 88.
[152] Id. paras. 5–6.
[153] Id. paras. 7–8.

The NATO ultimatum was, however, taken seriously by Belgrade and led to a cease-fire and a political settlement, brokered by Richard Holbrooke, which was signed on October 12 and under which the FRY agreed to comply with the demands of the Security Council. In addition a two-part verification agreement was signed wherein the FRY undertook to reduce its forces in Kosovo to pre-conflict levels and assented to mechanisms by which this process could be verified.[154]

The main agreement envisaged a political settlement to the crisis the background for which was a paper put forward by the Contact Group which proposed autonomy for Kosovo within the FRY. The Contact Group was keen to act on this settlement quickly. The agreement included a public commitment by the FRY to complete negotiations on a framework for a political settlement by November 2 and by November 9 the detailed rules and procedure for an election were to be agreed, the election itself to be held within 9 months under OSCE supervision.

Of the two verification agreements the first, signed on October 15 was the Air Verification Agreement (AVA)[155] which authorised unarmed flights over Kosovo by NATO aircraft to verify the cease-fire. It also provided for the withdrawal of government troops to pre-conflict levels. This was signed in Belgrade by the Chief of General Staff of the FRY, by NATO secretary General Javier Solana, and the NATO Supreme Commander in Europe, General Wesley Clark. The agreement had the NATO code name "Eagle Eye", and it compelled FRY forces to turn off all relevant radar systems while the verification flights were in progress.

The second verification agreement was again signed in Belgrade but this time on 16 October by the Minister of Foreign Affairs of the FRY and the OSCE Chairman-in-Office, Geremek[156] and it included an undertaking of the FRY to comply with resolutions 1160 (1998) and 1199 (1998).[157] This agreement established the Kosovo Verification Mission (KVM). This was the unarmed ground component, which was established to examine such things as the validity of check-points and road blocks in Kosovo. It was to be composed of 2,000 monitors to be overseen by the OSCE. This was more politically acceptable to Yugoslavia and indeed to Russia than a NATO verification process.[158] The mission was initially to be for one year but could be extended on the request of the head of the OSCE or the FRY government. It would also absorb the existing Kosovo Diplomatic Observer Mission (KDOM) when it became active.[159] The task of the Verification Mission was to verify compliance by all parties in Kosovo with Security Council resolution 1199 (1998) and to report instances of progress and/or non-compliance to the OSCE Permanent Council and the Security Council. As mentioned, the Verification

---

[154] The latter two agreements were signed on October 15 and 16. All three agreements were endorsed by Serbia.

[155] The agreement between NATO and the Federal Republic of Yugoslavia was annexed to a letter from the United States to the President of the Council dated October 22, UN Doc. S/1998/991.

[156] Bronislav Geremek was the Polish Foreign Minister.

[157] UN Doc. S/1998/978.

[158] However, the possibility of a NATO quick reaction force remained.

[159] The KDOM was a team of diplomats to whom Milosevic had allowed access to the province following agreement with Russian President Yeltsin in June, 1998.

Mission was also tasked to supervise elections in Kosovo in order to ensure their openness and fairness.

As part of the agreements the Security Council was requested to pass a resolution calling on the OSCE to establish the mission. Again this part of the process has considerable significance for NATO in its claim that the use of force in March 1999 was the culmination of a process of close co-operation with the Security Council. No explicit authorisation for the use of force was ever forthcoming from the Security Council, but NATO was keen, at the time of its intervention, to point to Res. 1203 (1998) which endorsed and supported the October Agreements.[160] It is notable that the Security Council welcomed both the verification agreements, and that the Resolution demanded "the full and prompt implementation of these agreements by the Federal Republic of Yugoslavia".[161] These agreements were achieved with the threat of force by NATO and accordingly NATO took the view that the Security Council endorsement of the October 15 Agreement, which envisaged a prominent role for NATO, provided some form of tacit support for its ultimate intervention in March 1999.[162]

It should be borne in mind however that SC Res. 1203 (1998), although it endorses the settlement agreed between Belgrade, the OSCE and NATO, gives no authorisation for the use of force by NATO should the FRY still fail to comply with Res. 1160 (1998). Indeed the Security Council initially met on October 6 to discuss the Secretary-General's report of the previous day but did not reach agreement on this. Russia for example remained consistently opposed to military action and threatened to veto any resolution attempting to authorise it, and although Res. 1203 (1998) contained no reference to military action Russia and China still abstained in the 12-0 vote in favour.[163] Indeed the Resolution is fairly even-handed in its approach to the conflict in issuing a strong condemnation of all acts of violence as well as terrorism, and in insisting that the Kosovo Albanian leadership condemn all terrorist acts.[164] This showed a clear reluctance on the part of certain Security Council members to be seen to be taking sides. Its reaffirmation of the commitment of all Member States to the sovereignty and territorial integrity of the Federal Republic of Yugoslavia is another example that it was not prepared to go too far in favour of the Kosovo Albanian position.

The aftermath of the October Agreements initially saw a stabilisation in the situation on the ground with a cautious welcome accorded to it by both sides.[165] Problems however continued to be reported by the Secretary-General. For example, it seemed that the KLA were attempting to take advantage of the Serbian withdrawals

---

[160] SC Res. 1203 *supra* footnote 28.
[161] SC Res. 1203 *supra* footnote 28, para. 1, and see Press Release UN Doc. SC/6588, October 24, 1998.
[162] Resolution 1203 also noted the endorsement by the Government of Serbia of the main accord reached by President Milosevic and Richard Holbrooke on October 12, 1998 and the public commitment of the FRY to complete negotiations on a framework for a political settlement by November 2, 1998. The Resolution also called for the full implementation of these commitments (para. 2).
[163] Press Release, UN Doc. SC/6588, October 24, 1998.
[164] SC Res. 1203 *supra* footnote 28, para. 10.
[165] UN Doc. S/1998/1068, November 12, 1998, paras. 6–11.

by reasserting authority over areas vacated.[166] Nonetheless the humanitarian situation began to improve with a return to villages by many people and the housing of almost all of those living in the open.[167] The Secretary-General was able to report that access by humanitarian agencies to internally displaced persons had generally improved since the time of his previous report.[168] By the end of December, however, there was still no progress on reaching a political settlement despite the deadline of November 9 having come and gone. The Secretary-General reported "alarming signs of potential deterioration",[169] and that violence had reached its highest level since the October 16 Agreement.[170] Similarly the humanitarian problems remained very severe with the UNHCR estimating that 200,000 people remained displaced within Kosovo.[171]

The October 16 Agreement had also not been implemented successfully. Once again in order to fulfil the Security Council's request that he report regularly to the Council regarding implementation of Resolution 1203 (1998), particularly in regard to the implementation of the Agreements of October 15 and 16, the Secretary-General suggested that the OSCE and NATO report to the Council through him as they had in respect of Resolution 1160 (1998).[172] In November he also suggested that the KVM should take over the reporting role carried out by the Secretariat, given that it was assigned the responsibility of reporting to the Security Council in terms of the October 16 Agreement.[173] This suggestion was rendered somewhat redundant since the Secretary-General in his report on December 24 1998 confirmed that "the operational date and deployment of the Verification Mission remain delayed and expectations of large-scale presence of international verifiers on the ground have not been met."[174] Furthermore, by now the KDOM was reporting breaches in the cease-fire by the FRY.[175]

6. RAMBOUILLET AND THE LEGALITY OF NATO INTERVENTION

The developing crisis throughout 1998 was met by a concerted international effort, involving a number of organisations, to resolve the security crisis and to reach a lasting political settlement which would resolve the national question in Kosovo. The eventual intervention of NATO was the culmination of the failure of this process.

---

[166] Id., paras. 13 and 15.

[167] Id., paras. 21 and 22.

[168] Id., para. 25.

[169] UN Doc. S/1998/1221, December 24, 1998, para. 4.

[170] In one day in December 34 violent deaths occurred, Id. para. 12. On November 27 the North Atlantic Council announced that it was "deeply concerned about the deteriorating security situation in Kosovo" and by incidents created by both Serbian security forces and armed elements such as the KLA. Press statement by the North Atlantic Council on Kosovo, November 27, 1998.

[171] Id. para. 7.

[172] UN Doc. S/1998/1068, November 12, 1998, para. 57.

[173] Id., para. 56.

[174] UN Doc. S/1998/1221, *supra* footnote 88, para. 26.

[175] The KDOM reported that FRY armed forces had flouted the cease-fire in the Podujevo area by attacking KLA positions. Kosovo Diplomatic Observer Mission, Daily Report, December 21, 1998, other violations were reported just before Christmas, Daily Report, December 24, 1998.

It is important in assessing the legal justifications advanced by NATO for its military action to consider the context of this ongoing attempt to resolve a nationalist crisis. This background is important because, through NATO's action, a precedent may have been set for the use of international military force in situations where demands for national autonomy are being denied.

From the beginning of 1999 ominous signs of a breakdown in the political process began to appear. Since October 1998, concerted efforts had been made to arrive at a detailed political settlement. This involved initially a proposal advanced by US Ambassador to Macedonia, Christopher Hill who, following a process of shuttle diplomacy over the summer of 1998 proposed a draft settlement on October 1, 1998 which would have guaranteed autonomy for Kosovo for an interim three year period at the end of which the agreement would be re-considered.[176] By the end of the year little progress had been made and by January 1999 Western patience was wearing thin particularly as atrocities continued to be committed by the security forces. The build up to the Rambouillet process and the final ultimatum from NATO which eventually triggered air strikes can be traced to a massacre reported on January 16, 1999 where at least forty five people from the village of Racak near Pristina were reported to have been killed by the security forces. President Clinton declared: "This was a deliberate and indiscriminate act of murder designed to sow fear among the people of Kosovo... it is a clear violation of the commitments the Serbian authorities have made to NATO. There can be no justification for it."[177] This set in motion the final diplomatic push for a solution to the crisis. NATO held an emergency meeting on January 17,[178] which was followed by a Contact Group meeting of January 22[179]

---

[176] Weller 1999: 219–220.

[177] US Ambassador William Walker, the head of the OSCE force monitoring the cease-fire accused Serbian security forces of mass murder. *Villagers Slaughtered in Kosovo 'Atrocity' Scores Dead in Bloodiest Spree of Conflict*, The Washington Post, January 17, 1999. Violence was not one-sided, however. On December 14, 1998 six Serb youths were murdered in a bar in Pec and on December 17, Zvonko Bojanic, the Serbian Deputy Mayor of Kosovo Polje, was kidnapped and executed. Condemnation of violence continued to be largely even-handed. For example, Bronislaw Geremek, chairman-in-office of the OSCE, condemned the recent violence and warned: "The Federal Yugoslav authorities and the people of Kosovo must commit themselves to negotiations, and not resort to further violence. Fighting will not lead to peace and prosperity, but to a future of instability". OSCE Press Release No. 78/98, December 15, 1998. A U.S. Department of State spokesman denounced the murder of Mr. Bojanic as "an act of savage brutality." U.S. Department of State Office of the Spokesman, Statement, December 18, 1998.

178 *US: NATO Set To Strike Vs. Serbs*, Associated Press, January 18, 1999. The OSCE also held an emergency meeting on January 18, *Kosovo massacre: OSCE calls emergency meeting,* Associated Free Press, January 18, 1999. On 30 January, the NAC agreed that Secretary-General Solana could authorise air strikes against targets on Yugoslav territory. He stated, "NATO stands ready to act. We rule out no option to ensure full respect by both sides in Kosovo for the requirements of the international community." Statement by NATO Secretary-General, NATO Headquarters January 30, 1999.

[179] *NATO Talks Tough, Big Powers Meet On Kosovo,* Reuters, January 22, 1999. In addition to compliance with the October Agreements, NATO now demanded acceptance of further limitations on the movement of military and police forces, and co-operation with the UN investigation of the Racak and other recent massacres, together with increased security for the OSCE monitors. However, there was still no agreement within NATO for air-strikes in the absence of a political settlement and hence the necessary conditions for deployment of a peacekeeping ground force. *Allies Balk At Bombing Yugoslavia. Europeans Want US In Ground Force*, The Washington Post, January 23, 1999.

and a call to both sides to come to peace talks soon followed. At a subsequent meeting on January 29, the Contact Group summoned representatives from the FRY, Serbia and the Kosovo Albanians to meet at Rambouillet by February 6, "to begin negotiations with the direct involvement of the Contact Group."[180] As these got underway at Rambouillet in France in February both sides were presented with a detailed agreement covering a new constitutional status for Kosovo and provision for an international peacekeeping force in the region. Washington made clear the likely outcome of the FRY rejecting an agreement signed up to by Kosovo Albanians. US State Department Spokesman James Rubin said that a peacekeeping force was an integral part of the Contact Group peace plan and was therefore non-negotiable. He was explicit in his assertion: "If the Serbs fail to agree to the ... plan and the Kosovar Albanians do – and a prime example of failing to agree would be to refuse to allow the peace implementation force – the Serbs will be subject to air strikes".[181] After weeks of negotiation the Kosovo Albanian side did indeed sign an agreement and the FRY's refusal to do so led directly to air-strikes, following a final intervention by the OSCE,[182] commencing on March 24 in Operation Allied Force.[183]

The legality of NATO's actions over Kosovo including the simulated air-strikes of June 1998, through to October 1998 when the ACTORDs were issued, and ultimately and most importantly culminating in the air-strikes of March 1999 has been a source of much controversy. Non-intervention as a principle of international law, is enshrined in Articles 2(4) and 2(7) of the UN Charter which reflect the accompanying principles of territorial integrity and political independence of states.[184] There are however, at least two exceptions to this principle, the Article 51 right of self defence, and the power vested in the Security Council by Chapter VII of the UN Charter to authorise the use of force.[185] A third possible exception is humanitarian intervention. NATO's action will be reviewed under each of these

---

[180] Contact Group statement, London, January 29, 1999. On the background to this meeting see, *Big Powers To Summon Kosovo Sides To Peace Talks*, Reuters, January 26, 1999; *US Discloses Plan To Impose Kosovo Settlement*, Reuters, January 27, 1999. At the same time NATO issued fresh warnings, and expressed its preparedness to back with force the final political initiative launched by the Contact Group on January 29. Javier Solana announced, "NATO stands ready to act and rules out no option... The North Atlantic Council has decided to increase its military preparedness to ensure that the demands of the international community are met." Hence an ultimatum was issued to both sides that they must agree to meet for peace talks within a week or face the consequences. *NATO Warns Both Sides in Kosovo*, Reuters, January 28, 1999, *Major Powers To Give Ultimatum On Kosovo*, Reuters, January 29, 1999.

[181] *Washington renews warnings to Serbs over accepting Kosovo agreement*, Associated Free Press, February 10, 1999.

[182] The OSCE reported that Chairman-in-Office Norwegian Foreign Minister Knut Vollebaek, telephoned President Milosevic on March 24 and urged him to accept the Rambouillet interim agreement and put an end to the excessive use of force by FRY and Serbian forces in Kosovo. OSCE Press Release, Vienna, March 26, 1999.

[183] Javier Solana, NATO Secretary-General announced the commencement of air operations against the FRY on March 24. NATO Press Release (1999)041, March 24, 1999. For a discussion of the Rambouillet process and the agreement see Weller 1999.

[184] Arts. 2(4) and 2(7), UN Charter. See Doswald-Beck 1985; Ryan 1991; Nanda 1992; Kresock 1994.

[185] This is referred to in Article 2 itself with 2(7) providing that the principle of non-intervention shall not prejudice the application of enforcement measures under Chapter VII. Art. 2(7) UN Charter.

headings and the implications of the intervention for self-determination will also be considered.

A. Article 51

There would seem to be no valid Article 51 justification for the NATO intervention. Article 5 of the North Atlantic Treaty enshrines a commitment to collective defence, and it is itself based upon Article 51 of the UN Charter. In terms of the Charter the exercise of self defence is only permissible in the case of "armed attack", and there was no attack on a Member State by the FRY.[186] NATO as has been mentioned, however, employed a more expansive interpretation of the principle particularly to include a right of collective self defence. In the resolution of the North Atlantic Assembly of November 1998, which followed the issuing of the October ACTORDS, there is a reference to Article 51 which it asserted was to be interpreted broadly to include the defence of "common interests and values".[187] Bruno Simma completely rejects the use of this doctrine as purported justification for the threat[188] of use of force against the FRY: "To thus widen the scope of self-defence, as a legal institution, is intolerable, indeed absurd, from a legal point of view and does not deserve further comment."[189] Indeed NATO has traditionally accepted that it should not act in this type of situation without Security Council authorisation.[190]

B. Chapter VII of the UN Charter

Under the UN Charter authorisation for the use of force can only be given in terms of Chapter VII which gives the Security Council authority to take action permitting the use of force in order to bring states into compliance with UN resolutions. For the Security Council to invoke Chapter VII, the dispute must not lie "essentially within the domestic jurisdiction" of the state (Art. 2(7))[191], and it must constitute a threat to

---

[186] Antonio Cassese notes that in previous actions by states without Security Council approval the states in question "have always tried to justify their action by relying upon (and abusing) Article 51. In the present instance, the member states of NATO have not put forward any legal justification based on the United Nations Charter". To invoke self defence as a justification for such action because of a "threat to peace" is unacceptable. "Even cursory consideration of the Charter system shows... that this argument does not constitute per se a legal ground for initiating an armed attack against a sovereign state." Cassese 1999: 24.

[187] Cited by Simma 1999: 16.

[188] Simma was writing before the air-strikes of March 1999 had commenced, but since Article 2(4) of the Charter proscribes both the threat and the use of force in equal measure, his comments can be taken to apply equally to the strikes themselves and to the threat which had pertained at the very least since the issuance of the ACTORDS of October 1998.

[189] Simma 1999: 16.

[190] In its 1994 Brussels Summit NATO leaders gave the following statement: "We reaffirm our offer to support, on a case by case basis in accordance with our own procedures, peacekeeping and other operations under the authority of the UN Security Council or the responsibility of the CSCE." Cited by Daalder 1999.

[191] Although as has been noted even this is qualified in Article 2(7) which states that "this principle shall not prejudice the application of enforcement measures under Chapter VII".

"international peace and security" (Art. 39).[192] States may intervene for this purpose if the Security Council determines under Chapter VII that such force is necessary and requests the state to use force. By Art. 39 only the Security Council can determine "the existence of any threat to the peace, breach of the peace, or act of aggression and shall make recommendations, or decide what measures shall be taken in accordance with Arts. 41 and 42, to maintain or restore international peace and security."[193] By Art. 42 the Security Council "may take such action by air, sea or land forces as may be necessary to maintain or restore international peace and security",[194] and by Art. 41 it can impose non-military sanctions to maintain or restore international peace and security. Finally, Art. 48 is explicit in providing that states may use force as the Security Council may determine.[195]

Neither Resolutions 1199 (1998) nor 1203 (1998) contain authorisation for the use of force. 1199 (1998) in a fairly oblique reference to future action states that the Security Council: "Decides, should the concrete measures demanded in this resolution and Resolution 1160 (1998) not be taken, to consider further action and additional measures to maintain or restore peace and stability in the region".[196] Similarly 1203 (1998) affirms that "in the event of an emergency, action may be needed to ensure their [i.e. the Verification Missions'] safety and freedom of movement".[197] No elaboration on the nature of this action is given and nor is there specific reference as to who ought to undertake it.[198]

C. Humanitarian intervention

The question remains whether in the absence of both an Article 51 right of self defence and of Chapter VII authorisation the NATO action might still have some legal justification. The argument that intervention in the affairs of other states on humanitarian grounds can be justifiable at international law is gaining ever greater acceptance. First, action including rescue may be possible to protect a state's own nationals, or even those of a third state or of the state being intervened in.[199] The issue confronting NATO is whether it is ever permissible to intervene in a dispute on general humanitarian grounds, and if so whether first, it can be permissible to do so without the authority of the Security Council under Chapter VII, and secondly, if such a unilateral right of intervention does on occasion exist, whether NATO can legitimately claim that its action falls within the acceptable limits of this exception.

One occasion when a right of humanitarian intervention may be justifiable is when a state has descended to a condition of virtual anarchy in which case intervention

---

[192] See also Art 2(4). The Security Council power to authorise the use of force also gains support from the preamble to the Charter which sets out one of the purposes of the Charter to be the prevention of the use of armed force except in the common interest.

[193] UN Charter Art. 39.

[194] UN Charter Art. 42.

[195] UN Charter Art. 48.

[196] SC Res. 1199 *supra* footnote 22, para. 16.

[197] SC Res. 1203 *supra* footnote 28, para. 9.

[198] This fact leads Antonio Cassese to conclude that NATO's intervention is unlawful. Cassese 1999: 25.

[199] Kresock 1994: 213.

is required to preserve a state's sovereignty. This clearly was not the case with the FRY where the mass dislocation of the civilian population in Kosovo and the campaign against the KLA since March 1999 was intended to strengthen the sovereignty and territorial integrity of the FRY and which but for NATO intervention would seemingly have done so.

Another argument is that humanitarian intervention is justified to prevent widespread human rights violations and indeed NATO used the serious human rights abuses perpetrated by the FRY in Kosovo as one of the main justifications for its actions.[200] A number of commentators now accept a right of intervention in such cases,[201] while others are either reluctant to go this far,[202] or reject the proposition outright. On this point Antonio Cassese contends that of the three overarching values of inter-state relations: peace, human rights and self-determination, "peace must always constitute the ultimate and prevailing factor."[203]

In defence of the right of humanitarian intervention in the case of serious human rights violations it is clear that human rights protection is an international concern. Both the preamble to, and Article 1 of, the UN Charter suggest this.[204] For example, Art. 1(3) contains an obligation on states to promote and encourage respect for human rights,[205] and Arts. 55 and 56, which create a duty to promote and respect human rights, also denote the importance ascribed to rights protection by the Charter.[206]

However, even if humanitarian intervention in the name of human rights is permissible the question remains whether it is permissible without a Chapter VII mandate. Certain proponents of humanitarian intervention argue that in cases of "gross and persistent violations of human rights" military action is justified even if not authorised by the UN.[207] Therefore, it is possible to argue that the primary importance of preserving peace may not be as clear-cut in its opposition to unilateral intervention as it would on its face appear. Cassese himself takes note of this argument (while not endorsing it) in the following way: "where atrocities reach such a large scale as to shock the conscience of all human beings and indeed jeopardise international stability, forcible protection of human rights may need to outweigh the necessity to avoid friction and armed conflict. To put it differently, "positive peace", i.e. the realisation of justice, should prevail over "negative peace", i.e. the absence of armed conflict."[208] On the basis of these trends, Cassese suggests that "under

---

[200] Javier Solana's letter of October 9, 1998 *supra* footnote 150.
[201] Ryan 1991; Kresock 1994; Nafziger 1991; Nanda 1991 and 1992.
[202] Kresock for example states: "Definitive authority does not exist... for the proposition that a state or international body may intervene to terminate human rights violations." Kresock 1994: 213.
[203] Cassese 1999: 24.
[204] The preamble reaffirms the faith of the peoples of the UN in fundamental human rights.
[205] UN Charter Art. 1(3).
[206] UN Charter Art. 55(c) and Art. 56.
[207] Ryan 1991: 57. Others argue that such a right ought to be developed. Kresock for example, suggests: "as the concept of "popular sovereignty" spreads and becomes the international norm, the ability to act unilaterally will help remove the political impediments that have prevented effective assistance of the crisis in Bosnia. Questions of the proper scope and means to address egregious human rights violations will devolve into political questions." Kresock 1994: 238.
[208] Cassese 1999: 26–27.

certain strict conditions resort to armed force may gradually become justified, even absent any authorisation by the Security Council."[209] These conditions involve egregious breaches of human rights which both the state in question and the Security Council are either unable or unwilling to resolve. In such a case a group of states, not a single state, having explored all peaceful avenues, may intervene in a proportionate way where "armed force is exclusively used for the limited purpose of stopping the atrocities and restoring respect for human rights".[210]

The "legal basis" NATO presented for its intervention has, per arguments which were first advanced in respect of the October ACTORDs, centred upon first, the "humanitarian catastrophe"[211] caused by the Serbian offensive of July-August 1998 which was never properly alleviated. NATO also focused upon the FRY's failure to comply with Security Council requirements, in particular the failure to secure a political settlement to the crisis, and thirdly, it claimed legitimacy for its actions from the Security Council's recognition that the situation posed a threat to peace and security.[212] Each of these three arguments will be addressed in turn.

(i) Humanitarian crisis

Turning first to the humanitarian crisis, NATO Secretary-General Javier Solana announced shortly before the October ultimatum: "NATO has to have the opportunity on a case by case basis to act, if necessary, under [its] own decision, always with an appropriate legal base, and always within the spirit of the [UN] charter.... There may be moments in which it is necessary to act for humanitarian reasons, when a UN Security Council resolution will not be necessary or will not be even appropriate because the UN charter does not contemplate humanitarian acts."[213]

The greater level of protection now accorded to human rights at international law is evident in Europe where the references to human rights in the UN Charter have been supplemented by, for example, the Helsinki Final Act and the Charter of Paris for a New Europe of 1990. These two documents elevate the importance of human rights and in doing so suggest that the view that peace is the ultimate and prevailing factor of inter-state relations is perhaps somewhat over-stated. The Helsinki Final Act for example, states that respect for "human rights and fundamental freedoms ... is an essential factor for the peace, justice, and well-being necessary to ensure the development of friendly relations and co-operation."[214] The Charter of Paris also places great emphasis on human rights and fundamental freedoms and declares that

---

[209] Cassese 1999: 27.

[210] Cassese 1999: 27. (This last point, known as purity of motive, is generally considered to be an essential precondition of legitimate humanitarian intervention). From Cassese's subsequent analysis of the Kosovo situation, it seems that, in his opinion, NATO met these criteria. Some justification for this view is perhaps provided by Solana's letter of October 9, 1998 in respect of the October ACTORDS *supra* footnote 150. It should be noted, however, that Cassese is still of the view that the NATO action is unlawful and he is also clear that within inter-state relations, peace constitutes the ultimate and prevailing value even over human rights concerns.

[211] SC Res. 1203 *supra* footnote 28, para. 11.

[212] SC Res. 1199 *supra* footnote 22, Preamble, and SC Res. 1203 *supra* footnote 28, Preamble; and see Solana's letter *supra* footnote 150.

[213] Cited by Daalder 1999: 15.

[214] Final Act of the Helsinki Conference, 1975 art. VII.

their "observance and full exercise are the foundations of freedom, justice, and peace." This level of emphasis on human rights as an "essential factor" and a "foundation" respectively, for peace, suggests that intervention to prevent egregious human rights violations might well be argued to be intervention in the pursuit of peace aimed at securing justice as a necessary precondition for peace, in other words involving the prioritisation of "positive peace" over "negative peace" in Cassese's terms. This argument perhaps derives some surprising support from the UN Secretary-General who on the night that the air campaign of March 1999 began, announced: "It is indeed tragic that diplomacy has failed... but there are times when the use of force may be legitimate in the pursuit of peace".[215]

In arguing that its intervention was founded both in humanitarian concerns and in the pursuit of peace, NATO can point to the elaborate process by which the Contact Group and the Security Council had since March 1998 identified the alleviation of humanitarian suffering as a main goal in their respective attempts to foster a political settlement.[216] The Contact Group, for example, consistently called for a mission to Kosovo to be undertaken by the United Nations High Commissioner for Human Rights and also as far back as March 1998 it supported the return of the OSCE long-term missions to Kosovo, and urged the office of the Prosecutor of the ICTY to begin gathering information related to the violence in Kosovo, an indication of the seriousness of the human rights violations which it suspected were taking place in Kosovo.[217]

The request for missions by the United Nations High Commissioner for Human Rights, and by the Personal Representative of the OSCE Chairman-in-Office for the FRY were also repeated by the Security Council in Resolution 1160 (1998) which also called for the withdrawal of the special police units and the cessation of action by the security forces affecting the civilian population.[218] The two subsequent Security Council resolutions also identified egregious human rights abuses by the FRY authorities as did successive reports by the Secretary-General all of which have been catalogued above. These included reports in September 1998 of mass

---

[215] UN Press Release, March 24, 1999. He did, however, also state: "under the Charter, the Security Council has primary responsibility for maintaining international peace and security, and this is explicitly acknowledged in the North Atlantic Treaty. Therefore, the Council should be involved in any decision to resort to force." But he placed the blame for the failure to find a political settlement firmly on the shoulders of the Yugoslav authorities, and on April 7, 1999 he went further stating that he believed an international norm against the violent suppression of minorities was emerging "that will and must take precedence over concerns of state sovereignty." *UN Secretary General Says Human Rights Norms Take Precedence*, IGEUWEB igeuweb@USIA.GOV 7 Apr. 1999.

[216] On the night the bombing began, Javier Solana announced: "We must stop the violence and bring an end to the humanitarian catastrophe now taking place in Kosovo. We have a moral duty to do so." NATO Press Release (1999)041, March 24, 1999. NATO can perhaps also point to the 1992 Constitution of the FRY which guarantees that the government will respect international law. Article 10 states: "The Federal Republic of Yugoslavia shall recognise and guarantee the rights and freedoms of man and the citizen recognised under international law."

[217] The unwillingness of the FRY to co-operate with the ICTY continued up to the Rambouillet process, for example on January 18, 1999 the Chief Prosecutor's staff were prevented by FRY border guards from entering the FRY to investigate the Racak massacre. *Peace-keeper ordered out of Kosovo*, Washington Post, January 18, 1999.

[218] SC Res. 1160 *supra* footnote 26, para. 16(b).

murder and the forced mass displacement of civilians. Hundreds of thousands of people were dislocated by the July-August offensive which both the Secretary-General and the Security Council concluded in September 1998 had resulted in a humanitarian catastrophe. There was no significant improvement in this situation by March 1999 and it appears that NATO viewed the Racak massacre of January as a final, glaring example of the abuses undertaken by the FRY forces. NATO did not enjoy specific Security Council authorisation for its intervention in March but one commentator concluded that NATO decided to act without such authorisation "out of overwhelming humanitarian necessity".[219]

(ii) The FRY's failure to comply with Security Council resolutions
NATO identified the repeated failure of the FRY to comply with other aspects of Resolutions 1199 (1998) and 1203 (1998), besides the humanitarian demands they contained. In particular, the FRY failed to reach a lasting political settlement with the Kosovo Albanians despite the numerous attempts by the Contact Group to foster talks starting with its attempts in March 1998 to secure a political agreement through the mediation of Felipe Gonzalez. NATO also attempted to invoke the UN Charter and Security Council Resolutions 1160 (1998) and 1199 (1998), and the FRY's failure to comply with them, in justifying its intervention, leading Bruno Simma to suggest: "The NATO threats of force continued and backed the thrust of SC Resolutions 1160 (1998) and 1199 (1998) and can with all due caution thus be regarded as legitimately, if not legally, following the direction of these UN decisions."[220] The fact that Resolution 1203 (1998) endorsed the October Agreements which were secured in the context of threats of military action, (and that they were also endorsed by the Secretary-General) allowed NATO to claim that its aims, if not ultimately its resort to force to secure them, were seen as positive and beneficial by both the Security Council and the Secretary-General in their efforts to secure a resolution to the crisis. It can even be argued that Res. 1203 (1998) amounted to *ex post facto* approval of the threat of force which preceded the October Agreements.[221] Similarly, when the Contact Group issued its demand on January 29, 1999 that the parties meet at Rambouillet, this was supported by a Security Council Presidential statement on the same day.[222]

---

[219] Simma 1999: 14. Kofi Annan in January 1999 appeared to suggest that NATO could act without Security Council approval. He endorsed the use of force when all other means have failed. Somewhat cryptically when asked if NATO could intervene in Kosovo without the express approval of the UN Security Council, he replied: "Normally, the approval of the Security Council for the use of force is required. I have always said that." However, he continued: "Let me ask only that we all – particularly those with the capacity to act – recall the lessons of Bosnia." This was seen by one commentator as "a pointed signal to NATO allies not to back off". Douglas Hamilton, *Annan Backs NATO Military Threat Over Kosovo* Reuters, January 28, 1999.

[220] Simma 1999: 12.

[221] This argument is discussed by Simma 1999: 10–11.

[222] UN Security Council Presidential Statement, January 29, 1999. See Weller 1999: 222. The Contact Group statement of January 29 had also repeated the demands that the FRY comply with existing Security Council resolutions.

If intervention is to be justified in pursuit of "positive peace" it must be clear that the pursuit of peace is the intention of those intervening, and in particular that they do not seek to undermine the territorial integrity of the state in question – in other words, as was noted above, humanitarian intervention must have purity of motive. Successive initiatives by the Contact Group which have dovetailed with EU, NATO and Security Council initiatives have made clear that their joint aim was for a settlement securing Kosovan autonomy within the FRY. Even as NATO prepared to intervene in June 1998, it was asserted by NATO that independence for Kosovo was not an option.[223] The need to secure the territorial integrity of the FRY was frequently restated by both the Contact Group and NATO as a priority, so much so that no action was taken in respect of the FRY offensive of July-August 1998 until the scale of the humanitarian disaster became apparent. Similarly, if it is accepted that NATO has 'followed the direction' of the UN Security Council resolutions 1160 (1998) and 1199 (1998), it can be recalled that both of these (and indeed 1203 (1998)) reiterated the respect of all member states for the FRY's territorial integrity.[224] British Prime Minister Blair justified the March 1999 air-strikes in part by reference to the FRY's failure to reach any political agreement.[225]

(iii) Threat to peace and security
Another argument which NATO has used is that the crisis and in particular, the July-August offensive which displaced hundreds of thousands of people and led to floods of refugees pouring into neighbouring states, particularly Albania, had destabilised the region, causing a threat to peace and security. Again NATO could point to Security Council Resolutions 1199 (1998) and 1203 (1998) which have of course invoked Chapter VII in declaring the existence of such a threat.

At various times in the year leading up to the air-strikes, this threat seemed real enough. There was a genuine fear that Albania might become involved particularly after May 1998 when as was noted above Albania put its forces on alert on the Kosovan border and warned that war might be imminent.[226] NATO has also claimed that its military plans met with little if any opposition from the UN. For example, when NATO announced forward plans in May 1998 which considered *inter alia* the

---

[223] This position was repeated on January 30, 1999 when the NATO Secretary-General announced that the NAC had authorised air strikes in Kosovo. "NATO's decisions today contribute to creating the conditions for a rapid and successful negotiation on an interim political settlement which provides for an enhanced status for Kosovo, preserves the territorial integrity of the Federal Republic of Yugoslavia and protects the rights of all ethnic groups." NATO press release, January 30, 1999.

[224] There were still attempts in November 1998 to bring the FRY back into the community of nations, despite its failure to implement the October Agreements. For example the UN Secretary-General stated: "The immediate crisis in Kosovo should not overshadow the necessity to assess the medium-term rehabilitation and reconstruction needs of the Federal Republic of Yugoslavia. As conditions allow, the World Bank, the United Nations Development Programme and bilateral donors should play a major role in this process, particularly in post-conflict projects in Kosovo." UN Doc. S/1998/1068, November 12, 1998, para. 55.

[225] "Nobody in the light of this history can say either that we have not tried to find a peaceful resolution to this conflict, or that Milosevic has not been warned of the consequences of continuing to repress the civilian population in Kosovo." Press Conference, Berlin, March 24, 1999.

[226] *supra* footnote 117.

military implications of further deterrent measures, these steps were confirmed by
the Secretary-General without criticism.[227] Reference has also been made to the
way in which Security Council Resolution 1203 (1998) supported the agreements
of October 1998 which were secured by the threat of force, and the Presidential
Statement of January 29, 1999 which welcomed the demands made by the Contact
Group on the same day, demands which carried with them the threat of NATO air-
strikes.[228]

NATO member states have, therefore, been forthright in suggesting that the
air-strikes were in line with UN SC policy. As US Secretary of State Albright declared
shortly after the bombing commenced: "Acting under Chapter VII the Security
Council adopted three resolutions — 1160, 1199, and 1203 — imposing mandatory
obligations on the FRY... And these obligations the FRY has flagrantly ignored. So,
NATO actions are being taken within this framework, and we continue to believe
that NATO's actions are justified and necessary to stop the violence."[229] It is also
noteworthy that on March 26, 1999 the Security Council voted by 12 to 3 against a
resolution introduced by Russia, Belarus and India that demanded an immediate
cessation of the use of force against the FRY.[230]

VII. CONCLUSION

The implications of NATO's intervention for international law are considerable,
raising as it does the fundamental issue of what is to be done when the norm of state
sovereignty clashes with the important values vested in the international protection
of human rights. Reactions by international lawyers to NATO's actions have been
surprisingly sympathetic given the lack of Chapter VII authorisation, and as such
this reaction perhaps highlights the growing importance accorded to human rights
protection at international law. It has also been noted that UN Secretary-General
Kofi Annan addressed this dilemma by stating his belief that an international norm
against the violent suppression of minorities is emerging which, as he puts it, "will
and must take precedence over concerns of state sovereignty... Will we say that
rights are relative, or that whatever happens within borders shall not be of concern
to organisations of sovereign states? No one that I know of can today defend that
position. Collectively, we should say no!"[231]

The full implications of NATO's intervention are yet to be digested. The support
it has enjoyed despite the lack of a Security Council mandate suggests that a new
norm may be developing which would permit limited intervention in a state
perpetrating serious human rights violations where efforts have been made to reach

---

[227] UN Doc. S/1998/470, June 4, 1998 paras. 26–7. It has also been noted how the October Agreements
were endorsed by SC Res. 1203 (1998).
[228] *Supra* footnotes 161 and 222.
[229] Press Briefing, State Department Report, March 25, 1999.
[230] Security Council Press Release, SC/6659, March 26, 1999.
[231] He continued: "We will not and we cannot accept a situation where people are brutalised behind
national boundaries. For at the end of the 20th Century, one thing is clear: a United Nations that will
not stand up for human rights is a United Nations that cannot stand up for itself." Press Statement
April 7, 1999.

a diplomatic solution and where the UN Security Council can't or won't respond appropriately. Such a development may be perceived as dangerous given that it could undermine the entire edifice of collective security enshrined in the United Nations project itself. Alternatively, the emergence of such a norm can be posited as an indictment of the Security Council's failure to act in such situations and as a challenge to the UN to address more seriously the human rights provisions in its own Charter. That the human rights violations committed in Kosovo were integrally related to the broader dispute over national identity and to the Kosovan claims to self-determination suggests that the preparedness of the international community to intervene in cases where serious human rights abuses are being committed may well hold important implications for minority groups whose aspirations for greater accommodation of their identity are being forcefully restrained through the use of force by internal authorities.

REFERENCES

Cassese, A. (1999). Ex iniuria ius oritur: Are We Moving towards International Legitimation of Forcible Humanitarian Countermeasures in the World Community? *European Journal of International Law* 10: 23-30
Cerovic, S. (1993-4). The Rise of Serbian Nationalism, *New York University Journal of International Law and Politics* 26: 527-530
Contact Group Statement (1998). Statement of the London Contact Group Meeting, March 9, 1998
Craven, M. (1995). The European Community Arbitration Commission on Yugoslavia, *British Yearbook of International Law* LXVI: 333-413
Daalder, I.H. (1999). NATO, the UN, and the Use of Force, *JURIST: The Law Professors' Network*, Brookings Institution, March 1999 – Internet publication, http://www.unausa.org/issues/sc/daalder.htm
Doswald-Beck, L. (1985). The Legal Validity of Military Intervention by Invitation of Government, *British Yearbook of International Law* LXVI: 189
Elsie, R. ed. (1997). *Kosovo: in the heart of the powder keg*
Gray, C. (1997). Bosnia and Herzegovina: Civil War or Inter-State Conflict? Characterisation and Consequences, *British Yearbook of International Law* LXVIII: 155-197.
Kofos, E. (1998). *The Two-Headed Albanian Question,* 43-98, in Veremis, T. and Kofos, E. (ed.) 1998., *Kosovo: Avoiding Another Balkan War.* ELIAMEP: Athens
International Crisis Group (1998). *Kosovo Report,* March 10, 1998
Kresock, D.M. (1994). "Ethnic Cleansing" in the Balkans: The Legal Foundations of Foreign Intervention, *Cornell International Law Journal* 27: 203-239
McGoldrick, D. (1996). Yugoslavia – The Response of the International Community and of International Law, *Current Legal Problems* 49: 375-394
Mertus, J. A. (1993-4). Nationalism and Nation-Building: Milosevic Turns to Montenegro and Kosovo, *New York University Journal of International Law and Politics* 26: 511-519

Nafziger, J. A. R. (1991). Self-Determination and Humanitarian Intervention in a Community of Power, *Denv. J. Int'l L. & Pol'y* 20: 9-39

Nanda, V.P. (1991). The Use of Force in the Post-Cold War era: An Introduction, *Denv. J. Int'l L. & Pol'y* 20: 1-8.

Nanda, V.P. (1992). Tragedies in Northern Iraq, Liberia, Yugoslavia, and Haiti – Revisiting the Validity of Humanitarian Intervention Under international Law – Part I, *Denv. J. Int'l L. & Pol'y* 20: 305

Rehn, E. (1996). *Situation of human rights in the territory of the former Yugoslavia: Special report on minorities*, periodic report submitted by Elisabeth Rehn, Special Rapporteur of the Commission on Human Rights, pursuant to paragraph 45 of Commission resolution 1996/71, Report of the Commission on Human Rights E/CN.4/1997/8, October 25, 1996, Chapters I and II

Rich, R. (1993). Recognition of States: The Collapse of Yugoslavia and the Soviet Union, *European Journal of International Law* 4: 36-65

Ryan, K. (1991). Rights, Intervention, and Self-Determination, *Denv. J. Int'l L. & Pol'y* 20: 55-71

Simma, B. (1999). NATO, the UN and the Use of Force: Legal Aspects, *European Journal of International Law* 10: 1-22

Stojanovic, S. (1995-6). The Destruction of Yugoslavia, *Fordham Journal of International Law* 19: 337-362

Surroi, V. (1999). *Kosova and the Constitutional Solutions*, 197-233, in Veremis, T. and Kofos, E. (ed.) 1998., *Kosovo: Avoiding Another Balkan War*. ELIAMEP: Athens

Tierney, S. (1999). In a state of flux: self-determination after Yugoslavia, *International Journal on Minority and Group Rights* 6: 197-233

Veremis, T. and Kofos, E. (ed.) 1998., *Kosovo: Avoiding Another Balkan War*. ELIAMEP: Athens

Vickers, M. (1998). *Between Serb and Albanian: A History of Kosovo*

Warbrick, C. (1992). Recognition of States, *ICLQ* 41: 473-82

Warbrick, C. (1993). Recognition of States Part 2, *ICLQ* 42: 433-42

Weller, M. (1992). The International Response to the Dissolution of the Socialist Federal Republic of Yugoslavia *AJIL* 86: 569-607

Weller, M. (1999). The Rambouillet conference on Kosovo, *International Affairs* 75: 211-251

National Identity and the
Construction of Constitutions

Scottish Devolution:
Accommodating a Restless Nation

*Colin R. Munro**

INTRODUCTION

Recently the Supreme Court of Canada delivered its opinion in *Reference re Secession of Quebec* (1998) 161 DLR (4th) 385. Amongst other things, it held that the principle of self-determination in public international law could support a claim by Quebec to secede unilaterally if Quebecers were 'a people ... subject to an alien subjugation, domination or exploitation outside the colonial context', a premise which the Court rejected as inapplicable. Still less we might think, except upon the most *Braveheart* view of things, could Scotland advance claims based on such a ground.

The precise meaning of the term 'people' is rather uncertain, and it may be doubtful whether the term is right to distinguish Scots. Here we enter murky waters. As Caucasians, the Scots are not distinct racially from other Western European people, for example. Moreover, some of our beliefs about sub-groups turn out to be romantic myths, when research by geneticists shows that almost all indigenous Britons share the same ancestral gene pool. The test for a group distinguishable by 'ethnic origins', for the purpose of the Race Relations Act 1976, was laid down by the House of Lords in *Mandla v. Dowell Lee* [1983] 1 A.C. 548, and in *Boyce v. British Airways plc* and *Northern Joint Police Board v. Power* [1997] IRLR 610 has been held by the Employment Appeal Tribunal to be inapplicable to distinguish Scots and English.

Another approach to the issue depends upon geography. There is an identifiable territory called Scotland, defined as such for various legal purposes too. That geographical entity *might* be called a region, and sometimes has been. There are works of constitutional law which deal with Scotland and Wales under the title 'regional government'. However, there can be emotional significance (and consequently political weight) attaching to choice of terms, and there are many people in Scotland and Wales who would regard that term as ill-chosen, perhaps even insulting. It was no doubt with some awareness of these sensitivities that the Royal Commission on the Constitution (1973) was set up with the remit of considering the constitutional position of the 'several countries, nations and regions of the United Kingdom'.

Professor of Constitutional Law, University of Edinburgh

Stephen Tierney (ed.), Accommodating National Identity: New Approaches in International and Domestic Law, 133–150
© 2000 *Kluwer Law International. Printed in Great Britain.*
First published in the International Journal on Minority and Group Rights, Volume 6 No. 1/2 1999.
The article has been revised for this publication.

In the wording of that remit, we may discern also an appreciation that, even if the European mindset since the eighteenth century has tended to assume an identity between nations and states, it is an assumption which may turn out to be questionable or unjustified. It has also become commonplace to suggest that the nutcracker of supranationalism (as exemplified by European integration) along with greater differentiation within states is leading to a decline in the importance of the historic nation-state (Marquand 1991). Lawyers too have noticed the effects of these tendencies on our thinking about law and about constitutions (MacCormick 1993; Himsworth 1996B).

Of course, some recent events are such as to suggest that the political idea of nationalism is enduring, not to say tenacious. What might certainly be agreed on is that the concepts of 'nation' and 'national identity' are far from straightforward (Smith 1991; Woolf 1996). Indeed, the analysis of such concepts is apt to give employment to scholars of anthropology, sociology, history and cultural studies, and no doubt several other disciplines, for whom it is stock in trade.

A constitutional lawyer steps into these waters with apprehension, but at least might answer the questions whether and to what extent a Scottish identity has been reflected in constitutional arrangements. A lawyer's first thought might be that, to judge from the criterion of citizenship laws, there is no Scottish nationality since, under the British Nationality Act 1981, most people who live in Scotland have citizenship of the United Kingdom (and incidentally citizenship of the European Union, under the EC Treaty). However, beyond that, the law may appear less monolithic. Another ground on which discrimination is unlawful in areas covered by the Race Relations Act 1976 is 'national origins', and in *Northern Joint Police Board v. Power* [1997] IRLR 610, the Employment Appeal Tribunal held (I believe rightly) that English and Scottish national origins were distinguishable and so relevant for the application of the law.

There is at least some legal justification, therefore, for regarding Scotland as a nation. In ordinary usage, the appellation is quite common. In so far as perceptions are important, polling evidence informs us that approximately nine out of ten persons in Scotland regard themselves as Scottish and two thirds give priority to that Scottish feeling over Britishness (Brown, McCrone, Paterson and Surridge 1999). Clearly, identities can be multiple or multi-layered, but we might perhaps infer from this evidence that some kind of Scottish identity is widespread, judged by Scottish perceptions.

The perception of the United Kingdom as composed of several nations corresponds well with the perception that the United Kingdom is better regarded, not as a unitary, but rather as a 'union' state (Rokkan and Urwin 1982). In a union state, these authors suggested, integration would be less than perfect, because the historical circumstances of union would be echoed in contemporary variations in governance. The United Kingdom does not conform to classic definitions of federalism, because it lacks a structure of co-ordinate institutions, each with exclusive areas of competence. However, rather than a rigidly unified pattern, the state has exhibited some flexibility in legal and institutional arrangements. Flexibility has been necessary (and advisable) with regard to Northern Ireland, as Brian Thompson's chapter in this collection demonstrates. Flexibility has also been shown with regard to Scotland, in hopes of accommodating within the state the demands of that 'restless nation' (Clements, Farquharson and Wark 1996). The means chosen, within the domestic constitution, have been measures of *devolution*. By that inexact but useful term, we mean the delegation of governmental powers from the centre without the relinquishment of sovereignty. The recently enacted Scotland Act 1998 is the latest (not the first) stage of this accommodation.

THE SCOTTISH NATION STATE

A criterion which may be thought relevant to the question of what counts as a 'nation', is whether the territory in question was once a state. As has been observed, the criterion is by no means conclusive (Marquand 1991). Wales may claim to be a nation, although the territory's statehood was tenuous, short-lived and distant. Hanover and Piedmont were states of sorts more recently than Scotland, yet are not usually classified as nations. However, a period of statehood may be relevant, and is favourable rather than otherwise to claims of nationhood. If nothing else, the historical circumstance may echo in political resonance.

On this criterion, it is worth remembering that Scotland had a long history of statehood. In the ninth century Kenneth MacAlpin, the King of the Scots in Dalriada, became King of the Picts too. In 1018 one of his successors, Malcolm II, conquered Lothian when he defeated the Angles at the battle of Carham, and in the same year succeeded to the Kingdom of the Britons in Strathclyde. He and his grandson Duncan I, who followed him, thus became Kings of all Scotland. From that date onwards, Scotland was a recognisable country with, two or three interregnal periods apart, a continuous line of succession to the throne.

Unlike Wales and Ireland, Scotland was able to maintain its independence. The overlordship of Edward I of England was briefly acknowledged when he was invited to adjudge upon rival claims to the Scottish throne in 1292. But within two years his chosen man, John Balliol, and his counsellors were rebelling. Edward defeated the Scots at Dunbar, but if he thought that he had subdued them, was soon disabused of that notion by the patriot William Wallace. Wallace routed the English army at Stirling Bridge (1297), was defeated at Falkirk (1298), but continued to harry the English forces until his betrayal and death. Robert Bruce, who was crowned king in 1306, carried on where Wallace left off, and his campaigns culminated in a brilliant victory over Edward II at Bannockburn in 1314. Liberation of the country was complete, although the Scottish barons' insecurity led them to send an address to the Pope (the Declaration of Arbroath) in 1320, asserting the rightfulness of King Robert's claim to the throne and soliciting recognition and support. England's King Edward III acknowledged Scotland's independence in the Treaty of Northampton (1328).

There were intermittent hostilities between Scotland and England in the sixteenth century, but the conversion of Scotland to Protestantism began to bring the people of the two countries closer. Then in 1603, when Elizabeth I died, James VI of Scotland became King James I of England too. He was the son of Mary, Queen of Scots, and the great-great-grandson of Henry VII of England.

What occurred in 1603 was merely a personal union of the Crowns, contingent on the different laws of succession to the throne in Scotland and in England. Following the personal union, some trade restrictions between the two countries were abolished, and a common citizenship was introduced. But there was no union of the countries or their laws, and the English Parliament could no more make laws for Scotland than could the Scottish Parliament or Estates (as it was more commonly known) legislate for England. In fact, the circumstance of personal union was not very popular in Scotland, because the seat of royal government had been removed to London. When discontents arose during the reign of Charles I, they were felt all the more keenly in Scotland. The Scottish Presbyterian force of Covenanters took up arms against the King before the English parliamentary forces, and, for the rest of the seventeenth century, events were to follow a broadly similar pattern in both countries. Indeed, when Cromwell's forces had succeeded in both, under the constitutions of the Commonwealth and Protectorate, there was a single Parliament for Scotland, England and Ireland. But the brief experiment of a united Parliament was premature, and separate Parliaments met again following the Restoration, which in this respect as in others signified a deliberate return to the principles and practice of government under law which had been developing in the sixteenth and earlier seventeenth centuries.

However, the restored Stuart kings proved to be unworthy recipients of the authority given them, not least because they seemed to pervert principles of legality by their exercise of the powers of suspending or dispensing with laws. In 1688, James VII of Scotland and II of England fled into exile from a land which would tolerate no longer the abuse of his powers in furtherance of his fellow Catholics' cause.

So in 1688 there was a need for a new constitutional settlement in England. A monarchy was thought desirable, but it had to be a Protestant monarchy. It had also to be a limited monarchy, subordinate in its powers to the Parliament. These points were taken for granted when an informal group of Lords, past members of the Commons (which had not been summoned since 1685), and authorities of the City of London invited William, Prince of Orange (who was married to James's daughter, Mary) to summon a Convention. This irregular assembly met, declared the throne vacant, and offered it to William and Mary jointly. The gift was not absolute, but conditional, and the terms were embodied in a constitutional document enacted by the newly constituted Parliament as the Bill of Rights.

The peaceful revolution in England was rather less peacefully and more uncertainly followed, but followed none the less, in Scotland, where in 1689 the Scottish Crown too was offered to William and Mary, upon terms that established a limited monarchy, governing with the Parliament's consent. The constitutional document which realised the arrangement was called the Claim of Right.

THE UNION

In the seventeen years that followed, the Scottish Parliament displayed a greater authority than it had ever before evinced. The greater assertiveness of the body, and the enhanced importance of both Parliaments as against the Crown, were amongst the causes of the progress to a more complete union. There were other underlying trends conducive to harmony, and perhaps unity, such as the geographical factor of sharing an island off the continent of Europe, common dynastic and religious influences, and economic interests (Campbell 1994; Morrill 1994).

There had in fact been several earlier attempts to bring about union. Commissioners representing the Scottish and English Parliaments had been appointed in 1604 and again in 1670 in order to negotiate on the matter, but on these as on other occasions the efforts did not bear fruit.

However, after 1688, when it became clearer that the monarchy was to be a limited monarchy, constitutionally responsible to a Parliament, it was not easy to see how the monarchy could be responsible at one and the same time to two Parliaments, each pursuing its own policies. These contradictions were exposed, and perhaps exploited, when in the midst of war against Louis XIV the Scottish Parliament passed an Act (the Act anent Peace and War of 1703) to the effect that no future Sovereign should have power to make war or peace without its consent.

By that time, feelings were running high on both sides of the border. There was resentment in Scotland of the Acts passed by the English Parliament which excluded them from trading with the English colonies. The attempt by Scots to found a trading colony of their own, the Darien scheme, had been a disastrous failure, for which the English were also blamed. In England, fearful of a Jacobite restoration, the Parliament had passed in 1700 the Act of Settlement, which declared that after Queen Anne's death the Crown would go to the Hanoverian line. However, its counterpart had not been consulted, and the Scottish Parliament responded with the Act of Security in 1704. Under its terms, the successor to the Scottish Crown was to be chosen by the Parliament 'provided always that the same be not successor to the Crown of England', unless in the meantime some conditions such as freedom of trade had been established between the two countries. The English Parliament retaliated with the Aliens Act of 1705, which threatened to prohibit trade and to treat native Scots as aliens. When a Scottish ship was seized on the Thames, and an English ship captured in the Firth of Forth, the two countries seemed to be on the brink of war.

Perhaps it was that which brought them to their senses. The two Parliaments asked the Queen to appoint Commissioners on their behalf, with a view to negotiating a treaty of union. The Commissioners met in Whitehall and reached early agreement on the three main points: an incorporating union, guarantees by the English of complete freedom of trade, and acceptance by the Scots of the descent of the Crown according to the Act of Settlement. With a compromise on Scottish representation in the new Parliament, the endeavour was completed in nine weeks.

The Commissioners on both sides made concessions, and the provisions of the union legislation which resulted are not such as to suggest a shotgun marriage. The position of Scotland's established church had, for example, been kept outside the Commissioners' remit, as being non-negotiable. The English Commissioners were obliged not only to concede freedom of trade and navigation, but to grant tax exemptions and payments in compensation. The Scottish Commissioners had to agree to the Hanoverian succession.

The Scottish Commissioners also had to settle for an 'incorporating' union, by which was meant that both countries merged their legislatures and identity. Such an arrangement was naturally seen by the statesmen of the time as offering the most suitable form of government. Some of the Scottish Commissioners, notably Andrew Fletcher of Saltoun, were attracted to a more 'federal' conception of union. What they seem to have had in mind was rather what we should call a confederation, a league of states without a supreme, central legislature, on the model of the Dutch United Provinces. But an arrangement like that would have been open to the same dangers as the status quo. A truly federal solution would have been a different matter, but that was scarcely in the Commissioners' contemplation, as there was not, until the American example in 1787, an obvious model for such a form.

Therefore, what was established was a full political and economic union. As the Crowns were to become one in law, the new state could justifiably be called a 'United Kingdom', and it was to be called 'the United Kingdom of Great Britain'. Yet the union was not designed to effect a complete assimilation. As one historian puts it: 'The men who negotiated the Treaty had no interest in creating a united British nation and therefore enabled the Scots to preserve their own national identity within the Union' (Levack 1987: 212). The Scottish Commissioners' proposals concerning their distinct legal system and courts, the royal burghs, and the heritable jurisdictions, engendered no difficulties, while the place of the Kirk had been assured from the outset. These were institutions more strongly rooted in the national affection than was the Parliament which was disappearing.

The union legislation consisted of a principal Act composed of 25 articles, and three associated Acts which provided for the continuance of the different established churches in Scotland and England and the precise manner of electing the Scottish representatives to the House of Commons and the House of Lords. These Acts of Union were separately enacted first by the Scottish Parliament, then by the English, which were legislating for their own demise, to be succeeded by the Parliament of Great Britain. The legislation is in Scotland often referred to as 'the Treaty'.

Some lawyers in Scotland have argued that (in the law of Scotland, if not in English law) the union legislation enjoys a special legal status, so that the United Kingdom Parliament is unable to alter it or at least unable to alter some of its more important terms (Smith 1957; Mitchell 1968). The argument was encouraged, if not inspired, by some *obiter dicta* in *MacCormick v Lord Advocate*, 1953 SC 396, when a challenge to the Queen's chosen designation as 'Elizabeth II' was dismissed, not entirely unsympathetically.

However, the argument is difficult to sustain, since numerous alterations have in fact occurred and the courts, if they are not powerless to intervene to prevent them, have never actually done so (Munro 1994). The evolution of society since 1707 has been reflected in the evolution of the union, notwithstanding the precise terms of the provisions as they were enacted then, which can evidently be repealed expressly or by implication. The creation of a devolved Scottish Parliament under the Scotland Act 1998 does not as such, it may be noticed, involve any alteration or breach of the articles of the union legislation (which provided for representation in the new Parliament of Great Britain, but did not in terms abolish the Scottish Parliament or the English). By contrast, it is easy to conceive that the Scottish Parliament, in exercise of its powers under the Act of 1998, might legislate inconsistently with provisions of the union legislation, or at least might be argued to have done so. So arguments of legal impediment to change might have been expected to be raised, even if we would expect them to be defeated. The prospect induced the draftsmen to insert a provision in the hope of precluding the advancement of such arguments, and s.37 provides that the union legislation shall 'have effect subject to this Act'. If the union legislation were really unalterable, this provision would be ineffective, whereas its being given effect should go far to settle the argument.

In the Union State

In the years immediately following 1707, the union was not popular on either side of the border. In Scotland particularly, there were grievances over taxation policies and over actions of the British Parliament such as its legislating for toleration in the Scottish Episcopalians Act 1711 and for the restoration of lay patronage in the Church Patronage (Scotland) Act 1711. These measures were regarded as violations of the spirit of the union agreement, and arguably of its letter as well. In 1713, when a proposal for dissolution of the union was introduced in the House of Lords, it was defeated by only four votes.

However, by the later eighteenth century, the benefits of the union were becoming more generally appreciated. Home and colonial markets had been opened to Scottish traders and venturers as well as English, and the advances brought by the agrarian and industrial revolutions were enabling the people of northern and southern Britain to take full advantage of them. The industrial success of Scotland, first within the customs union of Great Britain and then increasingly in an international free trade economy in the nineteenth century, in which Glasgow became 'the second city of the Empire', could hardly be gainsaid. Economically, socially and culturally, the Scottish people had in many respects assimilated to their southern neighbours, with whom interchange and communion had become commonplace.

Moreover, as historians have argued persuasively, there were powerful forces combining to form and shape a British political identity in the eighteenth and early nineteenth centuries, in particular Protestantism, the external threat posed by France, and the commercial opportunities of Empire (Colley 1992; Robbins 1998). However, the same historians observe that by the later nineteenth century those factors which had been propitious were altering or waning, and a consequent decline in the success of the branding of Britain was beginning to set in, even if the common experience of embroilment in the two World Wars may have helped to obscure and even to delay the process.

In one part of the British Isles, disharmony and disunion had been felt earlier, because if a British identity had been forged and fostered with some success on the mainland, it had in Ireland rather become a badge of division between disparate communities inhabiting the same island. By the middle nineteenth century, Irish nationalism was a strong political force which politicians such as Mr Gladstone sought to assuage with a more limited measure of domestic self-government or 'Home

Rule' (Bogdanor 1979). The failure of well-intentioned efforts along these lines was succeeded by a successful struggle for independence on the part of the larger portion of the island, which was to become the Irish Free State and later the Republic of Ireland. For that larger portion, what was on offer from the United Kingdom Parliament and Government under the scheme of the Government of Ireland Act 1920 was too little, too late.

Scotland has been spared the troubles which have disfigured Ireland's history, and it would be wrong to press any parallels too far. Nevertheless, it is worth noticing that a significant step in the process of devolving governmental power to Scotland was begun in 1885, when 'the Irish question' had become prominent in Westminster politics. With the warning of events in Ireland in mind, the main political parties evidently thought it prudent to give greater recognition to a Scottish dimension in politics, perhaps in hopes of accommodating a national identity which had not been entirely extinguished and which might re-emerge in more aggressive form.

ATTEMPTED APPEASEMENT

After the union of 1707, there was no reason of principle why special arrangements should be made for Scotland in the matter of executive government. However, perhaps because distance lent bewilderment, there were always differences. In the eighteenth century, political management made of Scotland virtually a separate satrapy, as in the long period from the 1760s to the start of the nineteenth century when the influence of Henry Dundas (later Viscount Melville) was paramount. In the nineteenth century government functions were often carried out separately in Scotland through agencies and boards such as the Board of Supervision (concerned with relief of the poor) and the Fishery Board or, like schools and policing, were essentially organised at local level. In aspects of civil society such as religion and education, distinctive traditions had been preserved and different practices developed from those south of the border.

Against this background, the decision to differentiate the handling of Scottish affairs more clearly within central government did not represent a sharp break from the past. The policy, initially formulated by Gladstone's Liberal Government, was actually implemented by its Conservative successor, in 1885, when a Scottish Office was created as a department of government, whose minister, the Secretary for Scotland, was to be responsible for law and order, education, and a few other matters. From 1892 onwards, it became the practice to allocate a place in the Cabinet to that person, and in 1926 the holder's office was raised in status to that of a Secretary of State. Since 1939, the principal base of the Scottish Office has been in Edinburgh, first at St. Andrew's House on Calton Hill and later in more modern, often less pleasing buildings.

These moves, from 1885 onwards, represented an arrangement which may be called administrative devolution, where the central government, without creating legislatures and executive governments derived from them in different parts of the state, arranges for aspects of its work to be conducted by a department which is defined *territorially* rather than *functionally*. What was devised in this fashion for

Scotland was later to be followed (more slowly, and in a rather more limited way) for Wales, and (in rather different circumstances) for Northern Ireland at some periods.

Over the years, the functions and importance of the Scottish Office have significantly, if gradually, increased (Donaldson 1976; Midwinter, Keating and Mitchell 1991). On the recommendation of the Gilmour Committee on Scottish Administration in 1937, some statutory boards with particular functions were abolished, and their powers vested in the Secretary of State. Some more functions were allocated to the Minister as a result of recommendations made by a Royal Commission on Scottish Affairs which reported in 1954, and others from time to time. By the end of 1998, the Secretary of State for Scotland, with six junior ministers and a Scottish Office organised in five main departments, had responsibilities extending to agriculture and fisheries, the arts, crofting, education, the environment, the fire service, forestry, health, housing, industrial assistance, local government, police, prisons, roads, rural and urban development, social work, sport, transport, tourism, town planning, some minor departments and some public corporations operating in Scotland, and some legal matters (with other functions in connection with the Scottish legal system falling to the Lord Advocate's Department and Crown Office, for which the Lord Advocate was responsible). There have also been some matters for which the Scottish Secretary was jointly responsible with an 'English' colleague.

Viewed in another way, it may be said that the Scottish Office by the 1990s had responsibility for most functions of the United Kingdom Government in Scotland, with the major exceptions of defence, foreign policy, taxation and social security. However, even in areas where they did not have sole or chief responsibility, Ministers of Cabinet rank who were recognised as being 'Scotland's Minister', with an interest in all matters affecting Scotland, could be influential. Just to cite one recent example, it appears that a decision by the Secretary of State for Defence late in 1998, to scale down the Territorial Army, may have been influenced by Scottish Office representations, with the effect that less drastic reductions are being imposed in Scotland.

Scotland has probably profited from the Secretary of State system. Certainly, it has enjoyed a higher expenditure per head of population than other parts of Great Britain, and it is reasonable to attribute this in part to the advantage of having a spokesman at Cabinet level, even if different infrastructures and land and housing factors may go far to explain and justify the differential. Administration has probably been better by reason of the Scottish Office civil servants being closer to the country's concerns and its people. Policies formulated in areas such as social work services and education have often compared favourably with the English equivalents. Policies which have been applied to the whole United Kingdom have at least sometimes been applied with Scottish conditions or preferences in mind, and tailored or tempered accordingly. For example, the Conservative Government which carried through the privatisation of water companies in England and Wales was persuaded to modify its policy for Scotland, albeit while nonetheless insisting on a reorganisation. The scope for administrative initiative within the Scottish Office has increased since 1978, when a change in the method of allocating funds enabled the Secretary of State to have greater freedom of action within the total budget.

At the same time, it is difficult to form an accurate picture. The collective responsibility doctrine and the secrecy surrounding British government, generally prevent (or delay) us from knowing when, for example, the Secretary of State has been instrumental in winning something for Scotland or when he has been frustrated or defeated by a Cabinet majority. One distinguished political scientist contended that, although the system certainly facilitated access to officials more locally, it had only produced marginal gains for Scotland in the round (Mackintosh 1964).

While the system of administrative devolution was the most obvious concession to Scottish identity within constitutional arrangements from 1885 to 1999, there are some other matters which may readily be looked at in a similar light. Most obviously, the continuance of a separate legal system, in the spirit of the union treaty, has throughout the period since 1707 served as a reminder that the state is a union of nations which retained some separate institutions and characteristics (and law, religion and education are often regarded as the chief totems of Scottish distinctiveness).

In legislative arrangements, where primary legislation had of necessity to be enacted by the united Parliament, there were some minor variations in the usual parliamentary processes available for Bills (or parts of Bills) which were exclusively Scottish in operation. Procedural rules of the House of Commons allowed for such proposals to be debated by the Scottish Grand Committee (a body set up regularly since 1907, and since 1980 consisting of all the MPs for Scottish seats only) at the second reading stage, instead of in the House itself. Another reform in 1957 allowed for a Scottish Standing Committee to be set up for the committee stage of such Bills. In 1980 the Scottish Grand Committee was enabled to meet in Edinburgh and there were other minor reforms in the handling of parliamentary business initiated by the Conservative Government in 1994 and 1995, including greater use of the Grand Committee, which was encouraged to meet in other Scottish cities and towns as well as Edinburgh. A Select Committee on Scottish Affairs had been established as part of the new system of 'departmental' Select Committees in 1979.

Generous representation for Scotland in the House of Commons can be viewed as another instance of differential treatment. The electorate of Scotland in 1997 was represented by 72 MPs in the House, amongst the 659 sitting there. However, if electoral area apportionment in the United Kingdom were carried out on a basis of strict arithmetical equality, Scotland would have had 58 or 59 constituencies rather than 72. It is interesting to be reminded that, on one review of the issue by a Speaker's Conference, any diminution of the numbers of Scottish or Welsh seats was rejected because it 'might give rise to a good deal of political feeling and would lend support to the separatist movement in both countries' (McLean 1995).

Thus it is by no means fanciful to see, in matters such as these, differences and tokens which can be regarded as nods in the direction of Scotland's nationhood, some perhaps mainly symbolic, some more substantial. These privileges and concessions could be justified according to some criteria, but the motivation was at least partly political, when they could be seen as helping to buy off some of the more moderate demands for home rule within the union state. If the term is not too pejorative, we might say that the reforms from 1885 onwards represented attempts to appease the restless Scottish nation.

THE FAILURE OF APPEASEMENT

However, if the constitutional concessions to Scottish identity may be explained as attempts to appease, we should be driven to the conclusion that appeasement, in that form, has failed.

It is difficult to say when the failure may be dated from, and perhaps it is worth remarking again that a decline in the success and cohesion of 'British' identity may have been obscured or delayed by the circumstances of war. What may certainly be observed is the decline of the Conservative Party in Scotland from its peak in the 1955 general election, when it won just over half of the available seats (36 out of 71). The party in Scotland, from 1912 to 1965, was officially the Scottish Unionist Party, which indicated something of its ideological opposition to Home Rule, whether Irish or Scottish, although it did not oppose recognition of nationhood by some of the means which have been noticed. Nor should it be assumed that changes in Scottish voting patterns depended entirely, or even strongly, on attitudes to constitutional issues, for opinion poll evidence suggested otherwise.

However, it is also true that there was a rapid growth in Scottish National Party support and membership in the 1960s. Following some success in local elections, there was a parliamentary breakthrough in 1967, when Mrs Winifred Ewing won the Hamilton by-election for the party. By 1974, the SNP had become the second largest party in votes in Scotland and at the general election in October of that year it won 11 seats.

The Labour Government of Mr Harold Wilson responded to these nationalistic stirrings (felt in Wales too) by setting up a Royal Commission on the Constitution in 1969. Its report, which did not appear until October 1973, was far from unanimous, but broadly supported a scheme of legislative devolution for Scotland and, less clearly, of further devolution for Wales, and these proposals did form the basis of reforms planned when Labour was back in government from 1974. The Scotland and Wales Bill 1976 failed, but under a parliamentary pact with the Liberals, a second attempt succeeded, and the Scotland Act 1978 (and the Wales Act 1978) became law. However, amongst the amendments which the Government had been forced to accept was one which proved fatal. The Government intended to hold referendums in Scotland and Wales, so as to give electors there an opportunity to say whether they wanted the provisions to come into effect. George Cunningham, a backbench Labour opponent of the reform, successfully proposed that if less than 40% of those entitled to vote were to vote 'Yes', then orders for the repeal of the legislation would have to be laid before Parliament. At the poll in Scotland, the result was equivocal and, from any perspective, unsatisfactory. A majority of those who voted were in favour of the Scotland Act 1978 proposals, because 32.9% of the electorate said 'Yes' and only 30.8% said 'No'. However, as 36.3% of the registered electorate did not vote, the threshold requirement set by the Cunningham amendment was not satisfied. The results led indirectly to a change of government because, when the SNP withdrew its support from the Labour Government in reaction to its acceptance of the results, the Government was shortly defeated on a vote of confidence, and so was obliged to advise a dissolution.

With the return of the Conservatives to government in 1979, constitutional reforms along such lines were predictably put on the back burner. The administrations led by Margaret Thatcher and John Major showed no interest in reviving any proposals for legislative devolution. On the whole, their disinclination towards substantial reform was to be expected, for the reason of principle that the party's philosophy was historically opposed to it, and perhaps for the practical reason that the party enjoyed its strongest support in England, especially south of a line from the Severn to the Wash. As already noticed, there were some minor reforms introduced in the parliamentary handling of Scottish business in 1994 and 1995. Beyond tinkering of that kind, the Conservative Governments could hardly go, without abandoning their opposition to a substantial measure of home rule. During this period, the Conservatives' decline continued in Scotland. The party, which had won 36 seats in 1955, won 23 seats in 1970, won 10 seats in 1987, and won no Scottish seats at all in the 1997 general election.

The reasons for that decline are various, but evidence from opinion polls suggested that, on constitutional issues, a majority of voters in Scotland wanted something different from the status quo.

Why might the system of administrative devolution fail to satisfy? Fundamentally, there was a weakness at the heart of the system, in that the executive and administrative powers were not properly matched by a legislature or political base. In this sense there was something of a 'democratic deficit'. The Secretary of State was a member of the United Kingdom Government. When the majority in the House of Commons and the majority of Scottish MPs come from different parties (as they did between 1959 and 1964, between 1970 and 1974, and from 1979 to 1997), then the Secretary of State had less of the appearance of being Scotland's Minister and more of the appearance of being a colonial governor. The problem was exacerbated (and quite naturally exploited in the rhetoric of the other parties) after the Conservatives won only 10 seats in the 1987 general election.

The system of administrative devolution involved problems of accountability as well as of legitimacy, because Scottish Ministers' appearance on the rota for question time in the House of Commons once every three weeks was hardly commensurate with the scale of Scottish Office activities. The establishment of a Select Committee on Scottish Affairs in 1979 improved matters to a degree, although difficulties in agreeing on composition prevented the formation of the committee from 1987 to 1992. The expansion of the role of the Scottish Grand Committee from 1994 could be presented as enhancing accountability, but the changes were arguably more cosmetic than real (Himsworth 1996A).

With regard to legislation, the numerical predominance of members for England and Wales constituencies in the House of Commons – even allowing that Scotland is over-represented – might explain, if not excuse, a tendency to 'Anglocentricity'. An inspection of the statute book might confirm that such a tendency had prevailed. Its symptoms, so far as Scotland is concerned, might be seen either in the failure to find sufficient parliamentary time for distinctive legislation or sometimes in an insensitivity to different legal traditions, when the law was being amended by means of an Act applying throughout Great Britain or throughout the United Kingdom.

Use of the Scottish Grand Committee and Scottish Standing Committees did permit Scottish legislative business to be dealt with in the main by Scottish members, but could not in itself remedy the problem of insufficient time in the parliamentary timetable at Westminster.

The system which operated from 1885 to 1999 was not without merits. Scotland, in acknowledgement of its nationhood, received some special consideration which was denied to regions of England, for example. Along with the preservation of some of Scotland's institutions and distinctive practices, the devolution of administrative powers and some allowances and special arrangements in parliamentary business, may have been enough to satisfy some of the weaker demands for recognition of Scottish identity in the constitution. However, on analysis the system of administrative devolution was also something of an untidy compromise, and from the 1960s its deficiencies came under more vigorous challenge. Its central premise, holding that powers to decide on Scottish law and administration should remain in the hands of the United Kingdom Parliament and Government (with their political complexion largely determined by voters outwith Scotland) became harder to defend, as people in Scotland became increasingly conscious of their Scottish, rather than their British, identity.

THE SCOTLAND ACT 1998: A NEW ACCOMMODATION

The Labour Party could not be entirely absolved from the suspicion that its actions in government from 1974 to 1979 had been driven by political expediency as much as clear principle. However, in its years in opposition the party became more sympathetic to greater decentralisation of power. Besides, for a party which held (after the 1987 general election) 50 seats in Scotland, there were obvious electoral advantages to be garnered from espousing the cause of a Scottish Parliament, if it were popular, and losses to be risked if it did not. Moreover, especially after Mr John Smith became the party's leader in 1992, there could be no doubt over the party's commitment to the cause. For John Smith, who had piloted the Scotland Act 1978 through the Commons, the project of Scottish home rule was, quite simply, 'unfinished business'.

Political parties' policies were important, because only a party (or coalition of parties) in government could deliver constitutional reforms. It was also significant that some pressure groups were formed in the wake of the 1979 referendum or later, which were influential in keeping the issue of reform in front of the public and the parties during the long period of Conservative governments. Out of one of these groups grew a body calling itself the Scottish Constitutional Convention, in which the Labour Party and the Liberal Democrats participated, along with the Greens and a few other minor parties, and representatives or delegates of local authorities, trade unions, churches and some other organisations. This body produced a report, *Towards Scotland's Parliament*, in 1990, and its final report, *Scotland's Parliament. Scotland's Right*, in 1995. The final report was notable for its thoroughness and attention to detail as well as principle, which meant that a sympathetic government could import the proposals more or less wholesale. The Labour Party entered the general election in 1997 with a commitment to legislate for a Scottish Parliament within a year of taking office, assuming affirmative referendum results.

The decision to subject their proposals on Scotland (and on Wales) to referendums represented a change of policy on Labour's part, which irritated the Liberal Democrats, their partners in the Scottish Constitutional Convention. However, in 1996 Mr Blair, who had become Labour's leader, committed the party to testing the Scottish electorate's view on the two questions of their support for a Scottish Parliament and on the principle of its possessing tax-varying powers, in advance of legislating. When the general election in May brought Labour to power, the new Government was quick to produce a White Paper (*Scotland's Parliament*, Cm. 3658) with its proposals, and the referendum was held on that basis (Munro 1997). On September 11, 74.3% of those who voted agreed that 'there should be a Scottish Parliament', and 25.7% disagreed, while 63.5% agreed that the 'Scottish Parliament should have tax-varying powers', and 36.5% disagreed. The way was clear for the introduction of a corresponding Bill to turn the proposals into legislative form (Himsworth and Munro 1998).

The Scotland Bill, introduced in December 1997, became the Scotland Act 1998 when it received the royal assent in November 1998 (Himsworth and Munro 1999). Provisions of the Act were brought into effect in stages. Following the first general election in May 1999, a Scottish Parliament met after a gap of nearly three hundred years. Unlike its ancient forbear, however, it will not be the legislature of a sovereign state. If earlier acknowledgements of Scotland's nationhood in constitutional arrangements were insufficient to appease Scottish demands, will the new accommodation represented by the Scotland Act 1998 succeed?

One reason to take note of the history is so as to see that the devolution measures in the Act are in themselves evolutionary rather than revolutionary. It is salutary to remind ourselves of this because, at least in Scottish political discourse, the term 'devolution' had virtually been hijacked in recent years, coming to be identified almost exclusively with the demand for a Scottish legislature.

Another reason to keep the history in mind is so as not to be deceived about the extent of change. The areas devolved under the Act are largely coterminous with the current responsibilities of the Scottish Office. Because the legal system has always been separate, Scots law is already different from English in land law, criminal law, family law and so on, either because the common law differs or because the Westminster Parliament has legislated separately for different jurisdictions.

What will of course be altered is that there will be a directly elected legislature sitting in Scotland, to exercise competence in the areas, which are considerable, where power is devolved to it, and from which a Scottish Executive (headed by a First Minister) will be formed. The Parliament is elected under an additional member system of proportional representation, so that 73 constituency seats filled under the relative majority system are topped up with 56 regional seats on a party list system, to give 129 members in total, initially. With different electoral arrangements and timetables, it is entirely likely that the Scottish Parliament in years to come will bear a different political complexion from the House of Commons and the government of the day in London.

For the avoidance of doubt – because legally it is otiose – the continuing competence of the United Kingdom Parliament to legislate for Scotland is restated in section 28 of the Scotland Act. This serves as a reminder that the scheme is not federal, and the Scottish Parliament is merely a devolved institution. There is no reason, legally, why the Scottish Parliament could not be abolished by a later Act of the Parliament at Westminster. However, as Conservative politicians too have conceded, the reality is that abolition is not foreseeable, politically, albeit that it is possible, legally. Moreover, as regards devolved matters, rather as occurred in relation to Northern Ireland while its Parliament was in being earlier in the century, the expectation will be that Westminster will not normally legislate for Scotland on these areas without the consent of the Scottish Parliament. Therefore, it may not go too far to suggest that the relation between Scotland and the United Kingdom could be described as semi-federal.

Under the Scotland Act, the Scottish Parliament will have power to vary the basic rate of income tax by up to three percentage points, upwards or downwards. The power is, therefore, carefully limited and since some of the political parties at least may be reluctant to use it, the arrangement smacks of tokenism. Certainly, its significance is dwarfed by the larger issue of the amount of block funding to be assigned each year from the United Kingdom Government, as to which section 64 of the Act merely provides that the Secretary of State may pay 'such amounts as he may determine'.

The Royal Commission on the Constitution (1973) considered that a scheme of legislative devolution was not incompatible with stability. On this question, however, the jury is still out. Some Conservatives decried the reform as a 'slippery slope to independence', and the plausibility of such judgments was apt to be increased when some, at least, of the members of the Scottish National Party supported a devolved Parliament on the ground that it would be a stepping-stone to independence.

It should be remembered that the Labour Party and the Liberal Democrats are (in this sense) unionist parties too. The Labour Government is hoping to satisfy what seemed to be the most preferred constitutional option amongst Scottish electors, and is doing so under a calculation that maintaining the status quo, when it failed to please, was more destabilising and threatening, while the provision of a new constitutional settlement could help to strengthen the union. However, it is reasonable to regard their policy as a calculated gamble. Significantly, polling evidence informs us that a majority of people in Scotland expect independence to follow within twenty years (Brown, McCrone, Paterson and Surridge 1999), and already some opinion polls, such as *The Scotsman*/ICM polls in June 1998 and September 1998, have shown over 50% saying that they would vote for Scottish independence in a referendum on the issue. The Select Committee on Scottish Affairs (1998) in a report published a few days after the Scotland Act became law, criticised the piecemeal nature of the Government's approach to constitutional reforms and pointed to areas of possible conflict which had the potential to encourage movement towards independence.

One of the most apparent dangers of the Government's strategy lies in the frustration of expectations which have been raised. Fiscal dependency may be relevant here. So may the scope of what is devolved. The Scottish Parliament's legislative competence is not inconsiderable, but it is limited not only by the extent of matters reserved to Westminster, but by Community law and the European Convention on Human Rights as imported via the Human Rights Act 1998. The Scotland Act itself is not (except in a few respects) amendable by the Scottish Parliament, which therefore cannot extend its own legislative competence without Westminster's concurrence. The Scottish Parliament may, however, discuss and debate and pass resolutions on matters (such as independence) which it lacks the power to legislate on. Whether this will defuse or engender frustration must be questionable.

It is even arguable (if doubtful, and the Government has been at pains to deny it) that the Scottish Parliament's competence could extend to legislating to arrange a referendum to test opinion on independence. Whether through that route or another, it is quite conceivable that the Scottish electorate's opinion on the issue will be tested specifically on some occasion, and conceivably, Quebec-style, on a series of occasions. Mr Blair's Government, by regarding a simple majority as conferring sufficient mandate for important constitutional changes, and by confining the vote to those resident in Scotland, has arguably set precedents in these respects, however questionable. Alternatively, as politicians of the main parties have sometimes conceded, it could be taken as a mandate for independence if the Scottish National Party were ever to win a majority of the Scottish seats in the House of Commons (or perhaps in the Scottish Parliament?).

Mention of Quebec prompts reflection on the *Secession Reference* case, discussed by Peter Oliver in his chapter in this collection. It is significant that the question of Quebec's right to secede was considered by the Court at all, and significant too that the Supreme Court of Canada discovered in the Canadian constitution important principles and constraints which were relevant to the disposition of the question. The decision throws into sharp contrast the relative absence of principles and constraints in the United Kingdom's more 'political' constitution. Whether the latest accommodation of Scottish nationhood, in the form of the Scotland Act 1998, will sufficiently satisfy so as to be an enduring settlement must be doubtful, not least because of the indeterminacy of the British constitution, quite apart from political factors.

REFERENCES

Bogdanor, V. (1979). *Devolution*. Oxford: Oxford University Press.
Brown, A., McCrone D., Paterson, L. & Surridge, P. (1999). *The Scottish Electorate*. London: Macmillan.
Campbell, R.H. (1994). A Historical Perspective on the Union, pp.64-75, in: P.S. Hodge (ed.), *Scotland and the Union*. Edinburgh: Edinburgh University Press.
Clements, A., Farquharson, K. & Wark, K. (1996). *Restless Nation*. Edinburgh: Mainstream Publishing.
Colley, L. (1992). *Britons: Forging the Nation 1707-1837*. New Haven: Yale University Press.

Donaldson, A.G. (1976). Administrative and Legislative Devolution, pp.45-68, in J.P. Grant (ed.), *Independence and Devolution: The Legal Implications for Scotland*. Edinburgh: W. Green & Son.

Himsworth, C.M.G. (1996A). The Scottish Grand Committee as an Instrument of Government, *Edinburgh Law Review* 1: 79-90.

Himsworth, C.M.G. (1996B). In a State No Longer: The End of Constitutionalism?, *Public Law*: 639-660.

Himsworth, C.M.G. & Munro, C.R. (1998). *Devolution and the Scotland Bill*. Edinburgh: W. Green.

Himsworth, C.M.G. & Munro, C.R. (1999). *The Scotland Act 1998*. Edinburgh: W. Green.

Levack, B.P. (1987). *The Formation of the British State*. Oxford: Clarendon Press.

MacCormick, N. (1993). Beyond the Sovereign State, *Modern Law Review* 56: 1-18.

Mackintosh, J.P. (1964). Regional Administration: Has It Worked in Scotland?, *Public Administration* 42: 253-275.

Marquand, D. (1991). Nations, Regions and Europe, pp.25-37 in: B. Crick (ed), *National Identities*. Oxford: Basil Blackwell.

McLean, I. (1995). Are Scotland and Wales Over-represented in the House of Commons?, *Political Quarterly* 66: 250-264.

Midwinter, A., Keating, M. & Mitchell, J. (1991). *Politics and Public Policy in Scotland*. London: Macmillan.

Mitchell, J.D.B. (1968). *Constitutional Law* (2nd ed.). Edinburgh: W. Green & Son.

Morrill, J. (1994). The English, the Scots and the British, pp.76-86, in P.S. Hodge (ed.), *Scotland and the Union*. Edinburgh: Edinburgh University Press.

Munro, C.R. (1994). The Union of 1707 and the British Constitution, pp.87-109 in P.S. Hodge (ed.), *Scotland and the Union*. Edinburgh: Edinburgh University Press.

Munro, C.R. (1997). Power to the People, *Public Law*: 579-586.

Robbins, K. (1998). *Great Britain: Identities, Institutions and the Idea of Britishness*. Harlow: Longman.

Rokkan, S. & Urwin, D. (eds.) (1982). *The Politics of Territorial Identity*. London: Sage.

Royal Commission on the Constitution (1973). *Report*, Cmnd. 5460. London: HMSO.

Select Committee on Scottish Affairs (1998). *The Operation of Multi-Layer Democracy*, HC 460-I, 1997-98. London: The Stationery Office.

Smith, A.D. (1991). *National Identity*. London: Penguin.

Smith, T.B. (1957). The Union of 1707 as Fundamental Law, *Public Law*: 99-121.

Woolf, S. (1996). *Nationalism in Europe, 1815 to the Present*. London: Routledge.

Constitutional Accommodation of Ethnicity and National Identity in Nepal

Surya P. Subedi*

I. INTRODUCTION

Nepal is a mosaic of numerous ethnic groups without a dominant majority group. It is a nation held together by different ethnic groups committed to preserving the long-cherished independence of the country. According to the 1991 census, there are 60 or so ethnic groups living in this small Himalayan kingdom.[1] Out of a total of 22 million or so people of Nepal, the largest ethnic group, i.e. the Chhetries, had about three million people and the smallest ethnic group, i.e. the Churoute, had a total of 1,778 people. Thus, the traditional concept of a majority and minorities does not seem to apply to the situation of Nepal. In a sense, all ethnic groups are minorities and each has learnt to live in peace and harmony with other minority groups.

The picture is slightly different when the population is divided in terms of the languages spoken by different ethnic groups as their mother tongue. There are 31 languages spoken as the mother tongue by different ethnic groups.[2] Nepali or some sort of a dialect of this national language is spoken as a mother tongue by 50.31 per cent of the people who themselves belong to some two dozen or so different ethnic groups. Perhaps only in terms of religion can one talk about a majority and minorities in Nepal. According to the 1991 census, 86.51 per cent are Hindus, 7.78 per cent are Buddhists, 3.53 per cent are Muslims, 1.72 per cent are Kiratis, 0.17 per cent are Christians, 0.4 per cent are Jains and 0.24 per cent are others and non-stated. Yet, strictly speaking, Hinduism is not only a religion, but also a culture which is all-encompassing and universalistic in character. What is more, included within this broad group of Hindus are followers of different sects, shades and aspects of Hinduism

---

* Professor of Law, Law School, University of Hull, UK
[1] They are: Rajbanshi, Dhimal, Gangain, Marwadi, Bengali, Dhanuk, Shikh, Dhusadh, Chamar, Khatway, Mushar, Kewat, Rajbhar, Kanu, Brahman (Hill), Chhetri, Yadav (Ahir), Kayastha, Kumhar, Bania, Dhobi, Sudhi (Kalwar), Kurmi, Brahman (Terai), Rajput, Tharu, Teli, Kushwha, Muslim, Haluwai, Mallah, Thakuri, Sanyasi, Newar, Limbu, Rai, Gurung, Thakali, Tamang, Magar, Danuwar, Jirel, Majhi, Sunuwar, Gaine, Chepang, Kumal, Churoute, Bote, Lepcha, Raute, Darai, Raji, Thami, Damai, Kami, Sarki, Wadi, Sherpa, Bhote, etc. Central Bureau of Statistics (1998). *Statistical Pocket Book.* Kathmandu: His Majesty's Government, National Planning Commission Secretariat, 22–28.
[2] These languages are: Nepali, Maithili, Bhojpuri, Newari, Gurung, Tamang, Abadhi, Tharu, Magar, Limbu, Rai/Kirati, Sherpa, Thakali, Rajbansi, Satar, Danuwar, Santhal, Hindi, Urdu, Chepang, Thami, Bengali, Majhi, Dhimal, Jhangar, Marwadi, Kumhale, Darai, Jirel, Byanshi, Raji, etc.

Stephen Tierney (ed.), Accommodating National Identity: New Approaches in International and Domestic Law, 151–171
© 2000 *Kluwer Law International. Printed in Great Britain.*
First published in the International Journal on Minority and Group Rights, Volume 6 No. 1/2 1999.

which are quite different from each other. Hinduism is not only the most ancient of all cultures and religions but also a faith which has not gone through any process of modernisation in modern times. Hindus themselves are divided into four castes and 64 sub-castes with their own values, customs, and traditions, making it virtually impossible to put all of them in one category.

It is easy for an outside observer or a data collector to jumble together within the category of Hindus everybody who has anything to do with any aspect of Hinduism. But within Nepal Hindus are not a homogenous religious group. Hinduism is a belief and a way of life of an individual rather than purely a religious concept. Hinduism may mean one thing to one Hindu and slightly another thing to another Hindu. Although 86.51 per cent of the population could have identified itself as Hindu for the convenience of the government data collector wandering around the remote villages located in difficult terrain of Nepal, many of them may very well believe in something which is quite different from the belief of another fellow Hindu. This is, because Hinduism is based on *dharma* and this term is generic meaning many things to different people, including duty, ethics, morality, rule of law, merit and pious acts etc.

Indeed, as is stated by Bista, '[w]hen the Nepali Bureau of Statistics states that 90 per cent of the population are Hindus, people do not understand this to mean that the bulk of the population are orthodox Hindus. Nepalis have never been orthodox nor are they ever likely to be. The State automatically assumes that everyone is Hindu unless they specifically declare themselves otherwise.[3] Therefore, from whichever perspective one looks at the definition of a minority, one can find no satisfactory definition of this term in the context of Nepal.

Nepal is a union of people belonging to numerous ethnic, religious, cultural and linguistic groups none of which has a history of suppression of others. Of course, the upper caste Brahmins and Chhetries are the dominant minority groups and have, in effect, ruled the country since time immemorial, but they have done so with the support of many other ethnic groups. Although the two groups have very many things in common and have found themselves in some sort of alliance, they themselves do not constitute a majority. The combined total population of these two castes would still be less than one third of the total population. What is more, the Brahmins themselves are divided into two quite distinct groups: Terai Brahmins (i.e., living in the Indo-Gangetic plains of Nepal) and Hill Brahmins along the foothills of the Himalayas. These two types of Brahmins have very little in common. But Brahmins and Chhetries are the two minority ethnic groups who have, traditionally speaking, enjoyed more privilege and power than any other ethnic groups. The constitutional laws of Nepal are designed to address this imbalance rather than to protect the minorities vis-à-vis a majority since there is no single majority dominant group within the country.

International law does not seem to contain rules applicable to a specific situation such as that to be found in Nepal. Although many of the 60 or so ethnic groups of

---

[3]   Bista, D.B. (1991). *Fatalism and Development: Nepal's Struggle for Modernization.* Calcutta: Orient Longman, 30.

Nepal may qualify both as a minority and a people,[4] it is not clear whether the law on minorities, which appears to presuppose the existence of a majority, would apply to these ethnic groups. Thus, strictly speaking, in terms of the ethnic composition of the country, the popular definition of a 'minority' does not appear to apply to Nepal since it has no majority ethnic group. According to Professor Walker's definition of 'minorities' given in his *Oxford Companion to Law,* minorities are 'groups of individuals within a state, belonging to a race or having customs, language, religious beliefs, or other practices *materially different from those of the majority* of the individuals in that state'.[5] Similarly, a publication by the UN Centre of Human Rights states that 'Minorities, obviously, must be numerically smaller than the rest of the population which constitutes the majority'.[6] Article 4(2) of the European Framework Convention for the Protection of National Minorities takes a similar tone.[7] In the absence of a majority group, a minority has to have its rights as a minority under international law of human rights exercised against other minority groups who in turn would have their own rights exercised against other minorities. This creates a very complex legal situation in a country where there is no majority group.

There is a considerable amount of literature on minority rights,[8] but very little is written about the situations of ethnic groups such as those to be found in Nepal.[9] Most of the writings focus on the racial, linguistic, ethnic, cultural, religious and other characteristics of minorities and their right to self-determination as well as the nature and scope of this right vis-à-vis a particular minority in a given State.[10] The law on minorities does not provide a definition of the term 'minority'[11] nor does it

---

4   See, for instance, Crawford J. (ed.) (1988). *The Rights of Peoples.* Oxford: Oxford University Press; Thornberry, P. (1991). *International Law and the Rights of Minorities.* Oxford: Clarendon Press; Hannum, H. (1990). *Autonomy, Sovereignty, and Self-Determination: The Accommodation of Conflicting Rights.* Philadelphia: University of Pennsylvania Press; United Nations (1991). *Study on the Rights of Persons Belonging to Ethnic, Religious and Linguistic Minorities.* New York: United Nations, 1991, UN Sales No. E91.XIV.2; Rehman, J. (1998). Minority Rights in International Law: Raising the Conceptual Issues, *The Australian Law Journal 72:* 615–634.
5   Walker D.M. (1980). *The Oxford Companion to Law.* Oxford: Clarendon Press, 843, (emphasis added).
6   Centre for Human Rights (1992). *Minority Rights (Fact Sheet No. 18).* Geneva: United Nations, 9.
7   It reads: 'The Parties undertake to adopt, where necessary, adequate measures in order to promote, in all areas of economic, social, political and cultural life, full and effective equality between persons belonging to a national minority and those *belonging to the majority.* In this respect, they shall take due account of the specific conditions of the persons belonging to national minorities'. (emphasis added) 34 ILM 351 (1995) at 354.
8   See Thornberry P. *et al.* (eds.) (1997). *World Directory of Minorities.* London: Minority Rights Group, and the materials cited therein.
9   See Rehman J. and Roy N. (1997). South Asia: Nepal, in Thornberry, P. *et al., ibid.,* 571–572.
10   Hannum, *op. cit.;* Kritsiotis D. (ed.) (1994). Self-Determination: Cases of Crisis, (occasional paper), Hull: Hull University Law School; Thornberry P., (1989). Self-Determination, Minorities, Human Rights: A Review of International Instruments, *ICLQ* 38: 867–889.
11   None of the international instruments dealing with minority rights provide a definition of the term 'minority'. The principal international instruments dealing with minority rights are: 1966 International Covenant on Civil and Political Rights; the UN General Assembly Declaration on the Rights of Persons Belonging to National or Ethnic, Religious or Linguistic Minorities GA Res. 47/135, 18 December, 1992; and the Framework European Convention for the Protection of National Minorities of 1995 34 ILM 351 (1995).

clarify whether the combination of a number of minority groups constituting more than 50 per cent of the total population of the country can be regarded as the majority against which a minority not included in the combination of the majority population have its rights exercised.

What is more, almost all ethnic groups in Nepal are scattered all over the country, resulting in a complex intermingling of people belonging to different ethnic groups. None of the ethnic groups is situated in one location thereby denying any meaningful claim to a territory as its own within the country. Even if one were to argue that these ethnic groups are as eligible for the rights of minorities under international law as any ethnic minority in any other country, the ethnic groups in Nepal do not demonstrate a high degree of homogeneity, let alone the viable ability to exercise their right to self-determination which is perhaps the most important right of a people.

However, this does not mean that the ethnic groups in Nepal are entirely unprotected by international human rights law. All individuals belonging to such ethnic groups have as many individual rights and freedoms as any other individuals under international law and all ethnic groups have as many group rights as any ethnic group situated in any other country. Even if we were to say that the 60 or so ethnic groups in Nepal do not come within the direct protection of the international law on minorities, they are protected against discrimination etc. by the general provisions of international law and international law of human rights. Accordingly, all ethnic groups of Nepal could be said to have a right to exist, to enjoy and develop their culture, to speak their language and to have it recognised by the state machinery, to have equal political representation in the governance of the country and to have autonomy to administer matters internal to the groups, at least in the fields of culture, education, religion, etc.[12] It is in the light of these provisions of general international law that an attempt will be made in this chapter to examine the plight of various disadvantaged ethnic groups in Nepal and the extent of protection accorded to them within the constitutional tradition of Nepal since international law seems to have left matters such as these to States themselves. The main concern of the chapter is to examine the extent to which the constitutional provisions of Nepal accommodate ethnicity while preserving national identity.

2.   THE FOUNDATIONS OF THE KINGDOM OF NEPAL

(i)   National independence

As stated by Shaha, 'centuries before the Christian era, Nepal had acquired a distinct territorial character'.[13] Sandwiched between two giants of Asia, namely, China and India, Nepal had to cultivate a strong national identity at the expense of ethnic equality to preserve its independence for centuries. 'Territorial expansion in the second half of the eighteenth and the first decade of the nineteenth centuries provided a sense of

---

[12]   UN Centre for Human Rights, *op.cit.* footnote 6.
[13]   Rishikesh Shaha (1993). *Politics in Nepal: 1980-1991*. New Delhi: Manohar, 18.

emotional unity and identity among the peoples of various ethnic and linguistic backgrounds who had just been brought together into one kingdom.[14]

It was this sense of unity and separate identity that made people fight hard in a major war in 1815 against the mighty and expanding British Empire. These people succeeded in preserving Nepal's independence when the rest of the South Asian sub-continent came under British rule. However, when the external threat to its independence receded in the aftermath of the British withdrawal from India, different ethnic groups staked their claim to power. It was against this backdrop that Nepal developed its own indigenous system of accommodating ethnicity in its Constitution, while solidifying the nationhood of Nepal. Indeed, Article 2 of the Constitution of Nepal defines the Nation of Nepal in the following words:

The Nation: Having common aspirations and united by a bond of allegiance to national independence and integrity of Nepal, the Nepalese people irrespective of religion, race, caste or tribe, collectively constitute the nation.[15]

(ii) The Monarchy

The monarch is seen in Nepal as a fatherly figure and even as a Godly figure by many people in this predominantly rural and agricultural country where the majority of the people are still illiterate. Article 27(2) of the Constitution states that: 'His Majesty is the symbol of Nepalese nationality and the unity of the Nepalese people'. Indeed, the institution of monarchy has served as the symbol of Nepalese nationality and the unity of the Nepalese people since the unification of the country by King Prithvi Narayan Shaha in 1769. Since then, the country has been ruled by his descendants by and large as benevolent rulers. There was a period of 104 years during which an oligarchical family, the Rana family, ruled the country keeping the Shaha monarchs in the sidelines but still on the throne. Apart from that period, the Shaha dynasty has effectively acted as the focal point of national unity.

The institution of monarchy is deeply rooted in the Nepalese psyche and the monarchs, especially after the overthrow of the oligarchical Rana regime, have been able to adapt to the new environment. For instance, when the demand was strong, Nepal subscribed to a Western style parliamentary system of governance in the aftermath of the independence of India and the Communist revolution in China. Although the experiment with the parliamentary system of government was short lived, King Birendra, the present king, who inherited the panchayat system from his father, tried to introduce some democratic norms into the system.

In spite of the opposition from the hard-liners from within the panchayat system, he called for a referendum in 1980 to ascertain whether the people wanted to have a parliamentary system of government or to retain the panchayat system with some reform. The people gave their verdict in favour of retaining the panchayat system and the leader of the democratic movement, B.P. Koirala, accepted the verdict of the

---

[14] *Ibid.*
[15] Law Books Management Board (1990). *The Constitution of the Kingdom of Nepal, 2047.* Nepal: Ministry of Law and Justice.

people. It was generally accepted by both national and international observers at the time that the referendum itself was by and large free and fair.

However, when a sizeable number of people began to grow dissatisfied with the panchayat system, he decided to reintroduce the parliamentary system of government in 1990. Thus, the monarchy has survived in Nepal always with the support of the people and the Shaha kings have listened to the people whenever the country is gripped by a crisis. Indeed, it was King Tribhuvan, the grandfather of the present king, who led a democratic movement in Nepal in 1949/1950 against the oligarchical Rana regime. Thus, whenever there has been a crisis in Nepal, the monarchs have led the way and preserved the unity and independence of the country. The Nepalese monarchy has served as a crucial institution in the development of a national society consisting of so many different castes, sub-castes, and ethnic, cultural and linguistic groups. The following observations of a well-respected Nepalese anthropologist are of interest:

> The King is a positive force for the country and active catalyst for the process of nationhood because all Nepalis share a tendency for paternal dependency, which, in social organisation, facilitates a kind of perspective that monarchy provides an ultimate beneficent paternal figure. This is both reassuring to the Nepali, and also becomes the basis of his developing sense of national identity. The nation includes all those that enjoy the munificence of this common father. It is an extension of family, of village, of clan, of ethnic group, that brings a new completion by incorporating all surrounding ethnic groups into a common fold. This is inherently good, because it acts to harmonize relations between groups.[16]

(iii)   Religious Tolerance

One would expect tension and conflict along racial, cultural and religious lines in a developing country like Nepal inhabited by so many people of so many religious orientations. On the contrary, ethnic harmony and religious tolerance seem to have acted as two of the principal pillars of Nepalese nationhood. Bista rightly states that '[r]eligion has always been a central feature of Nepali life but Nepal has never been plagued by any form of religious fanaticism. On the contrary, Nepalis love colourful rituals of all kinds and have welcomed a variety of religious traditions.[17] Indeed, in spite of the numeric Hindu majority, there has been no major religious conflict in the modern history of the country.

Traditionally speaking, Hinduism is by its very nature based on a universalistic outlook on the world and tolerance of other religions. Christianity is a recent phenomenon in this ancient kingdom. Nepal has never been a fertile ground for Islam. After Hinduism, Buddhism is the second major religion in the country. Even then Buddhism in Nepal is fused into Hinduism and Lord Buddha is regarded as the

---

[16]   Bista, *op.cit.* footnote 3, 162.
[17]   *Ibid.*, 3.

tenth incarnation of Hindu God Vishnu. Most Hindus in Nepal worship both Buddha and Hindu gods and celebrate both Buddhist as well as Hindu festivals and most Buddhists in their turn do the same. This religious harmony and tolerance has acted as a bedrock of the unity of this country.

(iv) Ethnic Unity

Nepal is a melting-pot of numerous ethnic groups. Ethnic conflict is by and large an alien concept for most Nepalese people. Although Nepal is not a homogeneous country in terms of its ethnic composition, it is not India or Sri Lanka in the making. In addition to the classification of the people into four Hindu castes, all people in Nepal could again be grouped in nearly five dozen or so ethnic groups none of which would be the majority group in this relatively narrow strip lying in the southern flanks of the Himalayas. None of the ethnic groups can present itself as a viable separate geographical entity since none of them has an exclusive geographical area to claim as its own.

There is no history of major ethnic conflict in this country. All ethnic groups are united under the banner of Nepalese nationhood. They all have a shared history of unbroken independence since time immemorial. No part of Nepal has ever come under any alien domination. There is a feeling that a country which is already quite small compared to its giant neighbours cannot afford to harbour any ethnic tensions. This deeply rooted belief and understanding has served the country well and preserved its unity. There has not been much ethnic political violence during elections in a country with four castes and numerous ethnic groups and there is not much support for communal, ethnic and regional parties.

Nepal was one of the first few developing States to embrace a democratic system of government in the aftermath of the fall of the Berlin Wall and the end of the Cold War. The transition to democracy has been quite encouraging and peaceful in this multiracial, multicultural and multi-ethnic country. Since 1991 the country has seen three largely peaceful general elections and nine changes of government either through the ballot box or through the support of the parliamentarians. There has been an accommodation of all interests within the new democratic structure of the country. So much so that Nepal became one of those rare countries which freely voted the Communists to power when they agreed to work within the parameters of the new Constitution based on constitutional monarchy.

3.   PROBLEMS OF INEQUALITY IN UNITY

(i)   Economic Disparity

In spite of its existence as an independent entity since time immemorial, Nepal still finds itself among the ten poorest countries of the world. Unlike most other developing countries, Nepal has no former colonial power to blame for its economic underdevelopment. The majority of the population is still illiterate and lives below the poverty line. The gap between the rich and poor is ever widening. Nepal has seen nine years of multi-party system at work. Yet, the power structure is still centralised with the caste system very much a fact of life. People have very high expectations of their government, expectations which the government is unable to meet. As a result, the electorate has switched its loyalty from one political party to another in the hope of a better government and there is no guarantee that one day people will not form political parties along ethnic lines or at least switch loyalty to such ethnic and communal parties. That day will be a day of chaos for the infant democracy of Nepal and the very survival of the nation as a union of ethnic minorities would come under question. This is because there are quite a large number of ethnic groups not able to benefit equally from whatever economic development there is in the country. They are very poor not only by Western standards but also by the standards of other more prosperous ethnic groups within the country. As stated by Shaha, '[f]or physical, psychological and historical reasons the central government in Nepal has failed to enforce an equitable distribution of goods and services throughout the society'.[18]

(ii)   Lack of Educational Opportunities

The ethnic problem of Nepal is not about the suppression of minorities by a majority. Nor is it about discrimination against minorities by a majority or by another stronger minority. The problem is about educating the people belonging to various disadvantaged ethnic groups. It is about empowering these ethnic groups and facilitating their equal participation in the governance of the country. People belonging to many disadvantaged ethnic groups are very poor and cannot afford education for their children. Poor families need their labour to sustain the family.

As a result of the historically unequal power relations between different ethnic groups brought about by a number of factors such as the traditional division of the population of the country into different castes, lack of education, or the isolation of certain communities situated in the hilly, mountainous and remote areas of the country, there have come into existence a large number of disadvantaged ethnic groups which have become more assertive.

(iii)   Weak Political Participation

The disadvantaged ethnic groups in Nepal have a desire to be recognised and have their voice heard in the decision making process of the country. Yet, even after the introduction of a democratic system of government in 1951, not much significant change has come about for these ethnic groups so far as their participation in the governance of the country is concerned. Shaha rightly states that, '[e]ven after the 1951 political change, the possibility of social mobility for various ethnic groups other than the three socially dominant castes of the Brahmins, Chhetries and Newars has been minimal'.[19] He goes on to state that, '[t]his chronic state of inequality,

---

18   *Ibid.*, 20.
19   Shaha, *op.cit.* footnote 13, 16.

which has tended to give the widest possible opportunity for government service and education to only three castes and to one small area of the country [i.e., the Kathmandu area], cannot be said to be consistent with the modernization goals of the country'.[20] For instance, as the following table demonstrates, the majority of the representatives sent to Parliament during the first free elections of Nepal held in 1959 came from the privileged Brahmin and Chhetri castes, themselves a minority constituting less than one third of the population. A similar pattern of representation was witnessed in the elections of 1967 for the National Panchayat (the National Assembly).

TABLE 1[21]   REGIONAL AND CASTE/ETHNIC GROUPS WITHIN THE 1959 PARLIAMENT AND THE 1967 NATIONAL PANCHAYAT

Regional and caste/ethnic groupings of representatives	1959 Parliament		1967 National Panchayat	
	No. of reps	Per cent of total	No. of reps	Per cent of total
Hill Brahmins	31	28.4	30	24.0
Chhetries	30	27.5	47	37.6
Newars	5	4.6	15	12.0
Low-caste hill people	1	0.9	1	0.8
Hill tribals	22	20.2	19	15.2
Hill people, sub total	**89**	**81.6**	**112**	**89.6**
Caste Hindus and Muslims from the plains	13	11.9	11	8.8
Plains tribals	7	6.4	2	1.6
Plains people, sub total	**20**	**18.3**	**13**	**10.4**
Total of all representatives	109	100.0	125	100.0

(iv)   Under-representation in Bureaucracy and Military

The representation of disadvantaged ethnic groups in the bureaucracy and military is way below a proportionate level. As stated by Pradhan:

the higher echelon of the bureaucracy is composed of the influential members of the Nepalese society. It is composed of the elite groups who enjoy a monopoly over educational opportunity in a country where the literacy rate is very low and there are not many job opportunities available to the people

---

20   *Ibid.*
21   Source: Gaige, F.H. (1975). *Regionalism and National Unity in Nepal.* Berkeley: University of California Press, 164, cited in Blaikie P. *et al.* (1980). *Nepal in Crisis: Growth and Stagnation at the Periphery.* Delhi: Oxford University Press, 91.

outside the government. The education that a man achieves is also determined by the class in which he was brought up. Higher education which is considered as one of the requirements to be in the higher echelons of the administration is not available to all.[22]

Indeed, according to a survey, 92.8 per cent of high officials in the civil service came from three minority ethnic groups – the Chhetries, Brahmins and Newars – who together constituted only 22.8 per cent of the population.[23] A similarly disproportionate picture appears also in the case of army officers. Chhetries occupied 74 per cent of the officer rank positions followed by 6.5 per cent each by hill Brahmin, Newar and Gurung. As stated by Bista, the issue of ethnicity in Nepal 'is not so much a matter of discrimination because of membership of an ethnic minority group, or because of low caste status, but is a form of social exclusion in the absence of other qualifications necessary for group membership. Ethnic minorities, then, are disadvantaged and excluded in Kathmandu by default'.[24]

4.   EVOLUTION OF THE CONSTITUTION AND CONSTITUTIONAL TRADITION IN NEPAL

(i)   *The First Constitutional Act of Nepal, 2004 (1946)*

Nepal has traditionally been ruled by the dicta of Hindu law and philosophy and by national and local customs and traditions. There was no constitution or a constitutional law in its modern sense until 1946, and the monarch ruled the country within the limits permitted at the time. This normally meant consulting some sort of an advisory council consisting of the representatives of the nobility for the governance of the country. According to Hinduism, the king is a person who has some attributes of God. He was made by God to preserve *dharma*.[25] There is no wonder that King Prithvi Narayan Shah, the founder of modern Nepal, described his newly created kingdom in 1769 in the following terms: 'This throne of Nepal

---

[22]   Pradhan, P. (1973). Development of Political Institutions in Nepal since 1951, in: Rana and Malla (eds.), *Nepal in Perspective*. Kathmandu: CEDA,162, cited in Blaikie *et al., ibid.*, 94–95.

[23]   *Ibid.*

[24]   Bista, *op.cit.* footnote 3, 57.

[25]   See generally, Younger P. (1972). *Introduction to Indian Religious Thought*. Philadelphia: The Westminster Press; Subramaniam, K. (1977). *Mahabharata*. Bombay: Bharatiya Vidya Bhavan; Bowes, P. (1977). *The Hindu Religious Tradition: A Philosophical Approach*. London: Routledge & Kegan Paul; Duncan J. and Derrett M. (1963). *Introduction to Modern Hindu Law*. Oxford: University Press; Chinna Durai, J. (1933). *Hindu Law in a Nutshell*. London: Sweet & Maxwell; *Bharuci's Commentary on the Manusmriti, Vol. II. The Translation and Notes* by J. Duncan M. Derrett (1975). Wiesbaden: Franz Steiner Verlag GMBH; Naresh Chandra Sen-Gupta (1953). *Evolution of Ancient Indian Law: Tagore Law Lectures 1950*. London: Arthur Probsthain; Radhabinod Pal (1958). *The History of Hindu Law in the Vedic Age and in Post-Vedic Times down to the Institutes of Manu, Tagore Law Lectures, 1930*. Calcutta: University of Calcutta; Barth A. (authorised translation by Rev. J. Wood) (1969). *The Religions of India*. Delhi: Chand & Co.; Harold Smith, F. (1934). *Outline of Hinduism*. London: the Epworth Press.

is a fort ... A fort built by God himself'.[26] This statement is in keeping with the traditional Hindu belief that God created the king to uphold righteousness on earth in accordance with *dharma*. From this perspective, a *dharmic* king could hold both temporal and spiritual powers in his hands.

However, Hinduism attaches a number of qualifications to this exercise of power by a king. First and foremost, the king himself must be a *dharmic* person. Although the Hindu monarchy is by and large hereditary and patriarchal, a king can deny the throne to his son if he is a wicked person. Second, a king should always be responsive to the wishes of the people and be guided by the advice of the elder statesmen of the society in making decisions.[27]

As stated by Rangarajan the seeds of constitutional or benevolent monarchy could be found in Kautilya's *Arthasastra*, a book on the Hindu polity, written circa 300 B.C.[28] It is this aspect of benevolent monarchy which is deeply rooted in the Nepalese psyche and has been recognised as such since the creation of the country. Indeed, the institution of monarchy has served as the symbol of Nepalese nationality and the unity of the Nepalese people since the unification of the country by King Prithvi Narayan Shah in 1769.

As stated earlier, there was a period of 104 years during which an oligarchy, the Rana family, ruled the country, keeping the Shah monarchs in the sidelines but still on the throne. When the Rana rule came under threat owing to popular demand for democracy, a very limited system of representation was introduced in 1946 through the Government of Nepal Act, 2004 (1946). It introduced for the first time in the history of the country the idea of fundamental rights and duties and provided for basic rights in Part II of the Act. It also provided for a bi-cameral central legislature. While all the members of the upper house were to be nominated by the hereditary Rana Prime Minister, the lower house was to consist of members both nominated and elected. Only two members of the council of ministers were to be chosen from the elected members of parliament. The other members of the council of ministers were to be appointed by the Prime Minister. The legislature had very limited legislative power as the power to veto any bill passed by parliament rested with the Prime Minister. In any event, this Constitutional Law never entered into force owing to its rejection by the members of the democratic campaign who were committed to overthrow the Rana regime rather than accept some sort of accommodation within it.

---

[26] See in Joshi, B.L. and Rose, L.E., (1966). *Democratic Innovations in Nepal: A Case Study of Political Acculturation.* Berkeley: University of California Press, 3.

[27] Verse 1.19.34 of Kautilya's *Arthasastra* has this to say about the duties of a king: 'In the happiness of his subjects lies the king's happiness; in their welfare his welfare. He shall not consider as good only that which pleases him but treat as beneficial to him whatever pleases his subjects'. See in Rangarajan, L.N. (1992). *Kautilya: The Arthasastra.* New Delhi: Penguin Books, x.

[28] *Ibid.*, 26.

(ii)   The Interim Government of Nepal Act, 2007 (1951)

Following a tripartite compromise reached between the Rana rulers, the King and the leaders of the democratic movement with the help of the Indian Government for the transfer of power from the Rana rulers to the people, an Interim Government Act designed to usher the country down the road to full democracy was promulgated in 1951. This was supposed to be an interim constitution to be replaced by a democratic constitution framed by a Constituent Assembly elected by the people for this purpose.

Among the principal provisions of the Act were provisions for the election of a Constituent Assembly, creation of a National Assembly elected by the people, and the establishment of an independent judiciary. After some ten years of experiment with different governments, King Mahendra, the father of the present monarch, decided in 1959, for the first time in the history of the country, to promulgate a proper Constitution based on a bi-cameral parliamentary system of government. However, this was to be done without holding elections for the Constituent Assembly which was intended to chart the future political organisation of the country.

(iii)   The First Democratic Constitution of 1959

This Constitution was modelled, by and large, after the British system of constitutional monarchy. Noted British constitutional lawyers of the time were consulted in the drafting of the Constitution by the King of Nepal, but despite this some Nepalese characteristics were enshrined in the Constitution, most significantly the retention of quite substantial powers in the hands of the King. In the end this Constitution was withdrawn by King Mahendra within two years of its establishment through a so-called 'bloodless coup d'etat'. It was claimed that the parliamentary system of government was based on foreign and Western models and was not suitable for a country like Nepal. It was alleged that the leaders of the party in power had become corrupt, that they were lenient to India to the detriment of the traditional policy of neutrality of Nepal vis-à-vis her two giant neighbours of Asia, and that the new system as a whole did not allow for the preservation of the unique social fabric and traditional strengths of the country which had kept Nepal united and independent since its unification in 1769.

(iv)   The Panchayat Constitution, 2019 (1963)

After pondering for two years about the future political organisation of the country, the King decided in 1963 to promulgate a new Constitution based on the indigenous age-old panchayat system of government under which no political parties would be allowed to operate, but periodic elections of individual candidates for the National Assembly – the legislative body – would take place, with the King becoming the executive head of the State. He would be assisted by a Council of Ministers chaired by a Prime Minister in discharging the day-to-day administration of the country. The principal functions of the National Assembly included recommending to the King bills for his assent and a name for appointment as Prime Minister. The King retained the final decision making power with regard to both the appointment of Prime Minister and approval of the bills presented to him.

Thus, the new party-less panchayat system carried the image of an indigenous Nepalese system of government within the country and appeared at the same time in tune with the concept of 'basic democracy' applied by some contemporary heads of the Non-Aligned Movement such as Nasser of Egypt and Sukarno of Indonesia. This move of the King did not meet with significant opposition within the country nor did it invite sharp condemnation from neighbouring or other countries. The only neighbouring country which could have made an impact was India, but this move of the King came at a time when India itself was engulfed in a subdued mood following her defeat at the hands of the Chinese during the Sino-Indian border war of 1962.

In fact, the panchayat system met with popular approval in its early years and the King carried out quite a few radical and ambitious reforms during this period. Notable among them were land reform, the introduction of a much revised Civil Code (which abolished the caste system and introduced the principle of equality before the law in terms of punishment for crimes committed),[29] a village development campaign, the huge expansion of primary and secondary education, and the introduction of healthcare and family planning provisions etc. After a long period of isolation the country was opening up in more or less every area of activity both internally and externally. It was in a way a period of Nepalese Renaissance in terms of the development of arts, culture, education, transport, communications etc.

It was under the panchayat system that people learnt the basic concepts of democracy and democratic traditions and customs. People learnt how to vote and whom to vote for. They learnt the basic element of democracy that there were people contesting elections to be elected to public positions. It was quite a novelty brought to them only in the second half of the twentieth century. The system did not ask them to run before they could walk. The approach adopted by the system was a gradual and progressive democratisation of the country. People were quite fascinated by the idea of elections for local bodies such as the village panchayats. Things began to go wrong only when attempts were made to make the system more rigid and more insular in the name of reforming it. The system became more oppressive and exclusive which in turn gave way to opposition and dissension.

As stated earlier, King Birendra, the present monarch, tried to inject vitality into the system by introducing some democratic norms and kept the system going for quite a while. He tried to maintain a balance between those who wanted more democratic reforms and those right-wingers who were keen to push the system even more to the right. However, by early 1990 the national and international tide and time was running against him and the panchayat system. Those opposed to the panchayat system were quick to exploit the situation. The King was wise in detecting the national and international mood and decided voluntarily in 1990 to restore the parliamentary system of government (abolished by his father some thirty years ago) by promulgating the present Constitution.

---

[29] For instance, prior to this revised Code, the upper caste Brahmins were either immune from certain types of degrading punishments or were subject to a lesser degree of punishment for the same type of crime committed.

(v)   The 1990 Constitution

(a) Background
When those opposed to the panchayat system were swept to power during the 1990 campaign for democracy, the leaders of the campaign asked the King to appoint a committee to prepare a draft Constitution. They did not consider holding elections for a Constituent Assembly to draft the Constitution. However, the Constitution Reform Committee appointed by the King upon the recommendation of an all party coalition interim government engaged itself in an elaborate process of consultation on the content of the future Constitution with people from every walk of national life and every section of the population. When the Committee drew up a draft Constitution on the basis of the opinion of all major political parties, the interim government recommended it to the King who in turn promulgated it in November 1990, paving the way for a fully democratic system of government, which remains valid to this day.

(b) Basic Principles of the Constitution
The preamble to the Constitution specifies the following as the principal pillars of the political organisation of the country: (i) constitutional monarchy; (ii) sovereignty of the people; (iii) the system of multiparty democracy; (iv) a parliamentary system of government; and (v) constitutional guarantees of fundamental freedoms of the people. The Constitution provides that no amendment to the constitution can ever alter this basic political organisation of the country. Thus, parliament in Nepal occupies a key position within the constitutional framework which cannot be undermined even by constitutional amendment.

The new Constitution states in the very first article that the Constitution is the fundamental law of the land and all laws inconsistent with it will, to the extent of such inconsistency, be void. Article 3 makes it clear that the people are the source of state power: 'The sovereignty of Nepal is vested in the Nepalese people and shall be exercised in accordance with the provisions of this Constitution.' The Constitution, in Part III, Articles 11–23, guarantees fundamental rights and freedoms such as the right to equality, the right to privacy, the right to constitutional remedy and freedom of speech and opinion to every citizen of the country. It includes quite an elaborate list of rights and freedoms guaranteed under the Constitution.

The Constitution provides for the separation of power among the three principle organs of the State: the executive, the legislature, and the judiciary. According to Article 35 of the Constitution, the executive powers are vested in His Majesty and the Council of Ministers. Article 35(2) provides that the executive powers of His Majesty under the present Constitution are to be exercised upon the recommendation and advice, and with the consent of the Council of Ministers. Articles 84–86 of the Constitution vest all judicial powers in the judiciary consisting of the Supreme Court, Appellate Courts, and District Courts. According to Article 86, the Supreme Court is not only the highest court in the judicial hierarchy but also a Court of Record.

(c) The Legislature

Article 44 of the Constitution provides for a bicameral legislature for the country: 'There shall be a Legislature, to be called parliament, which shall consist of His Majesty and two Houses, namely, the House of Representatives and the National Assembly.' The House of Representatives, the lower house, consists of 205 members and the National Assembly, the upper house, has 60 members. While the full term of the House of Representatives is five years, the National Assembly is a permanent body. All members of the House of Representatives are elected directly by the people on the basis of the 'first past the post' system. With regard to the National Assembly, 10 of the 60 members are nominated by the King. Out of the remaining 50 members, 35 are elected by the House of Representatives on the basis of a proportional representation system by means of the single transferable vote and 15 are elected by an electoral college consisting of chiefs and deputy chiefs of local authorities.

Along with the traditional principal powers of parliament such as its powers to enact legislation and elect the government, the Nepalese parliament is also vested with powers relating to: ratification or accession or approval of treaties and agreements concluded by the government; removal of Supreme Court judges from their office for reasons of incompetence, misbehaviour or failure to discharge duties of their office in good faith; and amendment of the Constitution itself.

With regard to the restrictions on the powers of parliament, the Constitution provides in Article 1 that no law could be enacted *ultra vires* of the Constitution. Any law enacted by parliament *ultra vires* of the Constitution will be declared null and void by the Supreme Court. Nor can any law be enacted or amendment to the Constitution be passed by parliament which might undermine the letter and spirit of the Constitution. In other words, parliament cannot pass laws that undermine the five principal pillars of the political organisation of the country mentioned above.[30]

(d) Political Organisations

No political party can put forward candidates in general or other elections without being recognised as a political party by the Election Commission, and the Constitution requires the Commission to withhold recognition from any political party or political organisation which has been formed either with the objective of promoting a one-party system of government or a system of single ideology, or one based on religion, communal beliefs, caste, tribe or geographical region.

According to Article 113(2) of the Constitution, all political parties must fulfil the following conditions to qualify for registration as a political party by the Election Commission:

1. The constitution and the rules of the political organisation or party must be democratic;

---

[30] They are: (i) constitutional monarchy; (ii) sovereignty of people; (iii) the system of multiparty democracy; (iv) parliamentary system of government; and (v) constitutional guarantees of fundamental rights and freedoms of the people.

2. The constitution or the rules of the organisation or party must provide for election of office bearers of the organisation or party at least once every five years;
3. The organisation or party must set aside at least five per cent of the total number of candidates contesting an election for the House of Representatives for women candidates;
4. The organisation or party must have secured a minimum of three per cent of the total votes cast in the election to the House of Representatives.

Apart from the above-mentioned requirement in favour of women, no other provision of the Constitution guarantees seats in the lower house for any ethnic groups or other sectors of society.

There have been three general elections since 1990 and the composition of Parliament has shown no sign of polarisation on the basis of ethnicity. Nor has any party, fighting elections on the basis of communalism, ethnicity or other divisive basis, attracted any phenomenal support. The composition of Parliament after the 1991 elections was as follows:[31]

Political Party	Number of Seats in Parliament
Nepali Congress	114
Communist Party (United Marxist & Leninist)	68
United People's Front	9
Nepal Sadbhavana Party	6
Communist Party (Democratic)	2
Nepal Worker's and Peasant's Party	2
Rastriya Prajatantra Party	4
Total	205

In spite of having an absolute majority in the newly elected Parliament, the Nepali Congress Party could not remain in power for the full five-year term due to a power struggle within the party itself. A mid-term poll was held in 1994 and the result was as follows:[32]

Political Party	Seats won in 1994	Seats won in 1991	Change
Nepali Congress	83	114	(-30)
Communist Party (UML)	88	68	(+20)
United People's Front	0	9	(-9)
Nepal Sadbhavana Party	3	6	(-3)
Communist Party (United)	0	2	(-2)
Nepal Worker's and Peasant's Party	4	2	(+2)
Rastriya Prajatantra	20	4	(+16)
Party Independents	7	0	(+7)
Total	205	205	

---

[31] As summarised in Singh, D.M. (1995), 'Recent Democratic Process in Nepal: Aspects of Stress and Direction', an unpublished paper presented by the author at a seminar at the Institute of Social Studies, The Hague, The Netherlands, on 25 April 1995 (the paper is on file with the present author).
[32] *Ibid.*

The Congress Party did, however, recover in the 1999 general election.

Political Party	Seats won in 1999
Nepali Congress	111
Nepal Communist Party (UML)	71
Rastriya Prajatantra Party	11
Nepal Sadbhavana Party	5
Rastriya Jana Morcha	5
Sanyunkta Janamorcha Nepal	1
Nepal Majdoor Kissan Party	1

The above tables demonstrate that the people are divided along ideological and political lines rather than communal, ethnic or religious ones. There is a feeling that a country which is already quite small compared to its giant neighbours cannot afford to harbour any ethnic tensions based on geographical divisions. This deep rooted belief and understanding has served the country well and preserved its unity. Compared to the violent climate that one normally witnesses in the neighbouring Indian states of Bihar and Uttar Pradesh during general elections, there has not been much ethnic or other violence during elections in Nepal, a country with four castes and numerous ethnic groups, and there is not much support for communal, ethnic and regional parties in the elections.

5. ACCOMMODATION OF ETHNICITY IN THE NEW CONSTITUTION

Unlike the previous constitutions, the new Constitution recognises the ethnic diversity of the country since, as observed by Bista, 'minority people struggle for an identity, and demand that the identity be publicly acknowledged as having import'.[33] Article 4(1) of the 1990 Constitution 33 outlines the foundations of the modern Kingdom of Nepal: 'Nepal is a multiethnic, multilingual, democratic, independent, indivisible, sovereign, Hindu and constitutional monarchical Kingdom.'[34] This very acknowledgement of the actual situation of the country has acted as a catalyst for the improvement of the situation of various disadvantaged ethnic groups in Nepal.

Although the mention of 'Hindu' rather than a 'multireligious' society in this article may raise some disquiet among certain non-Hindu Nepalese people, many people regard this as a statement of the actual situation on the ground since, as stated earlier, some 86.51 per cent of the total population has been classified as Hindus by the latest census held in 1991. Whether as many as 86.51 per cent of the population actually regard themselves as Hindu may be debatable, especially if we were to consider this figure in the light of the observations made by Bista, above. However, what is indisputable is that the royal throne of Nepal is a throne reserved for a Hindu monarch. The term 'Hindu' in this article may be taken to mean a Hindu

---

[33] Bista, *op.cit.* footnote 3, 161.
[34] Law Books Management Board (1990). *The Constitution of the Kingdom of Nepal 2047*. Nepal: Ministry of Law and Justice.

and constitutional monarchical Kingdom implying that the monarchy is Hindu rather than the State itself since there is no comma after the word 'Hindu' in the official English translation of this article.

Yet, if we were to go by the Nepali text of this article, there is a comma after the word 'Hindu' implying that Nepal is a Hindu Kingdom rather than just the monarchy itself. Even if the latter were to be the case not many people should have much objection since according to Article 27(1) of the Constitution the royal throne of Nepal is a Hindu throne reserved for a Hindu monarch: 'In this Constitution, the words 'His Majesty' mean His Majesty the King for the time being reigning, being a descendant of the Great King Prithvi Narayan Shah and an adherent of Aryan culture and the Hindu religion.' In terms of the religious character of the throne itself this provision is not much different from many other monarchies around the world which have clearly identified religious affiliations but at the same time lead a perfectly democratic multiracial, multicultural and multi-religious society. Great Britain itself is a good example where the monarch has to be by tradition a Protestant.

Shaha states that, '[a]n awkwardly phrased Article 4(1) in Part I of the Constitution has unnecessarily provoked the religious, ethnic and linguistic minorities against Nepal's Hindu majority and Hindu King. The article is self-consciously worded in an attempt to mollify the feelings of the minorities. Actually, it has had the opposite effect'. He goes on to argue that, '[a]s the position of the Hindu King is safeguarded in Article 27(1) of Part V, which deals with the kingship, there was no reason for calling Nepal a Hindu state in Part I. Not only does Article 4(1) have the effect of rubbing religious minorities the wrong way, it militates against the principle and practice of separation of religion and the State'.[35]

One does not necessarily have to agree with Shaha since, as stated earlier, this provision of the Constitution of Nepal, whichever way it is construed, is neither out of the ordinary nor one which poses any serious problem. Moreover, a mere declaration of the country as a Hindu State does not necessarily imply discrimination against people of other faiths if this declaration is there as a decoration merely for the satisfaction of the majority Hindus without being translated into laws which discriminate against people of other faiths. No one is stating that the latter is the case. As discussed in the preceding paragraphs, the Nepali version of Hinduism is not an orthodox one and fanaticism has never been part of the Nepalese culture. It is a society based traditionally on religious harmony and tolerance. Nowhere does the Constitution declare Hinduism as the official or national religion of the country.

Indeed, Part III of the Constitution guarantees all fundamental rights to all citizens of the country. For instance, the provisions relating to the right to equality in Article 11 read as follows:

Right to Equality: (1) All citizens shall be equal before the law. No person shall be denied the equal protection of the laws.

(2) No discrimination shall be made against any citizen in the application of general laws on grounds of religion, race, sex, caste, tribe or ideological conviction or any of these.

---

[35] Shaha, *op.cit.* footnote 13, 242.

(3) The State shall not discriminate among citizens on grounds of religion, race, sex, caste, tribe or ideological conviction or any of these.

Another way of accommodating the interests of various ethnic groups in the constitutional framework of the country is to recognise and develop their language and allow for school education in their own language. Article 6(2) of the Constitution provides that: 'All the languages spoken as the mother tongue in the various parts of Nepal are the national languages of Nepal'. Article 18 guarantees all ethnic communities the right to preserve and promote their language, script and culture:

Cultural and Educational Rights: (1) Each community residing within the Kingdom of Nepal shall have the right to preserve and promote its language, script and culture.

(2) Each community shall have the right to operate schools up to the primary level in its own mother tongue for imparting education to its children.

Similarly, Article 19 of the new Constitution guarantees the freedom of religion to every person residing within this Hindu Kingdom:

Right to Religion: (1) Every person shall have the freedom to profess and practise his own religion as handed down to him from ancient times having due regard to traditional practices, provided that no person shall be entitled to convert another person from one religion to another.

(2) Every religious denomination shall have the right to maintain its independent existence and for this purpose to manage and protect its religious places and trusts.

Thus, although Nepal is 'officially' the only Hindu country in the world, it is not a theocracy nor a country seeking strict adherence to one religion, Hinduism. Of course, the Constitution prohibits any kind of proselytisation or conversion from one religion to another and many people are inclined to think that this provision is here to provide State protection for the Hindu religion. Actually, the above provision affords protection to all illiterate and innocent people belonging to many ancient ethnic and religious groups from outside pressures of the modern world which might lead to their conversion to other religions, causing them to lose their culture and religion for good. This article should be read as a provision designed to protect the religious and cultural heritage of the ethnic and indigenous people of Nepal rather than just Hinduism. As stated by Bista, '[s]uch prohibition is the result of the perception of a connection between missionary activity and colonisation'.[36] It should be stressed that this article 36 does not prohibit conscious conversion by an individual to any other religion: it is designed to protect the illiterate ethnic and indigenous people from falling prey to outside forces or from being lured to other religions against their conscious will. Hindus cannot be converted to Christianity nor can Christians be converted to Hinduism. The same applies to the Buddhists and Muslims or persons of any other faith. But if a person belonging to any of these religions, including a Hindu, wishes to convert to another religion out of his/her own free will this constitutional provision creates no problem.

---

[36] Bista, *op.cit.* footnote 3, 30.

6. CONCLUSIONS

As described in the preceding paragraphs, Nepal appears to have accommodated ethnicity in the legal structure of the country while retaining national identity within a unitary system of government. Nepal's is quite a unique approach to ethnicity and accommodation of the interests of ethnic groups in the legal structure of the country. It is debatable whether the disadvantaged groups of minorities have a right to self-determination since the Constitution of Nepal appears to have accommodated the minimum interests and rights of minorities required under general international law. Nepal's is a case where it is doubtful to say with certainty whether its minorities come under the protection of international law on minorities. The Constitution of Nepal serves as an example of protection provided for minorities without any express or implied provision for the right of self-determination for them. While it is a nation of ethnic minorities, it is too complex a nation to have a federal system of government for each of the minorities.

However, the law does not seem to have gone far enough in addressing the problems faced by various disadvantaged ethnic groups in everyday real life. There are a large number of disadvantaged ethnic groups in Nepal for which there is neither, unlike in many other countries such as India, a provision for affirmative action nor a quota system or reservation etc. There exists a great degree of inequality in terms of opportunities and the level of political participation among different minority groups, but there is no programme of action to address this inequality either in law or in policy at this juncture of history. Both national and international law appear to be inadequate for various disadvantaged ethnic groups in Nepal. There is a need for additional measures, both legal and political, to address the problems of disadvantaged ethnic groups in heterogeneous societies like Nepal.

In spite of the restoration of a parliamentary system of government based on the system of multiparty democracy some eight years ago, not much has been done to devolve power to local institutions. The centralised power structure of the panchayat system is still quite intact.[37] This centralisation of power has given way to abuse of power and corruption. As Bista writes, 'the most important aspect of democracy is equality in opportunity and rights',[38] yet democracy has meant little for the majority of the people living in rural areas in this predominantly agricultural and rural country.

The changes that took place in 1990 have been seen by some as an elite and urban middle-class struggle for power and the way the country has been governed thus far has proved this argument to be correct: the tiny middle-class has ruled the country with little active participation by the illiterate vast majority. All major political parties have been in government since 1990 but all have lost popular confidence due to political in-fighting, corruption, mismanagement of scarce resources of this resource-poor country.

Perhaps the biggest challenge to democracy in Nepal is illiteracy. Experience has shown that the economic development of the country can accelerate only if the

---

[37] See the remarks of Sarita Giri and others in B.P. Koirala India-Nepal Foundation (1997). *Judiciary and Democratic Experiences in India and Nepal.* Royal Nepalese Embassy, New Delhi.
[38] Bista, *op.cit.* footnote 3, 113.

people have skills. An unskilled and uneducated population is a big handicap for development. What is more, democracy means little for those who are not fully aware of their rights or the ways of exercising them or the means of having them enforced by courts of law. In this predominantly agricultural country, a vast amount of land is still kept in the hands of the few and is tilled by a large number of landless people. The land reform process which began in the early years of the Panchayat government was not only limited in scope, but also not carried out with the degree of seriousness and sincerity needed to conduct such an ambitious scheme in a hierarchical society like Nepal.

To conclude, building and strengthening a strong national identity at the expense of ethnic diversity has been the priority in Nepal until recently, and a great deal of emphasis was put on cultural homogeneity. But with the lapse of time things have moved on and the advent of a fully-fledged democracy has led to calls for pluralism and the strengthening of national identity through the equal advancement of all peoples and ethnic groups. Indeed, as discussed above, the new Constitution of Nepal has laid down the foundations for pluralism not only in terms of political ideologies but also in sectors such as culture, religion, etc. This Constitution represents a significant shift in emphasis and a change in direction. What is needed is a fleshing out of these constitutional provisions by empowering all citizens, especially those belonging to disadvantaged ethnic groups, through education and literacy campaigns, through equal regional distribution of resources, through the provision of equal opportunities for all, and ultimately, through decentralisation of power to the people in this multi-ethnic society.

National Identity and Minority Rights:
the Interaction of International and Domestic Law

Accommodating an Emergent National Identity: The Roma of Central and Eastern Europe[1]

*Istvan Pogany**

1. NATIONAL IDENTITY IN 'EASTERN' EUROPE

Throughout the long, post-war decades of Communist rule the countries behind the Iron Curtain were generally referred to as 'Eastern Europe'. From the point of view of geography, that was never an accurate description. Poland, the former Czechoslovakia and Hungary are very much at the heart of Europe; Prague is west of Vienna and only a little to the east of Berlin. A significant tranche of Poland, including the towns of Szczecin, Pyrzyce and Jelenia Góra, lie to the west of Vienna, while Bratislava, the Slovak capital, is barely twenty miles eastwards. Even Budapest is only some hours by train from Vienna. So the stubborn insistence of politicians, journalists and scholars in referring to 'Eastern Europe' was, in one sense, plain wrong.

But, if 'Eastern Europe' was, in geographical terms, a misnomer, at least it expressed an identity of another kind. Prague may be west of Vienna but, until the 'velvet revolution' of 1989, it belonged to a very different orbit. Politically, economically and militarily, countries such as Czechoslovakia, Poland and Hungary *were* different to the states of Western Europe. What united the former with countries such as Bulgaria and Romania and, to a lesser degree, with Yugoslavia and Albania, was not so much geography as politics. 'Eastern Europe' expressed a crucial difference of ideology and of economic governance. While 'Western Europe' was defined, more or less, by a common commitment to liberal democracy, human rights and market economics,[2] 'Eastern Europe' designated an area dominated by variants of Communist ideology. Command economies, the denial of basic rights and an anti-

* Professor, School of Law, University of Warwick
1 I am grateful to the Legal Research Institute of the University of Warwick for awarding me a grant to undertake research for this chapter in Hungary in September, 1998. All translations from Hungarian-language texts are mine, unless indicated to the contrary.
2 Naturally, there were wide variations within Western, as well as Eastern, Europe. In particular, the onset of democracy was delayed by a matter of decades in Portugal and Spain by long-established authoritarian, right-wing regimes, while a military junta seized power in Greece in the late '60s. However, these were aberrations which do not detract from the underlying truth that most of Western Europe has been governed throughout the post-war period by democratically-elected governments which respect the rule of law and fundamental rights.

Stephen Tierney (ed.), Accommodating National Identity: New Approaches in International and Domestic Law, 175–188
© 2000 *Kluwer Law International. Printed in Great Britain.*
First published in the International Journal on Minority and Group Rights, Volume 6 No. 1/2 1999.

Western military alliance, the Warsaw Pact, defined the true meaning of 'Eastern Europe' for the West.

Perceptibly, since the collapse of Communism, Eastern Europe has been moving West. Journalists, politicians and scholars now talk about East Central or even Central Europe. Old terms, redolent of the Cold War, are being discarded as Europe unites around the core values which the West has consistently (well, since 1945) championed. It is no longer polite to talk about 'Eastern Europe' as if the ex-communist countries remained fundamentally different from us in the West. After all, the East European states have, like us, adopted democratic constitutions, instituted periodic multi-party elections and embraced the market (Pogany 1995).

Yet there are differences. It would be quite wrong to imagine that the two halves of Europe followed near identical paths of development until the formal division of Europe after World War II.[3] The Soviet Union was not the first 'empire' to have stifled the national aspirations of the peoples of Eastern Europe. The year 1956 was not the first time that Russian troops appeared in Hungary to crush a rebellion against foreign domination. In 1849 the Russian Tsar, Nicholas I, sent his armies to help put down a revolt by Hungary against the autocratic rule of the Habsburg emperors (Macartney 1968: 429–430).

Unlike much of Western Europe, with its centuries-old states enjoying an almost unbroken history of sovereignty, the process of state building in the East was mostly slow and tortuous. Hungarians fought their Habsburg rulers in a bloody and unsuccessful war of independence in 1848–1849, before settling for wide-ranging autonomy within the Habsburg Empire in 1867 (Macartney 1968: 552–556). Poles engaged in a protracted three-cornered struggle against Russia, Austria and Prussia, who had divided Poland between them in 1795 (Davies 1986: Chapter IV). An independent Polish state was only re-established in November 1918, while the borders of the new Poland remained uncertain until the conclusion of a brutal war with the Soviet Union in 1920 (Davies 1986: 116–118). Romanians, Slovaks, Croats and Serbs had to contend with an uncompromisingly chauvinistic Hungarian administration in the eastern half of Austria-Hungary from 1867 until the collapse of the Habsburg Empire (Macartney 1968: 721–734). The Czechs battled for recognition as a nation in the face of an uncomprehending German nationalism (Bideleux and Jeffries 1998: 307–314).

Even where statehood was achieved in Eastern Europe it often proved precarious. In 1939, Hitler and Stalin divided Poland between them. Systematically, the elements of Polish national existence were stripped away from the two occupied zones (Davies 1986: 64–67). Czechoslovakia, which had been laboriously constructed in the peace settlement following World War One, uniting the industrious and industrialised Czechs with the more backward, agrarian Slovaks, was dismembered less than twenty years later. The Sudetenland, with its large *Volksdeutsche* (ethnic German) population was annexed by the Reich while a German Protectorate was established over Bohemia

---

[3]   Of course, like an apple, Europe can be divided in a number of ways. The division of Europe into two halves, reflecting two different paths of development, does not necessarily equate with historical reality (Szücs 1983).

and Moravia (Rothschild 1974:132–134). The Slovaks were granted a nominal independence under a clerico-fascist regime headed by Msgr. Jozef Tiso, although ultimate power rested in Berlin, not Bratislava (Bideleux and Jeffries 1998: 489). Hungary, having grown weary of its costly alliance with the Axis powers, fell victim to German occupation in March 1944 (Rothschild 1974:187–188). Each of these countries, having witnessed the defeat and withdrawal of German troops, a process which often involved terrible and wanton destruction, found themselves simultaneously 'liberated' and occupied by the Soviet Red Army. In the wake of the Soviet troops, a new 'internationalist' ideology was introduced which left little scope for national self-determination.

Set against this historical background it is scarcely surprising that the peoples of 'Eastern Europe' should so often have an acute sense of their national identities. Recognition of nationhood was often achieved slowly and painfully, frequently against fierce opposition. Their experience as minorities, in empires as diverse as Tsarist Russia, Ottoman Turkey and Austria-Hungary, was commonly one of oppression, disempowerment or, at times, of forcible assimilation. Despite the efforts of international statesmen, the fate of national minorities did not always improve significantly after World War One in new or enlarged 'nation states' such as Romania or Poland. Commenting on the treatment of Ukrainians, Belorussians, Germans and Jews in inter-war Poland, for example, Joseph Rothschild observed:

> The Right, which by the 1930s had ideologically saturated Polish society, viewed all expressions of nationalism on the part of minorities as treasonable and to be stifled … the Right insisted that restored Poland either assimilate or expel her minorities. But they were too numerous, already too conscious, and still too rooted for either of these alternatives to be practicable at that time. They were simply alienated by the whole sterile paraphernalia of discriminatory devices which this program entailed: skewed census tabulation, boycott, *numerus clausus*, colonization, biased land reform, prejudicial tax assessment, and violence (Rothschild 1974: 45).

The treatment of certain minorities during World War II, particularly at the hands of Nazi Germany or by the USSR, far exceeded in cruelty and ruthlessness virtually anything that had gone before. Thus, in contemporary Eastern Europe, national identities are cherished precisely because they have been cultivated at great cost and with enormous effort *in opposition to* a succession of fiercely hostile, or at the very least unsympathetic, political orders.

2. NATIONAL IDENTITY AND THE ROMA, OR GYPSIES, OF EASTERN EUROPE

What is so telling about the condition of the Roma, or Gypsies, of Eastern Europe during the nineteenth century is that they can be left out of the historical narrative that has been offered here. This is, quite literally, what many highly regarded historians have done, even some of the most liberal and progressive-minded (Okey 1986; Bideleux & Jeffries: 1998). Histories of the region are often silent about the Gypsies because, quite simply, the Gypsies scarcely participated in the major economic, political, cultural and social developments that took place in Eastern Europe in this period. Historians have reflected the Gypsies' absence from these events by omitting *them*, consciously or unconsciously, from their narratives. Of course, the Gypsies were there and in growing numbers; but they were mostly silent and invisible bystanders while important social and political forces took shape all around them. At most, where Gypsies participated at all, they tended to do so *on behalf of* one or other of the national groups amongst whom they lived. But Gypsies did not try to copy these national groups by claiming national status for themselves.

Yet, during the course of the nineteenth century, ideas of national identity had gradually come to shape the political consciousness of virtually every other people in Eastern Europe. This placed an enormous and, in time, irresistible strain on the empires which continued to dominate the region (Okey 1986: 75–83, 138–147). Most people began to identify themselves, first and foremost, as Czechs, Slovaks, Ruthenes, Poles, Slovenes, Croats, Serbs, Romanians or Hungarians. They clamoured for recognition of their 'national rights', whether in education, religious observance or political representation. The 'logic' of nationalism led, ultimately, to demands not merely for minority rights but for secession and statehood, a vision which was imperfectly implemented in the political settlement following the First World War.

However, all of this had comparatively little effect on the lives and aspirations of the Roma. Political and cultural ideas which had seized the imagination of almost every other people in Eastern Europe scarcely penetrated Roma communities in the region. Unlike almost every other long-established people in Eastern Europe, most Roma remained stubbornly, impassively outside the main currents of political, social and economic development. At most, as during the Hungarian revolt against Habsburg rule, in 1848–1849, significant numbers of Gypsies aligned themselves with the Hungarian cause, often as musicians who provided music to boost the morale of the Hungarian troops (Fraser 1995: 202). However, there is no record of Gypsies developing a specific national consciousness of their own, whether in Hungary or elsewhere in Eastern Europe.

There are many explanations for the absence of a national consciousness amongst the Roma in this period of mounting nationalist fervour. These include the fact that levels of literacy amongst the Roma were much lower than amongst the non-Roma population, inhibiting the transmission of ideas from the outside world. According to a census conducted in 1893, a mere 8 per cent of the Roma in present-day Slovakia were able to read and write (Crowe 1996: 42). In Hungary, the figure was under 6 per cent (Crowe 1996: 84). The precarious conditions in which most Roma lived also played a part, compelling them to focus on day to day needs bound up with survival, such as obtaining food, shelter, a little income, leaving scant time or energy for reflections on abstract political ideals such as nationalism.

More fundamentally, perhaps, Gypsies were separated from the non-Gypsy world not merely by their comparative poverty and illiteracy but also by feelings of innate difference. These feelings were reinforced by the *marimé*, or pollution, code which Gypsy communities observed. Compliance with these rules ensured the virtual – and *self-imposed* – segregation of the Roma. As Angus Fraser notes in relation to

Gypsy communities even today, observance of this code 'serves to isolate those Gypsies who practise it from any intensive, intimate contact with *gadžé*' (Fraser 1995: 246).[4] Thus, the segregation imposed on the Roma by a frequently hostile and suspicious outside world has been mirrored by a quite voluntary separation effected by the Roma themselves.

However, there were undoubtedly additional reasons for the absence of a national consciousness amongst the Roma in this period. In contrast to Hungarians, Czechs, Slovaks and the myriad other peoples of Eastern Europe, the Roma were, and remain, a people without any national territory that they can claim as their own. In the language of contemporary international law, they are a 'non-territorial minority'. At no point in history had there been a Roma state which Roma elites could later use to galvanise the political imagination of the Roma 'masses'. No aspiration for statehood, or even nationhood, developed amongst the Roma in imitation of the nationalist agitation sweeping the peoples around them. Having entered Europe in successive waves from the Indian sub-continent, several centuries earlier, many Roma retained their traditional, nomadic life-styles well into the nineteenth century. However, increasing numbers had opted, or been coerced, into more sedentary patterns of behaviour. The lack of a national territory, or even of any consciousness of a 'lost' national territory, may go at least some way towards explaining why a national consciousness failed to develop amongst the Roma.

Most importantly, perhaps, the various communities casually identified as 'Gypsies' or 'Roma' by the outside world have never conceived of themselves as belonging collectively to a single cultural, let alone 'national', group. The characterisation as 'Gypsies' of musicians, wooden spoon and wooden trough carvers, brush makers, blacksmiths, coppersmiths, horse traders, smallholders, bear trainers, beggars and a host of other occupational groups living in, or moving between, numerous European countries with which they had been associated for varying lengths of time, and speaking a startling variety of languages and dialects, is an ascribed identity. It does not correspond with the Gypsies' view of themselves, neither then nor now. As Angus Fraser has pointed out, there is still 'no single Romani word corresponding to "Gypsy"' (Fraser 1995: 8). Instead, '[e]ach Gypsy grouping tends to look upon itself as being the authentic Gypsies' (Fraser 1995: 8). In view of the diversity of communities involved, displaying sharply divergent incomes, customs and life-styles, only one thing could be said to have united them – the fact that they 'looked the same', or 'seemed the same', to those who were labelling them. But they did not seem the same to one another.

Limited but illuminating parallels can be drawn with the experience of Europe's Jews. Jews, like Gypsies, had no national territory in Europe to call their own and were often regarded, like Gypsies, as an alien and barely tolerated presence. However, Jewish attitudes to nationalism were frequently very different to those of the Roma. Where local circumstances had permitted a significant degree of economic, cultural and sometimes political integration, many Jews grew to identify with the nation in whose midst they were settled and whose language, customs and culture they had

---

[4]   The term '*gadžé*', or '*gadžó*', is a Romani word for some, or all, non-Roma people.

adopted. This was, in general, more true of Western than of Eastern Europe as the pace of Jewish emancipation was mostly faster in the West (Johnson 1995: 312–313). However, in Eastern Europe, it could be said of Hungary where, in 1848, as many as 20,000 Jews had joined the Hungarian troops fighting for independence from Austria. Jews represented an estimated 11 per cent of the Hungarian army although they constituted only 2.5 per cent of the overall population (Patai 1996: 280). Although some Gypsies also identified with the Hungarian cause, their involvement tended to be more limited and, as far as can be ascertained, affected a significantly smaller proportion of the Gypsy population.

While many Jews, particularly in comparatively liberal societies, grew to identify with the nation amongst whom they were living, towards the end of the nineteenth century a new nationalist vision offered itself. Theodor Herzl, a Viennese Jewish journalist, propounded a doctrine of Jewish nationalism, Zionism (Gilbert 1978: 48–51). As a national minority without any territory of their own, Jews were encouraged by Zionism to view Palestine, their 'lost' or 'historic' national home, as the natural focus of their aspirations.

The development of an ideology of Jewish nationalism had represented a conscious and quite deliberate reaction to the persistence of anti-semitism in even the most apparently liberal European countries, such as France. Herzl, who had been the Paris correspondent of the Austrian *Neue Freie Presse* since 1891, was shocked by evidence of mounting anti-semitism in France, culminating in the notorious trial and conviction of Captain Dreyfus. Zionism, in the view of its proponents, offered the Jews the prospect of liberation from routine discrimination, hostility and suspicion by forging them into a nation in their own right, with their own homeland. As Herzl argued in his book, *The Jewish State*, published in 1896, the Jews are 'one people – our enemies have made us one' (Gilbert 1978: 49). A hundred years later, much the same argument is now being made by Roma intellectuals about the Roma.

However, Zionism was not borne simply of despair. It also represented one particular response to the problem of Jewish identity in a world which had come to emphasise secular rather than religious distinctions (Avineri 1981: 13). Zionism offered Jews a specifically Jewish national identity, a means of affirming their pride in their distinctive origins, history and culture, and a powerful secular alternative to either a confessional identity or to integration, far less assimilation, within Christian (or Moslem) societies. Zionism, like the later black consciousness movement in the United States, with its slogan 'Black is Beautiful', allowed a despised minority to invert the traditionally negative images which they evoked in the wider community and to make difference a source of pride and the basis of a self-ascribed identity.

I have dwelt, at some length, on the conditions under which a specifically Jewish national consciousness developed at the end of the nineteenth century, albeit amongst a minority of Europe's Jews. I have done so because, in many ways, they mirror the circumstances in which a Roma national consciousness has begun to form a full century later. Like Zionism, the stirrings of a Roma national consciousness can be understood as both a reaction to on-going discrimination and persecution as well as an attempt to respond to the 'challenge of ... identity' in a changing world (Avineri 1981: 13). There is another parallel with the Jewish, or Zionist, experience. Just as

Zionism was taken up by only a small minority of Jews at the end of the nineteenth century, so the notion of a specifically Roma national consciousness is currently shared by only a fraction of the Roma. However, the idea has, understandably, taken root amongst the Roma intelligentsia and amongst many Roma activists and community leaders. For example, one of a number of influential Roma NGOs operating in Europe, the Roma National Congress, has put forward a number of 'General Principles'; these include the assertion that the Roma 'are a European nation'.[5] Calling for a 'European Charter of Romani Rights', the Congress seeks recognition of the Roma's 'right to political representation as an ethnic minority in national legislatures and as a nation in multilateral organizations'.[6]

Recognition of the Roma as a 'nation' and as a 'national or ethnic minority' is, particularly in tactical terms, highly advantageous. The international community is familiar with these categories and Europe, in particular, has evolved an elaborate structure of inter-locking norms and institutions to articulate and safeguard the rights of such minorities (Pogany 1998: 166–176). National, or minority, status thus affords the Roma a range of substantive rights as well as sources of institutional support. Some of these will be examined in Part 3.

However, such intellectual and essentially *gadźó* (i.e. non-Gypsy) abstractions as a Roma 'nation' have little meaning, as yet, for the great mass of the Roma for whom identity is still defined much more narrowly and traditionally. For example, Péter Szuhay, a leading ethnologist and specialist in Roma affairs based at the Museum of Ethnology in Budapest, observes that, '[t]oday in Hungary – while the representatives of the intelligentsia of the various ethnic Gypsy groups are working on the creation of cultural integration of the groups in question – at the level of popular culture we can still discern trench warfare between the different groups' (Szuhay 1997: 674).

Szuhay notes that Hungary's Gypsies can be divided into three broad and often mutually antagonistic categories, Hungarian or 'musician' Gypsies, who comprise the great majority of Gypsies in Hungary and who are Hungarian speaking; the Vlach or '*Oláh*' community of Gypsies, who continue to speak Romani; and, finally, Romanian or '*Beás*' Gypsies, who speak an archaic form of Romanian (Szuhay 1997: 668). Inter-marriage between members of these distinct categories is minimal, while important sub-groups exist within each of the broader Gypsy classifications, based on factors such as occupation, income levels, life-style, familial or clan ties etc. Even inter-marriage between members of different sub-groups within one of the broader Gypsy categories, such as *Beás* Gypsies, is frequently discouraged. Szuhai concludes that, 'while the majority of people in society classify every person described as a Gypsy within a single category, Gypsies themselves use real and symbolic means to express their *differences from one another*, and their adherence to a particular group' (Szuhay 1997: 669).

---

[5] See 'General Principles', http://www.romnews.com. The Roma National Congress was set up specifically to represent the interests of Roma who have become stateless as a result of recent political developments in Central and Eastern Europe.

[6] See 'Why a European Charter on Romani Rights?', http://www.romnews.com.

A British anthropologist, Charles Stewart, who studied a Vlach, or *Oláh*, community in Hungary in the late '80s, concluded that identity for the Roma in the settlement where he was living was defined not by descent or 'ethnicity' but, primarily, by participation in their culture, an important element of which was the Romani language:

> ... when I asked Gypsies how one might become a Rom, the answer, as often as not, was 'if you learn to speak Romany' ... Knowing Romany shaped identity because of the relationships that this involved one in, and so here the two meanings of *romanes*, as language and culture, became one: It was by relating as an equal with other Rom that one established one's shared identity (Stewart 1997: 59).

Stewart goes on to argue that there are, in fact, different degrees or types of identity amongst the Roma:

> In some contexts all people who accepted the *gażó* definition of them as *Cigány* [Gypsy] might be included in the group of 'Gypsies'; more commonly all people who called themselves Rom would be 'in'. At lower 'levels' there were categories of identity generically called *nemzetos* ... *Nemzetos* were not really groups in any sense, but the term referred to a concept used to loosely define differences of style among bands of Gypsies who did things together (Stewart 1997: 60).

Therefore, whether in sociological or anthropological terms, talk of a Gypsy or Roma 'national identity' remains premature. However, in political and legal terms the notion of a Roma 'nation' is undoubtedly a valuable tool for securing enhanced recognition of, and provision for, Europe's Roma peoples. The concept of a Roma 'nation' is also a useful means of promoting cohesion amongst the often fractured Roma communities which exist at the present time and of encouraging greater pride and self-worth amongst the Roma in general. The obvious artificiality of the concept of a Roma 'nation' in no way detracts from its potential usefulness, or from the possibility that it may become a reality at some point in the future.

3.   ACCOMMODATING ROMA NATIONAL IDENTITY IN INTERNATIONAL LAW

a) Enhanced International Concern with Roma-related Issues

There is growing evidence, particularly in Europe, of an unprecedented international concern with Roma-related issues. In general, these have been either a reaction to reports of increasingly common physical assaults on Roma in Central and Eastern Europe, or to the severe social and economic problems experienced by Roma in the CEE states in the transition from Communism. In the often painful shift from command to market economies, the Roma have frequently been conspicuous casualties whether in terms of unemployment, housing, education or social welfare.

For example, at the end of 1993, 64 per cent of non-Roma men in Hungary, aged between 15 and 59, were in employment. By comparison, the proportion of Roma men in employment was only 29 per cent (Kemény 1997: 652). The reasons for this disparity are not hard to find. Under Communism, the Roma were *sedentarised* and *proletarianise*d. While Communist policy required the Roma to be integrated into the general work-force, this was almost invariably done at the lowest levels, often involving factory jobs which were both unskilled and unhealthy (Stewart 1997: Chapter 6). With the collapse of Communism and the closure or scaling-down of many of these uneconomic industries, the Roma have suffered disproportionately.

In terms of the housing and social problems experienced in recent years by the Roma, experts have noted a tendency in certain localities to introduce housing policies which have resulted in 'residential segregation and ghettoization of Romani groups' (OSCE 1998: 16). Such policies have not been confined to Eastern Europe; they have been observed, for example, in localities in Hungary, the Czech Republic, Slovakia, Spain and Greece.

International recognition of the mounting persecution and discrimination experienced by the Roma can be traced back to an important text adopted by the states participating in the Organisation for Security and Co-operation in Europe (OSCE) at a meeting in Copenhagen in June 1990. In the so-called 'Copenhagen Document', the participating states condemned 'totalitarianism, racial and ethnic hatred, anti-semitism, xenophobia' etc., while noting that, '[i]n this context, they also recognise the particular problems of Roma (gypsies)'.[7] Although the nature of these problems were not elaborated, it is clear that the OSCE participating states felt that they were the result of a form of racial or ethnic hatred that was, in some respects at least, comparable to anti-semitism.

Institutionally, the OSCE has become a valuable source of support for Roma-related initiatives. In 1994, in Budapest, the states participating in the OSCE agreed to establish a 'contact point' for Roma and Sinti issues within the Office for Democratic Institutions and Human Rights (ODIHR) of the OSCE. The mandate of the ODIHR was widened, accordingly, to 'act as a clearing-house for the exchange of information on Roma and Sinti (Gypsies) issues' and to 'facilitate contacts on Roma and Sinti (Gypsies) issues between participating states, international organizations and institutions and NGOs' (OSCE 1998: 126–127).

Comparable developments can be found within the Council of Europe. In 1994, the Secretary General of the Council of Europe appointed a Coordinator of Activities on Roma/Gypsies with responsibility, *inter alia*, for co-ordinating 'activities regarding Roma/Gypsies within the Council of Europe', for promoting 'dialogue on policies and problems relating to Roma/Gypsies', and for co-operating with other international organisations, such as the OSCE, which are concerned with Roma issues (Council of Europe 1998: 9). In September 1995, the Committee of Ministers of the Council of Europe established a Specialist Group on Roma/Gypsies, composed of nine

---

[7]   Detailed references to OSCE texts adopted before January, 1998, will not be provided as the entire range of OSCE documents issued between 1973 and 1997 are contained in a CD-ROM available from the OSCE.

permanent members, which meets twice a year to advise the Committee of Ministers and to undertake various other tasks (Council of Europe 1998: 11). In November 1998, with Council of Europe funding, an independent Committee of Jurists, composed of academic and practising lawyers from a variety of jurisdictions, met in Strasbourg to consider a range of legal issues of particular concern to the Roma.

b) Recognition and Accommodation of the Roma as a National or Ethnic Minority

During the Communist era, the Gypsy experience in Central and Eastern Europe was characterised, on the one hand, by a paternalistic concern for the social and economic needs of Gypsies as a *social* class while, on the other, denying their existence as a separate national or ethnic group. For example, a decision of the Political Committee of the Hungarian Communist Party, adopted on 20 June 1961, set the goal of assimilating the Gypsies within Hungarian society. Although the final draft of the decision did not use the term 'assimilate', the underlying aims of the decision were perfectly clear. Thus, the 1961 decision condemned, *inter alia*, perspectives which favoured the development of the Romani language, the establishment of Romani-speaking schools, colleges or co-operatives, because 'these viewpoints are not just wrong, they are also harmful as they conserve the separateness of the Gypsies and slow down their integration in society' (Sághy 1996: 57). Similarly, the 1961 decision had opposed 'the separation of Gypsy youth' from their non-Gypsy peers, whether through the establishment of separate youth organisations or other means. In economic matters, the decision reaffirmed the policy of integrating Gypsies, as far as possible, within the general work-force.

The collapse of Communism in the CEE states has ushered in a new era with regard to the recognition of minority rights. The Roma, along with many other groups, have been beneficiaries of this process. As an OSCE text issued in October 1998 notes, '[t]he increasing recognition of Roma as a national minority is one of the most remarkable achievements' of the decade (OSCE 1998: 6). As the OSCE report notes, the enhanced recognition of the Roma and of other national minorities in recent years has resulted from 'both internal pressures from more actively involved minorities, and external pressures' (OSCE 1998: 6).

Explicit acknowledgement of the Roma as a national minority can be found, for example, in successive Recommendations of the Parliamentary Assembly of the Council of Europe. Although 'soft-law' texts, and thus not directly a source of legal obligation, the Recommendations are of major importance as an expression of contemporary political thinking on the Roma. Of course, they may also be used by tribunals and by other international bodies as interpretative aids in evaluating the scope, *ratione personae*, of binding legal instruments concerned with national and ethnic minorities.

Recommendation 1203, adopted by the Parliamentary Assembly in February 1993, notes in paragraph 2 that '[a] special place among the minorities is reserved for Gypsies' and that they are 'a true European minority', while paragraph 6 emphasises that, '[r]espect for the rights of Gypsies ... and their rights as a minority, is essential to improve their situation'(Council of Europe 1998: 43). Recommendation 1353, on 'Access of Minorities to Higher Education', which was adopted by the Assembly in January 1998, confirms that the Roma have been recognised as a minority. The Recommendation notes that, 'the socio-economic situation of minorities is very often also an obstacle to their access to higher education. This is particularly true in the case of Roma/Gypsies'.[8]

As is well known, the Council of Europe's Framework Convention for the Protection of National Minorities, which entered into force in February 1998 and which has been ratified or acceded to by 31 states at the time of writing, contains no definition of 'national minorities'. More worryingly, it remains unclear whether the Committee of Ministers of the Council of Europe will even challenge decisions by individual contracting states as to which minority groups they have chosen to recognise for the purposes of the Convention. A number of states, including Germany, have made declarations emphasising that, as the Framework Convention contains no definition of the concept of national minorities, '[i]t is therefore up to the individual Contracting Parties to determine the groups to which it shall apply'.[9] A purely subjective determination of this sort, made by each party to the Framework Convention, could be detrimental to the interests of minorities such as the Roma who could find themselves arbitrarily excluded from the list of national minorities recognised by individual states.

A number of contracting states have made declarations expressly recognising that the Framework Convention will be applied to members of the Roma community living in their respective countries (Macedonia, Slovenia). More restrictively, the German declaration states that the Convention 'will ... be applied to the Sinti and Roma *of German citizenship*'.[10] Other declarations, while not referring to the Roma as such, emphasise that treatment in accordance with the Convention will be confined to members of minorities who are citizens of the states in question (Austria, Estonia, Luxembourg, Switzerland).

Linking citizenship, or even long-term residence, to the enjoyment of minority status under the Framework Convention has particular and possibly unique implications for the Roma. Unlike most other minority populations in Europe, the Roma are a non-territorial minority who traditionally enjoyed a nomadic way of life. Although the overwhelming majority of Europe's Roma have been sedentarised, voluntarily or otherwise, it is clear that essentially *gadžó* notions such as 'borders' or even 'states' do not have the same meaning for many Roma. Historically, the Roma have migrated from one country to another in an effort to flee persecution or in search of improved economic opportunities. Prominent migratory patterns, an apparent readiness to move on, remain a conspicuous feature of many Roma communities today and represent an aspect of Roma culture and identity. In part, of course, these patterns are also the legacy of the collapse of Communism in the CEE states and the greater opportunities for Romanian, Slovak and other Roma to move

---

[8] For details of Assembly Recommendations see http://stars.coe.fr/.
[9] All information relating to declarations made by parties to the Framework Convention have been obtained from the Council of Europe's website.
[10] My emphasis.

westwards. Consequently, significant numbers of Roma in Germany, as elsewhere in Western and Central Europe, do not possess the citizenship of the countries in which they are presently living.

As these difficulties demonstrate, acknowledging that the Roma constitute a European national minority is not the same as accommodating them. The latter would require states to take proper account of the cultural, social and economic features which distinguish the Roma from most 'traditional' national minorities. As Recommendation 1203 of the Parliamentary Assembly of the Council of Europe emphasises, the Gypsies 'are a true European minority, *but one that does not fit in the definitions of national or linguistic minorities'.*[11]

There is, as yet, little evidence of a widespread or systematic willingness to acknowledge the 'differentness' of Roma culture or to accommodate these differences adequately. The underlying conservatism of the judges of the European Court of Human Rights, for example, was exposed in *Buckley v. United Kingdom.*[12] The Court rejected the arguments of the applicant, a Roma woman, who had complained that the refusal of planning authorities to allow her to live in caravans with her children on land that she had bought infringed her right to respect for her 'home', within the meaning of Article 8 of the European Convention on Human Rights, or that it amounted to unlawful discrimination against her as a Gypsy (Article 14 in conjunction with Article 8(1)). The Court emphasised, instead, the importance of the doctrine of margin of appreciation, which allows each contracting state a significant measure of discretion in the implementation of particular rights (paras. 74–84). The Court concluded, with respect to Article 14: [13]

> More generally, it does not appear that the applicant was at any time penalised or subjected to any detrimental treatment for attempting to follow a traditional gypsy lifestyle. In fact, it appears that the relevant national policy was aimed at enabling gypsies to cater for their own needs.

The finding of the Court ignored evidence that the relevant 'national policy' did not meet the needs of the applicant, a single parent with young children, who was afraid to use the designated local caravan site because of unruly and violent behaviour by some of the residents (paras. 24–26).

More recently, in *Assenov and others v. Bulgaria,*[14] the European Court of Human Rights considered a case brought by a young Rom and his parents in which the applicants had alleged, *inter alia*, that police in Bulgaria had assaulted the young man, then aged 14, and that no proper investigation had been carried out by the authorities. Although the case raises a number of points of interest, it does not really

---

[11] My emphasis.
[12] *Buckley v. UK,* HUDEC Ref. No: REF00000664, available at http://www.dhcour. coe.fr/, the website of the European Court of Human Rights.
[13] *Ibid.*, para. 88.
[14] *Assenov and Others* v. *Bulgaria*, Ref. No: REF00001054   http://www.dhcour.coe.fr/. See also, *Velikova* v. *Bulgaria*, Ref. No: REF 00001501, *ibid.*

address the issues of acknowledging or accommodating Roma identity and will not be discussed further here.

4.   CONCLUSIONS

Despite the arresting title of Michael Stewart's book, published in 1997, it is hard to believe that we are witnessing 'the time of the Gypsies'. Nevertheless, this is undoubtedly a critical point in the often painful history of this minority. In an era of almost unprecedented concern for minority rights,[15] the Roma are now firmly recognised as one of the continent's largest, and most complex, minorities. In part, this perception has resulted from external factors; however, in part, it stems from the pressures exerted by a growing number of Roma NGOs, pressure groups, political and cultural organisations etc. In the eyes of the Roma intelligentsia, inter-governmental organisations and a growing number of states the Roma are a national, or at least ethnic, minority with all of the rights and entitlements that follow from this status. Of course, as argued above, the bulk of the Roma have yet to be convinced that they are truly 'a European nation' as proclaimed by the Roma National Congress in their General Principles. A genuine, and widely held, Roma national consciousness will take time to develop and may never fully crystallise if circumstances are unhelpful.

How has International Law accommodated the nascent or embryonic national identity of the Roma? At the level of rhetoric, International Law has taken giant strides. As noted above, a succession of international instruments now recognise the Roma as a national or ethnic minority. However, accommodation is something else. In an avowedly multicultural Europe, the strains of coexistence, let alone accommodation, are all too evident. As Recommendation 1203 of the Council of Europe's Parliamentary Assembly acknowledges, the Roma are *different* from other minorities in a number of important respects. The process of genuine and meaningful accommodation, as distinct from formal acknowledgement, has barely begun.

REFERENCES

Avineri, S. (1981). *The Making of Modern Zionism*. London: Weidenfeld & Nicolson.
Bideleux, R. & Jeffries, I. (1998). *A History of Eastern Europe*. London & New York: Routledge.
Council of Europe (1998). *Activities of the Council of Europe concerning Roma/ Gypsies and Travellers*. Strasbourg: Council of Europe.
Crowe, D. (1996). *A History of the Gypsies of Eastern Europe and Russia*. New York: St. Martin's Griffin.

---

[15] It would be wrong to suggest that the current concern for minority rights is entirely without precedent. The political settlement following the First World War was characterised, in part, by its attention to minority rights.

Davies, N. (1986). *Heart of Europe*. Oxford: Oxford University Press.

Fraser, A. (2nd ed., 1995). *The Gypsies*. Oxford: Blackwell.

Gilbert, M. (1978). *Exile and Return*. London: Weidenfeld & Nicolson.

Johnson, P. (1995). *A History of the Jews*. London: Phoenix.

Kemény, I. (1997). A magyarországi roma (cigány) népességről [On the Hungarian Roma (Gypsy) people], *Magyar Tudomány* 42: 644–655.

Macartney, C.A. (1968). *The Habsburg Empire 1790 – 1918*. London: Weidenfeld and Nicolson.

Okey, R. (2nd ed., 1986). *Eastern Europe 1740–1985*. London: Harper Collins Academic.

OSCE. (1998, Background Paper No. 4) *Public Policies Concerning Roma and Sinti in the OSCE Region*. Warsaw: OSCE/ODIHR.

Patai, R. (1996). *The Jews of Hungary*. Detroit: Wayne State University Press.

Pogany, I., (ed.) (1995). *Human Rights in Eastern Europe*. Aldershot: Edward Elgar.

Pogany, I. (1998). International Human Rights Standards and the New Constitutions: Minority Rights in Central and Eastern Europe, pp. 155–186, in: R. Mullerson, M. Fitzmaurice, M. Andenas (eds.), *Constitutional Reform and International Law in Central and Eastern Europe*. The Hague: Kluwer Law International.

Rothschild, J. (1974). *East Central Europe between the Two World Wars*. Seattle: University of Washington Press.

Sághy, E. (1996). A magyarországi cigányság története a Holocausttól az 1961-es párthatározatig – A politika tükrében [A History of Hungarian Gypsies from the Holocaust until the 1961 Party Decision – in the Mirror of Politics]. Typescript, ELTE University, Budapest, Hungary.

Stewart, M. (1997). *The Time of the Gypsies*. Boulder, Colorado: Westview Press.

Szücs, J. (1983). The Three Historical Regions of Europe, *Acta Historica Academiae Scinetiarum Hungaricae* 29: 131–184.

Szuhay, P. (1997). Akiket cigányoknak neveznek – akik magukat romának, muzsikusnak vagy beásnak mondják [Those who are called Gypsies and who call themselves Roma, musician or *beás*], *Magyar Tudomány* 42: 656–674.

The Rights of Ethnic Minorities in Pakistan: A Legal Analysis[1] (with particular reference to the Federally Administered Tribal Areas)

Shaheen Sardar Ali*

INTRODUCTION

The purpose of this chapter is to analyse rights of ethnic minorities in Pakistan from a constitutional/legal perspective. It will be argued that the position adopted by the founding fathers of the state vis-à-vis the multi-ethnic composition of the newly emergent Muslim state of Pakistan was flawed in its conceptualisation of a monolithic Muslim identity of its citizens to the exclusion of their diverse ethnic, linguistic and cultural identities. Using the example of the Federally Administered Tribal Areas (FATA) of Pakistan, the chapter will attempt to demonstrate the proposition that post-independence state structures were constrained to address this diversity among the population. Measures adopted to this end were however, based on political expediency rather than a genuine recognition and respect for special needs of these ethnic groups. Being half-hearted and *ad hoc,* these steps are held responsible by many for widening chasms between the ethnic groups at various levels.

Pakistan is a Federal State, and in studying the laws applicable to the various peoples, it is imperative to address the interplay between constitutional provisions according recognition and protection to minorities, and the governance structures formulated at the provincial level. Since 'formal' laws are not the sole regulatory norms governing the lives of the various groups of people living in Pakistan, it is also pertinent to look into the parallel legal systems (which are often informal and based on customary norms) working alongside the black letter law and regulations, and their impact on ethnic minority rights. After providing a brief overview of the various ethnic, linguistic and cultural groups in Pakistan, this paper will proceed to engage in an analysis of the constitutional provisions affecting recognition and protection of ethnic minorities. Part 3 of the chapter will attempt to present a

---

* *Professor of Law, University of Peshawar, Pakistan, presently Reader at the School of Law, University of Warwick, England*
[1] This paper draws on research undertaken for a World Bank project, co-authored with J. Rehman Cheema entitled *Ethnic Minority Issues in Pakistan: A Legal Perspective* submitted to the World Bank in November 1997.

Stephen Tierney (ed.), Accommodating National Identity: New Approaches in International and Domestic Law, 189–209
© 2000 *Kluwer Law International. Printed in Great Britain.*
First published in the International Journal on Minority and Group Rights, Volume 6 No. 1/2 1999.

description of the governance structures applicable to ethnic groups and analysis of the information on the Ministries in charge of minorities at both national and provincial level. Throughout the fifty-one years of the existence of Pakistan, courts have played an important role (arguably both negative and positive) in establishing fundamental rights and modes of governance of the people of Pakistan, including those belonging to ethnic minorities. This paper will also discuss some of these landmark cases in so far as they relate to issues of ethnic minorities.

1.   ETHNIC, LINGUISTIC AND CULTURAL GROUPS IN PAKISTAN: A BRIEF OVERVIEW

Pakistan, formally designated as the Islamic Republic of Pakistan, came into existence in 1947, when British colonial rule in the Indian subcontinent came to an end. It was carved out of the Indian sub-continent comprising areas inhabited by a predominantly Muslim population. Under its 1973 constitution, Pakistan is a federal state with four federating units (known as provinces), and some Federal territory. Punjab, meaning the land of five rivers and the home province of the Punjabi ethnic group, is the most populous and affluent of the provinces and administrative units of Pakistan.[2] It has a rich and fascinating history, where many races came and were absorbed in the 'melting pot' of Punjabi civilisation. Sindh, too, has a history going back thousands of years and is the home of the Indus Valley civilisations. Islam was introduced to the Sindhis in 711 AD when it was conquered by Arab Muslims. Baluchistan, the largest of the four provinces, is home to the Baluch, an ethnic group spread across three countries, Pakistan, Iran and Afghanistan. Pukhtuns mostly inhabit the North-West Frontier Province (NWFP) of Pakistan, some parts of Baluchistan and Afghanistan.

In addition to these four provinces, the country also has areas designated as the Federally Administered Northern Areas (FANA), and the State of Azad Jammu and Kashmir (AJ&K). Some of the tribal areas, located in NWFP and Baluchistan, are known as Provincially Administered Tribal Areas (PATA) and are under the control of the provinces; others the Federally Administered Tribal Areas (FATA) referred to above are under the administrative control of the Federal government. The inhabitants of PATA and FATA are mostly Pukhtun and Baluch.

2.   COMPOSITION AND GEOGRAPHICAL LOCATION OF FATA

Since colonial times certain border areas of the sub-continent had to be designated as tribal areas and 'controlled' rather than ruled, through specially designated personnel. After the creation of Pakistan, the government continued this practice. Tribal areas are defined by Article 246 of the constitution according to which:

---

[2]   Punjab, was divided at the time of the partition of India, the western flank becoming part of Pakistan and the eastern portion remaining as part of India.

(a) 'Tribal Area' means areas in Pakistan which, immediately before the commencing day, were Tribal Areas and include
 (i)   the Tribal Areas of Baluchistan and the North-West Frontier Province; and
 (ii) the former states of Amb, Chitral, Dir and Swat.
These tribal areas are further sub-divided into:
(b) 'Provincially Administered Tribal Areas' (PATA) which means
 (i)   the districts of Chitral, Dir and Swat (which includes Kalam) [the tribal area of Kohistan district] Malakand Protected Area, the Tribal Area adjoining [Mansehra] district and the former states of Amb; and
 (ii) Zhob district, Loralai district (excluding Duki Tehsil), Dalbandin Tehsil of Chagai District and Marri and Bugti tribal territories of Sibi district; and
(c) 'Federally Administered Tribal Areas' (FATA) which includes
 (i)   Tribal areas adjoining Peshawar districts;
 (ii)   Tribal areas adjoining Kohat district;
 (iii) Tribal areas adjoining Bannu district;
 (iv)   Tribal areas adjoining Dera Ismail Khan district;
 (v)   Bajaur Agency;
 (vi)   Orakzai Agency;
 (vii) Mohmand Agency;
 (viii) Khyber Agency;
 (ix)   Kurram Agency;
 (x)   North Waziristan Agency; and
 (xi)   South Waziristan Agency.

Article 247 of the constitution of Pakistan further reaffirms the separate legal status of the tribal areas, continuing in the tradition of the colonial powers of simply 'containing' the 'unruly tribals' rather than extending to them the rights and privileges which are theirs as responsible and equal citizens of an independent country. The executive authority of the Federation extends to the Federally Administered Tribal Areas (FATA), and that of the North West Frontier Province (NWFP) and Baluchistan to the Provincially Administered Tribal Areas (PATA). The President rules the tribal areas through his agent, the Governor of the province where the particular tribal area is situated and gives him directions in this regard. No act of Parliament applies to FATA or any part of it, unless the President so directs. Thus the President enjoys far-reaching legislative functions and powers in respect of making regulations for the peace and good government of a tribal area or any part thereof. The President also may, at any time, by Order, direct that the whole or any part of a tribal area shall cease to be a 'Tribal Area', and such order may contain such incidental and consequential provisions as appear to the President to be necessary and proper. Such an Order, however may only be made after ascertaining the views of the people of the Tribal Area concerned, as represented in tribal *jirga* but in a manner as considered appropriate by the President himself.

Neither the Supreme Court nor a High Court can exercise any jurisdiction under the constitution in relation to a Tribal Area, unless the Parliament by law provides otherwise. Thus, despite being integral parts of Pakistan, these territories are governed through special laws and not by the ordinary laws of the country, and are denied access to judicial forums of the country. An anomalous situation thus arises here in terms of whether persons belonging to FATA enjoy any fundamental rights of citizenship as envisaged in the constitution. Since these entitlements may be invoked primarily through the judiciary and, since inhabitants of FATA are denied recourse to courts, what is the status of other constitutional provisions affording rights to citizens of the state? The following section of the paper seeks to address this issue.

3. CONSTITUTIONAL PROVISIONS AFFECTING ETHNIC MINORITIES IN PAKISTAN: SCOPE AND APPLICATION TO FATA

In independent Pakistan, the constitutional and legislative apparatus reflects a considerable amount of hesitancy and ambiguity on the subject of ethnic and linguistic minorities. On the one hand, it provides an explicit recognition of the distinct status of what has been termed by Article 247 of the Constitution of the Islamic Republic of Pakistan 1973, 'Tribal Areas' and on the other, the State has betrayed a sense of nervousness in its constitutional practices on debates relating to the identification of ethnic and linguistic minorities in general. For purposes of our discussion the question that may be posed is: Are people of FATA a 'minority' to whom special protection may be offered or, are they simply 'different' to the rest of the population due to the sensitive geopolitical context in which they are located?

Although the term has been used in the 1973 Constitution on a number of occasions,[3] there is no definition of what constitutes a minority. The meaning of minority that was taken by the drafters of the constitution and has been subsequently adopted is that minorities necessarily means religious minorities.[4] It is also the case that none of the population census conducted in the country since 1961 attempted to provide a figure on the basis of ethnicity. In so far as linguistic identity is concerned, the official census since 1961 has not contained any specific question about the mother tongue of the respondents. Indeed while the language data from the 1972 census was not published at all,[5] the last census held in 1981 provides information relating to what is termed a family question on 'language commonly spoken in the household'.[6] The official census which according to the constitutional provisions

---

[3]   See e.g. the Preamble, Articles 2(a) and 36.
[4]   This view is confirmed through the proceedings of the Committee on the Elimination of All Forms of Racial Discrimination (which works in pursuance of the Convention on the Elimination of All forms of Racial Discrimination 1965) and the ensuing debate thereon. According to the International Commission of Jurists: 'It is only the non-Muslim religions that are formally recognised by the government as constituting minorities and for whom special, albeit not entirely favourable arrangements are considered appropriate. The only way in which the interests of various linguistic and cultural groupings in the province can be protected therefore, is through the constitutional provisions establishing provincial governments and assemblies'. International Commission of Jurists (1987). *Pakistan Human Rights After Martial Law*, Report of a Mission. Geneva, 115.
[5]   See Wirsing, R. (1981). The Baluch Frontier Tribes of Pakistan, pp. 271–312, 309, in: Wirsing, R. (ed.), *Comparative Perspectives Protection of Ethnic Minorities*. New York: Pergamon Press.
[6]   According to a United Nations Report the question was presented to a random sample of 10 per cent of the respondents. *UN Pakistan, Report of a Mission on Needs Assessment for Population Assistance* (Nov. 1979). Rep. No. 23, 26.

was due to be held in 1991 was postponed for a variety of reasons thus contributing to the difficulty in analysing accurate figures of ethnic minorities.[7]

The 1973 constitution of Pakistan as the main legal document, both in terms of providing substantive rights as well as laying down standard setting norms, contains a number of articles that may be usefully employed in protecting and promoting the rights of ethnic minorities in the country. The question for purposes of the present paper is the scope and extent to which these may be applied to ensure rights to persons belonging to FATA.

The preamble to the constitution declares that adequate provisions shall be made for the minorities to freely profess and practice their religions and develop their cultures, and that fundamental rights, including equality of status, of opportunity before law, social, economic and political justice, and freedom of thought, expression, belief, faith, worship and association, subject to law and public morality shall be accorded to all citizens. The preamble also makes a commitment for adequate provision to safeguard the legitimate interests of minorities and backward and depressed classes.

Article 2(a) inserted in the constitution under the Presidential Order No. 14 of 1985 is also known as the Objectives Resolution of 1949. It has always formed the preambular statement of successive constitutions of Pakistan until 1985 when it was made a substantive part of the constitution of Pakistan. It contains reference to safeguarding rights and interests of minorities.

A reading of the preamble to the constitution however, reflects the reluctance on the part of the framers of the constitution to acknowledge the existence of diverse ethnic, linguistic and cultural groups in Pakistan. It may be argued that there appears an indication of this reluctance in the preambular statement that: '... adequate provisions shall be made for the minorities to profess their religion and develop their culture'.

Although one may analyse and read the above provision in more ways than one, i.e., it may be interpreted to mean that religious minorities as well as cultural minorities are being indicated here, I would propose to interpret this as follows: in the absence of any recognition accorded to minorities other than religious minorities, the only logical and indeed permissible reading of the aforesaid statement is that adequate provisions shall be made for members of religious minorities to develop their religion and culture. There does not appear any clear reference to development of culture or identity apart from, and in addition to, the right given to religious minorities.

Other articles of general application to all citizens of Pakistan may also be applicable to members of ethnic, linguistic and religious minorities. Thus the right of individuals to be dealt with in accordance with law,[8] supremacy of fundamental

---

[7]   According to the Human Rights Commission of Pakistan 'the immigrant population settled in Sindh... strongly contested the figures that emerged from preliminary enumerations. Others disputed the 1981 count too. Representative bodies of Christians, for instance, put the present size of their community in excess of 5 million; Ahmadis claimed their number to be in the region of four million. Their grievance tended to be frequently voiced regarding the number of seats for minorities in the national and provincial legislatures which is fixed in proportion to their population, and there is a feeling amongst the minorities of being grossly underrepresented'. Human Rights Commission of Pakistan (1992). *State of Human Rights in Pakistan,* Lahore: Maktabi Jadeed, 119.

[8]   Article 4, constitution of the Islamic Republic of Pakistan.

rights,[9] security of the person, safeguards as to arrest and detention,[10] inviolability of the dignity of the person and privacy of the home,[11] freedom of movement,[12] freedom of assembly,[13] freedom of association[14] and freedom of speech.[15] With regard to whether these rights are extendible to FATA, the question arises as to whether one set of constitutional provisions may be used to nullify the effects of another. Article 247 clearly states that only those laws promulgated by the President and any other laws that he may deem appropriate, shall be extended to FATA. Since the ordinary courts of law do not operate within FATA, which forum would a citizen approach to seek a remedy?

The argument that the term 'minorities' contained in the constitution, is mainly interpreted to mean religious minorities as opposed to ethnic, and linguistic groups is further strengthened by the many constitutional provisions on the subject as well as a special seat allocation in Parliament. Thus the constitution provides for freedom to profess religion and to manage religious institutions,[16] safeguards against taxation for purposes of any particular religion[17] and safeguards as to attendance in educational institutions in order to receive religious instruction or take part in any religious ceremony, or attend religious worship, if such instruction, ceremony or worship relates to a religion other than his own.[18] In order to provide a voice to religious minorities, Article 51(2A) of the constitution provides for ten additional seats for persons belonging to the Christian, Hindu, Sikh, Buddhist, Parsi and Qadiani religious communities in the National Assembly. A similar reservation of seats is made in provincial legislatures under Article 106(3) for members of the above mentioned religious minorities.[19]

Next we have three articles that constitute the equality and non-discrimination articles of the constitution. These include the fundamental right to equality before law and equal protection of the law,[20] non-discrimination in respect of access to public places,[21] and safeguards against discrimination in services.[22] It is submitted that these articles, as justiciable provisions of the chapter on fundamental rights in the constitution have the potential for providing a strong foundation for protection of minority rights in Pakistan. To date however, the equality and non-discrimination

---

[9]   *Ibid.*, Article 8.
[10] *Ibid.*, Article 9.
[11] *Ibid.*, Article 14.
[12] *Ibid.*, Article 15.
[13] *Ibid.*, Article 16.
[14] *Ibid.*, Article 17.
[15] *Ibid.*, Article 19.
[16] *Ibid.*, Article 20.
[17] *Ibid.*, Article 21.
[18] *Ibid.*, Article 22.
[19] Note the explanation to Article 106 of the constitution which states that 'where no independent seat is allocated to a minority in a province for being very small in number, the seat allocated jointly to all other non-Muslims in that province shall be deemed to include that minority'. Why is the reference to a minority in the constitution of Pakistan always a reference to a religious minority and not to ethnic, linguistic or racial minorities?
[20] Article 25, constitution of the Islamic Republic of Pakistan.
[21] *Ibid.*, Article 26.
[22] *Ibid.*, Article 27.

articles of the constitution have not been upheld by any court in Pakistan to accord equal access to its jurisdiction to inhabitants of FATA.

One of the few indicators that Pakistan has diverse elements other than religious groups in its polity, appears in Article 28 of the constitution where it has been conceded that sections of communities possessing a distinct 'language, script or culture' shall have the right to preserve the same. It is primarily on the strength of this article that one may argue for the rights of ethnic minorities in Pakistan. Furthermore, Article 28 is the only justiciable article in the constitution relating to ethnic minorities in Pakistan, appearing as it does in the chapter on Fundamental Rights. The provisions of this article however, are attenuated in a number of respects as they are subject to those of Article 251 which accords Urdu the status of national language. Urdu remains the official language, which leaves a considerable proportion of the population at a disadvantage.

In Chapter II of the constitution relating to Principles of Policy, articles likely to affect rights of ethnic minorities are enumerated. These include Article 33 which states that the State shall discourage parochial, racial, tribal, sectarian and provincial prejudices among citizens. Article 36 pledges protection of minorities by safeguarding their 'legitimate rights and interests, including due representation in Federal and Provincial services'. Here too, one may be inclined to draw the inference that it is religious minorities that are being referred to, particularly in relation to the provincial services. Finally, Article 37 provides for the promotion of social justice and eradication of evils whereas Article 38 declares the intent of the State to promote the social and economic well-being of the people. It is pertinent to bear in mind that Articles 33–38 fall under the principles of policy and, unlike fundamental rights that are enforceable in a court of law, Principles of Policy are statements of intent and therefore merely standards the Government hopes to achieve progressively.[23]

Language was to emerge as one of the main obstacles in the integration of the Pakistani nation, primarily due to the insensitive manner in which the issue was approached upon attaining independence. At the time of the creation of Pakistan, Urdu was the mother-tongue of only 5 per cent of the population (mainly of the North Indian immigrants). Bengali was spoken by 51 per cent of the people (in East Pakistan), Punjabi in Punjab, Pukhto in the North West Frontier Province, Sindhi in Sindh, Baluchi and Brahvi in Baluchistan, Pahari and other Kashmiri dialects in Azad Kashmir along with virtually a dozen other languages in the Northern Areas of Pakistan. But Urdu was declared the only national language. This led to vehement protests from Bengalis and other non-Urdu speakers. It has to be acknowledged that five decades down the line, Urdu has now acquired the status of a *lingua franca* and is widely spoken and understood around the country, but the insensitive manner in which the language was initially imposed on people for whom it was totally an alien mode of communication created problems for the people of the diverse ethnic groups. It was argued that native Urdu speakers acquired an unfair head start as they could

---

[23] In India however, the past decades have witnessed an increasing trend in litigation by human rights activists successfully invoking the equivalent Directive Principles of Policy as enforceable rights. See for instance the various cases in the area of public interest litigation.

communicate with ease and confidence as well as write and read it, and that 95 per cent of the population were reduced to illiterates in their own country as Urdu was made a compulsory part of the curriculum from primary to high school levels.

Although Pakistan was created on the express belief that Muslims formed one nation and ethnic differences and diversity among its people could be disregarded, by 1973, it was evident that some acceptance of the multi-ethnic identity of the population had to be made. The constitution of Pakistan provides for a Council of Common Interests under Article 153 to enable provinces to air their grievances vis-à-vis the Federation as well as each other. The purpose of this forum is also to ensure a just distribution of assets among the federating units. Cases in point are revenues acquired from the vast natural gas deposits from Sui in Baluchistan and hydroelectric power in the NWFP. Another forum known as the National Economic Council has been provided for under Article 156 of the Constitution the purpose of which is to oversee the economic development and interests of the country.

The discussion surrounding constitutional obligations incurred by the state for protecting rights of FATA therefore tends to become nullified. On the one hand a catalogue of fundamental rights are afforded to every citizen in the state, yet by virtue of another set of constitutional provisions their access to these rights is debarred due to the overriding rule that FATA will only be subject to rule by the President and the Governor/s of the provinces where these areas are located. This rule is facilitated by some institutional mechanisms outlined below.

4.   INSTITUTIONAL ARRANGEMENTS FOR PROTECTION OF ETHNIC MINORITIES IN PAKISTAN, WITH PARTICULAR REFERENCE TO FATA

It is evident that while residents of FATA are citizens of Pakistan and hence governed by the constitution of Pakistan, this status is undermined by the 'special' status accorded to these areas largely due to their contiguity to Afghanistan, a historically 'hostile' neighbour of the British Empire. The independent sovereign state of Pakistan, in continuation of this trend of 'containing' Afghanistan and by extension the former Soviet Union, devised means to curtail the freedom of the people of the tribal areas. At the same time, governments also realised that some semblance of patronage must be seen to be extended to the tribals in lieu of their 'loyalty' to the Pakistan government. This section provides an outline of the institutional structures responsible for governing FATA,[24] including the Ministry of States and Frontier Regions (SAFRON), the informal dispute resolution forums, *jirga*, the *jirga* under the Frontier Crimes Regulation 1901 (FCR), and the FATA Development Corporation (FATADC).

---

[24]   Two other ministries, the Ministry for Kashmir Affairs and Northern Affairs (KANA) and the Ministry of Religious Affairs and Minority Affairs deal with 'special' areas and issues of minorities in Pakistan. KANA oversees the State of Azad Jammu and Kashmir, and the Northern Areas whereas the Ministry of Religious Affairs and Minority Affairs has as its brief: to safeguard rights of minorities as guaranteed under the constitution; promotion of welfare of minorities; protection of minorities from discrimination; representation in international bodies and conferences, including the UN Sub-Commission on Prevention of Discrimination and Protection of Minorities; international commitments and agreements, and implementation of those agreements concerning minorities.

The Ministry of States and Frontier Regions (SAFRON)

This Ministry was created and named on 1 July 1948 by the founder of Pakistan, Muhammad Ali Jinnah less than a year after the creation of Pakistan. Initially it was charged with the responsibility of dealing with the affairs of the Tribal Territories of the North West Frontier, Baluchistan, Baluch Tribals adjoining Dera Ghazi Khan District of the Punjab, the excluded areas (Northern Areas and Azad Jammu and Kashmir) and Princely States who had acceded to Pakistan at the time of partition of India. Subsequently, a separate Ministry for Kashmir and Northern Affairs (KANA) was created, thus narrowing the jurisdiction of SAFRON. By the end of the 1960s, all princely States in Pakistan had been merged with the administrative set-up of the rest of the country, which more or less confined the area of operation of the Ministry to the Tribal Areas of Pakistan. (Additional functions relating to Afghan refugees were, however, taken on by SAFRON due to the war in neighbouring Afghanistan and the resulting refugee exodus since 1979).

As an administrative Division of the Federal Government, SAFRON performs the following functions:

i. Tribal Areas

(a) Administrative and Political Control in the Federally Administered Tribal Areas (FATA);
(b) Development Plans and Programmes of FATA;
(c) All Matters Relating to the FATA Development Corporation;
(d) Issuing of Policy Directives to the Governments of North West Frontier Province and Baluchistan Regarding Tribal Areas;
(e) Matters Relating to the Durand Line;
(f) Anti-subversion Measures;
(g) Agreements with the Tribals.
(h) Application of Laws to, Regulations for, and Alterations in the Tribal Areas;
(i) Administrative Reforms;
(j) Issue of Import Licences to the Tribes;
(k) Visits of Foreigners to the Tribal Areas;
(l) Policy Regarding Detribalisation of the Tribal Areas;
(m) Powindah Policy;
(n) Payment of Maliki Allowance and Individual Service Allowance; and
(o) Nomination of Candidates from the Federally Administered Tribal Areas for Admission to Various Medical Colleges Against Seats reserved for those Areas.

ii. Administrative Control of the Contingents namely:

(a) The Frontier Constabulary;
(b) The Khasadars; and
(c) The Levies.

iii. Employment of the Contingents at ii above, in the Tribal Areas of the North West Frontier Province and Baluchistan iv. Postings and Transfers of Officers in FATA

v. Afghan Refugees

The organisational set-up of SAFRON is as follows:

SAFRON is headed by a Minister who is required to be a member of either House of Parliament (National Assembly or the Senate). On the administrative side, SAFRON has a Secretary as well as a Parliamentary Secretary. The Secretary is assisted by two Joint Secretaries; one dealing with Afghan Refugees and the other in charge of Administration. Each Joint Secretary is in turn assisted by a number of Deputy Secretaries and Section Officers. The FATA Development Corporation, which is an autonomous body created to institutionalise developmental work in the Tribal Areas comes under the purview of SAFRON as well. Since early 1997, the FATA Development Corporation has become the cause for controversy and protest in many quarters of FATA as the Federal Cabinet has decided to wind up this institution. Its final fate is yet awaited.

The FATA Development Corporation:
Its Formation, Life and Impending Demise[25]

Established in 1972 for the economic uplift and development of FATA, the Charter of the Corporation requires it to undertake development schemes in water supply, minerals, industries, agriculture, land reclamation, power and other allied sectors. Prior to the establishment of this Corporation, development work in FATA was being carried out by the line departments of the provincial government. But since the administrative, political and judicial control of the area rests with the Federal government, this arrangement resulted in a duality of authority and responsibility that did not allow these departments to carry out their work efficiently. It was also argued at the time that the provincial line departments responsible for implementation of projects were virtually under the direct control of the political administration in FATA, resulting in more emphasis on political, rather than economic considerations. FATA Development Corporation (FATADC) thus came into existence against this backdrop of heightened concern for execution of development projects based on technical and economic considerations.

According to FATADC sources, the institution has in over 25 years of its existence achieved a great deal towards implementing its mandate of the economic uplift of FATA. It has completed 630 schemes in the water supply sector bringing under irrigation 317,000 acres of previously barren land; 691 tubewells have been drilled out of which 494 have been commissioned, and 11 industrial units were set up

---

[25] This section is based on a number of documents, including the following: the Federally Administered Tribal Areas Development Corporation Regulation 1970; the Federally Administered Tribal Areas Development Corporation Rules 1971; Government of Pakistan Ministry of States and Frontier Regions FATA Development Corporation, Annual Report 1995–1996; articles and briefs published in various national newspapers and magazines on behalf of SAFRON as well as journalists and employees of FATA Development Corporation.

throughout FATA creating 1,200 direct jobs. Almost the whole region (of FATA), has been geologically surveyed and mapped, resulting in identification of 19 precious minerals.

Despite these claims of achievements by the FATADC, the Federal Cabinet took a decision in 1996 to wind up the Corporation on two main counts, i.e., that it has become over-staffed, and its non-development expenditure has exceeded its development allocation. Following this decision of the government of Pakistan,[26] an intensive and prolonged campaign of protest took off using a variety of strategies and methods ranging from approaching the judiciary for redress, to petitioning government bodies, hunger strikes and protest marches. Prominent coverage was given to the issue in the Pakistani press and the support of the people of FATA was also solicited. The government however is abiding by its decision and is seeking a number of alternatives to minimise the effect of this winding up on the employees of FATADC, including absorption into other departments and offering a 'golden handshake' for those opting for early retirement.

A number of issues, however, arise in the context of the formation, working life and now impending demise of an institution that was created to achieve the uplift of a grossly under-developed and backward part of the country. Firstly, was there a basic drawback in the structure, composition and working of FATADC? Was there a slackness on the part of SAFRON in monitoring the organisation leading to its impending demise? If so, why did this lapse go unnoticed for twenty-five years? And, last but not least is the sensitive issue of participation and owning of the FATADC by the people whom it was meant to serve. Has twenty-five years of FATADC made any substantive difference in the lives of the millions of citizens of the area? Has there been any empowering effect of the various projects undertaken by the Corporation on the people of the area? Why does there appear only very lukewarm support for the continuance of an institution from the people who are supposed to have benefited immensely from it?

It is submitted that the attitude of institutions such as SAFRON appears typical of most government departments and ministries i.e., lack of commitment to providing better services and quality of life for the people they are meant to serve. Most of the employees of FATADC were themselves tribals, with the difference that functionaries in decision-making positions were either an urbanised elite who had long since moved away from the area and used their tribal identity only as a 'passport' to the job, or belonged to non-FATA areas. It is worth posing the question as to how relevant this factor has been in the present predicament of the working of SAFRON in general and FATADC in particular? And last, but not least, to what extent is this seeming apathy and lack of commitment a manifestation of tokenism regarding integration of people of FATA as equal citizens of Pakistan?

---

[26] The decision was taken under Article 42(1) of The Federally Administered Tribal Areas Development Corporation Regulation 1970.

The Federally Administered Tribal Areas: Governance Structures

FATA, as defined in Article 246(c) of the constitution of Pakistan comprises areas located in the North West Frontier Province (outlined above). These territories had a unique position prior to the creation of Pakistan and their relationship with the British Crown rested mainly on the treaties and agreements which the tribes of these areas had executed with the Government of India. The agreements with the tribes made them territorially responsible for keeping peace with the government, and for protecting the means of communication passing through their areas, and in lieu thereof they were assured payment of allowances by the government.

On attaining independence in 1947, the government of Pakistan rather than shedding that particular colonial legacy of ruler and ruled, continued with the pre-independence arrangement. The government executed fresh agreements with the tribes who declared their territories as an integral part of Pakistan and the tribesmen inhabiting these areas as its citizens. The tribes, or to put it more accurately, the tribal elders, were assured that they would continue to 'enjoy' the position in the pre-independence period, which consisted of giving them allowances etc. in return for their pledge of loyalty to the government of Pakistan.

Since FATA was not part of the 'settled' areas of Pakistan, the normal civilian government did not function within its borders. The following administrative, political and legal arrangements have been made for the governance of FATA:

- The Governor of the North West Frontier Province has been appointed as agent to the President of Pakistan in FATA and he exercises immediate executive authority in these areas.
- The Chief Secretary, Government of NWFP has been appointed as head of the local administration of FATA.
- The services of the provincial departments are utilised to meet the needs of FATA within their respective spheres of jurisdiction. For this purpose, each Secretary of the provincial government acts as the Secretary to the local administration. The Finance Secretary acts as Financial Adviser to the agent of the President in respect of FATA.
- Special Cells created in the provincial government departments attend exclusively to the affairs of FATA.

The department at the federal level co-ordinating these activities in FATA is SAFRON. In actual terms, governance in FATA is carried out through a Political Agent who governs the area by a number of measures foremost being through the 'co-operation' of the tribal leaders of the area the various mechanisms of which are discussed below.

Maliki is an allowance for the head/s of a tribe and is hereditary, subject to 'good conduct' of the heir of the Malik (head of the tribe), and approval of the government. *Lungi* is a personal allowance for individual service and may be modified on the death of a *lungi* holder. *Mawajib* allowances are those which are paid out to the entire tribe bi-annually.

The main objective of the *malik, lungi* and *muwajib* allowances is to maintain amiable political relations with the tribes, to bind them to the government of Pakistan by excluding other 'influences' and hence outside interference in the area. A further objective is to preserve law, order and security of life and property within the tribal areas, and to keep mountain passes and roads open for trade and communications at all times.

The essence of political control by the mechanisms employed as described above is to maintain law and order in the tribal areas by enforcing tribal and territorial responsibility through accredited representatives of tribes i.e., tribal maliks and elders who are in receipt of allowances. It is intended to use the system for upholding official influence and implementing development programmes.

The Maliks and Elders who receive allowances of a tribe/section are perceived as the political medium and are required to restrain and control their tribesmen from committing any act hostile or subversive to the State. The government policies are implemented in the area through the maliks and elders. The government maintains that it is following a policy of peaceful progress through development by the opening of schools, dispensaries, roads and other development works in the tribal areas with their help. Since the creation of Pakistan, governments in neighbouring Afghanistan had been hostile and were blamed for assisting and abetting Pukhtun demands for a separate homeland for which the term 'Pukhtunistan' was coined. The Pakistan government sought to counteract Afghan propaganda and influence with the help of allowance holders, the maliks and elders.

From a purely legal perspective, FATA has been governed since colonial times through the Frontier Crimes Regulation of 1901 (FCR), the purpose of which was primarily to control and suppress crimes in the tribal areas and not to provide or promote justice. This practice has continued in the post-independence era. However, from time to time and after due consultation with the provincial government, tribal elders, etc. some laws are extended to the area. To date about 365 federal and provincial laws have been extended to FATA.

FATA may be divided into directly administered areas, protected areas and inaccessible tribal territory. The Political Agent uses a different mode of administration for each of these areas depending upon the amount of control that he can exercise therein. For the maintenance of law and order, the FCR is applied in the administered areas. Administered areas are those where the judicial jurisdiction of the Political Agent extends under the FCR, and any offence committed on government roads, offices or other government installations is duly registered and disposed of through a Council of Elders appointed under the Regulation (FCR). In the remaining areas, the Political Agent administers by other means at his disposal, including executive action. The tribes regulate their lives through tribal '*riwaj*' (custom) which differs from tribe to tribe and from agency to agency.

The un-administered areas are those where the tribes take cognisance of civil and criminal disputes and decide them through '*jirgas*' under tribal customs. Finally, there are large chunks of inaccessible areas in every agency of FATA which are governed indirectly by the political agents. All civil and criminal disputes in these areas are decided by the tribesmen themselves.

It has been the policy and stated position of every regime in Pakistan that the FCR has stood the test of time and pressure of destabilising forces generated by various elements in FATA as a result of having a long unmanned border with Afghanistan. Until the Soviet invasion of Afghanistan in 1979, relations with that country were far from cordial and the FCR was seen as an effective 'iron-hand' with which to balance the activities of an unfriendly neighbour. Therefore, despite the persistent demand of the tribals for repeal of the FCR, successive Pakistani governments did not relent. Although the situation has changed radically government functionaries are still of the view that the FCR with its *jirga* system 'suits the genius of the people and has stood the test of time'.[27] Various briefs prepared by SAFRON state that withdrawing the FCR summarily and substituting it with any half-baked measure without introducing a proper alternative legal system would create an administrative vacuum as well as chaos and confusion. Therefore, in the opinion of the government it is neither desirable nor advisable to withdraw the FCR from FATA.

Informal Governance Structures: The Jirga System

In this section it is proposed to trace the historical development, composition and working of the dispute resolution forum of the Pukhtuns and Baluch known as the *jirga*. Contrary to popular belief, the *jirga* does not have a monolithic, uniform identity but is functioning in different forms under different sets of laws, both statutory and customary. The *jirga*, like the *Panchayat* in Punjab and Sindh, was used, with modifications, by the British to enforce law and order (under the FCR), in certain parts of the NWFP and Baluchistan. The traditional *jirga*, nevertheless, continues to exist parallel to the one constituted by the British.[28]

The Traditional Jirga:

The institution of traditional *jirga* of the Pukhtuns and Baluch, has fascinated scholars and lay persons alike through the centuries. Any study on the people of the area, invariably deals at some length with the subject. A particularly lucid description of the *jirga* as given by James W. Spain[29] is reproduced in the following paragraphs:

'A *Jirga* in its simplest form is merely an assembly. Practically all community business, both public and private, is subject to its jurisdiction. In its operation, it is probably the closest thing to Athenian democracy that has existed since the original. It exercises executive, judicial, and legislative functions, and yet frequently acts as an instrument for arbitration or conciliation. Mogul ambassadors, Sikh generals, British administrators unrepentant tribesmen,

---

[27] Quoted from an interview with Lt. General (retd) Muhammad Arif Bangash reported in The News on Sunday, 16 November 1997.

[28] Another category of *jirga* constituted under certain special laws, was a post-independence development, applicable to PATA of NWFP and Baluchistan (now repealed).

[29] Spain, W.J. ed., (1962). *The Pathan Borderland.* New York: Prager.

Pakistani politicians, and American celebrities have stood before *jirgas* during the years.

Elphinstone found the *jirga* in a remarkably high state of organisation when he passed through the Frontier on his way to Kabul in 1809. He describes something like a system of soviets, in which the *kundi* (ward or hamlet) *jirga* sent representatives to a village Jirga, which selected members to a *khel* (clan) *jirga*. This in turn was represented in the main tribal *jirga*. Ultimately, the best representatives of each tribe sat in the *Loe* (Great) *jirga*, which advised and on occasion selected or overturned the Amir or King of Kabul.[30]

The *jirga* system of today is not very different, though the division of the Pathans into nationals of two separate states has eliminated the *Loe jirga* as a practical representation of the entire Pathan community.[31] In an important *jirga*, each *kundi, khel*, and tribe must be represented. There are no elections and no credentials committees. Representatives are usually chosen on the spur of the moment, almost always on the basis of age, shrewdness, and reliability.

The *jirga* is essentially a round table conference. There is no chairman or presiding officer. Everyone whose interest may be affected has a right to speak. Decisions must be unanimous and solemnised by a prayer. If this cannot be achieved, the *jirga* breaks up. A *jirga* may meet under the shade of a solitary tree by the side of a dusty road in Waziristan, or on the spacious green lawns of the Government House at Peshawar.

The *jirga* as it operates today, has three main functions. In its broadest and purest form, it regulates life at all levels within a tribal society requiring community attention, e.g., the choice of a site for a new mosque, punishment for domestic infidelity, settlement of a blood feud, or a decision to take up arms against a neighbouring tribe. Secondly, the *jirga* provides a mechanism by which the decisions or opinions of the tribe are communicated to the Government and the decisions of the government passed to the tribe. In this sense, the *jirga* handles the foreign relations of the tribe and has the authority to commit it to a course of action. A third form, the so-called 'official' *jirga*, composed of men appointed by an officer of the Government of Pakistan, has little to do with *Puktunwali* in the traditional sense. It acts as an advisory jury to an officer in trying crimes under the Frontier Crimes Regulations.

There is seldom any voting in a *jirga*. The 'sense of meeting' is usually abundantly apparent, although its import would frequently curdle the souls of

---

[30] Elphinstone cited by Spain (1962) *ibid.*, 143.
[31] The Government of Afghanistan has incorporated the *Loe jirga* into its political structure. However, it meets seldom and usually only to confirm the policies of the government. Its membership has been revised to represent various groups within Afghanistan rather than only Pathan clans.

the peaceful Friends who coined the term. The armed membership of the *jirga* is its enforcing agency if enforcement is needed. The sanctity accorded the *jirga* is indicated by the fact that very rarely does it break up into a fight. In view of the volatile nature and heavy armament of the Pathan, this is truly a triumph of tradition over instinct.

A subtle point, which is frequently obscured by the semi-judicial role of the *jirga*, is that the body's function is to settle peacefully an existing situation more than to judge right or wrong, determine guilt, or pass sentence. The parties, who in a western court would be plaintiff and defendant, appear as equals. One has usually acted against the other and the nature of the act is generally known and agreed upon by all concerned. The function of the *jirga* is to determine whether what was done was rightly done, and if not, what the party acted against is entitled to do to square accounts.[32] In working out the proper settlement, the *jirga* members take into account the requirements of *Puktunwali*, the circumstances in the particular situation, and the character of the individuals concerned. They are also guided by the generally accepted scale of monetary compensation which an injured party can honourably accept, if he so chooses, instead of retaliation in kind.

Decisions are usually very simple: Mahmud had a right to kill Afzal because Afzal had killed Mahmud's uncle, and no more is made of the affair; Alamgir had acted correctly in killing his wife because she had committed adultery, and his father-in-law had no complaint against him; Hukmat acted unjustly in killing Bashir without cause, and Bashir's relatives are entitled to kill Hukmat, unless they are prepared to accept Rs. 4,000 *nagah* (blood-money) from him, in which case the matter is finished and no *badal* may be taken. When complex disputes over property or inter-tribal feuds are involved, settlement is more complicated, and recourse is usually had to *Shariat*.'[33]

While the detailed account of the traditional *jirga* given above remains essentially valid, a number of factors have contributed in bringing about a slow but sure change in this institution. It will be evident from the discussion below that only the name of this forum has been adopted for dispute resolution under FCR, without incorporating the spirit behind the institution.

Jirga under The Frontier Crimes Regulation

As mentioned above, on attaining independence, Pakistan inherited alongside 'settled' areas and princely states, some tribal or Frontier Districts that had never properly been made part of the British Empire. These were areas considered as a threat to the colonial powers. Therefore, special laws were promulgated for the tribal or Frontier

---

[32] Elphinstone, the first Englishman to observe the system, grasped this point immediately.
[33] Elphinstone cited by Spain (1962) *op. cit.* 143.

Districts the purpose of which was the suppression of crime'.[34] This law called the Frontier Crimes Regulation (FCR) came to be known as the 'black law' due to its extremely harsh, inhuman and discriminatory provisions.[35]

This legal system was designed by the British to rule through a class of local notables who not only enjoyed social influence and status within society but were also loyal to the British.[36] The object was to depict a policy of non-interference in their centuries old system of *Riwaj*;[37] while giving efect to the real purpose which was to deny them a universally recognised judicial system and the basic human right of equality before law and equal protection of laws.[38] The rulers therefore nominated members of the *jirga* which formed part of the dispute resolution mechanism to which the Deputy Commissioner was empowered to refer cases under the FCR. A *jirga* constituted under the FCR must thus be distinguished from the traditional *jirga* applying customary laws of the area.

Unfortunately, the FCR was retained and applied to the tribal areas even after independence and emerged as the first parallel judicial system in Pakistan. It is based on the premise of suppression of crime by infliction of the severest possible punishment. The administration of justice is neither its aim nor purpose.

The FCR, denies the accused due process of law. The entire procedure is based on a system of inquiry conducted by the *jirga* rather than a process of presenting evidence, examination and cross-examination of witnesses etc. It also is not permitted to engage counsel. Appeals to the superior judiciary i.e. the Supreme Court and High Court which are the constitutionally guaranteed right of every citizen of Pakistan, are denied to persons subject to the FCR. The most tragic part of the enforcement mechanism under the FCR, is that an institution as important and revered as the *jirga* has been corrupted and distorted to suit the rulers, first alien and now our own.

The provisions of the FCR have been challenged at different times in the superior courts of the country. In the case of *Toti Khan vs. District Magistrate Sibi and Ziarat*,[39] provisions enabling executive authorities to refer any criminal case to a hand picked *jirga* was challenged as repugnant to Article 5 and void under Article 4 of the 1956 constitution (then in force). S.A. Rehman, C.J., (as he was then) accepting the contention, was of the opinion that the provisions were ex facie discriminatory.

Similarly in *Khan Abdul Akbar Khan vs. Deputy Commissioner Peshawar*,[40] certain provisions applicable to Pathans and Baluchis only, were challenged as violative of Article 5 of the 1956 constitution (then in force) in so far as they did not provide equal protection of law to these communities. Kayani J., ruled that this

---

[34]   Preamble, Frontier Crimes Regulations (Regulation III of 1901).
[35]   For details see text of Frontier Crimes Regulations.
[36]   Per Amir-ul-Mulk Mengal J., speaking for the court in *Balochistan Bar Association vs. Govt. of Balochistan* PLD 1991 Quetta 7.
[37]   Customary law.
[38]   *Op.cit.* in PLD 1991 Quetta 7.
[39]   PLD 1957 (W.P.) Quetta 1.
[40]   PLD 1957 (W.P.) Pesh 100.

amounted 'to racial discrimination and is open to criticism as discrimination between a Negro and a white man'.

Soon after these judgements, Martial Law was imposed in the country (1958), and the 1956 constitution of Pakistan abrogated. Accordingly, fundamental rights were suspended and once again the FCR reigned supreme. In 1979, it was again challenged before the Shariat Bench of the Baluchistan High Court and found repugnant to Islam.[41] The situation as it stands today is that the FCR along with this 'official' *jirga*, still holds sway over FATA, and the citizens of the area labour under all the disabilities resulting from such retrogressive and repressive laws.

Extension of Right to Vote to FATA: The Beginning of a New Era?

In November 1996 when a caretaker government took charge in Pakistan, its main brief was to hold fresh elections within 90 days. A long-standing demand of the people of the tribal areas had been the right to vote on the basis of adult franchise like their counterparts in the rest of the province, and indeed, the country. The caretakers acceded to this demand and for the first time in the history of Pakistan, the people of the tribal areas were allowed to choose their own representatives for Parliament. The Political Parties Act of 1962 was however, not extended to FATA and elections were held on a non-party basis. The enfranchisement of the tribals in the 1997 elections has raised hopes of a qualitative change for the better in their lives by giving them a voice and a political choice. The interesting development of this right to vote has been the massive registration of female voters, who, contrary to the popular belief that women do not participate in the electoral process, were registered and came out in their thousands to cast their votes. It has been argued that this trend in areas like Kurram and South Waziristan was motivated more by the political, tribal and sectarian pressures for each side to outdo their rivals than by a regard for women's rights. But there can be no denial that the inevitable has happened: FATA has 'opened up' to the rest of the country and this initial step will have important implications for the people of the area to seek their legitimate share in the economic resources and institutions of Pakistan.

The Inter-relation of Rights and Duties: A Bitter Pill to Swallow for FATA?

The extension of adult franchise to the tribal areas as well as a number of other laws has given rise to very grave issues in terms of governance and control of the government over FATA. To date the 'special status' card was used by the tribals for not paying any taxes or bills to the federal or provincial government. But in recent years this has led to an impossible situation of millions of rupees worth of loss to the national exchequer due to this non-payment. The area appears to have been caught up in a no-win situation. On the one hand, seeking greater choice in governance is their desire, yet the deep neglect of all governments in Pakistan has resulted in an

---

[41]   *Maulvi Mohammad Ishaque Khosti vs. Govt. of Balochistan* PLD 1979 Quetta 217.

economic crisis that is unparalleled. Barring a few affluent people, the predominant population of the area suffers from unemployment, underdevelopment in all spheres of life such as education, health, water supply and sanitation. The tribals are protesting at the insistence of the government to make them pay their electricity bills; it has been argued that Warsak Dam located in the tribal areas produces electricity and thus is an 'indigenous' resource. But in a recent interview the Governor of the NWFP has stated that Warsak only produces 100 MW of electricity whereas the FATA consumes 400 MW. Where, he queries, will the shortfall come from? Similarly, the Customs Act has also been extended to FATA which the tribals are actively resisting. The government insists that the law is required to control smuggling into the province and the rest of the country.

Yet another major cause for concern in the debate concerning the integration of FATA lies in the fact that the 'special' status of FATA has been exploited by unscrupulous absconding criminals, drugs traffickers and arms smugglers. The people of FATA use the pretext of unemployment and dire economic conditions in the area as reasons for participation in these activities. It is imperative to sense the gravity of the situation and address the grievances of the people if any real progress in arresting the current situation is to be made.

Denial of Fundamental Rights to the Citizens of FATA

The people of FATA have, over the years, developed a sense of isolation from the rest of the country. The recently accorded right to vote has, in the initial period, instilled a sense of hope for a better future in the minds of the people of the tribal areas. But until all structures such as The Political Parties Act, 1962, and access for all political parties to propagate their views freely in the area are put in place, this positive step may suffer a setback.

An important basic right currently denied to the people of FATA is access to the ordinary courts of the land. The FCR implemented by government officials and hand-picked elders cannot be a substitute for the formal court system which needs to be extended to FATA. The sense of alienation in terms of development opportunities in areas of education, health, roads and clean drinking water has aggravated the already unhappy situation. The future of the Tribal Areas appears bleak and with it is endangered the integrity of Pakistan. Unfortunately this very simple fact does not seem to get across to the people in power. Fifty years of independence for Pakistan is meaningless for the Tribals as they simply changed masters, from the British to Pakistani rulers. They have lagged behind not only in the lack of access to basic civic amenities but also in terms of integration into national life. This issue needs some hard thinking and courageous steps on the part of elected representatives to bring about the appropriate constitutional amendments needed to bring the tribal areas into line with the rest of the country.

Concluding Remarks

A significant theme that runs through Pakistan's chequered legal and constitutional history is the politics and sociology of ethnicity and ethnic minorities. Law is not an autonomous entity divorced from the socio-economic and historical background of a people. The legal status of ethnic minorities in Pakistan therefore can only be appreciated if the rationale and context against which laws were formulated, is understood and analysed. This chapter, using the example of FATA, has attempted to analyse laws affecting ethnic minorities in Pakistan by placing the debate in perspective relative to historical events, and to the political and socio-economic compulsions of various governments and key actors.

Incised from British India in August 1947, Pakistan's founding fathers placed an unrealistically high premium on the Islamic character of the new State. Their view was of a State where Islamic values and identity would overshadow and subsume all differences including those based on ethnic, linguistic and cultural diversity. The reality however, as history tells us, turned out to be very different and it was only after the country was truncated (by the secession of East Pakistan to become Bangladesh) and insurgent movements had shaken Baluchistan, that a slow realisation of the multiple identities of the people of Pakistan began to gain a reluctant acceptance. Even so, the official position even today focuses on religious minorities rather than ethnic and linguistic groups distinct from the dominant population.

This reluctance to concede the existence of ethnic groups within the geographical borders of Pakistan is reflected in the inadequacy of the laws which address the issue. Although some constitutional provisions may well be construed and used to attain rights of ethnic groups, these provisions still lie mainly within the non-justiciable chapter of the constitution under the heading of Principles of Policy. It would require an ingenious human rights activist to seek an alternative interpretation as has been the case in India and elsewhere under the rubric of public interest litigation.

The constitution of Pakistan sought to achieve the improvement of the less developed ethnic groups including FATA, by resorting to affirmative action measures. By virtue of these laws, seats have been reserved for various provinces and administrative groups in professional institutions such as Medical, Law and Engineering Colleges and Universities. A fixed employment quota is also in place. These special measures were put in place for a period of 20 years from the commencing day (of the constitution) with the hope that in this period a certain measure of uniformity in development and access to jobs etc. would have been achieved.

These measures have clearly not had the desired effect and have in fact had the opposite result, creating resentment among the dominant ethnic group, the Punjabis. The Central Superior Services of Pakistan entrance examination result 1997 acted as an incentive for candidates from that province to seek an injunction from the court and declare that henceforth all jobs were to be awarded on merit and no reservation would be made for marginalised ethnic groups. The case is still not resolved although the federal government hastened to set things 'right' by passing an appropriate law extending the period of affirmative action measures.

The above example reinforces our earlier comment that attempting to understand certain laws without their context can be an exercise in futility. On the one hand members of the less 'advantaged' groups demand a fair share in the country's resources and decision-making bodies for which they see reservation of jobs as an effective measure. On the other hand, the dominant ethnic group refuses to be denied access to jobs in order to accommodate people with lesser 'merit' than themselves, simply because these people have historically not partaken in mainstream national life. The dilemma is one that impinges on legality in conjunction with political and socio-economic factors and is typical of problems of a nation-state comprising a multi-ethnic population.

A further legal issue that we are faced with is the position of the tribal areas of FATA. Are these an integral part of the country, and are its people citizens of the state of Pakistan? If the answer is in the affirmative then why have we faltered in the whole-hearted integration of these ethnic groups into mainstream national life? Why are these areas governed by different laws? Why are they denied access to ordinary courts of the land? And although not strictly a legal issue, but certainly inter-linked and crucial for the previous questions posed, why are the people of the tribal areas left to suffer from extreme economic deprivation, unemployment and without the basic facilities of decent living?

In summation it may be submitted that widespread illiteracy and under-development gives birth to prejudices of racial, ethnic and linguistic chauvinism. A balance has to be struck between pride in one's ethnic identity and respect and tolerance for other ethnic groups. Black letter law is but one of the many tools of social engineering to create this balance but this can only be effectively implemented taking on board the political and socio-economic undercurrents of the country.

Ancient Peoples and New Nations in the Russian Federation: Questions of Theory and Practice

Bill Bowring

1. INTRODUCTION

The Russian Federation is a political formation of unprecedented complexity. This is so precisely because of the unique way in which national identities have been accommodated in both the recent and more distant past. My chapter explores a number of issues, practical and theoretical, arising from the Russian predicament. Following an analysis of the constitutional position, there is a brief account of the history of nationalities policy in the Tsarist Empire and Soviet Union, and of the construction of the present Federation. This sets the scene for a discussion of the intense theoretical discussions surrounding these issues, especially the work of Valeriy Tishkov, a central actor in both spheres. Against this background, I attempt a closer look at some legal issues arising in areas where ethnic minorities are concentrated. Particular regard is had to the plight of the indigenous "small-in-number" peoples of the Russian North, whose very existence is now in jeopardy.

THE PARADOXES OF RUSSIAN FEDERALISM

The Russian Federation is the largest and most differentiated in the world. It has no less than 89 "subjects of the Federation", each of which has formal equality under the 1993 Constitution, as well as formidable legislative and executive competence. These subjects are as follows. First, and most important for our purposes, Russia has 21 ethnic republics, the successors of the "autonomous republics" of the USSR, named after their "titular" people, with their own presidents, constitutions, and, in many cases, constitutional courts. Next, there are 6 enormous *krais*, a word often translated as "region", with their own elected governors. In fact, these are very large territories, whose name suggests that they are on the "edge" of the federation. The most numerous subjects of the Federation are the 49 *oblasts*, territorial formations inhabited primarily by ethnic Russians, also with elected governors. The 10 "autonomous *okrugs*" are also ethnic formations, and reflect a relative concentration of the indigenous peoples which give them their name. For all their formal constitutional equality, they are for the most part located *within* other formations

---

*   Pan-European Institute, University of Essex, UK.

Stephen Tierney (ed.), Accommodating National Identity: New Approaches in International and Domestic Law, 211–230
© 2000 *Kluwer Law International. Printed in Great Britain.*
First published in the International Journal on Minority and Group Rights, Volume 6 No. 1/2 1999.

(*krais* and *oblasts*), with consequences which will be explored later in this chapter. There is a Jewish autonomous *oblast*, located in the Russian Far East. Finally, two "cities of federal significance", Moscow and St Petersburg, are also subjects of the federation. However, it is important to remember that of at least 150 nationalities in the Russian Federation, only 32 have their own territorial units (Kempton, 1996: 609).

This extraordinary ramification reflects both the Soviet nationalities policy, and also the character of the Tsarist Empire, themes which will be explored in this chapter.

For the present, it should be noted that the phrase "*Rossiskaya Federatsiya*" (Russian Federation) cannot be accurately translated into English. The Russian language has two words which are translated into English as "Russian". The first is "*russkii*", which means "ethnic Russian", while the second is "*rossiskii*", which means "civic Russian". The Federation is the "*Rossiskaya*" Federation, not the "*Russkaya*" Federation – it is the country not of ethnic, but of civic Russians, that is of bearers of citizenship under the Constitution.

This is of the greatest importance, since the Federation embodies a striking paradox. As Khazanov points out (1997:135), ethnic Russians comprise more than 83% of the total population of about 150 million, making the Federation ethnically more homogenous than, say, Britain or France. The next most numerous are the Tatars (3.8%), Ukrainians (2.3%), Chuvash (1.2%), Bashkir (0.9%), Belorussians (0.7%) and Mordovians (0.6%). There are almost 200 ethnic groups in Russia today, but most exist in relatively and absolutely tiny numbers. (Pain, 1999).

NATIONAL IDENTITY IN RUSSIAN HISTORY

The impression is sometimes given, in discussions of the conflict in Chechnya, that Russia is a homogenously Slav, Orthodox Christian, nation facing a Moslem opponent, engaged in a geo-political showdown. In reality, Russia is, amongst other things, a Moslem state: Islam is one of the four "traditional" religions of Russia – the others are Orthodox Christianity, Buddhism, and Judaism. This is one of the formulations of the controversial Federal Law of 26 September 1997 "On Freedom of Conscience and on Religious Associations" (on which the Russian Constitutional Court adjudicated on 23 November 1999 – in favour of Jehovah's Witnesses.) According to its preamble, the Law recognises "the special role of Orthodoxy in the history of Russia, and in the formation and development of its spirituality and culture", and respects "Christianity, Islam, Buddhism, Judaism, and other religions, which make up an integral part of the historical heritage of the peoples of Russia".

The importance of Islam in Russia is linked to its earliest history. The development of the Russian state was made possible by Ivan the Terrible's victories over the Moslem Khanates of Kazan in 1552, and Astrakhan in 1556. However, as Khenkin points out (1997: 2), the fundamental task of Russia was not cultural or regional assimilation, but the security of the state. Even before Ivan, the Finno-Ungric tribes that populated the Oka basin and the upper Volga (whose descendants are the 'titular' nations of the republics of Marii El and Mordoviya) served the first Moscow princes (Tsimbaev, 1998: 59). On entering the Russian Empire the Turkic Moslems of the

Volga region and the North Caucasus, and the Buddhists of South Siberia and the Kalmyk steppe, retained their way of life, language and religion. Tsimbaev argues (1998:59) that "the heart of Russia's policy with respect to the peoples it annexed was not national but social assimilation". That meant that the local ruling elites were not annihilated or driven out, but incorporated into Russia's own elite, retaining their own language, religion, and rights and privileges. In return, they were to give devoted service to Russia. The only religious practice persecuted was defection from Orthodoxy. "Catholics and orthodox Moslems were an organic part of the ruling class as long as they belonged to their faith by birth and upbringing, but any Russian noble who became a schismatic would lose all estate privileges." (Tsimbaev, 1998: 61). It followed that the "fundamental principle of the Russian Empire was social and class division rather than nationality or religious division." Pershits and Smirnova note (1997: 792) that prior to October 1917 three legal systems coexisted in the North Caucasus – Adaty, Sharia (for Moslems in the region) and Russian laws. However, the accession of Tsar Nicholas I meant the abandonment of any attempt to create a *rossiiskii* (civic Russian) state, and a decisive shift to a *russkii* (ethnic Russian) path. This official ideology had three components: orthodoxy, autocracy and nationality (*narodnost*), meaning Russianness (Tsimbaev, 1998: 67).

The Soviet Union, too, applied an ethnic, rather than civic, criterion, with surprising and paradoxical results. As Khazanov shows (1997: 126), the Union was a "pseudofederation of ethnoterritorial republics", in which most of the nationalities were allowed various degrees of autonomy. Thus, state-controlled ethnic identity became decisive, through the connecting of nationality with specific territories, often arbitrarily mapped, linking the political and cultural-linguistic positions of nationalities with a degree of autonomy, through a hierarchy of union republics (Ukraine, Belarus, Moldova etc), autonomous republics, autonomous regions, and autonomous districts.

Even during the Soviet period, and despite the often repressive effect of central Party rule, the goal of leaders of the "titular" nationality in a particular territory was to preserve as much as possible of its ethnic character and territorial integrity in order to gain advantageous positions as against other nationalities. Of course, the ethnic populations which did not receive their "own" territory, especially the indigenous peoples of the North, lost out in this competition. Dowley points out that "[e]lites in the ethnic autonomous republics and national level republics were appointed to represent the ethnic group interests in the larger state, and thus, their natural political base of support was supposed to be the ethnic group. Other political appointments in these regions were made on the basis of ethnicity, a Soviet form of affirmative action for the formally, institutionally, recognised ethnic groups referred to in the early years of the Soviet Union as *korenizatsiya* or nativisation." (1998: 363). The Chairmen of the Supreme Soviets of Tatarstan and Bashkortostan, both of which aspired to the status of "union republics", were always members of the Presidium of the Supreme Soviet of the USSR, along with those of the Union Republics – the only two "autonomous republics" so represented (Shaimiev, 1996a: 1). By the end of the 1970s, more than half of the professional cadre in half of the Union Republics and 11 of the 21 autonomous republics in the RSFSR was composed of the titular ethnic group. Social mobility of ethnic groups was higher than that of Russians (Drobizheva, 1996: 2). As the Soviet Union weakened and finally collapsed, in December 1991, it is hardly surprising that the same leaders sought to turn symbolic authority into real power, and had a strong base for doing so.

Two scholars, one Russian, the other American, have generated, separately, but with remarkable agreement, satisfying analyses of the nature of the Soviet experiment in accommodating national identity. I will return to both these writers. Valerii Tishkov mirrors the analysis presented above: "The nation-building process in Imperial Russia was abruptly halted by the Bolshevik regime, and the whole vocabulary was changed in favour of Austro-Marxist ethnonational categories. Now the 'socialist nations' were proclaimed and constructed in the Soviet Union on the basis of existing or invented cultural differences. Soviet ideology and political practice, while pursuing declaratory internationalism, also enforced mutually exclusive ethnic loyalties on the principle of blood, and through the territorialisation of ethnicity on the principle of 'socialist' (read; ethnic) federalism. The very process of civic nation-building lost its sense, replaced by the clumsy slogan of "making the Soviet people from many nations, instead of making one nation from many peoples." (1997: 250).

This is very close to the analysis of Rogers Brubaker (1996: 29), "... the Soviet union was neither conceived in theory nor organised in practice as a nation-state. Yet while it did not define the state or citizenry as a *whole* in national terms, it did define component *parts* of the state and the citizenry in national terms. Herein lies the distinctiveness of the Soviet nationality regime – in its unprecedented displacement of nationhood and nationality, as organising principles of the social and political order, from the state-wide to the sub-state level. No other state has gone so far in sponsoring, codifying, institutionalising, even (in some cases) inventing nationhood and nationality on the sub-state level, while at the same time doing nothing to institutionalise them on the level of the state as a whole."

NATIONS IN THE FORMATION OF THE NEW FEDERATION

It is possible (Kossikov, 1996:1) to identify three phases of the development of the present Russian Federation. The first was the period between 1990 and March 1992, which has been described as the "parade of sovereignties". Led by Tatarstan, Bashkortotstan, and Sakha-Yakutiya, a number of the "autonomous republics" sought to gain recognition as independent republics within the Russian Federation, in the context of the dissolution of the Soviet Union itself in December 1991. They were encouraged by the real independence achieved by the former "union republics" – Armenia, Azerbaijan, Belarus, Estonia, Georgia, Kazakstan, Kyrgyzstan, Latvia, Lithuania, Moldova, Tajikistan, Turkmenistan, and Ukraine. Both Boris Yeltsin and Mintimer Shaimiev were democratically elected on12 June 1991 – the former as the first President of the RSFSR, the latter as the first President of Tatarstan (Shaimiev, 1996a: 2). One of the factors which precipitated the abortive putsch of August 1991 was the real threat of ethnic separatism, even within the (former) Russian Socialist Federation of Soviet Republics (RSFSR). The putsch leaders, leading officials of the Communist Party of the Soviet Union, believed they were saving the Union.

At this crucial moment, as the Soviet Union dissolved, the Russian Federation itself was saved from dissolution. In March 1992 a "Federation Treaty" was concluded, which represented the maximum possible compromise of the central authorities and the regional ruling elites, consistent with preserving the territorial integrity of the Federation within its existing borders. Two "autonomous republics", Tatarstan and the Chechen Republic, refused to sign the Federation Treaty. It is highly instructive to note the very different trajectories of the two republics since then.

The history of the Chechen Republic, and the wars of 1994-5 and 1999-2000, comprise in one sense an exception which proves the rule. The Chechen Republic was one of the most ethnically homogenous of all the Russian republics. The Chechens defied the Russian Empire until 1864. This people has its own special history of repression and injustice – especially the brutal deportation by Stalin of the whole Chechen population in 1944. On June 9, 1991, the second Congress of the National Congress of the Chechen People announced that the Chechen Republic, arbitrarily carved out of Chechno-Ingush Republic, was planning to secede from the USSR and RSFSR. Dudayev's seizure of power did not automatically mean the use of armed force by Russia, but there was no possibility of compromise. This was not least because of the gross injustices suffered by Chechens in this and past centuries. (Pain & Popov, 1999). Conflict followed almost as a matter of course.

The trajectory of Tatarstan has been quite different. On 30 August 1990, well before the dissolution of the Soviet Union, Tatarstan adopted a Declaration of Sovereignty, in which state sovereignty was declared as the "realisation of the inalienable right of the Tatar nation, of all people of the republic to self-determination" (Tishkov 1997, 56). President Shaimiev stresses the fact that the "people of Tatarstan" was not divided into ethnic groups (1996a: 5). In a referendum of that time, no less than 62% of its population, Tatars and Russians, supported this stance. Tatarstan, like Chechnya, refused to sign the Federation Treaty in March 1992, but, unlike the Chechen leadership, entered into lengthy negotiations with the Russian government. On 15 February 1994, Tatarstan signed the Treaty "On the Demarcation of Competences Between the Government of the Russian Federation and the Government of the Republic of Tatarstan" and 12 agreements with Moscow, affirming its constitution and presidency, republican citizenship, a significant degree of sovereignty over oil and other natural resources, special provisions for military service and other rights and powers (Tishkov 1997, 243).

This history shows that war and secession are not the only modalities for the accommodation of national identities in Russia. Thus, Articles 11 and 78 of the 1993 Constitution provide for regulation of relations between federal centre and federal subjects by agreement. One of the unique features of Russian federalism is the proliferation of treaties between the Federation and its subjects. The first was the Treaty between Tatarstan and the centre of 15 February 1994 (see above). Further examples are the Treaties with Kabardino-Balkariya (June 1994), Bashkortostan (August 1994), Udmurtiya (October 1995), and Omsk Oblast (May 1996) – see Shulzhenko, 1998: 68, and Lysenko, 1996: 2). As at June 1998, more than half of the regions had concluded some 46 similar treaties (Alekseyev and others, 1998a: p.334).

These treaties do not even pretend to conform to the norms of the Russian or any other constitution. As Lysenko points out (1996: 2), the 1994 treaty with Tatarstan contains neither a provision stating that Tatarstan is a constituent part of the Federation, nor recognition of the superiority of the 1993 Constitution and federal laws over republic laws. In his view, it "has created a dangerous precedent of exceeding the region's authority above the limits set by the federal constitution, arbitrarily redistributing authority and jurisdiction without regard for consistency with the federal constitution, and delegating certain concessions and benefits to a region which are denied to others." (1996: 3). This has helped to give rise to the phenomenon described as "asymmetrical federalism". Nevertheless, it is certain that more serious conflict has been avoided, as is also the case with Bashkortostan and Sverdlovsk Oblast (see Easter, 1997, as to the attempt in July 1993 to create a new "Urals Republic" on the basis of the Oblast).

But there are already a number of Russian commentators who predict the final departure of the whole of the North Caucasus, colonised by Russia in the 18th and 19th centuries. Indeed, it is not just the North Caucasus which is in turmoil at present. Some Tatar writers see the increasing confidence and international presence of the Republic of Tatarstan as the harbinger of the final disintegration of the Russian Federation. Thus the journalist Sabirzyan Badretsinov argues in her article "How Tatars Can Contribute to Russia's Disintegration" – that ... "the survival of the Tatar nation depends on whether Tatarstan will become an independent country. Due to Tatarstan's geographical position, her independence can be achieved only if Russia breaks up into a number of independent states. Fortunately, Russia is already in the process of political disintegration: the governors of many Russian regions openly defy Moscow's authority; many parliaments of mainly ethnic Russian regions continue to pass legislation that directly contradicts the federal Constitution; some local newspapers openly support separatist tendencies in the regions." (1998)

THE ETHNIC NATURE OF THE NEW FEDERATION

The 21 ethnic Republics – Adygeya, Altai, Bashkortotstan, Buryatiya, Dagestan, Ingushetiya, Kabardino-Balkar Republic, Kalmykiya – Khalmg Tanch, Karachayevo-Cherkess Republic, Kareliya, Komi, Marii El, Mordoviya, Sakha – Yakutiya, North Osetiya, Tatarstan, Tyva, Udmurtiya, Khakasiya, Chechen Republic, Chuvash Republic – and other ethnic autonomous formations comprise about 53% of the whole territory of the Federation. According to Khazanov (1997:135), the 9 million ethnic Russians who live in non-Russian republics of the Federation have in most cases – especially in Tatarstan, Bashkortotstan, Udmurtiya, Buryatiya, Tyva, Komi and Sakha-Yakutiya – already lost their former dominant status. This is despite the fact that only in Dagestan (Russians 9%), Chechen Republic (23%), Chuvash Republic (26%), Tyva (32%), Kabardino-Balkar Republic (31%), and Tatarstan (43%) are ethnic Russians in a minority. In all the others they are have an absolute or relative majority.

Of the 27 million non-Russians, about 18 million live in "their own" national states, though in no case except Chechnya with anything like ethnic homogeneity. Only in four republics – Osetiya, Tyva, Chechnya and Chuvashiya – does the "titular" people have more than 50% of the population. In three – Kabardino-Balkarskaya, Kalmykiya and Tatarstan – they have a relative majority, 48.3%, 45.7% and 48.5% respectively, while in 12 republics ethnic Russians have an absolute or relative majority – Adygeya 67.9%, Altai 60.3%, Bashkortostan 39.3%, Buryatiya 70%, Karachaevo-Cherkasskaya 42%, Kareliya 73.6%, Komi 58%, Marii El 47.5%, Mordoviya 61%, Sakha – Yakutiya 50.3%, Udmurtiya 59%, and Khakasiya 79% (Umnova 1998, 92). The Mordva constitute only 27% of the Mordovian Republic, and Karels only 10% of the Karelian Republic. Of the 26 million people living in all of the territorial autonomies in Russia in 1989, the proportion of "titular" groups was 37.5%, with 11.8 million Russians living there making up 45.7% (Tishkov 1997, 232).

However, the regional elites are already bringing about a decisive shift in favour of the "titular" nation. For example, in Tatarstan, where Tatars are 51% of the population, they have 92% of ministry heads, and 76% of regional administrators. In Sakha-Yakutiya, where the titular nation are 37% of the population, they held 69% of ministry positions in 1996 (Drobizheva, 1996: 6). With the exception of Kareliya, Komi, Khakassiya and Udmurtiya, political power in all the ethnic territorial formations is in the hands of the elites of the indigenous nationality, even where these are an absolute minority of the population, as in Sakha-Yakutiya and Adygeya.

REGIONAL INEQUALITY – FEDERAL ASYMMETRY

This all takes place against a background of the greatest inequality between one region and another. There are only 10 "donor" regions, which contribute more to the federal centre than they receive in grants. These are Bashkortostan Republic, Khanti-Mansinskii Autonomous Okrug, Krasnodar Krai, Lipetsk Oblast, the City of Moscow, Nizhnii Novgorod Oblast, Samara Oblast, Sverdlovsk Oblast, Tatarstan Republic, and Yamalo-Nenetskii Autonomous Okrug. The remaining 79 subjects of the federation are "*dotatsionnii*" – they could not survive without federal subsidies.

The contrasts are even greater in terms of purchasing power of per capita monetary income. According to the Ministry of Labour and Social Development (*Obshchaya Gazeta* 23 December 1999), in the first half of 1999 the top ten subjects in these terms were as follows: City of Moscow, Yamal-Nenetsk Autonomous Okrug, Khanty-Mansi Autonomous Okrug, Tyumen Oblast, Samara Oblast, Murmansk Oblast, Komi Republic, Krasnoyarsk Krai, Irkutsk Oblast, and Perm Oblast. The bottom ten (Chechnya is excluded) were: Karachay-Cherkessia Republic, Ivanovo Oblast, Tyva Republic, Komi-Permyak Autonomous Okrug, Kalmykia Republic, Chita Oblast, Dagestan Republic, Ingushetia Republic, Ust-Orda Buryat Autonomous Okrug, and the poorest of all, Aga Buryat Autonomous Okrug. It is notable that there are ethnic republics and autonomous okrugs in both the top and bottom ten, and that the second and third are autonomous okrugs named after small indigenous peoples, and located within the fourth, Tyumen Oblast.

THE IMPORTANCE OF THEORY

At this point I turn to the role of scholars in shaping the new arrangements – and to a controversial proposal. In 1996 President Shaimiev of Tatarstan recognised at a seminar that without the work of leading scholars like Emil Pain, Vyacheslav Mikhailov, and Valery Tishkov, there would be no concept of a Russian nationalities policy at all (Shaimiev, 1996a: 4). Indeed, scholars have played an exceptionally important role in determining the nature and relative success (with the exception of Chechnya) of the Federation. Tishkov, a former Minister of Nationalities, and long-time Director of the Institute of Ethnology and Anthropology, combines an extraordinary breadth of practical experience with an engaged knowledge of nationalism theory as it has developed in the West. For example, the "Concept of the State Nationalities Policy" adopted by the Russian government on 11 April 1996, was formulated by the Ministry of Nationalities and the Institute of Ethnology and Anthropology (Tishkov 1997, 67). Many books and articles are now being published by him and others on the questions of the "Russian idea", and Russia's orientation (see for example Alekseyev & others, 1998a and b).

This chapter naturally focuses on developments in law and legal institutions. For the Russian Federation, these are heavily influenced by the large body of international law to which Russia has adhered. This includes practically the whole body of UN treaty law. More recently, Russia has been accepted into membership of the Council of Europe in 1996, and has ratified the 1950 European Convention on Human Rights in 1998 and the 1995 Framework Convention on the Rights of National Minorities in 1999. There is a burgeoning Russian literature on minority and group rights.

However, there is one notable difference between Russian and Western scholars in this field. Although increasing attention is paid by Western legal theorists to the work on citizenship of Will Kymlicka (1995), Jurgen Habermas (1995), and others, there is almost no reference to nationalism theory. Thornberry's classic work on the law of minority rights (1992) does not mention the field at all – perhaps not surprising, in a work which does not seek to address theory. But the absence of an explicit methodology is unfortunate, given that the most acute problems of minority rights – those in which states have reason to fear secession (a point noticed by Thornberry (1992: 387) – "… in some ways it is remarkable that the institution of the protection of minorities survives, in view of the apparent threat posed to States by dissident groups perhaps wishing to secede…") – are those linked precisely to nationalist discourse and nation-building.

Even where the disciplines are brought together, these areas of theory do not seem to meet. Thus, a recent collection on human rights in global politics (Dunne & Wheeler, 1999) hardly refers to nationalism. In his essay on the "social construction of human rights" (his argument is that human rights are not just abstract values but a set of particular social practices to realise those values) Jack Donnelly refers several times to a "resurgence" (twice on Donnelly 1999: 96), indeed a "major resurgence" (92) in nationalism, as a "plausible alternative" to stronger cosmopolitan sentiments, and as a threat to human rights. But he does not further elucidate the notion, nor does he refer to any of the scholarly literature. He simply states that strong international reactions to nationalism suggest that "such arguments have little appeal beyond those who see themselves as specially chosen" (97). And the leading scholars of nationalism have either failed to notice or have been repelled by the law and practice of minority rights.

TISHKOV AND NATIONALISM THEORY

Tishkov has succeeded in bringing together both bodies of theory, as well as his substantial practice. In a recent theoretical article provocatively entitled "Forget the Nation" (Tishkov, 1998) he discerns a number of fundamental approaches in the enormous literature of nationalism theory. The first, dominant view, he describes as "Weberian" (Eugène Weber, that is) or historical, which sees nationalism as the process of development, over a long period of historical time, of a phenomenon or an "ideal type". According to this view, the main proponents of which are Anthony D. Smith (Smith 1986) and Miroslav Hroch (Hroch 1985), nationalism has its own roots, moment of birth, stages of growth and fundamental characteristics. This is reflected in the typically Russian conception of the "ethnos", regarded as a sociological paradigm by a number of leading authors (Kravchenko *et al*, 1997). Tishkov makes the ad hominem point that the three authors in question, respectively Armenian, Belarussian and Jewish, teach their students about the "ethnos" with its "stable particularities of culture and psychology" without asking which "ethnos" they inhabit.

He sees the historical approach as being a mix of Weberian positivism and Marxist historical determinism, but it was also at the centre of non-communist Russian thought at the turn of the century, especially in the work of the philosopher Nikolai Berdyaev. Tishkov notes that this approach has spawned a whole discipline, exemplified by the London journal "Nations and Nationalism", with its own meta-categories. In Tishkov's (1998, 7) view the "historical" approach is closely affiliated to the functionalist interpretation of nationalism linked to Ernest Gellner, in which it is seen as having played a key role in the process of modernisation (for which read industrialisation). Within this camp, dissidents have emerged, who contend that it is not modernisation, but its failure, which gives birth to nationalism. This is the approach which has appeared to prove most useful in analysing the events of the last few decades in the region of the former USSR, but in fact suffers from the same serious weakness, namely its connection of nationalism with the historical process of modernisation (or its failure).

Close to Gellner's interpretation, but more contemporary and popular, is the "constructivist" interpretation of nationalism, to be found in Benedict Anderson's *Imagined Communities* (1983). For Tishkov, this is interesting for two reasons. It breaks from the historical-determinist and primordialist view of ethnicity and the concept of nation, and it only weakly lends itself to the analysis of the Soviet and Russian experience, while at the same time that experience contains wonderful illustrative materials for it. In this approach, the concept of the nation is seen as a social construct. This approach has proved especially useful to Tishkov, since it has enabled him to change his focus from the fundamental category of Russian ethnology, "ethnic processes", to the phenomenon which Tishkov would prefer to call "the process of ethnic process" (*etnicheskaya protsessual'nost'*). Through this new "prism", the development of Soviet "ethnic engineering" is thrown into sharp relief.

Tishkov's conclusions are twofold. First, in the formation of the ethnic policy of the USSR, primordialism ceased to be simply a marginal, empirical approach, but came to be used as the source of state policy, and in nationalist discourse. Second, although the ethno-nationalism of a community is an imagined construct, this does not prevent it from becoming a harsh reality and the basis for collective action. It is this ever-present reality of the contemporary Russian state which has prevented the government from properly working out its legal relationship with its own citizens, notoriously in relation to the new passport, and whether this should continue to contain a statement of the bearer's ethnic identity ("nationality").

Thus, what Tishkov is proposing (1998, 9) is not a construction of ethnicity or nationalism, but possibilities for its deconstruction or a process *back* from nationalism. He is convinced that the apparent irreversibility of nationalism is a chimera.

However, he recognises that a number of authors exist whose orientation is post-structuralist, post-modernist, indeed post-colonialist – followers of Anderson, such as Partha Chatterjee (1993), whose aim is to reinstate an "indigenous nationalism". This is a line of inquiry discussed by Smith in his recent work under the heading "fragmentation and hybrid identities" (Smith, 1998: 203), but Tishkov has a more severe critique. In his view, the difference between Russian theorists and their Americanised Indian counterparts is merely the greater education and subtlety of argument of the latter. They do not display the para-scientific naiveté of analysis (in the manner of Lev Gumilev (1990)) which is so often found in the writings of Yakut, Tatar, Bashkir, Ossetin and many other authors in the Russian Federation, especially when these are writing in their native languages.

Indeed, Tishkov believes that the liberal West would not have enjoyed such an easy victory over "communism" had it not enjoyed the support of a very powerful ally. This was the Soviet understanding of the word "nation" in its ethno-cultural sense, especially since the word "nation" is so closely tied to notions of statehood and self-determination. He sees a number of current arguments for the further break-up of Russia. First, the naïve conception of ethno-nations as bio-social or ethno-social organisms, finding their realisation in statehood. Second, the common Western conception that Spain is the country of self-determining Spaniards, England the land of the self-determining English, and so on, leads to the conclusion that just as the Russian Empire and its Soviet successor broke up, so must Russia itself disintegrate – as a colleague said to Tishkov – "what Russia grabbed, it must give back". Third, is what Tishkov (1998, 10) would call the falsified or imprecise reading of international law norms and declarations on the protection of the rights of peoples and on self-determination. This is especially ironical since the USSR was the long-term supporter of the ideology of national self-determination for colonial peoples, of the "international national liberation movement". What is missed is that colonial independence was always strictly territorial, and was absolutely anti-ethnic, anti-tribal and did not permit a single new state to emerge from within established colonial borders.

Tishkov notes the readiness of Western scholars and politicians to make use of the language of their former ideological opponents to construct an intriguing scenario:

first, there was the break-up of the USSR, and now, a series of perspectives for a second round of disintegration on Russia's account. Thus, many Western scholars, regardless of discipline, regularly insist that "multi-national Russia" does not contain ethnic or even national minorities, but status-less nations, or even "nations without states" – see the work of Bremmer and Taras (1993).

He is also highly suspicious of the fact that in Council of Europe and OSCE documents and practice, there appear to be "ethnic" and "linguistic" minorities in Western Europe, but "national" minorities in Eastern Europe and the former USSR. Why, he asks, does Max van der Stoel, the OSCE's High Commissioner on National Minorities, concern himself with the Gagauz in Moldavia, the Crimean Tatars in Ukraine, the Tatars in Russia, but not the Basques in Spain, the Tirolese in Italy, or the Irish in Ulster?

A further example is the support given by the US State Department and others to organisations such as UNPO (the Unrepresented Nations and Peoples Organisation – see http://www.unpo.org/member/), founded in 1991. It is noteworthy that current members of UNPO include Bashkortostan, Buryatia, the Chechen Republic, the Chuvash Republic, Ingushetia, Komi, Mari, Sakha -Yakutia, Tatarstan, Tyva and Udmurtiya, all of which happen to be subjects of the Russian Federation.

Tishkov finds support and significance in the recent work of Rogers Brubaker, who wrote: "Nationalism can and should be understood without invoking "nations" as substantial entities. Instead of focusing on nations as real groups, we should focus on nationhood and nationness, on "nation" as practical category, institutionalised form, and contingent event. "Nation" is a category of practice, not (in the first instance) a category of analysis. To understand nationalism, we have to understand the practical uses of the category "nation", the ways it can come to structure perception, to inform thought and experience, to organise discourse and political action." (Brubaker 1996: 7) Tishkov is delighted to find that this view exactly coincides with his own conclusion, published in the same year (Tishkov, 1996), that "nation" does not constitute a scientific category, and ought to be expelled from the discourse of science and politics.

Thus, Tishkov ends with a recommendation (1998, 26): either all ethnic communities should call themselves nations, if this continues to have any significance whatever in the world of contemporary politics – or none of them should. If none of them do, then politicians and scholars should stop using the term too, and their theory and practice would not suffer. Indeed, Tishkov argues, the abolition of this category would help in the understanding of the nature of human coalitions, their cultural differences and political configurations. Tishkov's slogan is: forget about *Nations*, in the name of *peoples, states and cultures*, even if future scholars cast doubt on these last definitions as well.

A REALIST CRITIQUE

For Tishkov, Anthony D. Smith is the leader of the "orthodox" camp in nationalism theory. Yet it is Smith who has paid the most carefully detailed attention to the role of discourse, myth and imagination in the formation of nations and nationalism, and would scarcely deny the socially constructed nature of concepts of nation and nationalism. Neither, however, would he be willing to forego, on principle, any examination of the historical events, landscapes and artefacts on which myth and sentiment flourish, nor would he wish to legislate against a theory of nationalism. Thus, Smith notes (1998: 219) the contemporary turning away from any 'grand narrative' like modernism or perennialism at the very moment when ethno-nationalism is resurgent and when the national state and national identity have once again become central to arguments about the direction of politics and society. "Without an explicit theory of the character, formation and diffusion of nations and nationalism, such arguments will lack depth and validity."

Smith's recent critique of Brubaker seems to have equal significance for Tishkov:

"… Brubaker is right to remind us that… the 'nation' (like the 'state') is a concept, but to confine its referents to form, practice and event is to strip it of those attributes that give it so much potency and appeal. How could we account for the widespread powerful feelings of attachment to mere forms and practices, even when these are backed by the panoply of state institutions and the international system? 'Nationalism' cannot be so readily separated in this fashion from nations – as communities." (Smith 1998, 77).

The consequence, it seems to me, of Smith's position, with which I broadly speaking agree, is that a more robust approach is needed to Russian realities. Nation-building and its accompanying rhetoric cannot simply be wished away, or legislated out of existence. Even lawyers do not, for the most part, suffer from such delusions.

THE INDIGENOUS SMALL-IN-NUMBER PEOPLES OF RUSSIA

Tishkov is of course referring to the already constituted ethnic political formations of Russia, and their demands for autonomy and statehood. Yet this is one set of peoples, the "indigenous small-in-number peoples", whose future is very much in the balance in Russia, and whose very existence may well be conditional upon their recognition as "nations", even if they have no prospect, ever, of nation statehood. At one level, that of the Constitution of the Russian Federation, these peoples are protected. According to Article 69 of the 1993 Constitution: "The Russian Federation guarantees the rights of indigenous small-in-number peoples in accordance with the generally recognised principles and norms of international law and the international treaties of the Russian Federation."

There is to date only one binding international treaty on the rights of indigenous peoples, the International Labour Organisation's Convention No.169 of 26 June 1989, the "Convention Concerning Indigenous and Tribal Peoples in Independent Countries". Although Russia has not yet ratified this Convention, many of its principles, especially that of self-identification, are reflected in Russian legislation. Article 1.2 of the Convention states that "Self-identification as indigenous or tribal shall be regarded as a fundamental criterion for determining the groups to which the provisions of this Convention apply."

Witness the Federal Law of 19 June 1996 "On the Fundamentals of State Regulation of the Social and Economic Development of the North of the Russian Federation". This contains, in Article 1, the following definition of the approximately 29-30 peoples concerned – Aleut (702 members, according to Sokolova & others, 1995: 86), Dolgan (6,932 members), Ket (1,113 members), Nents (34,665 members), Khant (22,521 members), Mans (8,461 members), Chukch (15,184 members), and others:

> "…peoples residing in territories of the traditional residence of their ancestors, preserving their distinctive style of life, with a population in Russia of less than 50,000, and identifying themselves as independent ethnic communities." (Kryazhkov, 1997: 18).

These principles are not new. In fact, the self-determination of the indigenous peoples of the North within the boundaries of the Russian State was formulated in law in the 19th century (Sokolova & others, 1995: 75). The *"Ustav ob upravlenii inorodtsev (Charter on government of aboriginals)"* adopted in 1822 elaborated and strengthened the principles of their autonomous self-determination. During the early 20th century these principles collided with the Soviet economic exploitation and industrial development of the North. In 1925-26 the Soviet state legislated a list of 26 "small peoples of the North", defined by reference to their means of subsistence rather than their culture. This formed the basis for the establishment, noted above, in 1930 of the various "autonomous okrugs" as administrative rather than self-determination units.

Despite legal and legislative guarantees, the position of these peoples, who together number some 200,000 (Kotlyakov & Agranat, 1999: 3) has continually deteriorated. The State Duma, in its *Postanovleniye* (Decree) of 26 May 1995 "On the crisis situation of the economy and culture of the small-in-number indigenous (aboriginal) peoples of the North, Siberia, and Far East", recognised that traditional economic activities were continuing to collapse, with a corresponding rise in unemployment and impoverishment. The mortality of these peoples was one and a half times that of other Russians, with a very low birth-rate, and threatening levels of alcoholism and crime. Only 2-3% of the territory of the Russian Arctic has special protection, while the optimum would be 25% (Kotlyakov & Agranat, 1999: 6). Degradation of the environment proceeds unabated. Yablokova (1996) asserts that "within 30-50 years the country may lose practically all the natural riches of the vast Arctic region and will already be in no position to save even part of the nature of the Arctic or its population, especially the small-in-number peoples". As Kotlyakov and Agranat point out, this is a question of universal human importance. These peoples are the bearers of cultures which are extraordinarily well adapted to the extreme conditions of the Arctic.

A Federal Law "On the Status of Indigenous Small-in-number Peoples" was in preparation for more than 7 years. The Council of the Federation, the Russian Parliament's upper house, made up of the governors and presidents of the subjects of the Federation, failed to adopt its most recent version in 1996 (Kryazhkov, 1997: 18).

According to Kryazhkov, the following arguments were heard: the principle of non-discrimination meant that there were no grounds for additional guarantees; subsidies would violate the equal rights of citizens; inequality on the basis of national characteristics would incite social tension.

A short Federal Law, of a framework nature, "On Guarantees of the Rights of Indigenous Small-in-number Peoples of the Russian Federation", was finally enacted by the State Duma on 16 April 1999, approved by the Federation Council on 22 April 1999, and signed by President Yeltsin on 30 April 1999. It outlines the role of the Federation and its subjects in protecting the primordial habitat, traditional way of life, agriculture and hunting of these peoples. Many of its provisions dealing, for example, with self-government and political representation, require further legislation at the regional level. However, on 25 November 1999 President Yeltsin refused to sign a draft Federal Law, enacted by the Duma on 27 October 1999 and approved by the Federal Council on 11 November 1999, "On the General Principles of Organisation of Communities of Indigenous Small-in-number Peoples of the North, Siberia and the Far East of the Russian Federation". The grounds on which he did so included incompatibility wth the Constitution and a number of laws including the Law on Guarantees, not least because of its restriction to certain territories only, in addition to the points made by Kryazhkov. President Putin wishes to curtail the powers of the regions; it is as yet unclear what relevant legislative initiatives, if any, will be made by him or his government.

The discussion so far has not touched on the role of civil society. Indeed, there was no place for civil society, in the sense of self-organisation independent of the State, in the Soviet system. It is therefore especially significant that a new voice is being heard in the Russian Federation: a unified voice of the indigenous peoples. A document of 4 March 1996, "Discrimination Against Indigenous People of the North, A Statement by Social Organisations and Movements of Indigenous People of the North" has been widely distributed, including publication in the English language on the Internet, at <http://arcticcircle.uconn.edu/ArcticCircle/SEEJ/russia_indig.html>. The Statement was published by the Association of Indigenous Peoples of the North, Siberia and Far East, and signed by leaders of the Associations of Indigenous Peoples of Yamalo-Nentsk and Khanti-Mansinsk Autonomous Okrugs, the Republics of Sakha-Yakutiya and Buryatiya, Krasnoyarsk Krai, and Kamchatka and Sakhalin Oblasts, as well as the Association of Ket People, and others.

The Statement starts with a highly significant reference to international law. It recalls Russia's membership of the Council of Europe (1996), and signature (now ratification in 1998 and 1999 respectively) of the 1950 European Convention on Human Rights and 1995 Framework Convention on the Rights of National Minorities. The Association mourns the loss of such peoples as the Ain, Vod, Kamasinets, Kerek, Omok and Yug. It points with horror to the fact that such peoples as the Aleut (702 members), Ket (1,113 members), Iganasan (1,278 members), Negidalets (622 members), Orok (190 members), Oroch (915 members), Tofalar (731 members), Enets (209 members) and Yukagir (1,142 members) are on the verge of extinction.

A sharp contrast is drawn between the late Soviet period, 1989-1991, when there were 18 indigenous representatives in the Supreme Soviet of the USSR and RSFSR, and the 1995 State Duma, in which only two indigenous deputies were elected. The Statement points out that no action was taken following the State Duma's May 1995 Decision noted above. Demands include the enactment of the proposed Federal laws "On the Foundations of the Legal Status of Indigenous Peoples of Russia" and "On the Status of the Peoples of the North". Further, the authors want procedures for licensing of and compensation for exploitation of resources in their territories, minimum representation in federal and regional legislative and executive bodies, and a fully empowered federal agency to advance the rights of the indigenous peoples of the North.

THREE CASE-STUDIES

In order to comprehend the precarious position of the indigenous peoples in two very wealthy subjects, it is worth reflecting for a moment on the two autonomous okrugs in the "top ten" wealthiest, referred to above. They were both established in December 1930, as part of Stalin's nationalities policy. Both are very large and sparsely populated. Recall that the United Kingdom as a whole is 242,910 square kilometres, with a population of just over 59 million. Khanti-Mansinsk has an area of 523,000 square kilometres, while Yamalo-Nenets has 750,300. The former has a population of 1,371,500, of whom 66.3% are Russians, and only 1.5% the indigenous "titular" peoples – Khanti comprise 0.9%, Mansi 0.5%, and Forest Nentsi 0.1% of the total. There are more Tatars than there are indigenous peoples – 7.6%. The latter, half again larger in area, has a population of 497,000, of whom Russians comprise 59.2%, Ukrainians 17.2%, Tatars 5.3%, and Belorussians 2.6%. Again, the numbers of the indigenous peoples are tiny, a total of only 6.1% of the total population comprise "peoples of the North": just 4.2% are Nentsi, 1.5% Khanti, and 0.3% Selkupi.

Their "host" oblast, Tyumen, by contrast, has a total area of 1,435,200 square kilometres (of which 1,273,300 is made up of the two okrugs, the northern part of the oblast), more than 8% of Russia. However, it has a population of 3,228,100 (most of whom therefore live in the south of the Oblast), of whom 83% are Russians, 9.4% Tatars, 1,8% Ukrainians, and 1,4% Germans (All statistics from http://www.society.ru/bibl/polros/).

Both the autonomous okrugs are very wealthy in natural resources, especially oil. This brought them into conflict with Tyumen, in a case which reached the Russian Federal Constitutional Court on 14 July 1997. The case was bought by the legislative bodies of all three protagonists, and sought a definitive interpretation of Article 66 point 4 of the 1993 Constitution:

> "The relations of autonomous okrugs located within the territory of krais or oblasts may be regulated by federal laws and by treaties between organs of state power of the autonomous okrug and, correspondingly, the organs of state power of the krai or oblast."

The legislative bodies of the two autonomous okrugs argued that their status as equal subjects of the Federation meant that they retained full competence within their territories, with matters concerning the oblast as a whole to be decided jointly by all three parties, by agreement. Their view prevailed (for a full discussion, see Tyumen International Institute, 1997).

Note that this issue had nothing to do with the indigenous peoples after whom the *okrugs* are named. The wealth of the *okrugs* is much more likely to work to the detriment of these peoples than to contribute to their survival.

The Republic of Sakha-Yakutiya is also emblematic, and has received considerable scholarly attention. It is enormous, even by Russian standards – 3,103,200 square kilometres, 18.2% of the Federation as a whole, with a population of 1,062,000, only 0.71% of the Federation. The Sakha (Yakut) people have Turkic linguistic and cultural roots, and arrived in the territory some 500-700 years ago (Balzer & Vinokurova, 1996: 103, 105), greatly outnumbering the aboriginal peoples. In 1989 Russians comprised 50% of the population, with 33% Sakha (Yakut), 7% Ukrainian. Of the indigenous populations, the "peoples of the North", only 1.3% Evenk, 0.79% Even, 0.06% Yukagir, and 0.04% Chukchi remained. Russians are leaving, and by 1996 Russians were 46.8% and Sakha (Yakut) 40%. The aboriginal populations continue to decline.

Sakha-Yakutiya became an autonomous republic in April 1922, and adopted a "Declaration on Sovereignty" in September 1990. In December 1991, Mikhail Nikolaev, an ethnic Sakha, was elected President, having become chairman of the Supreme Soviet in 1990. Sakha-Yakutiya's 1992 Constitution places republic laws above Russian Federal laws, and has a provision for the Republic's "right to leave the Russian Federation". Both provisions clearly violate the 1993 Federal Constitution. It has colossal mineral resources – it produces 99% of Russia's diamonds, 24% of its gold, and 33% of its silver. An agreement of 31 March 1992 between the federal centre and Sakha provides that the Republic and the centre each receive 32% of all diamond profits, on the basis of a new enterprise, *Almazy Rossii-Sakha* (Diamonds of Russian and Sakha) (Kempton 1996: 593). Furthermore, the majority of Sakha-Yakutiya's tax revenues were to remain in the Republic. Another bilateral agreement of 29 June 1995 gave Sakha-Yakutiya an even greater share of its mineral wealth, with unprecedented economic leeway in making foreign contacts, distributing profits, and allocating taxes (Kempton, 1996: 606). Much of this success has been due to Nikolaev's skill in negotiation with President Yeltsin, based, of course, on the Republic's extraordinary wealth.

In all three cases, there are ample territorial and economic foundations for the independent ambitions of local leaders, and, as in the case of Sakha-Yakutiya, the "titular" people. But the original inhabitants, the "small-in-number peoples of the North", have been entirely left out of the equations of federation and nation building.

CONCLUSION

What is Tishkov's prognosis for the future of Russia? He wants to see Russia recognised both internationally and domestically as a nation of its own, containing a large number of ethnic, linguistic, religious and other minorities. He argues (1997: 260-1) that there are good reasons for supposing that a pan-Russian (perhaps

"Rossiyan", rather than "Russian", meaning ethnic Russian) identity can be forged. Thus, Russia is a UN member, recognised as a "nation" in this context, and presenting itself as such. Moreover, Russia within its new borders is an historical fact, with recognised borders, and administrative and other configurations developed before and during the Soviet period. Third, the population as a whole, despite containing over a hundred ethnic groups, has a high degree of cultural cohesion, and is a culturally homogenous state in which all the people can communicate in the same language.

Thus, there are good reasons for giving conditional support to Tishkov's optimistic prognosis for Russia. The Russian Federation already defies the existing international legal models. The nature and complexity of arrangements in the new Federation, and the extraordinary degree of decentralisation which now exists, exceed previous concepts of federalism. If the aspirations of Tatars and Bashkirs can be accommodated within the new Federation, and their own minorities can be effectively protected, then great gains will have been made in the practice of conflict avoidance. Of course, the very survival of the "small in number" peoples will require appreciation of their own special nationhood, in ways which the present federal organisation of Russia renders extraordinarily difficult. *Pace* Tishkov, all this means that due recognition must be given to the fact that the discourse of nations and nationalism retains considerable, even perhaps growing, organising and mobilising potential, precisely because of the vivid reality of the subjects of this discourse. But in this field above all, theory and its concepts will never be adequate to the ever dynamically changing object of study. What is required is recognition combined with the most acute criticism.

REFERENCES

Alekseyev, S. *et al.* (1998a). *Ideologicheskiye Orientiry Rossii* (Russia's Ideological Orientation"). Volume 1. Moscow: Kniga i Biznes

Alekseyev, S. *et al.* (1998b). *Ideologicheskiye Orientiry Rossii* (Russia's Ideological Orientation"). Volume 2. Moscow: Kniga i Biznes)

Anderson, B. (1983). *Imagined Communities.* London: Verso

Badretsinov, S (1998). How Tatars Can Contribute to Russia's Disintegration, copy in the possession of the author

Balzer, M. M. & Vinokurova, U. A. (1996). Nationalism, Interethnic Relations and Federalism: The Case of the Sakha Republic (Yakutia), *Europe-Asia Studies* 48: 101–120

Bremmer, I. & Taras, R. (1993). *Nations and Politics in the Soviet Successor States.* Cambridge: Cambridge University Press

Brubaker, R. (1996).*Nationalism Reframed. Nationhood and the national question in the New Europe.* Cambridge: Cambridge University Press

Chatterjee, P. (1993). *The Nation and its Fragments. Colonial and Postcolonial Histories.* Cambridge: Cambridge University Press

Donnelly, J. (1999). The social construction of international human rights, in: Dunne, T. and Wheeler, N. (eds): *Human Rights in Global Politics.* Cambridge: Cambridge University Press

Dowley, K. (1998). Striking the Federal Balance in Russia: Comparative Regional Government Strategies, *Communist and Post-Communist Studies* 31: 359–380

Drobizheva, L. (1996). Power Sharing in the Russian Federation: The View from the Center and from the Republics, in *Preventing Deadly Conflict. Strategies and Institutions. Proceedings of a Conference in Moscow*. Carnegie Corporation, at http://www.ccpdc.org/pubs/mosvcow/moscow6.htm

Drobizheva, L. (1997). *Natsionalismy v respublikakh Rossiiskoi Federatsii: ideologiya elity i massovoye coznaniye* (Nationalism in the republics of the Russian Federation: ideology of the elite and mass consciousness), *Panorama-Forum* 1 (8)

Dunne, T. & Wheeler, T. (1999). *Human Rights in Global Politics*. Cambridge: Cambridge University Press

Easter, G. (1997). Redefining Centre-Regional Relations in the Russian Federation: Sverdlovsk *Oblast, Europe-Asia Studies* 49: 617–635

Gellner, E. (1983). *Nations and Nationalism*. Oxford: Oxford University Press

Gorenburg, D. (1999). Regional Separatism in Russia: Ethnic Mobilisation or Power Grab? *Europe-Asia Studies,* 51: 245–274

Gubayeva, T. V. and Malkov, V. P. (1999). Gosudartsvenniy Yazyk i yevo Pravovoi Status (The State Language and its Legal Status), *Gosudarstvo i Pravo* (State and Law) 7: 5–13

Gumilev, L. (1990). *Geografika etnosa i istorichekii period (The geography of the Ethnos in the Historical Period)*. Leningrad: Nauka

Habermas, J. (1995). Citizenship and National Identity: Some Reflections on the Future of Europe, in Beiner, R. (ed) *Theorising Citizenship*. New York: SUNY Press

Hall, J. (ed). (1998). *The State of the Nation: Ernest Gellner and the Theory of Nationalism*. Cambridge: Cambridge University Press

Hroch, M. (1985). *Social Preconditions of National Revival in Europe*. Cambridge: MA

Kempton, D. R. (1996). The republic of Sakha (Yakutia): The Evolution of Centre-Periphery Relations in the Russian Federation, *Europe-Asia Studies* 48: 587–613

Khazanov, A. (1997). Ethnic Nationalism in the Russian Federation, *Daedalus* 126:121–142

Khenkin, S. (1997). Separatizm v Rossii – pozady ili vperedi? (Separatism in Russia – backwards or forwards?"), *Pro et Contra* 2, at http://pubs.carnegie.ru/p&c/ Vol2-1997/2/01henkin.asp

Kossikov, I. (1996). Federalism and Regionalism in Contemporary Russia, speech delivered in September 1996 at the 13th International Seminar European Union, at http://www.eurplace.org/federal/kossikov.html

Kotlyakov, V. M. and Agranat, G. A. (1999). Rossiskii Sever – Krai Bolshikh Vozmozhnostei (The Russian North – Region of Great Possibilities), *Vestnik Rossiskoi Akademii Nauk (Bulletin of the Russian Academy of Science)* 69: 3–15

Kravchenko, S. A., Mnatsakanyan M. O. and Pokrovskii N. E. (1997). *Sotsiologiya: Paradigmy i temy (Sociology: Paradigms and themes)*. Moscow: Nauk

Kranz, J. (ed.) (1998). *Law and Practice of Central European Countries in the Field of National Minorities Protection After 1989*. Warsaw: Center for International Relations

Kryazhkov, V. A. (1997). Pravo Korennikh Malochislennikh Narodov Rossii: Metodologiya Regulirovaniya (The Rights of Indigenous Small-in-number Peoples of Russia: The Methodology of Regulation), *Gosudarstvo i Pravo (State and Law)*. 5: 18-23

Kymlicka, W. (1995). *Multicultural Citizenship*. Oxford: Clarendon Press

Lankina, T. (1999). 'Local self-government' or local political control in Russia? The case of Bashkortostan, *EWI Rossisskii Regionalni Bulleten (Russian Regional Bulletin): Local Government*, 26 July

Lysenko, V. N. (1996). Distribution of Power: The Experience of the Russian Federation, in *Preventing Deadly Conflict. Strategies and Institutions. Proceedings of a Conference in Moscow*. Carnegie Corporation, at http://www.ccpdc.org/pubs/mosvcow/moscow6.htm

Mastyugina, T. and Stelmakh, V. (1994). Maliye narody severa i dalnevo vostoka. Osnovy pravovovo statusa v svete printsipov mezhdunarodnovo opyta. (Minor peoples of the north and far east. Foundations of their legal status in the light of international law and foreign experience), *Rossiiskii Byulletn' po Pravam Cheloveka (Russian Bulletin for Human Rights)* 4: 156–171

Memorial (1997). *Pravo Narodov na Samoopredeleniye: Ideya i Voploshcheniye (The Rights of Peoples to Self-Determination: Idea and Realisation)*. Moscow: Svenya

Mikhaleva, N. A. (1996). Constitutional Reforms in the Republics of the Russian Federation, *Russian Politics and Law*, 67–79

Miller, D. (1997). *On Nationality*. Oxford: Clarendon Press

Murashko, O. A. (1998). Etnoekologicheskii Refugium: Kontseptsiya Sokhraneniya Traditsionnoi Kulturi i Sredi Obitaniya Korennikh Narodov Severa (The Ethnic-Ecological Refugium: The Concept of Preserving the Traditional Culture and Means of Existence of the Indigenous Peoples of the North), *Etnographicheskoye Obozreniye (Ethnographic Observer)* 3: 74–89

Pain, E. A. (1999a). Russia: The Ethnic Dimension, *Russia* December, at http://www.russia-all.ru/society_general.htm

Pain E. A. and Popov A. A. (1999b). "Chechnya – From past to present", at http://www.amina.com/article/history.html

Pershits, A. I. and Smirnova, Ya. S. (1997). Etnologiya Prava (The Ethnology of Law), *Vestnik Rossiskoi Akademii Nauk (Bulletin of the Russian Academy of Science)*. 67: 792–807

Shulzhenko, Yu. (1998). *Institut Konstitutsionnovo Nadzora v Rossiskoi Federatsii (The Institution of Constitutional Review in the Russian Federation)*. Moscow: Institute of State and Law

Shaimiev, Mintimer (1996a). Conflict Prevention and Management: The Significance of Tatarstan's Experience, in *Preventing Deadly Conflict. Strategies and Institutions. Proceedings of a Conference in Moscow.* Carnegie Corporation, at http://www.ccpdc.org/pubs/mosvcow/moscow6.htm

Shaimiev, Mintimer (1996b). Opyt vzaimootnoshenii Tatarstana i Rossii (Experience of the interrelations of Tatarstan and Russia), *Panorama-Forum* 6

Shustov, V. B. (1996). Discrimination Against Indigenous People of the North, A Statement by Social Organisations and Movements of Indigenous People of the North, 4 March, http://arcticcircle.uconn.edu/ArticCircle/SEEJ/russia_indig.html

Smith, A. D. (1983). *Theories of Nationalism.* London: Duckworth
Smith, A. D. (1986). *The Ethnic Origin of Nations.* Oxford: Oxford University Press
Smith, A. D. (1998). *Nationalism and Modernism. A critical survey of recent theories of nations and nationalism.* London: Routledge
Sokolova Z. P., Novikova N. I., Sorin-Chaikov N. V. (1995). Etnographi pishut zakon: kontekst i problemy (Ethnographers write a law: context and problems), *Etnographicheskoye Obozreniye (Ethnographic Observer)* 1: 74–88
Sokolovskii, S. V. (1998). Ponyatiye 'Korennoi Narod' v Rossiskoi Nauke, Politike i Zakonodaltelstvo (The Concept of 'Indigenous People' in Russian Science, Policy and Legislation), *Etnographicheskoye Obozreniye (Ethnographic Observer),* 3: 74–88
Tishkov, V. (1996). O natsii i natsionalisme (On the nation and nationalism), *Svobodnaya Mysl (Free Thought)* 3
Tishkov, V. (1997). *Ethnicity, Nationalism and Conflict in and after the Soviet Union. The Mind Aflame.* London: Sage
Tishkov, V. (1998). Zabyt o natsii. Post-natsionalisticheskoye ponimaniye natsionalism (Forget about the nation. A post-nationalist understanding of nationalism), *Voprosii Philosophii (Questions of Philosophy)* 3–26
Thornberry, P. (1992). *International Law and the Rights of Minorities.* Oxford: Clarendon Press
Tsimbaev, N. I. (1998). Russia and the Russians (The Nationality Question in the Russian Empire), *Russian Studies in History* 37: 53–68
Tyumen International Institute of Economics and Law (1997). *Sovremenniy Federalizm: kraya, oblasti v sostave Rossiiskoi Federatsii (status, modeli vzaimootnosheniya c federanym Tsentrom) (Contemporary Federalism: krais, oblasts in the Russian Federation (status, models of interaction with the Federal Centre),* Tyumen: Vektor Buk
Umnova, I. (1998). *Konstitutsionni Osnovy Sovremennovo Possiiskovo Federalizma (The Constitutional Foundations of Contemporary Russian Federalism).* Moscow: Dyelo
Vishnyakov, V. G. (1998). Konstitutsionnoye Regulirovaniye Federativnikh Otnoshenii (The Constitutional Regulation of Federal Relations), *Gosudartsvo i Pravo (State and Law)* 20–28
Weber, E. (1979). *Peasants into Frenchmen: The Modernisation of Rural France, 1870–1914.* London: Chatto & Windus
Yablokova, A. V. (ed) (1996). *Rossiskaya Arktika: na poroge katastrophi* (The Russian Arctic: on the verge of a catastrophe). Moscow; cited in Kotlyakov and Agranat (1999), above

National Identity:
the Territorial Question in
International and Domestic Law

Transcending Territory:
Towards an Agreed Northern Ireland?

*Brian Thompson**

INTRODUCTION

Given that for many people the 'troubles' in Northern Ireland are perceived as being a religious conflict between catholics and protestants, there is tremendous symbolism in the fact that agreement in the multi-party talks was reached on one of the most important days in the Christian calendar, Good Friday. On the first Good Friday Jesus Christ was crucified. He died but he was resurrected and this sequence of loss followed by renewal and hope may be repeated in Northern Ireland. The parties in the negotiations have had to compromise, to yield significant aspirations in order to reach an agreement, which holds out the longed for prospect of an end to the conflict.

This paper will argue that the Good Friday Agreement or the 'Belfast Agreement' as it is termed in the Northern Ireland Act 1998 is an extremely sophisticated one. It appears to give enough to the various parties to have passed the initial hurdles of being approved in referendums and to offer the possibility of peace, if it can be operated according to its principles.

THE NORTHERN IRELAND PROBLEM[1]

Put at its simplest, the north eastern corner of Ireland, comprising six of the nine counties of the ancient province of Ulster is contested territory. There are broadly, two communities, which have differing allegiances. The nationalist community desires to be part of the Irish republic, in which all of the territory of the island would be unified in one state. Whereas the unionist community desires to retain its links with Great Britain and remain in the United Kingdom of Great Britain and Northern Ireland. The two communities owe their antagonistic origins primarily to the colonisation or 'plantation' of Ulster in the early 17th century. The 'planters' from Britain were mainly protestant, and the indigenous community or 'gaels' were catholic. The period of British rule in Ireland had several bloody episodes from Cromwell[2] through to the

---

* Liverpool Law School, University of Liverpool, UK
[1] There is a vast literature on Northern Ireland. The following are recommended: Whyte 1990; McGarry & O'Leary 1995; O'Leary & McGarry 1996. There are also many volumes on the history of Ireland and Northern Ireland: Beckett 1966; Lyons 1973; Foster 1988; Lee 1989; Bardon 1992.
[2] The massacres at Drogheda and Wexford in September and October 1649.

Stephen Tierney (ed.), Accommodating National Identity: New Approaches in International and Domestic Law, 233–256
© 2000 *Kluwer Law International. Printed in Great Britain.*
First published in the International Journal on Minority and Group Rights, Volume 6 No. 1/2 1999.

Anglo-Irish War or War of Independence 1919–1921[3] and the two communities suffered from earlier bouts of 'troubles' before the 30-year period from 1968 and these have been etched into each community's collective memory.[4]

Matters are slightly complicated by the fact that there were earlier periods of invasion and settlement such as the Norman in the 12th century and this community was catholic and came to be known as the 'old English'. The Stuart plantation had more Scots than English and the Scots were predominantly Presbyterian or 'dissenters'. Policy and its implementation, for example the 'Penal Laws' which favoured the 'planters', did focus on religion, and this promoted Anglicanism, the English established church. This helps to explain why some of the Irish nationalist and republican heroes included protestants such as Wolfe Tone, one of the leaders of the 1798 uprising. This rebellion, and its aborted predecessor in 1796, which did not receive the anticipated assistance from the French due to bad weather affecting the ships bringing troops, persuaded the government in London to abolish the Irish Parliament and incorporate Ireland, like Scotland, into a United Kingdom. Both Acts of Union were accomplished through patronage and bribery. The protestant elite on the whole accepted the union and became unionist. The majority catholic population did not embrace the union, with the failure to keep the promise of simultaneous catholic emancipation being an important factor. Under the leadership of Daniel O'Connell they unsuccessfully sought the repeal of the union. O'Connell died before the potato famine which led to a great decline in the population through death and emigration. The London government did not do much to relieve the misery caused by the failure of this staple food and this led to great bitterness which fuelled anti-British feeling in Ireland and amongst the descendants of those who emigrated, particularly to the United States of America. The famine did not affect Northern Ireland as badly as the rest of Ireland and this region was further distinguished from the rest of the island by its industrialisation. Belfast grew along with, for example, Glasgow and Birmingham, as a major manufacturing city, with ship-building and linen being especially prominent. The movement to regain governmental power in Ireland, 'home rule', was predominantly catholic and the church supported it despite attempts by the British government to woo the catholic hierarchy. Gladstone was converted to home rule and it took the Liberal party three attempts before Irish home rule legislation was passed, the opposition in the House of Lords being by-passed by means of the procedures in the Parliament Act 1911. Opposition in Ireland to home rule was mainly concentrated in Ulster and this included the formation of the Ulster Volunteers who armed themselves and thus induced the counter-formation of the National Volunteers. Implementation of the Government of Ireland Act 1914 looked as if it would be a bloody affair but it was suspended because of the First World War. During the War an uprising was somewhat inefficiently attempted in Dublin over Easter 1916. It was ruthlessly put down. In the 1918 general election the great majority of Irish seats were won by Sinn Féin. Unionist Members of

---

3   The actions of the British army auxiliaries or 'Black and Tans', particularly in Cork in late 1920.
4   For example the 'Battle of the Diamond' in Co. Armagh in 1795 which led to the founding of the protestant Orange Order.

Parliament were concentrated in Ulster. A provisional government was formed in Dublin and a war of independence followed which eventually resulted in the partition of the island into the Irish Free State and Northern Ireland. The Irish Free State was separate from the United Kingdom but was part of the British Empire having 'dominion' status like Australia, Canada, New Zealand and South Africa.[5] The new 'British' political entity, Northern Ireland, comprised the counties of Antrim, Armagh, Down and Londonderry which all had protestant/unionist majorities and also Tyrone and Fermanagh which had nationalist/catholic majorities. Overall Northern Ireland had a ratio of unionist/protestant to nationalist/catholic of 2 to 1.

The constitution for Northern Ireland was the Government of Ireland Act 1920. This created a bicameral legislature which was given competence in transferred matters, expressed as power to make laws for the 'peace, order and good government ... of Northern Ireland'. There were two other categories of legislative power, excepted and reserved. Excepted matters included foreign affairs, defence and naturalisation which were the sole competence of the Westminster parliament. Reserved matters were also to be legislated for by Westminster. In the original scheme envisaged by the 1920 Act, reserved matters had been intended to be given to an all-Ireland parliament. The postal service, the Supreme Court of Judicature of Northern Ireland and registration of deeds were amongst the matters in the reserved category.

During the life of the Northern Ireland Parliament, the government was always formed by the Unionist party and it exercised hegemonic power. Discriminatory actions were taken which included replacing the original proportional voting system for the parliament of Northern Ireland with the plurality, 'first past the post' method. Discrimination also occurred in the local councils of Northern Ireland, particularly in employment practices and the allocation of housing. In the 1960s a civil rights campaign sought to secure equal rights for the minority community. While some changes were made under the reforming Northern Ireland prime minister Terence O'Neill, sectarian tensions were aroused and disorder broke out which was not always dealt with professionally by the police force, the Royal Ulster Constabulary and some of its reserves, the 'B' Specials. In 1969 the UK government in Westminster authorised the use of the army to assist the Northern Ireland government in keeping order. The Northern Ireland government decided to deal with the threat posed by the terrorist activities of the Irish Republican Army (IRA) by interning suspects without trial under the Civil Authorities (Special Powers) Act (Northern Ireland) 1922. This was not successful, innocent men were detained and it served to boost the support for the IRA and increased the number of its volunteers. Finally in March 1972 the Northern Ireland parliament was prorogued, and Northern Ireland was governed under 'direct rule' through the Northern Ireland Office under a Secretary of State who is a member of the British Cabinet.

---

[5] The Irish Free State became Éire, a republic in 1937, and left the Commonwealth in 1949.

POLICY RESPONSES TO NORTHERN IRELAND

In sketching the main lines of the British and Irish governments' policy responses much is omitted. It must be recognised that the two governments have not always worked together, and where they have agreed on objectives, this has not always been reflected in the implementing actions. The route to the Belfast Agreement, signed on 10 April 1998, can be expressed within a matrix composed of themes and initiatives:

Themes
*   devolved, consociational institutions of government
*   values: consent, inclusiveness, diversity, democratic methods
*   three-stranded relationship
*   acknowledgement of ethnic foundation
*   values to guide institutional design
*   law protects & promotes

Initiatives
*   Sunningdale Agreement 1973 &
*   Anglo-Irish Agreement 1985
*   Brooke Talks 1990–1992
*   Joint Declaration 1993
*   Framework Documents 1995
*   Mitchell/Forum/Talks 1996–1998

Themes
It is not always easy to identify the exact point at which these themes crystallised. It took a little time for the British to move from one style of constitution-making to another, which it is suggested was more appropriate to Northern Ireland. One analysis propounded that, at first, a pragmatic empiricist approach was used which was subsequently replaced by a constitutional idealist model (McCrudden 1989). The Government of Ireland Act 1920 exemplifies the former approach as it sought to transplant the Westminster model of constitutional and political practice. This did not work because the political entity of Northern Ireland and its institutions were not supported by the nationalist community which comprised around a third of the population. McCrudden states that the constitutionalist idealist approach has substantive and procedural aspects. The substantive aspect focuses upon the values of liberty, equality and justice and upon the institutions which are likely to secure those values. The procedural aspect highlights institutions, process and methods. For the British government a major policy objective was the creation of acceptable devolved institutions in Northern Ireland which would have an executive drawn from both communities. Such a power-sharing executive, (a form of con-sociationalism[6]) was agreed at Sunningdale in 1973 and it is notable that this model

---

[6]   The leading theorist of consociation, Lijphart, suggests that it has four features: a power-sharing coalition which enjoys more than a simple majority of voters; the different communities must have

is also a feature of the Belfast Agreement. The early attempt at consociationalism marks a move away from the Westminster model of the pragmatic empiricist approach as there was not a great deal of attention devoted to values. Subsequently with the full acknowledgement of the ethnic basis, of the different national identities, the foundation of values was articulated. Both of the communities in Northern Ireland are minorities. The nationalists are a minority within Northern Ireland and the unionists are a minority within Ireland. The two communities must be reassured and protected. The civil society must be one in which diversity is not simply tolerated and protected, but also embraced and promoted. These values should not just be imposed on Northern Ireland by the two governments but be part of their own constitutional arrangements. Thus an important insight by John Hume, the leader of the Social Democratic and Labour Party (SDLP) is that the Northern Ireland problem is concerned with three sets of relationships or three strands. The first deals with the relationships between the two communities within Northern Ireland; the second with the relationship between the two parts of Ireland and the third with relations between the two governments. One factor which necessarily takes in all three strands is the claim in the Irish constitution that Northern Ireland was part of the territory of the Irish state.[7] This was deeply offensive to unionists. It affected their relationship with the nationalist community in Northern Ireland, and their attitude to the Irish government. However, action upon it by the Irish government would necessarily involve the Irish republic's relations with both communities in the north and the British government.

Returning to the values upon which a settlement depends, because the violence was not of such an extent and intensity as to constitute a war with a clear victory which would determine the settlement, the two governments had to uphold the primacy of democracy so that objectives could only be obtained by peaceful means. The principle of consent, therefore carries with it the idea of inclusiveness. It is acknowledged that without the participation of the majority of the parties, there cannot be a settlement, or a settlement that has any chance of working. Accordingly hostilities must be stopped in order that negotiations can be held.

Initiatives

All of the themes identified above are, as we shall see, present in the Belfast Agreement but they are also to be found, in varying degrees, in the first major initiative, the Sunningdale agreement. Most of its elements were prefigured in the white paper *Northern Ireland Constitutional Proposals*.[8] The Northern Ireland Assembly Act 1973 had provided for elections to an assembly using the single transferable vote variant of proportional representation. The Northern Ireland Constitution Act 1973, provided for the devolution of power to the assembly and an

---

some degree of autonomy; there must be proportionality in the public sector in government institutions, public employment, public expenditure and finally, there is required to be a system of protection for minorities by mutual vetoes or concurring majorities (Lijphart 1968; 1975; 1977).

[7]   Article 2, for text of original and amendment see below.

[8]   Cmnd 5259.

executive drawn from it. The devolution was conditional upon the formation of an executive which was likely to 'be widely accepted throughout the community'.[9] The Constitution Act through section 1 declared that Northern Ireland was part of the UK and that this status would not cease without a vote by a majority of the people of Northern Ireland. Hadfield points out that this is not the source of the constitutional guarantee which is to be found in Article 1 of the Anglo-Irish Acts of Union (Hadfield 1989: 105).

After the elections to the assembly which used the single transferable vote system of proportional representation (STV), negotiations were held to see if a power-sharing executive could be formed. Agreement was formally reached at Sunningdale by three of the parties, and the British and Irish governments. This was not a settlement which fully met the ideas of the three-stranded relationships. The experiment in consociational government was brought down by a political strike prompted by action to begin the Council of Ireland, an institution which would now be classified as Strand 2. The Council of Ireland was to have comprised 14 'ministerial' members, seven each from the Northern Ireland executive and the Irish government, with a secretariat and a consultative assembly of 30 Northern Ireland assembly members and 30 members drawn from Dáil Éireann, the lower chamber of the Irish parliament. Resolutions of the Council would require unanimity. Its main role was consultative, with a view to possible harmonisation. It was, however, a step too far for some unionists who could not countenance contact, never mind co-operation with the Irish government. While it was unionists who destroyed the Sunningdale agreement, it was not without its nationalist critics. Paragraph 5 of the Sunningdale agreement contained parallel declarations by the two governments:

> The Irish government fully accepted and solemnly declared that there could be no change in the status of Northern Ireland until a majority of the people of Northern Ireland desired a change in that status.

The British government solemnly declared that it was, and would remain, their policy to support the wishes of the majority of the people of Northern Ireland. The present status of Northern Ireland is that it is part of the United Kingdom. If in the future the majority of the people of Northern Ireland should indicate a wish to become part of a united Ireland, the British Government will support that wish.

The Irish government's declaration was challenged in the courts by a former Irish government minister on the basis that it was not in conformity with Articles 2 and 3 of the Irish Constitution. The Supreme Court ruled in *Boland* v. *An Taoiseach*[10] that as the Sunningdale agreement was an act of executive power it could not be subjected to judicial review for unconstitutionality. Fitzgerald C. J. and O'Keefe P. held that the reference to the status of Northern Ireland in paragraph 5 was to *de facto* status and did not amount to a recognition of Northern Ireland as being *de jure* part of the United Kingdom, which would be incompatible with the Irish constitution.

---

[9] Section 2(1)(b).
[10] (1974) IR 338.

The ruling did not reassure unionists and reinforced the point for the two governments that the constitutional claim limited what the Irish government could do.

The next major initiative[11] with which we deal is the Anglo-Irish Agreement 1985 (AIA). This is significant because it articulated important values, which would recognise and legitimate the aspirations of the two communities in Northern Ireland. This was partially undermined by the fact that it was negotiated over the heads of the people of Northern Ireland. Whilst there were lines of communication between the nationalist community and the Irish government, this was not the case between unionists and the British government. Indeed part of the idea of the AIA was that it broke what was perceived as being the unionist veto. The arrangements in the AIA were designed so that they could not founder through a unionist boycott. Senator Mary Robinson, later to become the President of Ireland, resigned from the Labour party, which supported the AIA, because the unionist community had not been consulted.

The AIA created inter-governmental institutions: a conference jointly chaired by the Northern Ireland Secretary and the Foreign Minister, serviced by a Secretariat. It also envisaged an Anglo-Irish parliamentary body. The AIA established institutions and a process in which the two governments could discuss the following topics concerning Northern Ireland: political matters, security and related matters, legal matters including the administration of justice, and cross-border co-operation on security, economic, social and cultural matters. This conferred upon the Irish government a consultative role in the governance of Northern Ireland which was anathema to unionists, but it was not joint sovereignty which was one of the options proposed in the report of the New Ireland Forum.

The AIA tried to balance matters between the unionists and the nationalists. In Article 1:

The two Governments
  (a) affirm that any change in the status of Northern Ireland would only come about with the consent of a majority of the people of Northern Ireland;
  (b) recognise that the present wish of a majority of the people of Northern Ireland is for no change in the status of Northern Ireland;
  (c) declare that, if in the future a majority of the people of Northern Ireland clearly wish for and formally consent to the establishment of a united

---

[11] There were several initiatives tried between the collapse of the executive in 1974 and the 1985 Anglo-Irish Agreement. A Constitutional Convention was elected in 1975, it reported in that year, was reconvened and abolished in 1976; the British and Irish Prime Ministers met in summits in 1980 and an Anglo-Irish Intergovernmental Council established in 1981; a policy of 'rolling devolution' was also tried under which, if there was cross-community support, more powers would be conferred to local institutions. *Northern Ireland: A Framework for Devolution* Cmnd. 8541, (1982) enacted in the Northern Ireland Act 1982, however, as the Social, Democratic and Labour Party, which enjoyed the largest support in the nationalist community boycotted the work of the assembly the initiative did not succeed. The SDLP did participate in the New Ireland Forum which was established by the Irish political parties and which issued a report in 1984 which proposed 3 models for the future of Ireland: unitary Irish state, federal Irish state, and British and Irish joint authority over Northern Ireland. Although all of these were rejected by British Prime Minister Thatcher, they contributed to the making of the Anglo-Irish Agreement.

Ireland, they will introduce and support in the respective Parliaments
legislation to give effect to that wish.

Once again a challenge was made in the Irish courts but this time it was made by
unionists.[12] It was not successful. The AIA carefully did not stipulate what the present
constitutional status was and so the finding of conformity with the Irish constitution
was not a surprise. What was a surprise was the holding by the Supreme Court that
the reintegration of Northern Ireland within the national territory was a constitutional
imperative, and not a political aspiration.

Article 1 of the AIA was not that different from Paragraph 5 of the Sunningdale
agreement. Articles 4 and 6 were significant as they committed the governments to
work for the accommodation of the rights and identities of the two traditions which
exist in Northern Ireland, to promote reconciliation, respect for human rights, co-
operation against terrorism and the development of economic, social and cultural
co-operation.

The strategy of the AIA then was to bind the governments together, to proclaim
that the two traditions had a right to co-exist and to be respected by the governments
and by any institutions in Northern Ireland which might subsequently be created.
This involved what has been termed 'coercive consociationalism' (O'Leary 1989),
which offers the unionists incentives to agree to a power-sharing executive because
that would reduce the consultative role of the Irish government in the inter-
governmental conference. There would still be an irreducible role which was designed
to reassure the nationalists, so that they would have the Irish government as their
guarantor. For the unionists the union would only end if that was the majority wish
of the people of Northern Ireland, and the AIA promised better co-operation between
the two states' security forces against terrorism and the Irish government agreed to
ratify the 1977 European Convention on the Suppression of Terrorism, which reduces
the political offence exception in extradition proceedings. Nationalists were to be
reassured by the consultative role which the Irish government would play in the
administration of justice, which was intended to be a confidence-raising point.

The unionists were not reassured by the AIA despite the overwhelming support it
received in the Westminster Parliament. They resolved to remove it. The AIA was
also criticised by the Irish opposition party, Fianna Fail, but when they came into
government they operated it with the same commitment as their Fine Gael-Labour
predecessors had.

As the unionists were not reconciled to the AIA a new initiative was tried by
Northern Ireland Secretary Peter Brooke. His idea was to create the conditions for
talks amongst the Northern Ireland political parties. The major point to come out of
this initiative was the idea of the three-stranded relationship. As we have seen aspects
of it were present in previous initiatives but from now on it was the framework
within which negotiations would be conducted.

John Hume of the SDLP had been talking to Gerry Adams the leader of Sinn
Féin, regarded as the political representatives of the IRA. His efforts led to the Irish

---

[12] *McGimpsey* v. *Ireland* (1990) 1 IR 110.

and the US governments being able to persuade the British government that the only way forward was to create a process by which the paramilitaries would stop their campaign of violence, the so-called 'armed struggle', enabling Sinn Féin to participate in multi-party talks. The Joint Declaration for Peace, or Downing Street Declaration, of December 1993[13] was designed to achieve this. In addition to reiterating that a change in Northern Ireland's constitutional status from being part of the UK to part of a united Ireland could only arise from the wish of the majority of the people living there, the British government stated that it had no 'selfish strategic or economic interest in Northern Ireland'.[14] The two governments made it clear that the achievement of peace must involve a permanent end to the use of, or support for, paramilitary violence. Parties that were committed to exclusively peaceful methods and could demonstrate that they abided by the democratic process could 'join in' dialogue in due course between the governments and the political parties on the way ahead.[15]

The following year saw the announcement of IRA and Loyalist paramilitary cease-fires. Whilst the governments were talking to the various political parties including Sinn Féin and the Progressive Unionist Party and the Ulster Democratic Party who had close links to the paramilitaries, the formal multi-party talks had not been commenced. In February 1995 the two governments produced the Framework documents[16] which indicated the possible contours of agreements on the three strands. These were based on the governments' assessments of the positions which the parties had put forward in their contacts with the governments. Strand 1 would see a fairly complicated system of committees overseeing the work of the Northern Ireland departments. This was full of safeguards so that neither community could be damaged by the other. This gave unionists some of what they wished for, but it was linked to Strand 2 which gave nationalists what they wanted, which was an institutional link to, and expression of, all-Ireland relationships. Various topics were identified where consultation and possible harmonising and executive action could take place. The two governments would maintain their links in new inter-governmental arrangements.

Despite these signs of what the agreement might cover, the talks which could lead to it had not been set in motion. The issue of the decommissioning of paramilitary weapons was a sticking point for the unionists and the British government. An international body chaired by former US Senator George Mitchell was convened to investigate the attitudes of the parties. The Mitchell report[17] indicated that none of the paramilitaries were prepared to yield their weapons before multi-party talks began. The report suggested that one way forward might be to have decommissioning take place during the talks. The report also recommended that certain principles should be subscribed to by parties who would participate in the talks. These principles

---

[13] Cm 2442.
[14] *Ibid.*, paragraph 4.
[15] *Ibid.*, paragraph 10.
[16] *Frameworks for the Future* (Belfast 1995) comprises *A Framework for Accountable Government in Northern Ireland* by the British government and *A New Framework for Agreement* by the British and Irish governments.
[17] *Report of the International Body on Arms and Decommissioning* (Belfast, 1996).

were: commitment to democratic and exclusively peaceful means of resolving political issues; the giving of undertakings by all paramilitary organisations to the total disarmament of these organisations, which would be verifiable to the satisfaction of an independent commission; the renouncing of the use of force or threats of force to influence the course of negotiations, and the opposition to any efforts by others to use force or the threat of it in this way; to agree to abide by the terms of any agreement reached in negotiations and to resort to democratic and exclusively peaceful methods in trying to alter any aspect of that outcome with which they might disagree; and to take effective steps to prevent punishment killings and beatings. The two governments had diverged in their reaction to the Mitchell report. The British prime minister John Major decided that the way forward might be one of the items considered by the International Body, namely an elective process. In the month after the publication of the Mitchell report the IRA broke its cease-fire. The governments agreed a response arranging for election to a Northern Ireland Forum which would allow for entry into talks but only to those representatives in the Forum who had eschewed violence.[18] Elections were held and although Sinn Féin had representatives returned it could not join the talks. After the election of the Labour government almost a year after the Forum elections, a timetable for the talks was set and assurances given that if the cease-fire was renewed then Sinn Féin could participate in the talks. A cease-fire was announced, Sinn Féin was permitted to join and the Ulster Unionist Party decided not to withdraw although other unionist parties did. The negotiations began and concluded in agreement on Good Friday 1998.

THE BELFAST AGREEMENT[19]

The following are the headings in the agreement:

Constitutional Issues
        British legislation
        Irish legislation
Strand 1   Democratic institutions in Northern Ireland
Strand 2   North-South Ministerial Council
Strand 3   British-Irish Council
        British-Irish Intergovernmental Conference
Rights, Safeguards and Equality of Opportunity
        Human Rights
         UK legislation
         New institutions in Northern Ireland
         Comparable Irish steps

---

[18] Northern Ireland (Entry to Negotiations) Act 1996, *Northern Ireland: Ground Rules for Substantive All-Party Negotiations* Cm 3232 (1996).

[19] *The Belfast Agreement: Agreement Reached in the Multi-Party Negotiations on Northern Ireland*, Cm 3883 (1998). References will be given to the statutory implementation of the Belfast Agreement's provisions, primarily in the Northern Ireland Act 1998.

Joint Committee
Reconciliation and Victims of violence
Economic, Social and Cultural issues
Decommissioning
Security
Policing and Justice
Commission on Policing for Northern Ireland
Review of Criminal Justice system
Prisoners
Validation, Implementation and Review

In this chapter, dealing as it does with national identity, the focus will not be on those parts of the Belfast Agreement dealing with decommissioning and prisoners. This is not to deny the importance of these topics. Decommissioning has already proved to be a stumbling block and for the unionists some action on this point is being called for before other elements of the agreement can be implemented. The agreement provides for accelerated release of those imprisoned for 'scheduled' offences (terrorist offences, including murder) but these prisoners must be aligned to groups which have committed to the cease-fire.[20]

The themes identified earlier are all present in the Belfast Agreement. It is carefully crafted with a balancing of points for the two communities. Accordingly, it is quite in keeping that the first item concerns constitutional issues, in particular the amending of Articles 2 and 3 of the Irish constitution.

Original Article 2
The national territory consists of the whole island of Ireland, its islands and the territorial sea.

Amended Article 2
It is the entitlement and birthright of every person born in the island of Ireland, which includes its islands and seas, to be part of the Irish nation. That is also the entitlement of all persons otherwise qualified in accordance with law to be citizens of Ireland. Furthermore the Irish nation cherishes its special affinity with people of Irish ancestry living abroad who share its cultural identity and heritage.

Original Article 3
Pending the re-integration of the national territory, and without prejudice to the right of the Parliament and Government established by this Constitution to exercise jurisdiction over the whole of that territory, the laws enacted by that Parliament shall have the like area and extent of application as the laws of the Saorstat Eireann and the like extra-territorial effect.

---

[20] The Agreement p. 25, implemented in Northern Ireland (Sentences) Act 1998.

Amended Article 3
1. It is the firm will of the Irish nation, in harmony and friendship, to unite all the people who share the territory of the island of Ireland, in all the diversity of their identities and traditions, recognising that a united Ireland shall be brought about only by peaceful means with the consent of a majority of the people, democratically expressed, in both jurisdictions in the island. Until then, the laws enacted by the Parliament established by this Constitution shall have the like area and extent of application as the laws enacted by the Parliament that existed immediately before the coming into operation of this Constitution.

2. Institutions with executive powers and functions that are shared between those jurisdictions may be established by their respective responsible authorities for stated purposes and may exercise powers and functions in respect of all or any part of the island.

The Irish territorial claim to the whole island is now removed.[21] The amended articles pronounce the values of consent, diversity and inclusivity. The Irish nation is not only associated with the island of Ireland but also with those of Irish ancestry, the Irish diaspora. The older concept of Irish nationalism with its twin markers of gael and catholicism is replaced with one which recognises the unionist tradition and identity. This inclusive concept of nationality transcends territory and allegiance but not in an irredentist, expansionist fashion. The people of Northern Ireland will only be part of a united Ireland if they and the people of the Republic vote for it.

This constitutional change is balanced by British legislation which would repeal the Government of Ireland Act 1920 and amend section 1 of the Northern Ireland Constitution Act 1973 along the lines of the AIA so that a vote by the people of Northern Ireland for Northern Ireland to cease to be part of the UK and to be part of a united Ireland would be given effect.[22]

The aim is to reassure both communities in both the short and long term. Thus the governments recognise the right of people in Northern Ireland to identify themselves as Irish, British or both as they choose. They can currently, and will continue to be able to, hold both British and Irish citizenship. Thus nationalists can be Irish citizens while Northern Ireland remains part of the UK and if Northern Ireland becomes part of a united Ireland, unionists could continue to be British citizens.

Strand 1
The arrangements for democratic institutions in Northern Ireland create an assembly with legislative and executive power. The assembly's 108 members will be elected using STV.[23] The legislative competence of the assembly is defined by reference to

---

[21] Article 29.7 makes it clear that the amendments to Articles 2 and 3 are conditional upon the implementation of the Agreement.
[22] Northern Ireland Act 1998, section 1 on the status of Northern Ireland, section 2 repeals the Government of Ireland Act 1920.
[23] Northern Ireland (Elections) Act 1998.

transferred, excepted and reserved matters. Transferred matters[24] are those not in the excepted and reserved categories. Excepted matters are those which Westminster retains and reserved matters may be legislated upon by the assembly with the Secretary of State's consent and subject to parliamentary control. Excepted matters include the Crown, international relations treaties, defence, control of nuclear, biological and chemical weapons, dignities, treason, nationality, UK-wide taxes, national insurance, appointment of the judiciary and the Director and Deputy Director of Public Prosecutions, elections, the franchise, registration of political parties. Reserved matters include navigation, the foreshore and seabed, domicile, postal service, disqualification from membership of the assembly, criminal law matters including the creation of offences and penalties, prevention and detection of crime, detention, treatment of offenders, surrender of fugitive offenders to Northern Ireland, maintenance of public order, police matters, the Emergency Powers Act (Northern Ireland) 1926, matters relating to the Supreme Court of Judicature of Northern Ireland, trade outside the UK, various matters under the Pension Schemes Act 1993, financial services, regulation of anti-competitive practices, units of measurement, telecommunications, the National Lottery, xenotransplantation, surrogacy, Human Fertilisation and Embryology Act 1990, human genetics, Data Protection Act 1984, nuclear installations, regulation of activities in outer space, oaths and declarations.

This tripartite arrangement repeats the model established in the Government of Ireland Act 1920 and the Northern Ireland Constitution Act 1973. It will be possible for matters to be moved in and out of the transferred and reserved categories but such changes will be subject to safeguards. The safeguards include special voting procedures described below. The assembly will not have the power to make legislation which infringes the European Convention on Human Rights, or the equality provisions of the agreement, or European Community law.[25] Scrutiny of Bills for conformity with the European Convention on Human Rights can be carried out, on reference, by the Judicial Committee of the Privy Council,[26] a committee of the assembly,[27] and the Northern Ireland Human Rights Commission.[28] The assembly committee would have the power to call for persons and papers. Its report would be considered by the assembly and be determined using the special procedures.

There will be mechanisms based on those proposed for the Scottish parliament, to ensure co-ordination, and to avoid disputes between the assembly and Westminster.[29] The Westminster Parliament's power to make legislation for Northern Ireland will remain unaffected.[30] Westminster would legislate for excepted matters and reserved matters not given to the assembly. Thus Westminster would ensure that

[24] Northern Ireland Act 1998, schedules 2 and 3 define excepted and reserved matters respectively.
[25] Northern Ireland Act 1998, section 6(2).
[26] Reference by Attorney General for Northern Ireland, Northern Ireland Act 1998, section 11.
[27] Northern Ireland Act 1998, section 13(3).
[28] Northern Ireland Act 1998, section 13(4).
[29] These include scrutiny of proposed legislation by the two devolved legislatures' Presiding Officers and by the Judicial Committee of the Privy Council, Northern Ireland Act 1998, sections 10, 11, and Scotland Act 1998, sections 31, 33.
[30] Northern Ireland Act 1998, section 5(6).

the UK's international obligations are met in Northern Ireland.[31] The work of the Secretary of State would be scrutinised through the House of Commons Northern Ireland Select and Grand Committees.

Some decisions will be subjected to special procedures so as to ensure that they are taken on a cross-community basis. These may be either: parallel consent in which not only must there be a majority of those present and voting, but this must constitute separate majorities of both the unionist and nationalist designations present and voting; or a weighted majority requiring 60 per cent of those members present and voting, with at least 40 per cent of each of the nationalist and unionist designations present and voting.[32] Accordingly, for these procedures to work they require members to register their designation as nationalist, unionist or other. Some decisions which will be subject to these procedures will be nominated in advance and will include: the election of the chair/presiding officer of the assembly and the First and Deputy First Ministers, and agreement on the assembly's standing orders and on budget allocations. The special procedures could also be triggered by a petition from 30 of the members.[33] There will also be an Equality Commission[34] to monitor the statutory obligation to promote equality of opportunity[35] in specified areas and parity of esteem between the two communities and also to investigate complaints against public bodies.[36]

There will be an executive committee[37] which will comprise the First and Deputy First Ministers[38] chosen using the special procedure, and the subsequent ministers will be chosen under the d'Hondt system. The ministers will agree a programme of work with its associated budget[39] and this programme will be scrutinised by the relevant departmental committees and then be subject to approval by the special procedures. All of the ministers will, as a condition of appointment, have to affirm a pledge of office[40] which will require the discharge of duties in good faith, a commitment to non-violence and to exclusively peaceful and democratic means; to serve all of the people of Northern Ireland equally; to comply with the obligation upon government to promote equality and prevent discrimination; to participate with colleagues in the preparation of a programme for government; to operate within the framework of that programme when agreed within the executive committee and endorsed by the assembly; to support and to act in accordance with, all decisions of the executive committee and assembly and to comply with the ministerial code of conduct.

---

[31] Northern Ireland Act 1998, section 26 confers power on the Secretary of State to stop action incompatible with, and to require action to give effect to, international obligations.
[32] Northern Ireland Act 1998, section 4(5).
[33] Northern Ireland Act 1998, section 42.
[34] Northern Ireland Act 1998, section 73.
[35] Northern Ireland Act 1998, section 75, schedule 9.
[36] Northern Ireland Act 1998, schedule 9.
[37] Northern Ireland Act 1998, section 20.
[38] Northern Ireland Act 1998, sections 16, 20.
[39] Northern Ireland Act 1998, section 20(3) which implements paragraphs 19 and 20 of Strand 1 of the Belfast Agreement.
[40] Northern Ireland Act 1998, section 18(8), the pledge is in schedule 4.

The ministerial code derives from the work of the UK's Committee on Standards in Public Life and obliges the ministers to follow the seven principles of public life adumbrated by that committee.[41] The code is concerned with propriety and regularity in the stewardship of public funds. Ministers are to be accountable for their actions, are not to use public office for personal gain and are to promote good community relations and equality of treatment.

There is also provision for the establishment of a consultative Civic Forum.[42] It would comprise representatives of the business, trade union and voluntary sectors, and such other sectors as the First and Deputy First Minister agree. These ministers will agree on administrative support for the body and establish guidelines for the selection of the representatives. The remit of the body will be social, economic and cultural issues.

Elections were to be held for the assembly in June 1998 at which point a transitional period would commence during which no legislative or executive powers would be devolved.[43] The assembly would elect its Presiding Officer and the First and Deputy First Ministers and determine its standing orders and working practices and generally prepare for the operation of the new institutions in all of the three strands. A shadow executive committee would be established and all of the shadow ministers would have to commit to non-violence and exclusively peaceful means, to work in good faith to bring the new arrangements into being and to observe the spirit of the pledge of office for ministers.

The democratic institutions in the Belfast Agreement are closer to the Sunningdale model than those envisaged in the 1995 Framework documents. There is an executive which will operate as a kind of cabinet with the requirement to agree a programme of work. In the Framework proposals, there would have been two sets of elections: one for the assembly and one for a three-person panel which would oversee the work of the assembly and which would have been more of a safeguard than a real institution of executive government. The Belfast Agreement's executive committee will be a form of power-sharing because membership of it is derived from the proportionate party strengths in the assembly. It has been suggested that the d'Hondt variation of proportionality will favour the larger parties and so they prefer the Saint-Laguë variant (McGarry and O'Leary 1995: 374–375). The STV method used to elect the assembly will also favour the larger parties, however, this may be offset by the fact that the assembly is to have 108 members and not the 90 proposed in the Framework documents. The electoral method used to elect the Forum in 1996 used a mixture of STV and a 'top-up' party list which allocated a further twenty seats to the ten parties with the highest totals of votes. This gave the smaller parties, which did not have candidates elected in the multi-member constituencies, two members. In effect this system was designed to ensure that the smaller parties such as the Progressive Unionist Party, and the Ulster Democratic Party which had close links with loyalist paramilitaries and the Women's Coalition, would have representation

---

[41] *First Report from the Standing Committee on Standards in Public Life* Cm 2850 (1995) (London, HMSO) p. 14.
[42] Northern Ireland Act 1998, section 56.
[43] *The Agreement* Strand 1, paragraph 35.

in the Forum and thus qualify for inclusion in the multi-party talks. The smaller parties have secured representation in the assembly but it is not sufficient for inclusion in the executive committee.

It is possible that the special cross-community procedures with their stipulated majorities might lead to gridlock. The thinking must be that as consensus is required this will influence the assembly and the executive committee into learning how to compromise, something which is new to Northern Ireland's politicians who have not been involved in any meaningful form of government for a long time.

Strand 2

The North/South Ministerial Council has the remit to 'develop consultation, co-operation and action within the island of Ireland – including through implementation on an all-island and cross-border basis – on matters of mutual interest within the competence of the administrations, North and South. Participation in the council is to be a responsibility attaching to posts in the two administrations.[44] Where a minister fails to participate normally then the Taoiseach in respect of the Irish government, and the First and Deputy First Ministers in the case of the Northern Ireland administration, are to be able to make alternative arrangements. The council may meet in different formats: (a) as a biannual plenary body; (b) in specific sectoral formats on a regular and frequent basis with each side represented by the appropriate minister; and (c) in an appropriate format to consider international or cross-sectoral matters, including European Union matters, and to resolve disputes.

The council will exchange information and discuss and consult with a view to co-operating on matters of mutual interest; will use best endeavours to reach agreement on the adoption of common policies where there is a mutual cross-border and all-island benefit, and which are within the competence of both administrations, with the administrations making determined efforts to overcome any disagreements; to take decisions by agreement on policies for implementation separately in each jurisdiction in relevant meaningful areas within their competences; to take decisions by agreement on policies and action at an all-island and cross-border level to be implemented by bodies some of which will be existing bodies in each jurisdiction and some of which will be bodies agreed on a cross-border or all-island level.

By 31 October 1998, the transitional Northern Ireland administration was to have agreed with the Irish government, a work programme, in consultation with the British government, with a view to identifying and agreeing 12 subject areas where co-operation and implementation for mutual benefit would take place. The council was also to have identified and agreed at least six matters for co-operation and implementation in each of the following categories: matters where existing bodies will be the appropriate mechanisms for co-operation in each jurisdiction; and matters where co-operation will take place through agreed implementation bodies on a cross-border or all-island level.

These areas could include matters in the following list:

---

[44] Northern Ireland Act 1998, section 52.

1. Agriculture – animal and plant health;
2. Education – teacher qualifications and exchanges;
3. Transport – strategic transport planning;
4. Environment – environmental protection, pollution, water quality and waste management;
5. Waterways – inland waterways;
6. Social Security/Social Welfare – entitlements of cross-border workers and fraud control;
7. Tourism – promotion, marketing research, and product development;
8. Relevant EU programmes such as SPPR, INTERREG, Leader II and their successors;
9. Inland Fisheries;
10. Aquaculture and marine matters;
11. Health: accident and emergency services and other related cross-border issues; and
12. Urban and rural development.[45]

The two governments are to make the necessary arrangements which will ensure that the bodies agreed as part of the council's work programme will function at the time of the inception of the British-Irish Agreement, or as soon as possible thereafter, and that the transfer of powers (to the assembly) is to include legislative authority for these bodies.[46] Other arrangements will also commence contemporaneously with the transfer of powers to the assembly.

The council is to have a standing secretariat staffed by members of the Northern Ireland Civil Service and the Irish Civil Service. Consideration is to be given to the creation of supplementary bodies: a parliamentary forum comprising an equal number of members from the assembly and the Oireachtas (Irish parliament) for discussion of matters of mutual concern; and an independent consultative forum representative of civil society, comprising the social partners and others with expertise in social, cultural, economic and other issues.

The key points are the locking together of Strand 1 and Strand 2, the goals and timetables. If Strand 1 gives the unionists some of what they want then the price for that is co-operation with the Republic which is what the nationalists want. The architecture bears some resemblance to European Union Institutions. The biennial

---

[45] The 31 October deadline for the agreement of matters of North-South co-operation and implementation was missed but agreement was reached on 18 December 1998. Six implementation bodies were agreed: Inland Waterways, Food Safety, Trade and Business Development, Special EU Programmes, Language (Irish and Ulster Scots), Aquaculture and Marine Matters. The six areas for co-operation include some aspects of Transport, Agriculture, Education, Health, Environment and Tourism. Agreement was also reached on the number of Departments and thus the size of the Northern Ireland executive committee but appointments to the ministerial posts were not agreed because of Ulster Unionist Party concern about the lack of progress on decommissioning of weapons, particularly by the IRA.

[46] Northern Ireland Act 1998, section 55 gives the Secretary of State power to make orders to confer powers and functions on implementation bodies and the new Article 3.2 of the Irish constitution authorises these bodies to carry out functions.

plenary body shares the frequency of meetings of the European Council and the participation of nominated parliamentarians along the lines of the original European Assembly/Parliament. The sectoral meetings seem to be modelled on the sectoral Council of Ministers, and the consultative bodies resemble the Economic and Social Committee, and the Council of the Regions, not least with the use of the European terminology of social partners. Given that Strand 2's remit covers EU matters, it is entirely appropriate that it should have European influences in its design.

The Framework documents were more explicit about the different levels of the work in Strand 2 using the labels consultative, harmonising and executive. All of these are in the Belfast Agreement's terms of cooperation, consultation and action. Perhaps it was thought that spelling out so clearly the possibility of executive action being taken would be unduly provocative to those unionists concerned about the role and influence of the Irish government in Northern Ireland's affairs. Nationalists may be reassured by the details of Strand 2 and the fact that the transfer of power to the Strand 1 institutions will not occur until the Secretary of State is satisfied that the agreement is working satisfactorily, and so insufficient progress on Strand 2 would block Strand 1. Momentum on Strand 2 is to be generated by the interim targets such as the 31 October deadline at which point there is supposed to be agreement on six matters of North-South cooperation. The areas of co-operation identified in the Framework documents are mostly repeated in the Belfast Agreement, although industrial development, energy and consumer and economic policy have disappeared since 1995.

Strand 3

There are two bodies the British-Irish Council (BIC)[47] and the British Irish Intergovernmental Conference (BIIGC).[48] The BIC is to comprise representatives of the British and Irish governments and the devolved institutions in Northern Ireland, Scotland and Wales, plus representatives from the Isle of Man and the Channel Islands.

The BIC will exchange information, discuss, consult and use best endeavours to reach agreement on co-operation on matters of mutual interest. Early suitable candidates would include transport links, agricultural issues, environmental issues, cultural issues, health issues, education issues, and approaches to EU issues. It is open to the BIC to agree common policies or common actions and their means of implementation. Implementation will require unanimity, otherwise it will operate by consensus. It will also be possible for two or more members to develop bilateral or multilateral arrangements.

The BIIGC subsumes the Anglo-Irish Inter-governmental Council and the Inter-governmental Conference established under the 1985 AIA. Whilst the remit can cover bilateral co-operation at all levels on matters of mutual interest, particular concern will be given to non-devolved matters on which the Irish may put forward views and proposals and this could include cross-border and all-island non-devolved

---

[47]   Northern Ireland Act 1998, section 52.
[48]   Northern Ireland Act 1998, section 54.

matters. Relevant ministers from the Northern Ireland executive will be involved in conference meetings and in the reviews of the working of the British-Irish agreement dealing with non-devolved matters.

The balancing achieved in Strand 3 is that for unionists the detested AIA is superseded by the new institutions in which the ministers from the executive committee will be able to play a part. For the nationalists the Irish government can still act as a guarantor and it will continue to have a consultative role in the important non-devolved issues of justice, prisons and policing in Northern Ireland. If the people of Northern Ireland were to vote to join a united Ireland then the unionists could still enjoy British citizenship and through the BIC could be part of a wider set of relationships beyond the new, more pluralist, united Ireland.

Rights
The parties to the agreement all affirmed their commitment to the mutual respect, the civil rights and to the religious liberties of everyone in the community. In particular they affirmed: freedom of political thought, the right to freedom of and expression of religion, the right to pursue democratically national and political aspirations, the right to seek constitutional change by peaceful and legitimate means, the right to choose freely one's place of residence, the right to equal opportunity in all social and economic activity, regardless of class, creed, disability, gender or ethnicity, the right to freedom from sectarian harassment and the right of women to full and equal political participation.

The UK would complete its incorporation of the ECHR with direct access to the courts and their jurisdiction will include power to overrule assembly legislation on grounds of inconsistency. A statutory obligation will be placed upon public authorities in Northern Ireland to promote equality of opportunity in relation to religion and political opinion, gender, race, disability, age, marital status, dependants and sexual orientation. The public bodies would be obliged to devise statutory schemes to implement this obligation and would cover arrangements for policy appraisal, including an assessment of impact on relevant categories, public consultation, public access to information and services, monitoring and timetables. A new Northern Ireland Human Rights Commission would be created[49] and it would consult upon and then advise on the scope for defining in Westminster legislation supplementary rights to the ECHR which would reflect the particular circumstances of Northern Ireland. These additional rights would reflect the principles of mutual respect for the identity and ethos of both communities and parity of esteem. Together with the ECHR these rights would constitute a Bill of Rights for Northern Ireland.[50] The Commission will consider the formulation of the obligation upon public bodies to respect the identity and ethos of the two communities in Northern Ireland and a clear formulation of, (a) the right not to be discriminated against, and (b) the right to equality of opportunity in the public and private sectors.

---

[49]   Northern Ireland Act 1998, section 68.
[50]   Northern Ireland Act 1998, section 69.

The Commission will be established by Westminster legislation, be independent of government, and reflect the community balance in its membership. Its remit will be wider than the Standing Advisory Commission on Human Rights which is dissolved.[51] Its powers will include: monitoring the effectiveness and adequacy of laws and practices; making recommendations to government; consideration of draft legislation on reference by the assembly; the provision of information and promotion of awareness of human rights, and in appropriate cases the bringing of court proceedings or provision of assistance to individuals who litigate. Following public consultation, the British government decided to create a unified Equality Commission which would replace the Fair Employment Commission, the Equal Opportunities Commission (NI), the Commission for Racial Equality (NI) and the Disability Council.[52] The remit of this body would be to advise on, validate and monitor statutory obligations and to investigate complaints of default. It would be open to the assembly to bring together the responsibilities in these areas in a Department of Equality.

The Irish government will take action within its jurisdiction to strengthen further the protection of human rights. This will take into account the work of the All-Party Oireachtas Committee on the Constitution and the report of the Constitution Review Group. This will include consideration of incorporating the ECHR. Measures to be brought forward would ensure at least an equivalent level of protection of human rights as will pertain in Northern Ireland. The Irish government commits itself to establishing a Human Rights Commission equivalent to that in Northern Ireland, to proceed to the speedy ratification of the Council of Europe Framework Convention on National Minorities (which has been ratified by the UK), to implement enhanced employment equality legislation, to introduce equal status legislation and to continue to take further active steps to demonstrate its respect for the different traditions in the island of Ireland.

It is envisaged that the two Human Rights Commissions would establish a joint committee to consider human rights issues in the island of Ireland. It would consider, amongst other things, the possibility of establishing a charter open to signature by all democratic political parties, reflecting and endorsing agreed measures for the protection of fundamental rights of everyone living in the island of Ireland.

It is obvious that human rights should be protected in Northern Ireland and that the rights go beyond the individualistic ones protected in the ECHR. The Northern Ireland political parties have for some time agreed that protection of human rights was necessary and have accepted that incorporation of the ECHR would be a minimum step. Equivalent action by the Irish government is required, again to reassure unionists, that if unification came about, they and their ethos and traditions would not only be respected but protected.

The UK has been prepared to do more to protect human rights in Northern Ireland than in Great Britain. The Conservative governments were opposed to incorporation of the ECHR but would have enacted a Bill of Rights for Northern Ireland despite

---

[51] Northern Ireland Act 1998, section 72.
[52] Northern Ireland Act 1998, section 73.

the precedent it might have set for the rest of its jurisdiction. The current Labour administration has not included the establishment of a commission in the Human Rights Act 1998. It is unfortunate that the protection of human rights will be stronger in Ireland than in Great Britain.

Economic, Social and Cultural Rights
The British government will pursue broad polces for sustained economic growth and stability in Northern Ireland and for promoting social inclusion including community development and the advancement of women in public life.

   The parties recognise the importance of respect and understanding and tolerance in relation to linguistic diversity, which in Northern Ireland includes the Irish language, Ulster-Scots and the languages of the various ethnic communities all of which are part of the cultural wealth of the island of Ireland. The British government is considering whether the UK ought to sign the Council of Europe Charter for Regional and Minority Languages. The British government will, in relation to the Irish language, take action to promote the language, facilitate and encourage the use of the language in speech and writing in public and private life where there is appropriate demand, and seek to remove, where possible, restrictions which would discourage or work against the maintenance or development of the language. It will also make provision for liaising with the Irish language community, representing their views to public authorities and investigating complaints, place a statutory duty on the Department of Education to encourage and facilitate Irish medium education in line with current provision for integrated education, explore urgently with the relevant British authorities, and in co-operation with the Irish broadcasting authorities, the scope for achieving more widespread availability of the Irish language television channel Teilifis na Gaeilige in Northern Ireland, seek more effective ways to encourage and provide financial support for Irish language film and television production in Northern Ireland and encourage the parties to secure agreement that this commitment will be sustained by the new assembly in a way which takes account of the desires and sensitivities of the community. All participants acknowledge the sensitivity of the use of symbols and emblems for public purposes and the need, in particular in creating the new institutions, to ensure that such symbols and emblems are used in a manner which promotes mutual respect rather than division. Arrangements will be made to monitor the issue and consider what action might be taken.

   The British government has made different levels of commitment on the Irish language. There is a general obligation to respect it, but action to promote and facilitate its use in speech and writing in the public and private sectors is qualified by reference to appropriate demand. It is important that the respect for linguistic diversity does do more for the small but growing European and Asian ethnic communities in both parts of Ireland. It is open to debate whether the Belfast Agreement would have considered gender and a commitment to encourage women to enter public life if the Women's Coalition had not been participants in the multi-party talks.

CONCLUSIONS

The Belfast Agreement seeks to bring to an end an ethnic conflict in a frontier region by reassuring the two communities that they have a right to their identity, ethos and aspirations and that this must be reciprocated by respecting the other community's rights. The region will have powers devolved to it which are tempered by safeguards to ensure that one community cannot injure the other. International human rights norms, and new national rights which will also focus on collective rights, will further strengthen the two communities and these rights will continue to apply if the region moves from one state, the UK, into another, Ireland. Thus the arrangements have to ensure that they can cope with the new position of devolution within the UK and also with a possible process leading to, and the actuality of, a united Ireland.

The parties therefore are engaged in a process of construction, of state-building and nation-building. This time they must avoid the mistakes of the past which caused the Northern Ireland problem. Amongst the failures in state and nation-building are the years of neglect of Northern Ireland by the British government; the narrow conception of Irish nationality employed by the new Irish state and the desire to complete the unfinished business of Irish unification. This desire was perceived as an external threat by the unionist community in Northern Ireland. They were clearly not defined as Irish but their home was the subject of the irredentist claim in the 1937 Irish constitution and in a sense the unionist community mirrored the Irish nation and its state-building process with its own narrow view of citizenship. Therefore, those who wished to leave the UK for a united Ireland were not committed to the political institutions of the region and constituted an internal threat to this unionist home. Suspicion and fear were mutually reinforcing and led to discriminatory and partial government. Such discrimination added to the feeling of alienation and injustice and increased the desire on the part of the nationalist community for a united Ireland.

Does the Belfast Agreement offer a realistic prospect of turning a vicious circle into a virtuous one? The importance of the foundational values of consent, diversity, parity of esteem, and commitment to exclusively peaceful means cannot be overstated because fear motivates people to do terrible things.

National identity is comprised of several components which combine to form this shared identity. These components can include the idea of nationality or citizenship, territory, religion, language, race and culture. National identity is strong if all of these are shared, as they reinforce the common identity. If these factors are not shared but in fact create differences within society then the state is likely to be fissile unless there is something stronger binding it together.

The possible lessons which might be learnt from the Belfast Agreement begin with the values and their influence in institutional design. One of the interesting things about consent is the way in which it was obtained. The international law principle of self-determination refers to peoples. Some republicans would argue that the appropriate self-determining unit is the people of the island of Ireland, whilst the unionist community would consider it to be the people of Northern Ireland. As we have seen since the Sunningdale agreement the British and Irish governments have agreed that it is the people of Northern Ireland who constitue 'the people' for this purpose. The way in which the Belfast Agreement achieved its consent was by simultaneous referendums in the two parts of Ireland. In Northern Ireland what was sought was approval for the agreement, while in Ireland the issue was amendment of the constitution, and in particular Articles 2 and 3. It will be recalled that the amended Article 3 proposes that the unification of Ireland will be obtained through 'the consent of a majority of the people, democratically expressed, in both jurisdictions in the island'. The holding of the simultaneous referendums enabled one to say that the people of the island of Ireland had agreed to unification by consent achieved through peaceful methods. This helps to delegitimise extreme republicans who seek to argue that giving the people of Northern Ireland self-determination justifies resort to force because Northern Ireland was created to have a unionist majority.

There is at the heart of the Belfast Agreement a paradox. We have a territory, an ethnic frontier, in which two communities have different national identities. Uniting the island of Ireland is now to be achieved by tolerance and protection of diversity of people and their traditions and identities and ethos. In other words the integration of the territory and entity of Northern Ireland into a state whose boundaries are those of the whole island, is to be done by transcending territory by uniting the diverse peoples. The common link of sharing the island is not enough to create a nation and a state and yet the notion of the island as a state is a very strong one.

Perhaps in the Belfast Agreement there is recognition that identity is complex and can be multi-faceted. In Great Britain unionist Scots and Welsh can cope with the idea of being Scottish or Welsh and British. The nationalist Irish, Scots and Welsh can cope with an additional European identity. Perhaps it is the case that if one is content with one's core identity, then one has no difficulty with other outer layers of identity. So perhaps for the project of European integration, one must ensure that the outer European layer is not perceived as a threat.

Back to Northern Ireland, the solutions to its problem which enjoyed the most support were either, allowing one community to enjoy its aspirations as to the state it was part of, or a formulation involving joint sovereignty between the UK and Ireland. The Belfast Agreement may be said to combine both, in that the region remains in the UK until the majority of the people wish to become part of a united Ireland, and that the two governments exercise a kind of sharing of sovereignty beyond the territories of their states in both of those circumstances. There may be quibbling about the Belfast Agreement's institutional superstructure but if it is going to succeed it will be because of the values which form its foundations.

REFERENCES

Bardon, J. (1992). *A History of Ulster.* Belfast: Blackstaff Press.
Beckett, J.C. (1966). *The Making of Modern Ireland 1603–1923.* London: Faber and Faber.

Foster, R. (1988). *Modern Ireland 1600–1972*. London: Allen Lane.

Hadfield, B. (1989). *The Constitution of Northern Ireland*. Belfast: SLS Publications.

Lee, J. (1989). *Ireland 1912–1985, politics and society*. Cambridge: Cambridge University Press.

Lijphart, A. (1968). *The Politics of Accommodation*. Berkeley: University of California Press.

Lijphart, A. (1975). The Northern Ireland Problem: Cases, Theories and Solutions, *British Journal of Political Science*, V: 83–106.

Lijphart, A. (1977). *Democracies in Plural Societies*. New Haven: Yale University Press.

Lyons, F.S.L. (1973). *Ireland since the Famine*. Glasgow: Fontana.

McCrudden, C. (1989). Northern Ireland and the British Constitution, pp. 297–342, in: Jowell, J. & Oliver, D. (eds.) *The Changing Constitution*. Oxford: Clarendon Press.

McGarry, J. & O'Leary, B. (1995). *Explaining Northern Ireland*. London: Blackwell.

O'Leary, B. (1989). The Limits to Coercive Consociationalism in Northern Ireland, *Political Studies*, XXXVII: 562–588.

O'Leary, B. & McGarry, J. (1996). *The Politics of Antagonism*. London: Athlone.

Whyte, J. (1990). *Interpreting Northern Ireland*. Oxford: Clarendon Press.

National Identity & The International
Law of Self-Determination:
the Stratification of the Western Saharan 'Self'

Joshua Castellino

INTRODUCTION

When forces claiming to represent Biafra engaged the Nigerian army in civil war, the international community sat back and waited for the result of the war. Early recognition in favour of the Biafrans was not likely since it would have been seen to infringe upon Nigerian sovereignty. At the same time, the Biafrans, strategically adept, were winning the war of propaganda abroad.[1] However, just as it looked like overwhelming support for the separatist movement was being garnered, the might of the Nigerian army wiped out any hope of a separate homeland. Biafran identity would have to seek recognition within the sovereign state of Nigeria.[2] A few years later Bangla nationalists sought to overthrow what they perceived as the mantle of neo-colonialism from the western wing of Pakistan. Allegations of repression and genocide were made, but easily defeated as the Pakistani army sought to reinforce its sovereignty. Meanwhile, hostile neighbour India intervened, using force of dubious legality, and while the United Nations Security Council was hamstrung by India's ally Russia, independence was gained for the new state of Bangladesh, with Pakistani sovereignty blatantly violated.[3]

Modern crises in the form of Chechnya and Kosovo still allow us glimpses of what essentially remains the same problem. A 'national liberation' movement seeks to express its agenda for a separate state, usually by calling on the norm of self-determination. They deem this an expression of 'national' identity and demand accommodation as a separate state at the expense of the state they are within. This is usually met with overwhelming physical strength by the state from which it wishes to secede. The process is, from time to time, affected by action from the international community, driven by various motives of national interest.[4]

---

*   Irish Centre for Human Rights, University College, Galway, Eire.
[1]   Heraclides 1991: 82
[2]   For general reading on Biafra see Nayar 1975:321
[3]   For a general reading see Nanda 1972:321; also see Sisson & Rose 1990
[4]   E.g. in Kosovo where the threatened refugee crises of enormous magnitude arguably put pressure on the Western European states within NATO to back the bombing campaign.

Stephen Tierney (ed.), Accommodating National Identity: New Approaches in International and Domestic Law, 257–284
© 2000 *Kluwer Law International. Printed in Great Britain.*

Despite the turmoil caused by secession movements, the law surrounding them remains ambiguous. Initially the idea of 'self-determination' set in motion the wheels of the decolonisation process. To rid a territory of a foreign oppressor was seen as necessary and justifiable.[5] International law applauded this process and provided help in every form to subjugated peoples who attempted to emancipate themselves.[6] However, the emancipation was to take place along pre-determined parameters.[7] In addition, once achieved, this emancipation was believed to be exhausted: from that point onward doctrines of unity were called upon to help solidify 'identity' within the new sovereign state. For this purpose the international community fully endorsed the concept of *nation-building* which was believed to provide the basis for international order.[8] The doctrine of nation-building basically postulates that 'narrow' cleavages between peoples, whether ethnic, racial, cultural or religious should not be permitted to impede the development of the sovereign state. It also endorses ideas of universalism and fraternity that see people of different kinds coming within the common identity of the sovereign state. This was the process that informed the early years of post-colonialism, and for a while, notwithstanding the attempted secession of Katanga, Biafra and Bangladesh, it seemed to be working. However, recent fragmentary forces have once again re-opened the issue of the accommodation of national identity within the confines of the post-colonial state.[9]

This chapter is primarily concerned with such expressions of 'national identity' and will focus on the particular case of the Western Sahara. The paper itself is divided into three sections. The first section will seek to lay down the norms of international law that have served to create the system described above. This particular section looks at the theoretical aspects of the norm of self-determination and the manner in which it creates the fixed model of representation i.e., statehood within which all national identity must be accommodated. The second section then examines the specific case of the people in the Western Sahara – a population of nomads with a confusing array of allegiances. Within this it is hoped to demonstrate that national identity is dynamic; and in doing so highlight some of the unresolved issues in the Western Sahara Case, as well as the broader implications for the theory and discourse of international legal self-determination. The third section will then examine the manner in which the International Court of Justice (ICJ) adjudicated on the allegiances between the territory and the *Sherifian* state (the precursor to modern Morocco). In doing so it is hoped to highlight the manner in which international legal discourse seems to examine 'identity' through the manifestation of external acts of recognition. The concluding section will then re-assert some of the points highlighted and seek to draw out the implications of these for the discourse of self-determination and expressions of 'national' identity.

---

[5]   See generally, Sureda 1973; Cassese 1979
[6]   See GAOR 1514 (XV); 1541 (XV); and 2625(XXV)
[7]   See Kaikobad 1983:119; Shaw 1996:75; Ratner 1996: 590
[8]   See Deutsch 1963
[9]   As epitomised by the creation of Eritrea, the continuing agitation in Chechnya, Kosovo, Kashmir and East Timor which have been challenged by strong-arm tactics of state militaries.

PART 1
ACCOMMODATING NATIONAL IDENTITY WITHIN INTERNATIONAL LAW:
THEORETICAL ISSUES

The modern law of self-determination is at best, ambiguous.[10] It seems to foster the negotiation of Kosovan self-determination at international level, while the not dissimilar quest for Chechnyan independence is met with relative indifference.[11] International law values the concept of order above others[12] and the modern international right to self-determination can be seen as being framed with respect to this caveat.[13] It will not be possible in this paper to examine the intricacies of this norm in any depth.[14] However it needs to be mentioned that the 'right' as we recognise it, derives from the American Declaration of Independence, and was rejuvenated and introduced to international law by US President Wilson at the Versailles negotiations.[15] These largely western ideals were instrumental in the surge for re-negotiation of the map of Europe after the First World War. A more recent manifestation of this right was seen in the process of decolonisation, where swathes of territory previously under colonial rule, were emancipated as the right took root, driven by the recognition that colonialism was abhorrent to humanity.[16] Thus former colonial peoples were encouraged to free themselves of these shackles and constitute themselves as sovereign states acceptable within international law and politics. This was seen as the ideal way of accommodating colonial peoples within an international system that was increasingly stratified on grounds of 'statehood' and 'nationality'.[17] From the perspective of the typical colonial 'state', anything was better than being ruled by foreigners who sought to exploit resources and impose an alien culture. In addition, the transition from colonies into states was relatively simple since international law laid down the framework for statehood, which the new entities had to adhere to.[18] Problems were rife with this but by and large the exercise was believed to have prevented the significant bloodbaths which many expected to follow the departure of colonial rulers from certain territories.[19]

As these newer entities entered the UN, they put pressure on existing members to support the cause of self-determination further. As a result, the fledgling norm expressed by Wilson gradually began to take on legal substance. It was the focus of the United Nations General Assembly's 1960 'Declaration on the Granting of Independence to Colonial Peoples and Territories' that laid the groundwork for

---

[10] For general opinions on self-determination see Baker & Dobbs(eds.) 1925–7; Cassese 1995; Cobban 1969; Crawford 1979; Cristescu 1981; Emerson 1971:459; Franck 1990; Fukuyama 1992; Gellner 1983 & 1994; Gros-Espiell 1980; Hannum 1980; Hobsbawm 1990; Notter 1937; Kirgis 1994:304; Kohn 1957; White 1981: 147–171; Brilmeyer 1991: 177–302
[11] See Gaeta 1996:563; and [Editorial] 1998:125
[12] Bull 1995:7; Lung-Chu 1991:1286
[13] Mazrui 1975:9
[14] For further reading see Tomuschat (ed.) 1993
[15] Whelan 1994:100
[16] See Sureda 1973:21
[17] See generally, Anderson 1993
[18] See the discussion originating with Jackson 1990 and the response – Grovogui 1996
[19] Heraclides 1991:27

subsequent development by declaring that colonialism was abhorrent to peace-loving states.[20] This was backed by the enshrining of the right in the joint International Bill of Rights;[21] and also recognised as an important principle of international law in the 1970 'Declaration on Principles of International Law Concerning Friendly Relations and Co-operation among States in Accordance with the Charter of the United Nations'.[22] Since then the status of self-determination has been uncertain: the prime reason perhaps is that traditional *salt-water* colonialism is ended.[23] The norm was significant in the emancipation of former colonies, which are today recognised as fully-fledged members of the international polity. It was through the working of this norm of self-determination that their subjugated identities were allowed to emerge in the recognisable form of a 'national identity' expressed in terms of citizenship of a sovereign state. This process was accompanied by the reiteration of two other important international legal norms: i) territorial sovereignty[24] and ii) the doctrine of *uti possidetis*. The former dictated that once the territory has been decolonised the new rulers were considered sovereign, and no interference with their affairs was tolerated.[25] As a result these rulers had more or less *carte blanche* in terms of the means available to them in developing the former colony into a state. In addition, separatist movements were by and large repressed by the strength of the state machinery while the international community refused to aid their agitation for what they believed was 'self-determination'. As far as the international polity was concerned 'self-determination' had resulted in the creation of the new state in the first place, and was a one-off right that had been exercised. Once this right was deemed exercised, the international community mobilised behind the newly formed state, demanding respect for its sovereignty.

The other accompanying norm that helped this process was the doctrine of *uti possidetis*. The doctrine of *uti possidetis* is perhaps the single greatest influence on the shaping of the map of the world today. It has, in one form or another, been the biggest contributor to the constitution of nearly 80 per cent of states that currently exist, and perhaps the most important factor in the creation and maintenance of modern post-colonial national identities.[26] The doctrine basically states that 'new states will come to independence with the same boundaries that they had when they were administrative units within the territory or territories of one colonial power'.[27] This doctrine, when applied to self-determination suggests that newly created

---

[20]   GAOR 1514 (XV)

[21]   The article on 'self-determination' forms the joint article 1 in both the International Covenant for Civil and Politics Rights, 1966 as well as the International Covenant for Economic, Social and Cultural Rights, 1966.

[22]   See Declaration on Principles of International Law concerning Friendly Relations and Co-operation among States in Accordance with the Charter of the United Nations (GAOR 2625 (XXV); also see Warbrick and Lowe (eds.) 1994; Rosenstock 1967:713

[23]   See the discussion about the Belgian Thesis UNDOC A/Ac.67/2, pp. 3–31; also see 89 Rec.des Cours 321, *The Question of Aborigines Before the United Nations: The Belgian Thesis 1954* (UNDOC A/C.4/SR.257), para 11, quoted in Thornberry 1989:874

[24]   As protected by art. 2(7) of the UN Charter, 1945

[25]   Motyl 1992:307

[26]   See generally Macartney 1987; Neuberger 1986

[27]   Shaw 1996:97

ex-colonial states will inherit the boundaries created for them by their colonial rulers. Thus while underlining the principle of stability of boundaries it also provides a territorial limitation to the exercise of sovereign power in relation to its neighbours by means of a demarcated boundary line. The norm, which originated in *ius civile*, was basically in place to prevent the 'disturbance of the existing state of possession of immovables as between two individuals'.[28] Thus, the *status quo* would be preserved irrespective of the means by which possession had been gained. International law picked up on the doctrine of *uti possidetis* for the first time to allow consolidation of the *de facto* situation following hostilities as the Spanish withdrew from Latin America.[29] This was convenient since it allowed the simple conclusion of peace without attempting redress. Thus, in the case of belligerent occupation, the doctrine would require peace to be concluded by the simple decision to allow the aggressor to continue possession of the territory gained by conquest, and the *status quo* to be maintained from that point onward. The doctrine thus has the effect of trying to stop the clock at a situation and carry on in peace. To allow re-definition during transition would be chaotic since, inevitably, new claimants to power would arise due to the fact that the nature of colonialism did not allow for the grooming of successors to take over power on colonial abdication. The doctrine, therefore was merely recognition that in the interests of short-term order, the snap-shot of the territory at independence would have to be taken as given, so that development could be pursued.

At the time of the decolonisation of Africa in the middle of the twentieth century, this norm was once again rehabilitated with accommodation being made for the particular situation in Africa. The African example, as will be highlighted in some depth in this chapter in looking at the Western Sahara Case, was particularly fragile due to the nature of the boundaries drawn by the colonial rulers in the grab for land in the preceding century.[30] This had created artificial entities on the continent, and the administrative units drawn and left behind by colonial powers bore little resemblance to the history or geography of the region, often placing antagonistic tribes within the same boundary. So the dilemma faced was either to allow re-negotiation of boundaries along more acceptable lines, or to simply accept the situation created, and pursue development without running the risk of fragmentation. The logic of the situation was clear to the post-independence African leadership who extended the doctrine of *uti possidetis* to the African continent, expressing it in the language of the Cairo Declaration in 1964. This has been subsequently re-enforced in numerous international law cases.[31]

The legitimation of the principle also held firm outside the decolonisation process in that by freezing international boundaries for posterity, it prevented smaller movements, post-independence, from trying to carve up sovereign states. While

---

[28] Shaw 1996:109
[29] See generally, Picon-Salas 1962
[30] See Neuberger 1986; Baker & Dobbs (eds.) 1925–7
[31] See: Rann of Kutch in 50 ILR:407 (Bebler's dissenting opinion); Burkina Faso Mali case *ICJ Reports* 1986:565; Guinea-Bissau/Senegal case 83 ILR:35; El Salvador Honduras case *ICJ Reports* 1992:351, 386; Libya Chad Case *ICJ Reports* 1994:83 (esp. Judge Ajibola's Opinion)

this was perhaps necessary to prevent the immediate unravelling of the sovereign state at a time of transition, the doctrine went further and legitimised these boundaries for all time. With the African application of the doctrine being deemed a success by the international community – measured solely in the currency of post-independence blood-baths which had been assumed imminent but were avoided; the doctrine was readily extended in the nineties to the unravelling of the Soviet Empire, Yugoslavia and Czechoslovakia. In all three cases, the parent states, artificial entities themselves, broke down under pressure from different peoples within who had gained their right to freedom of expression.[32] The international community was once more faced with the threat of destabilisation to order and once more responded by calling on the doctrine of *uti possidetis.* Thus new entities claiming statehood could only do so along the fault-lines that already existed when they were administrative units within the parent state.[33]

Thus the discourse of self-determination encourages subjugated peoples to emancipate themselves. However the decolonisation process was forced into respecting certain norms, the foundation of which was the need for order.[34] This order basically dictated that expressions of 'national' identity among colonial peoples would be accommodated within the realms of a sovereign state, irrespective of their validity as separate minority rights. As a result more often than not 'national' identity within post-colonial states is largely artificial: the result of the freedom struggle against the colonisers. Meanwhile, the physical boundaries of this sovereign state were assumed to be unchallengeable irrespective of the manner in which they were constituted. The ideal of the 'nation-state' was meant to be the vehicle that could contain *all* expressions of national identity. The fledgling states that came out of this process, not always coherently defined in kin terms, were forced to accommodate and manufacture an identity that could be perceived as being common to all its subjects. Thus the modern decolonised state was required to conform to the Montevideo Convention requirements for statehood:[35] with the highly problematic requirement that the 'defined territory' and the people as a consequence, were colonially demarcated. This was considered a valid expression of 'national identity' even though the 'nation' was externally defined. Worse, the rhetoric emanating from the decolonisation process suggested that this was the ultimate fruit of liberation processes that would yield vibrant and forthright democratic states.[36]

---

[32] Shaw 1996:110
[33] Shaw 1996 *ibid.*
[34] See Bull 1995:7
[35] See Article 1, Montevideo Convention, 1933. (The state as a person of international law should possess the following qualifications: (a) a permanent population; (b)defined territory; (c) government; and (d)capacity to enter into relations with other States)
[36] For more on the 'democratic entitlement' see Franck 1992:46

PART 2
THE WESTERN SAHARA CASE AND THE ACCOMMODATION OF 'NATIONAL' IDENTITY.

The Western Sahara is that fringe of the Saharan Desert on the coast of the African continent. It includes the areas of Sakiet El-Hamra in the north and Wadi Ed Dahab (Rio de Oro) in the south, covering a total area of 284,000 square kilometres. It shares borders with Morocco in the north, Mauritania in the south and a small common border with Algeria in the east. As is the case with most African 'states', the borders of the entity were drawn and agreed between the colonial powers of Spain and France that were influential in this part of the *Maghreb*.[37]

As established elsewhere, the current position of international law is that self-determination is only valid in situations of *salt-water* colonisation.[38] The Western Sahara is an interesting case in that the colonial issue has never been resolved despite the active interest of the UN Security Council.[39] A colony of Spain at the time of decolonisation, the area known as the Spanish Sahara was entitled to exercise the right of self-determination in the same way as other post-colonial entities in the region and around the rest of the world.[40] However with the national interests of Spain, Morocco and Mauritania clashing, compounded by the fact that the actual residents of the region were nomadic, the situation has thus far evaded resolution. Spain, the colonial ruler was responsible for the smooth transition of the region from its own administration to that of the people of the area.[41] However the *Saharawis* have traditionally been nomads who have wandered across the region that included Morocco and Mauritania for centuries without having to worry about borders. The stratification of 'identity' within the limits of the statehood and sovereignty discourse forced a change in this life-style. As a result they, like other nomadic peoples such as the gypsies of Central Europe and the itinerants of the Republic of Ireland, have been forced into an area that corresponds to a sovereign 'state'. However what really brings the issue to an impasse is the intricacy of the history and identities within the region, and the claims of Morocco and Mauritania (since dropped) to the Western Sahara. As early as 1966[42] Mauritania and Morocco, both newly independent, called for the 'self-determination' of the region, certain that exercise of this 'right' would see the region being integrated into their respective states.[43] This claim was

---

[37] Treaties were signed between the two powers in 1900, 1904, and the Treaty of Fez in 1912 – see Rézette 1975:31
[38] See Thornberry 1989:867–889
[39] See S/RES/1163, 17 April, 1998; S/RES/1148, 26 January, 1998; S/RES/1133, 20 October, 1997; S/RES/1131, 29 September, 1997; S/RES/1108, 22 May, 1997; S/RES/1084, 27 November, 1996; S/RES/1056, 29 May, 1996; S/RES/1042, 31 January, 1996; S/RES/1033, 22 December, 1995; S/RES/1017, 22 September, 1995; S/RES/1002, 30 June, 1995; S/RES/995, 26 May, 1995; S/RES/973, 13 January, 1995; S/RES/907, 29 March, 1994; S/RES/809, 2 March, 1993; S/RES/725, 31 December, 1991; S/RES/690, 29 April, 1991; S/RES/658, 27 June, 1990; S/RES/621, 20 September, 1988; S/RES/380, 6 November, 1975; S/RES/379, 2 November, 1975; S/RES/377, 22 October, 1975
[40] Sureda 1973
[41] As required under the UN Charter, 1945 Chapter XI Article 73
[42] Shaw 1978:119–154 at p.123
[43] Chopra 1994; Rézette 1975:29

unsurprising and, irredentist as it might seem, was based on the traditions and lifestyle of the nomads who traversed across these territories throughout their history largely unhindered by considerations of statehood and boundaries.[44] When this nomadic lifestyle is superimposed onto the concept of the 'greater *Maghreb* identity' it throws up complications which serve to reduce the right of self-determination to one easily manipulated by the harnessing of shrewd political forces. These political claims arising out of specific perceptions of historic identity, are compounded by the territorial 'prize' of the Western Sahara – an area perceived to be rich in phosphates – which some authors claim is the prime purpose for the struggle over it.[45]

By the time of the Spanish withdrawal from the territory in 1974, the stage was set for a battle between itself, Morocco and Mauritania, in trying to engage the international community in awarding the Western Sahara itself or parts of its mineral wealth to the three powers. The details of the events unfolding thereafter are documented elsewhere;[46] however what is of particular importance for this chapter is that the matter was referred by the United Nations at the behest of King Hassan, to the United Nations Fourth Committee. This Committee after extensive discussion[47] addressed the International Court of Justice with two vital questions:

I.   Was Western Sahara (Rio de Oro and Sakiet El-Hamra) at the time of colonisation by Spain a territory belonging to no one (*terra nullius*)?

If the answer to the first question is in the negative,

II. What were the legal ties between this territory and the Kingdom of Morocco and the Mauritanian entity?[48]

The manner in which the Court dealt with these questions is indicative of the way that international law treats issues of identity, allegiance and nationhood. It is therefore instrumental to view some of the issues arising out of this case, in a bid to examine the fault-lines present in the current international legal position on self-determination and the accommodation of 'national' identity. An important issue that needs to be borne in mind before examining the issues raised by the case is that while the pleadings of the Security Council went unheeded, King Hassan called upon Moroccan citizens to march into the desert to re-claim land that belonged to them.[49] Thus an important and perhaps vital factor in the Western Sahara imbroglio, is the presence of nearly 200,000 Moroccan citizens who marched peacefully into the territory of the Western Sahara and took up residence. This factor is partially responsible for the delay in implementing what all

---

[44]   Rézette *ibid.*
[45]   The exploitation of mineral wealth was suddenly an issue in the decade leading up to colonial abdication. The region is blessed with an abundance of Phosphates that has given this otherwise desolate part of the desert its economic importance.
[46]   Chopra 1994
[47]   Shaw 1978:124
[48]   See *ICJ Reports* 1975:14 at para 1
[49]   Chopra 1994; Rézette 1975:47, Abun-Nasr 1975

parties involved in the process consider a reasonable manner of resolving the problem. This can be phrased in the words of Judge Dillard in the ICJ case '...it is for the people to determine the destiny of the territory and not the territory the destiny of the people'.[50] However the referendum that the parties believe must be held to thus determine the 'destiny' of the territory stalls on the basic question that was first highlighted by Robert Lansing, US Secretary of State in his original criticism of the Wilsonian vision of self-determination. `On the surface it seemed reasonable: let the people decide. [But] It was in fact ridiculous because people cannot decide until someone decides who the people are'.[51] The problem at the time seemed simple to him: 'When the President talks of self-determination what has he in mind? Does he mean a race, a territorial area, or a community? Without a definite unit which is practical, application of this principle is dangerous to peace and stability'.[52] What this chapter suggests is that more than seventy-five years later, the norm of self-determination has evolved to such an extent that it defeats in totality, the original albeit flawed norm that Wilson sought to ideate. The best example of this is that minorities, who were at the heart of the original Wilsonian conception of self-determination, today only acquire the right of self-determination under great difficulty. Thus the doctrine, initially expressed with the aim of helping minorities, today excludes them from the fruits of external (i.e. secession) self-determination.[53]

Perhaps the main argument in support of the notion that the Western Sahara has yet to exercise traditional 'self-determination' (colonial emancipation resulting in the formation of an independent state) is that the territory was never given a choice of independence on Spanish withdrawal. Since what was at stake in 1975 was classical *salt-water* self-determination, the Western *Saharawis* (or the residents of the Western Saharan region) ought to have had the following choices:

1.   Emergence as a sovereign state;
2.   Free association with an independent state; or
3.   Integration with an independent state.[54]

However political expediencies overtook this legal entitlement and the process was never allowed to go ahead. Arguably if 'self-determination' is to be exercised there needs to be some calculation of the will of the people; perhaps best gauged at this stage by a referendum. While both Morocco and the Frente de Popular Para Liberacion who are fighting the cause of Saharawi independence[55] agree to the holding of a referendum, the difficulties of deciding 'who' the people are, is confused by population migrations from the north.[56] Nonetheless the argument

---

[50]   ICJ Reports 1975:122; also see Higgins 1983:387
[51]   Jennings 1956:55–56
[52]   Lansing *Self-determination* in the Saturday Evening Post, 9 April 1921 p. 7, as quoted in Whelan 1994:102
[53]   See Whelan 1994:110; Thornberry 1989:867–889
[54]   See *ICJ Reports* 1975:32 at para 57; also see GAOR 1541 (XV)
[55]   For the Mauritanian withdrawal from the process see Chopra 1994
[56]   See Dunn in Gellner & Micaud 1972:85–107

for self-determination is technically one that is subscribed to by both sides to the conflict. The problem is reaching agreement on what 'self-determination' entails. While the Polisario,[57] demand that independence is the only way of maintaining *Saharawi* identity and integrity, Morocco claims that by the principle of self-determination, the Western Sahara ought to be integrated within Morocco. The evidence for the emergence of a separate state as a matter of right is significant. The doctrine of *uti possidetis*, outlined in the first section of this chapter suggests that by state practice, former colonial entities have usually gained statehood within the boundaries drawn for them by the colonial ruler. This argument appears to support the Polisario case that on Spanish withdrawal, the territory, with its borders demarcated by the Treaty of Fez, ought to have become an independent country. The Polisario argues that political expediencies were allowed to overtake the process, and the appropriate manner of resolving the conflict would be to prevent Moroccan interference in the 'sovereign' affairs of the Saharan Arab Democratic Republic (SADR) which they proclaimed on the 27th February 1975.[58] It appears that this argument is supported by the Organisation of African Unity, which granted recognition to the SADR on the 12th of November 1984 at its 20th Summit in Addis-Ababa.[59]

The Moroccan side to this particular argument is equally compelling and is based on a historical reading of the conflict. This history was dealt with in great depth during the proceedings at the Hague, where the Polisario were, of course, not allowed to appear. Morocco claims with historical authority that the demarcation of the territory of the *Maghreb* between Spain and France was illegal to start with. While this is clearly incontestable, the *intertemporal* rule would suggest that actions of colonisation cannot be judged by today's standards of international law. However Morocco, while accepting this argument suggests that the only way to rectify this situation would be to allow integration of the territory within the Kingdom of Morocco to which it belongs. The arguments put forth in the case sought therefore to engage the second of the questions asked of the Court; i.e. determination of the ties between the entity and the Kingdom of Morocco.[60]

The treatment of the first question too is interesting and merits attention. The Court defined *terra nullius* as 'a legal term of art employed in connection with "occupation" as one of the accepted legal methods in acquiring sovereignty over territory'. This is followed by the explanation that occupation was 'legally an original means of peaceably acquiring sovereignty over a territory otherwise than by cession or succession'. It went on to suggest that '…it was a cardinal condition of a valid "occupation" that the territory should be *terra nullius* – a territory belonging to no-one – at the time of the act alleged to constitute "occupation".'[61] Having defined the

---

[57] *Frente Popular para la Liberacion de Saguia el-Hamra y de Rio de Oro* henceforth referred to as Polisario
[58] See http://www.arso.org.html
[59] http://www.arso.org/03-1.html. This was merely confirmation of the recognition of the SADR by the Secretary-General of the OAU on February 22 1982
[60] For a criticism of this process see Shaw 1978:141, 149
[61] ICJ Reports 1975:39 at para 79: also see *Legal Status of Eastern Greenland, PCIJ Series A/B, No. 53 pp. 44 f and 63 f.* for which the Court relied for this definition.

concept thus the Court quotes state practice of the 'relevant period' as indicating that 'territories inhabited by tribes or peoples having a social and political organisation were not regarded as *terrae nullius*'.[62] Thus territory in such cases was acquired not through occupation, but through negotiation with local rulers. The Western Sahara was deemed not to be *terra nullius* due to the fact that 'local rulers' signed agreements with the occupying Spanish; a tenet of the judgement that fails to take adequate account of the role of coercion that may or may not have rendered these agreements void.[63] Nonetheless, the Court finds a more important reason for declaring that the territory could not have been *terra nullius*: '...at the time of colonisation Western Sahara was inhabited by peoples which, if nomadic, were socially and politically organised in tribes under chiefs competent to represent them'.[64] Thus the Spanish proclaimed that the King was taking Rio de Oro under his 'protection' on the basis of agreements which had been entered into with the chiefs of local tribes. These agreements consisted of a series of documents signed by these 'tribes' with the representative of the *Sociedad Española de Africanistas*. The Court accepts this scenario without raising the question as to what the legal entitlement was in this supposed agreement. It is clear that the Spanish gained a safe coast across the Canary Islands that would protect their fishing industry; in return the local rulers arguably gained protection. But it is not clear, and was not questioned why this protection was required. What the Spanish argued was that the land was not Moroccan territory but ought to be handed back to the 'people' – the local rulers that had control over it before the signing of these agreements.

Experts such as Gellner, who have studied the area of the *Maghreb* offer us clues to as the cultural make-up of this part of North West Africa. This is interesting because it gives an indication of the complex factors involved in the formation of the 'identity' of the peoples that traversed the vast territory of the Saharan Desert. Many authors advance the belief that there is some merit in the historic claim Morocco advanced. The *Sherifian* State – the precursor to modern Morocco, spread across current Morocco but also gained allegiance from regions further south. This was based on one vital factor: the entire region professed Islam of the *Maliki* rite; and according to *Shari'a* law, the entire region belonged to the Sultan (and thereby his successor the King).[65] There is tacit acceptance that the Sultan was recognised as the spiritual head of the region. Intriguingly however, the state was divided along a *Makhzen-Siba* axis. The former, the *Blad Makhzen* (or land of acceptance) consisted of the regions around the Imperial cities of Féz and Marrakech. In these regions the populations accepted the Sultan as their Head, paid taxes to him and accepted protection from his army. Meanwhile the *Blad Siba* (land of dissidence) consisted of the outer penumbra of territories in the *Sherifian* State. In these regions, the mainly Berber tribes that existed seemed to have accepted the Sultan as spiritual leader, however they withheld taxes from him. Gellner narrates that early *Sherifian* history

[62] *ICJ Reports* 1975:para 80
[63] Vienna Convention on the Law of Treaties, (1969) Art. 51, 52
[64] *ICJ Reports* 1975: para 81
[65] Seddon in Gellner & Micaud 1972

was a constant tussle of the *makhzen* trying to assert its power over the *siba*.[66] The current disagreement stems from the fact that the Polisario insist that while the Sultan may have been the spiritual head of the region he was never recognised as being its temporal head. In addition they question whether the territory of the Western Sahara could be considered to be within the realms of the *Sherifian siba*, whose boundaries remain indeterminable. And it is on these points that the two parties fail to agree. Thus the appeal to history fails to provide us with conclusive evidence as to the nature of the allegiances of the time. What is interesting however is that it gives us a view of two of the ancient entities that existed in this region: the *Sherifian* State and the *Bilad Shinguitti*. In doing so, it also gives us a glimpse via the Pleadings of the parties in the Court case as well as the work of ethnographers, of the components of 'identity' that remain central to the issue today.

The *Sherifian* State was recognised as being a state even at the time of Spanish colonisation as early as 1884. Thus the Moroccan argument that it is the only genuine state in the *Maghreb* has some merit, in that the neighbouring entities were all results of colonisation which gave them their current boundaries.[67] Morocco claims that as the successor to the *Sherifian* State it exercises territorial claims over the entire *Maghreb*. A prime facet of this is the profession of the *Maliki* rite of Islam that arguably unites the region. This hold was, they claim affected by colonisation which demarcated the area of the *Maghreb* between, primarily France and Spain; and the new entities that came to independence through the decolonisation process were artificial to that extent.

In contrast to the argument presented by Morocco, the *Bilad Shinguitti*, the precursor to modern Mauritania, claimed that south of the *Sherifian* Empire was *Shinguitti* country: 'a distinct human unit, characterised by a common language, way of life and religion'.[68] The *Bilad Shinguitti* presents an interesting platform to question the validity of expressions and formulations of national identity. It did not have a defined territory, a fixed population, a sovereign government, or the capacity to enter into relationships with other states.[69] In addition it did not even conform to the requirements of statehood of the time, and unlike the *Sherifian* state could not be identified as having a single authority that tribes swore allegiance to or contested taxes against. The Mauritanian entity functioned differently and while the Mauritanian argument was negated by the Court in this case it throws up a direct challenge to the perception of identity within non-European communities. The *Bilad Shinguitti* could be perceived as a distinct human unit. It had a uniform social structure, composed of three 'orders': warrior tribes with political power; marabout tribes engaged in religious activity, teaching, cultural, judicial and economic activities; and client-vassal tribes under the protection of either a warrior or marabout tribe. The marabout tribes were given great importance within *Shinguitt* culture, since they created a strong written cultural tradition in religious studies, education, literature and poetry

---

66   Gellner 1972:7
67   Rézette 1975:29
68   *ICJ Reports* 1975:55
69   As given by the Montevideo Convention, 1933

renowned through the Arab world.[70] *Shinguitt* culture also encompassed two types of political systems, emirates and independent tribes that did not form part of the emirates. In its Pleadings before the Court, Mauritania argued that one of the Emirates, the Emirate of Adrar, around the town of *Shinguitt*, was a centre of *Shinguitti* culture and proved an attraction for the nomadic *Saharawi* tribes. The argument presented to the Court was that at the time of colonisation of the Western Sahara by Spain, the Emir of Adrar was the most important political figure of the north and northwest *Shinguitt* country [which by implication in the Mauritanian Pleadings included the Western Sahara]. It also mentions the testimony of Captain Cervera who concluded a treaty with the Emir at Ijil, by which Spain would have recognised the Emir as the sovereign over the stated lands.[71] The parties to that treaty, according to Mauritania included not just the Emir but also several tribal chiefs, not only from the Adrar but also from the west of the Emirate. It is these tribal chiefs who allegedly represented the tribes that existed within the Western Sahara, and hence the origin of the claim of a territorial link between the Emir of Adrar and the nomadic tribes that traversed the desert immediately north of the Emirate.

According to Mauritanian Pleadings before the Court, neither the Emirates nor the independent tribes bore any tie of territorial allegiance to the Sultan of the *Sherifian* state although he might have been acknowledged as the spiritual head. It is clear from uncontested evidence presented in the case, that the Emirates and tribal groupings were autonomous; they signed treaties with explorers without 'higher consent' of the Sultan of the *Sherifian* state. Nonetheless, 'the emirs, sheikhs, and other tribal chiefs were never vested by outside authorities and always derived their powers from the special rules governing the devolution of power in the *Shinguitti* entity'.[72] Each emirate or tribal group was 'autonomously administered', and interestingly the rulers derived their power from the *Juma'a* – the locally elected participatory system that functioned as a governing council for each tribe. It appears from the evidence presented by Mauritania as well as by the work undertaken by Gellner and others on the subject, that the Saharan tribes[73] had a degree of autonomy that would have fulfilled the original Wilsonian vision for 'self-determination'. The relationship between this and the norm of self-determination post-Wilson, is a clear demonstration of the limitations of international law. While the Wilsonian vision of 'self-determination' was based on the 'self-governance' of people, when this 'self-governance' is manifest in other forms (such as the *Juma'a* or *Jemm'a* in the Western Sahara) it fails to gain acceptance as a valid right.

---

[70] *ICJ Reports* 1975:57–58 para 132
[71] It appears that this treaty was never ratified, and thus is not of legal standing in the procedures. Nonetheless Mauritania advances it as an indication of custom encountered by the explorer on reaching the territory subsequently known as Mauritania. *ICJ Reports* 1975:58 para 133
[72] *ICJ Reports* 1975:59 para 134
[73] This is used to refer to tribes that exist in this part of the Saharan Desert, rather than *Saharawi* tribes – used to refer specifically to the tribes that claim to be represented by the Polisario.

PART 3
EXTERNAL MANIFESTATION OF SOVEREIGN POSSESSION:
MOROCCAN 'NATIONAL IDENTITY' IN THE DESERT

One of the means by which Morocco sought 'possession' of the Western Sahara was by seeking to demonstrate that its authority over the region was internationally accepted. It thus tried to prove that the territory was within the ambit of the *Sherifian* state. This was important since, if Morocco could demonstrate that the region was historically recognised as being part of the *Sherifian* state, it would have a strong case as the Court could reasonably rule that externally recognised ties of a sovereign nature did exist between the Western Sahara and Morocco. The utility of going down this road is highly questionable since the region, as a post-colonial unit, would still have had the right to self-determination; i.e. the right to choose whether it wished to maintain separate status, associate with the Moroccan state or be integrated into it. Nevertheless, Morocco sought to plead external recognition of its sovereignty over the region by reference to a number of treaties, and the Court seemed happy to engage this question. The Moroccan demonstration of external sovereignty was argued on the basis of the following sets of treaties:

(a) A series of Moroccan treaties towards the protection and return of shipwrecked mariners on the coast of Wad Noun and its vicinity;
(b) A Moroccan Treaty signed with Great Britain in 1895 allegedly defining the territorial limits of Morocco;
(c) Diplomatic correspondence with regard to implementation of Article 8 of the Treaty of Tetuan, which it is claimed, shows Spanish acceptance of Moroccan sovereignty as far south as Cape Bojador; and
(d) A Franco-German exchange of letters allegedly suggesting the extent of Morocco's territorial sovereignty.[74]

The first category includes treaties such as the Treaty of Marrakech which concerned a fishing project by Canary Islanders, and was signed between the King of Spain and the Sultan of the *Sherifian* state in the Imperial city of Marrakech in 1767. Article 18 of the treaty, according to Morocco, refers to the setting up of a trading and fishing post by the islanders on 'the coasts of Wad Noun'. The Spanish, however, based their claim on the Spanish text of the treaty in which the operative clause reads: 'to the south of the river Noun'. Reading of the actual texts[75] reveals significant differences:

According to the Arabic text presented by Morocco, Article 18 reads as follows:

His Imperial Majesty warns the inhabitants of the Canaries against any fishing expedition to the *coasts of Wad Noun and beyond*. He disclaims any responsibility for the way they may be treated by the Arabs of the country, to

---

[74] See *ICJ Reports* 1975:49 para 108
[75] English translation of the Arabic and Spanish texts; accepted by the ICJ

whom it is *difficult to apply decisions*, since they have no fixed residence, travel as they wish and pitch their tents where they choose. The inhabitants of the Canaries are certain to be maltreated by those Arabs.[76]

This text suggests that the Sultan was concerned about the security of the Canary Islanders during expeditions beyond the coasts of Wad Noun. He warns that the Arabs there may mistreat them and in the event of such mistreatment, remedies may not be available. The reason cited for this difficulty is that the inhabitants have no fixed abode and wander across the region. The text does not suggest that the Sultan *cannot* apply his decisions to them in the event of maltreatment, but merely that it is difficult to do so in view of their nomadic leanings. Another interesting feature in the treaty text is the reference to the people 'on the coasts and beyond' the Wad Noun as 'Arabs'. Anthropologists state that migratory movements in the region suggest that the Arabs in the north gradually pushed the Berbers further southward into the Atlas Mountains. At the same time, harsh Saharan conditions forced Berbers from the south further north. While it seems generally true in modern day Morocco that Berber villages exist primarily in the Atlas Mountains, at the time of the treaty in 1767 it is unclear as to whether they had retreated that far. Thus, the use of the term 'Arab' in the text is unclear as is the reference to these Arabs as 'Arabs of the country' thereby implying a connection between their identity and where they lived.

The Spanish text however differs considerably from the Arabic text and reads:

His Imperial Majesty refrains from expressing an opinion with regard to the trading post which His Catholic Majesty wishes to establish *to the south of the River Noun*, since he cannot take responsibility for accidents and misfortunes, because *his domination (sus dominios) does not extend so far...* Northwards from Santa Cruz, His Imperial Majesty grants to the Canary Islanders and the Spaniards, the right of fishing without authorising any other nation to do so.[77]

According to this text, there is apprehension allegedly expressed by the Sultan with regard to the population that inhabits the area. For a start even the area under consideration is disputed since the Spanish text allegedly indicates that the area to the 'south of the River Noun' was beyond the control of the Sultan. It goes beyond the Arabic text of merely a lack of powers to enforce decisions (due to the nomadic nature according to the Arabic text); clearly suggesting that his *domination* did not extend as far. Thus, the difference between the two texts is considerable. Further, the contrast between the situation 'south of the River Noun' and 'northward from Santa Cruz' is also striking. In the case of the latter region the Sultan seems to clearly act in the role of the sovereign of the territory by granting the Canary Islanders and the Spaniards fishing rights to the exclusion of all other nations.

Thus the controversy in the case arose since Spain disputes the meaning of crucial words in the Arabic text and held that the meaning found in the Spanish text was

---

[76]   *ICJ Reports* 1975:50 para. 108 *emphasis added*
[77]   *ICJ Reports* 1975:50 para 110 *emphasis added*

authoritative. This is allegedly backed by subsequent diplomatic correspondence between the Sultan and King Carlos III, as well as by the Hispano-Moroccan Treaty of 1799. For the Spanish therefore, Article 18 is clearly read to mean that the Sultan disavows any pretensions to authority in the area. Morocco, on the other hand, questions the meaning attributed in the Spanish text, and holds that the Arabic text is the official version. In the absence of such evidence, it could be assumed in a bilateral treaty, that the two texts have equal weightage since they were agreed to and signed by both concerned parties. The Court failed to rule on this difficult issue and instead avoided the matter completely on the premise that the treaty was not altogether pertinent since it was not close to the period in question, namely 'at the time of colonisation by Spain in 1884'.[78] It nonetheless did not consider Morocco to have established beyond doubt that it extended sovereignty to the region under dispute, also suggesting that the later Hispano-Moroccan Treaty of Commerce and Navigation signed in 1861[79] would supersede the Treaty of Marrakech.

Article 38 (Arabic version) of this treaty reads:

> 'If a Spanish vessel of war or merchant ship get aground or be wrecked on any part of the coasts of Morocco, she shall be respected and assisted in every way, in conformity with the laws of friendship, and the said vessel and everything in her shall be taken care of and returned to her owners, or to the Spanish Consul-General. ...If a Spanish vessel be wrecked at Wad Noun or any other part of its coast, the Sultan of Morocco shall make use of his authority to save and protect the master and crew until they return to their country, and the Spanish Consul-General, Consul, Vice-Consul, Consular Agent, or person appointed by them shall be allowed to collect every information they may require...'.[80]

According to the arguments presented by Morocco this clearly entails recognition of Moroccan authority in the area of Noun as well as further southwards in the Western Sahara. It suggests that since the Sultan could call upon effective action through his appointed governors in the region this demonstrates evidence of the exercise of sovereign authority. This authority is considered by the Government to be spreading southwards to include the Sahara since even in cases of shipwrecks in this area the Spanish authorities 'receive permission to enquire into the fate of shipwrecked mariners and derive that permission from the Sultan'.[81] The Moroccan argument is buffeted by the presentation of diplomatic documents relating to a particular incident that occurred on the coast in 1863. A Spanish vessel the *Esmeralda* had been captured while fishing, by so called 'Moors of the frontier coast'. The incident according to documents is said to have occurred 180 miles south of Cape Noun. Therefore it could be considered to have occurred within the realms of what is considered the Western Saharan coast. In the incident, the Spanish Minister of

---

[78] *ICJ Reports* 1975:50 para. 111
[79] *Ibid.* para 111
[80] As quoted in the *ICJ Reports* 1975:51 para 112
[81] *Ibid.* para 112

State instructed his Minister in Morocco to approach the Sultan with the necessary request towards the recovery of men and material as governed under Article 38 of the Hispano-Moroccan Treaty. The Sultan was meant, according to the text of the Article quoted above, to 'use his powers to rescue the captive sailors'. The Court's Judgement reveals that in 'due course the sailors were reported to have been freed and to be in the hands of Sheikh Beyrouk of the Noun'.[82]

The controversy between the two parties over this issue stems from a different reading of the situation. The Spanish claimed that the shipwreck was caused by the specific lack of control of the *Sherifian Makhzen* over the *Siba*, and more specifically the tribes residing in and around the Noun region. Spain then read the treaty as giving birth to two separate systems for the protection and return of shipwrecked mariners along the north African coast.[83] The 'general section' as Spain referred to it (i.e. the first part of the article), was valid in areas where the direct authority of the Sultan prevailed. Under this part of the agreement the Sultan would be required to use his normal powers to ensure protection of foreign nationals from harm within his territorial jurisdiction. However, the second part of the article is alleged to refer to a different kind of mechanism, referred to by Spain as the 'special regime' applied exclusively to Wad Noun and further south. Under this mechanism within the treaty, the Sultan was to *try* to liberate the shipwrecked persons, rather than 'order' or 'protect' them.[84] For this purpose he was required to do what he could, and use 'his influence with the peoples neighbouring on his realm and negotiate the ransoming of the sailors, usually with the local authorities'.[85] Spain strongly disputed this 'special regime' as being an exercise of the Sultan's sovereign authority, but considered it rather as the use of his good offices. In addition Spain claimed that diplomatic correspondence suggested that the Minister of Spain in Morocco negotiated the release of the mariners directly. This negotiation is meant to have taken place between the Spanish Consul at Mogador and Sheikh Beyrouk (Sheikh of Wad Noun). Sheikh Beyrouk is alleged to have exerted great influence in these parts that were out of the reach of the Sultan's authority; and the mariners were delivered to him. Towards this end the Spanish also provided diplomatic evidence suggesting that, on one occasion, Sheikh Beyrouk informed the Spanish authority of his resistance to the efforts of the Sultan to gain control of the prisoners, as he preferred to negotiate directly with the Spanish nation. It is indeed questionable however, whether the decision of the Sheikh to negotiate the release of the mariners directly with Spain is a suggestion of a different sovereignty over this part of the north African coast. This is especially problematic in view of the existing scenario where tribes within the *Blad Siba* withheld taxes from *Makhzen* forces in any case; and the financial reward for dealing with the Spanish in this case would have been considerable. Nonetheless it perhaps dents the display of effective sovereignty of the Sultan over Wad Noun.

---

82 *ICJ Reports* 1975: 51 para 113 Sheikh Beyrouk was the sheikh for Wad Noun
83 *ICJ Reports* 1975:52 para 115
84 *Ibid.* para 115
85 *Ibid.* para 115

The Court also questioned the implicit assertion in Moroccan claims that phrases such as 'to the south of Wad Noun' and the 'coasts of Wad Noun', refer to the Western Sahara and claimed that the matter was open to a narrow and broad interpretation. The former, a narrow reading where the events were located in the Wad Noun itself, which was accepted as being part of the *Bled Siba* and thereby as part of the *Sherifian* State but not including the region of Sakiet El-Hamra. The latter, a broader reading, would refer to a wider area covering not just the Wad Noun but also the River Draa and Sakiet El-Hamra which is integral to the Western Sahara region. Spain contested the latter and suggested that from accounts of travellers and explorers there is no evidence of the broader use of the term.[86] Spanish arguments centred around evidence it claimed to have that the Sultan only asserted direct sovereign rule northwards of Agadir. From the south of Agadir onwards to the Noun, Sous and Draa, they allege that the Sultan could only act by negotiation with local powers and his capacity to 'order' in these parts was questionable.[87] This is borne out by the understanding of the Moroccan Vulgate as being split along the lines of the *makhzen-siba* divide. It also needs to be highlighted that the geographic part referred to above falls within the boundaries of modern day Morocco, and the disputed region of the Western Sahara lies further south with the Draa valley forming the frontier between the regions.

The Court ruled that the onus of proving the special meaning of the term and evidence for the broader rather than narrower interpretation of the phrases remained on Morocco – a decision parallel with the judgement in the *Eastern Greenland Case*.[88] It also stated categorically that Morocco had failed to demonstrate this beyond reasonable doubt and that therefore could not be considered to have presented sufficient evidence. Nonetheless it recognised the condition implicit in the treaty, that had Spain not believed the Sultan exerted any influence in the territory at all, it would not have had this special provision in the first place. The Court ruled that 'it is a quite different thing to maintain that those provisions implied international recognition by the other State concerned of the Sultan as territorial sovereign in Western Sahara'.[89]

Another treaty suggested by Morocco which remained controversial in the case was the Anglo-Moroccan Agreement of 13 March 1895 which was cited by Morocco as evidence of British recognition of Moroccan sovereignty as far south as Cape Bojador. The treaty dealt with the purchase by the Sultan of a trading company from the North West African Company at Cape Juby.[90] According to the Court's Judgement, the treaty of 1895 provided *inter alia* that, if the Moroccan Government bought the trading station from the company, 'no one will have any claim to the lands that are between Wad Draa and Cape Bojador, and which are called Terfaya above named, and all the lands behind it, because this belongs to the territory of

---

[86] See Burke in Gellner 1972:177
[87] *ICJ Reports* 1975:52 para 116
[88] *PCIJ Series A/B, No.* 53: 49
[89] *ICJ Reports* 1975:53 para 118
[90] This contract was also negotiated by Sheikh Beyrouk, who seems to demonstrate effective rule over the area immediately south of Wad Noun

Morocco'.[91] A further clause suggests that the Moroccan Government under this contract also undertook not to give away any part of the land 'without the concurrence of the English government'. This treaty is equally controversial in light of differences of opinion between the Spanish reading and the Moroccan reading, and also in the view of the Dissenting Opinion of Judge Ammoun who suggests the existence of a conspiracy between the colonial powers.[92] However one aspect that seems rarely questioned is the legal propriety of the title held by the 'English' government to these lands that would transfer to Morocco on purchase of a trading company. Even taking into account intertemporal law with regard to colonisation, it is highly problematic that one type of customary law is met with scepticism i.e. the presence of the non-territorial based allegiances of *Bilad Shinguitti* and the *Sherifian* State; while customary law applicable to colonial occupation and title to territory seems to be accepted without comment. This is of special concern in a case where regional custom, whilst being negated to a certain extent, might appear best placed as far as an international judicial decision is concerned. With regard to the treaty though, it appears that the Court felt that other documents provided suggested that Britain did not view Cape Juby as being within the jurisdiction of the *Sherifian* State. As a result, the ruling suggested that the treaty demonstrated Britain's acceptance of the interests of the Sultan in the area, rather than his sovereignty over it. This seems a rather contrived reading of the substance of an international treaty that does not seem to have room for contentious interpretation.

Morocco also cited the Treaty of Tetuan of 1860, and an alleged agreement in 1900 communicated via a diplomatic note of October 19, 1900 from the Spanish Ambassador in Brussels to the Belgian Foreign Minister which deals with the issue of Moroccan sovereignty.[93] The Court dismissed these documents on the basis that both Spain and Mauritania doubted the validity and possible existence of any Protocol to the treaty that Morocco based its claims upon. Other documents considered by the Court in its ruling and found to be inconclusive included the exchange of letters between France and Germany (November 4, 1911) which allegedly sought to define the territorial limits of Morocco. These, while clearly stating that Rio de Oro was part of the Spanish colony, did not specify the same for Sakiet El Hamra.[94] Spain countered this by quoting from Article 6 of a Franco-Spanish Convention of October 3 1904, which sets out the geographic limits of Morocco.[95] One would have to question this particular treaty for a number of reasons, not least because it constituted a treaty between two colonial powers over territory that did not belong to either. Also, the critique expressed by Burke with regard to the shaping of western discourse and stereo-typing that took place in the definition and understanding of Morocco by French officials at the turn of the century is worth bearing in mind.[96] It also needs to be questioned whether these officials were competent to understand and define tenets

---

[91] *Ibid.* p.53 para119
[92] See Dissenting Opinion Judge Ammoun *ICJ Reports* 1975:83–101
[93] See paras 121–123
[94] *ICJ Reports* 1975:55 para. 124
[95] *Ibid.* para 125
[96] See Burke in Gellner & Micaud (eds.) 1972:177

of culture that were so different from their own, and then allocate and legalise the territory that they believed merited such separation. In addition, the validity of definition of territory by geographic tools of latitude and longitude, without respect for natural features on the ground, needs to be questioned. Latitude and longitude while being vital tools in navigation, are arguably not ideal guidelines in the definition of territorial allegiance and subsequent identity, especially bearing in mind the complexities of ethnicity and history that have intermingled for centuries within this region. Another important aspect of such treaties was also highlighted by the Court in its judgement (paragraph 126) with regard to the purpose. 'Their [the treaties] purpose, in their different contexts, was rather to recognise or reserve for one or both parties a "sphere of influence" as understood in the practice of that time.' In other words, once a party granted to the other freedom of action in certain defined areas, it effectively promised non-interference in an area claimed by the other party. Such agreements were thus essentially contractual in character which explains why one party might be found acknowledging in 1904, vis-à-vis Spain, that the Sakiet El-Hamra was "outside the limits of Morocco" in order to allow Spain full liberty of action in regard to that area, and yet employing a different geographical description of Morocco in 1911 in order to ensure complete exclusion of Germany from that area'.[97] In light of this, one has to question the validity of the treaties cited here as proof of international boundaries since they would clearly remain open to differing interpretations by some of the parties concerned, as political tools for exerting or preventing the exertion of power within a given region.

Thus, after having examined the documents relating to the external recognition of Moroccan frontiers by the various treaties, the Court concluded that it had insufficient evidence to draw any inference towards those boundaries in question. It therefore ruled that no tie of territorial sovereignty could be suitably established. At the same time however, it admitted that there were indications 'of international recognition at the time of the colonisation of authority or influence of the Sultan, displayed through Tekna caids of the Noun, over some nomads in the Western Sahara'.[98]

This engaging of the second question i.e. the link between the entity and the *Sherifian* Kingdom is an excellent example of the treatment of questions of 'national identity' in international law. The Court seemed to consider that the territory of the Western Sahara, notwithstanding its ruling on the first question, remained a possession. This possession could be proven to belong to somebody, and it is this quest that the Court seemed to have engaged in by addressing the second question put forth at the instigation of Morocco.[99] It has to be borne in mind that the result of the Court's Judgement was highly significant to King Hassan's view that the people of his Kingdom were entitled to 'march peacefully' into the desert and re-claim land that historically belonged to them. This is once more an indication of the nature of the self-determination process. If true emancipation was intended then the options

---

[97] *ICJ Reports* 1975:56 para 126
[98] *ICJ Reports* 1975:57 para 128
[99] See Shaw 1978:141

available have to include all three options suggested by General Assembly Resolution 1541. To merely accept the integration of the territory into the Kingdom of Morocco cannot be considered true self-determination. Nor can the Polisario suggest that only the creation of a separate state would be a valid expression of self-determination since this would once again suggest a pre-judgement of the 'will of the people'. Within this case we already see the problem of being forced to accept the external demarcation of the territory as given. A Utopian expression of self-determination would see the element of territorial demarcation open to negotiation as well. Under the current international regime of self-determination that would however, not be possible. And thus the reality of the colonial legacy is apparent. Nonetheless even accepting this external demarcation as given, we have to question the valid interpretation of 'national' identity. Clearly as stated in General Assembly Resolution 1541, the process of self-determination must culminate in some form or another of the re-enforcement of the state. In this case the options available are: a) integration with Morocco, and b) universal recognition for the separate state of the SADR. The third option i.e. association with another state is at present not a political possibility. It would involve association with either Morocco or Mauritania which would be unacceptable to the parties to the conflict. Thus there is no political will to even consider that aspect of 'self-determination'. Instead the stakes in the Western Sahara are set for a battle in the referendum process, with both parties going for their chosen option, and one side bound to lose out. As far as the process of self-determination is concerned though, this is a *zero-sum* game since in allowing the process to go ahead we are forced to legitimise the boundaries constructed by colonial regimes in ignorance.

CONCLUSION

Franck, in his article draws a neat link between the concept of the 'democratic entitlement' and the American Declaration of Independence.[100] The latter as mentioned above, was the main inspiration for the initial formulation of Wilsonian ideas about self-determination. Criticism of his vision notwithstanding, Wilson understood 'self-determination' as being access to this right of the democratic entitlement.[101] The thrust of this argument is that people need to govern themselves, if government is to be legitimate. The transition of Europe post World War I to a more 'democratic' polity promoting the principle of self-determination was accompanied by a train of ethnographers and anthropologists who sought to define the units that would be allowed the right to self-governance.[102] In sharp contrast no such 'experts' accompanied the process of decolonisation, which as discussed, took place along strictly drawn physical parameters of the colonial state.[103] Thus the norm had already been altered significantly. However if one seeks to isolate the concept of the 'democratic entitlement' as being central to the concept, then it remains

---

[100] Franck 1992:46
[101] Franck 1992:48
[102] Whelan 1994:110
[103] Shaw 1996; also 1997:478

applicable in the Western Sahara even with the caveat that the boundaries will have to be accepted *de facto* and *de jure*. In the Pleadings before the ICJ Mauritania made an interesting argument: they claimed that the tribes and emirates that were 'autonomous', had their own governing structure independent from any central control. The legitimacy for this structure came from within the *Juma'a*. This is similar to the existence of the *Jema'a* within the Western Sahara, set-up albeit by the Spanish in a late attempt to try and revive official institutions of statehood in the territory. The concept of the *Jema'a* seems very similar to that of the *Juma'a* in *Shinguitti* culture and was probably inspired by it. The governing structure of each tribe is chosen by the tribe from within itself, and this act of choice gives the structure its external legitimacy. This was described by Franck as the flavour of 'democratic entitlement' that inspired Wilsonian ideas in the first place.[104] However, international law seems averse to making such comparisons, and instead attempts to measure local institutions by standards that emanate from within western political and legal institutions against which they are constantly found wanting.

In the case before the ICJ, if the largely uncontested evidence about tribal governance structures within the *Bilad Shinguitti* is taken at face value, it would raise interesting questions about the perception of the pre-colonial state. It would be difficult to locate this perception within international law of that time, or within modern international law. Mauritania itself recognised that the independent tribes that comprised *Shinguitti* culture were not in any hierarchical structure. It stated that '... the *Shinguitti* entity could not be assimilated to a State, nor to a federation, nor even to a confederation, unless one saw fit to give that name to the tenuous political ties linking the various tribes'.[105] But it then bows to the assimilatory process of international law by stating that this was not, in itself 'sufficient basis for saying that the *Shinguitti* entity was endowed with international personality, or enjoyed any sovereignty as the word was understood at that time'.[106] This quote whilst showing the extent to which Mauritania understood international legal discourse, also demonstrates the manner in which the rigid role of the discourse strait-jackets expressions of identity that do not fit within its Statist ambit. Clearly, Mauritania feels that the tribes and four emirates were a 'community having its own cohesion' and 'special characteristics' along with customary Saharan law that governed the use of water-holes, grazing lands and the sparse agricultural land available. In addition, it also had mechanisms that regulated inter-tribal hostilities and a process for the settlement of disputes. However explorers and colonialists perceived such a structure as being threatening to order.[107] It clearly was threatening since instead of functioning as one whole that represented all the different parts within the structure of the colonial state governed from Europe, it attempted to re-fragment into different structures and systems, dynamically, rather than statically. Without going into arguments of cultural relativism, it needs to be acknowledged here, that the 'State' at the heart of international legal discourse of self-determination, is located within a

---

[104] Franck 1992:46
[105] See Pleadings, also quoted in *ICJ Reports* 1975:59 para 135
[106] *Ibid.* para 135
[107] See Burke in Gellner & Micaud 1972:179

European context.[108] However this is perhaps not the only entity capable of accommodating national identity and guaranteeing that the consent of the governed makes for legitimate government. In addition, allegiance to the state cannot always be understood in pure territorial terms; nor can the identity emanating from it. The Saharan region was unique in the conditions it presented to people hardy enough to live there. The arid desert life and paucity of water resources dictated a way of life that was different from that of European nations around whom international law, as we know it, developed. To a large extent climatic conditions dictated Saharan (and *Saharawi*) culture and ways of thinking. Life often centred upon the quest for suitable pastures and watering holes; 'and each tribe [had] a well-defined migration area with established migration routes determined by the location of water-holes, burial grounds, cultivated areas and pastures'.[109] These factors rather than territoriality dictated by artificial concepts such as latitude and longitude had a great say in dictating concepts of identity and allegiance. However in the process of colonisation, all these conditions were ignored and the Westphalian State was super-imposed loosely and in arrogance over a region where it seemed ill-suited. In the words of the Court's ruling, in discussing Mauritanian pleadings: 'The colonial Powers... in drawing frontiers took no account of these human factors and in particular of the tribal territories and migration routes which were, as a result, bisected and even trisected by those artificial frontiers. Nevertheless, the tribes, out of necessity, continued to make their traditional migrations, traversing the *Shinguitti* country comprised within the territory...'[110] Further, the facts of nomadic life were recognised by Spain and France at the time, and were even the subject of an administrative agreement between them in 1934.[111] But typically, from an international legal perspective, these agreements while acknowledging the existence of such life and promising not to affect it, nonetheless forced it within the strait-jacket of a boundary regime.

One of the final issues that needs to be addressed briefly is the nature of identity – national or otherwise, in the territory of the Western Sahara. The components of this are difficult to identify since they relate to the existence of a nation. One of the central problems with the discourse of self-determination is that while 'all peoples' have the right to self-determination,[112] this right is only given to a colonially defined people. Outside this process it is very difficult to attribute 'peoplehood' to a group seeking 'national' liberation. UNESCO experts, in drawing up a list of factors that could be considered relevant in the recognition of a 'people' with a right to self-determination came up with an interesting list.[113] To conclude we shall now briefly examine this list against the situation in the Western Sahara in a bid to highlight the complexities of 'national' identity in the region.

---

[108] For interesting reading on cultural overtones in international law see Ali 1997:219
[109] *ICJ Reports* 1975:59–60 para 137
[110] *ICJ Reports* 1975:64 para 152
[111] *ICJ Reports* 1975 para 137
[112] See joint art. 1 International Covenant for Civil & Political Rights (1966) & International Convention for Economic, Social & Cultural Rights (1966)
[113] See Thornberry in Warbrick & Lowe (eds.)1994:175

One of the first criteria suggested was that a 'people' to be classed as such, needed to share a common historical tradition. In the case of this region, this could be seen either as the common tradition of being residents in northwest Africa, i.e. the *Maghreb* identity, or can be narrowed to suggest the *Saharawi* historical tradition of nomadism. The latter claim can be dismissed by Morocco on the basis that Morocco is essentially a mixture of different peoples, all with different historical traditions, dictated by the terrain they reside in. Thus the Berbers of the Atlas Mountains too, have a common historical tradition independent of other Moroccans but that does not suffice for separate statehood.[114] The second factor identified is racial or ethnic identity. There remains confusion over this issue since the entire region is a mixture between Berberic, Arabic and Moorish ethnicity.[115] These have mixed over centuries and it is hard to ethnically identify or separate them in the region. A third factor considered important to a 'shared identity' is cultural homogeneity. Once again the *Saharawi* people could be said to have a distinct cultural homogeneity. Amongst these, is the fact that they have traditionally been referred to in the history of the region as the 'Blue People' owing to the kind of clothing that they traditionally wear; which fades easily in the desert. Once again, this argument is weakened since different peoples within Moroccan borders have independent traditions and cultures without separate statehood. Linguistic unity is a fourth factor suggested as being necessary in a 'people'. This, the Polisario alleges is one of its strongest claims to a separate 'national' identity for the *Saharawis*. They speak a language known as *Hassaniya* that Moroccans cannot understand. This, they put forth, as evidence of difference. While it is difficult to fully examine the merits of this claim, the Moroccan government contends that *Hassaniya* is not a language but a dialect of Arabic. Religious or ideological affinity is another of the criteria. Despite claims emanating from various sources suggesting this as a ground for difference, it has to be stated categorically that the entire region is united in its respect for Islam.[116] Religious practices do vary, but the religion came to the entire region with the Arabs, who have settled down and are very much part of both *Saharawi* as well as Moroccan identities. The sixth criterion suggested by UNESCO, is the presence of a common economic life. This will, naturally, follow cultural traditions. The *Saharawis*, being nomadic have a different economic life from that of other peoples in the region. But that difference arises out of the basic differences between nomadic and settled peoples. Finally, and most importantly, there is the factor of the territorial connection which is examined in great depth above.

Whether these factors are to be considered as definitive remains open to question. The Court stated emphatically that the presence of ties between the territory and the two claimant states did not in itself suggest that the peoples were *subject* to Morocco – merely that connections existed. That particular ruling as discussed above reveals the rigidity of international law. It defines values and parameters it perceives as being important; but usually does so with reference to a specific cultural

---

[114] For ethnicity in Morocco see generally, Gellner 1972; & 1969
[115] See Abun-Nasr 1975
[116] Abun-Nasr1975:74–101

context whilst being ignorant of other traditions that perhaps embrace similar values with alternative approaches. When faced with a scenario that is inherently different to the one perceived as being ideal, it seems to categorise the *Other* in the noble quest of attempting to understand better. However in doing so it also tries to subjugate and conquer the *Other* thereby running the risk of missing the intricacies within. Thus in examining expressions of 'national' identity within post-colonial countries, it is extremely tenuous to resort to strict legal norms that may have been formulated under regimes that do not bear comparison with the case in question. While reliance on the territorial norm may be the most conducive to short-term order, it has longer term implications as can be seen vividly in the on-going crises of separatism that are constantly unwinding within the international community. Coping with this separatism will require re-formulations of aspects of international law; or else it will merely mean that the law follows political processes dictated by the 'national interests' of the players concerned rather than a belief in international order and justice.

SELECT BIBLIOGRAPHY

Abun-Nasr, A. (1975). *History of the Maghrib* 2nd edition, Cambridge: Cambridge University Press

Ali, S.S. (1997). Conceptual Foundations of Human Rights: A Comparative Perspective, *European Public Law* 3:219

Alonso W. (1995). Citizenship, Nationality & Other Identity, *Journal of International Affairs* 48:585

Anderson, B. (1993). *Imagined Communities: Reflections on the Origin and Spread of Nationalism.* Ithaca: Cornell University Press

Baker & Dobbs (eds.) (1925-7). *The Public Papers of Woodrow Wilson* 6 vols. London: Harper

Burke, E. III (1972). The Image of the Moroccan State in French Ethnological Literature, 177-211, in Gellner & Micaud (eds.) *Arabs and Berbers: From Tribe to Nation in North Africa.* London: Duckworth Trinity Press

Brilmeyer, L. (1991). Secession & Self Determination: A Territorial Interpretation, *Yale Journal of International Law* 16:177

Bull, H. (1995). *The Anarchical Society: A Study of Order in World Politics.* New York: Columbia University Press

Cassese, A. (1979). *UN Law Fundamental Rights: Two Topics of International Law.* Leiden: Sijhoff

Cassese, A. (1995). *Self-determination of Peoples: A Legal Reappraisal.* Cambridge, Cambridge University Press

Chopra, J. (1994). *The United Nations Determination of the Western Saharan Self.* Oslo: Norsk Utenrikspolitisk Institut

Cobban, A. (1969). *The Nation State and Self-determination.* London: Collins

Crawford, J. (1979). *The Creation of States in International Law.* Oxford: Clarendon

Cristescu, A. (1981). *The Right of Self-determination: Historical and Current Development on the Basis of the United Nations Instruments.* UN Doc. E/CN.4/ Sub.2/404/ Rev.1

Damis, J. (1983). The Western Sahara Conflict: Myths and Realities, *Middle Eastern Journal* 17:172

Damis, J. (1990). Morocco & the Western Sahara, *Current History* 89:165

Deutsch, K. & Foltz, W. (1963). *Nation-Building.* New York, NY: Atherton Press

Dunn, R. (1972). Berber Imperialism: the Ait Atta Expansion in Southeast Morocco, pp.85-107, in: Gellner & Micaud (eds.) *Arabs and Berbers: From Tribe to Nation in North Africa.* London: Duckworth Trinity Press

[Editorial] (1998). 'The Crisis in Kosovo,' *International Peacekeeping* 41:125

Emerson, R. (1971). Self-determination, *American Journal of International Law* 65:459

Emerson, R. (1960). *From Empire to Nations: The Rise to Self Assertion of Asian and African Peoples.* Cambridge, MA: Harvard University Press

Emerson, R. (1964). *Self-determination Revisited in the Era of Decolonisation.* Cambridge, MA: Harvard University Press

Franck, T. (1990). *The Power of Legitimacy Among Nations.* Oxford: Oxford University

Franck, T. (1992). The Emerging Right to Democratic Governance, *American Journal of International Law* 86:46

Franck, T. (1996). Clan and Super Clan: Loyalty, Identity and Community in Law and Practice, *American Journal of International Law* 90:359

Fukuyama, F. (1992). *The End of History and the Last Man.* NY: Macmillan International

Gaeta, P. (1996). The Armed Conflict in Chechnya before the Russian Constitutional Court, *European Journal of International Law* 7:563

Gamberale, C. (1995). National Identities and Citizenship in the European Union, *European Public Law* 1: 633

Gellner, E. (1969). *Saints of the Atlas.* London: The Trinity Press

Gellner, E. & Micaud, G. (1972). *Arabs and Berbers: From Tribe to Nation in North Africa* London: Duckworth Trinity Press

Gellner, E. (1983). *Nations and Nationalism.* Ithaca: Cornell University Press

Gellner, E. (1994). *Conditions of Liberty: Civil Society and Its Revival.* London: Hamish Hamilton

Gros-Espiell, H. (1980). *The Right to Self-determination: Implementation of the United Nations Resolutions.* UN Doc. E/CN4/Sub.2/405/Rev.1

Grovogui, S. (1996). *Sovereigns, Quasi-Sovereigns and Africans: Race and Self Determination in International Law.* Minneapolis: University of Minnesota Press

Hannum, H. (1980). *Autonomy, Sovereignty and Self-determination: The Accommodation of Conflicting Rights.* Philadelphia: University of Pennsylvania Press

Heraclides, A. (1991). *The Self-determination of Minorities in International Politics.* London: Frank Cass

Higgins, R. (1983). Judge Dillard and Self-determination, *Virginia Journal of International Law* 23:387

Herbst, J. (1989). The Creation and Maintenance of National Boundaries in Africa, *International Organisation* 43:673

Herbst, J. (1992). Challenges to Africa's Boundaries in the New World Order, *Journal of International Affairs* 46:17

Hobsbawm, E.J. (1990). *Nations and Nationalism Since 1780: Programme, Myth, Reality*. Cambridge/New York: Cambridge University Press

Jackson, R. (1990). *Quasi-States: Sovereignty, International Relations and the Third World*. Cambridge: Cambridge University Press

James, A. (1986). *Sovereign Statehood: Basis of International Society*. London: Allen & Unwin

Jennings, I. (1956). *The Approach to Self Governance*. Cambridge: Cambridge University Press

Kaikobad, K.H. (1983). Some Observations on the Doctrine of Continuity and Finality of Boundaries, *British Yearbook of International Law* 49:119

Kirgis, F.L. (1994). The Degrees of Self-determination in the United Nations Era, *American Journal of International Law* 88:304

Kohn, H. (1957). *The Breakdown of Nations*. New York: Rinahart

Lung-Chu, C. (1991). Self Determination and World Public Order, *Notre Dame Law Review* 66:1286

Macartney, A.(ed.) (1987). *Self Determination in the Commonwealth*. Aberdeen: Aberdeen University Press

Mazrui, A. (1975). *Cultural Forces in World Politics*. London: Currey

Motyl, A. (1992). The Modernity of Nationalism: Nations, States and Nation-States in the Contemporary World, *Journal of International Affairs* 45:307

Neuberger, R.B. (1986). *National Self Determination in Postcolonial Africa*. Boulder, Colorado: L. Rienner Publishers

Nanda, V. (1972). Self-determination in International Law: The Tragic Tale of Two Cities, *American Journal of International Law* 66:321

Nayar, K. (1975). Self Determination Beyond the Colonial Context: Biafra in Retrospect, *Texas Journal of International Law* 10:321

Notter, H. (1937). *The Origins of Foreign Policy of Woodrow Wilson*. Baltimore, John Hopkins Press

Picon-Salas, M. (1962). *A Cultural History of Spanish America from Conquest to Independence*. Berkeley, California University Press

Post, M. (1968). Is there a Case for Biafra? *International Affairs* 44:181

Ratner, S. (1996). Drawing a Better Line: Uti Possidetis and the Borders of New States, *American Journal of International Law* 90:590

Rézette, R. (1975). *The Western Sahara and the Frontiers of Morocco*. Nouvelles Editions Latines, Paris

Rosenstock, S. (1967). The Declaration of Principles of International Law Concerning Friendly Relations: A Survey, *American Journal of International Law* 61:713

Saxena, J.N. (1978). *Self Determination: From Biafra to Bangladesh*. Delhi: University of Delhi

Seddon, D. (1972). Local Politics and State Intervention: Northeast Morocco from 1870 to 1970, pp. 211-259, in Gellner & Micaud (eds.) *Arabs and Berbers: From Tribe to Nation in North Africa*. London: Duckworth Trinity Press

Shaw, M. (1978). The Western Sahara Case, *British Yearbook of International Law* 49:119

Shaw, M. (1996). The Heritage of States: The Principle of *Uti Possidetis Juris* Today, *British Yearbook of International Law* 67:75

Shaw, M (1997). People, Territorialism and Boundaries, *European Journal of International Law* 8:478

Sisson, R. & Rose, L. (1990). *War and Secession: Pakistan, India, and the Creation of Bangladesh.* Berkeley: University of California

Sureda, R. (1973). *The Evolution of the Right to Self Determination: A Study of the United Nations Practice.* Leiden: Sijhoff

Thornberry, P. (1989). Self Determination, Minorities, Human Rights: A Review of International Instruments, *International and Comparative Law Quarterly* 38:867

Tomuschat, C. (ed.) (1993). *Modern Law of Self determination.* Dordecht: Martinus Nijhoff

Warbrick, C. and Lowe, V. (eds.) (1994). *The United Nations and the Principles of International Law: Essays in Memory of Professor Michael Akehurst.* London/ New York: Routledge 175

Whelan, A. (1994). Wilsonian Self Determination and the Versailles Settlement, *International and Comparative Law Quarterly* 43:100

White, R. (1981). Self Determination: Time for Re-assessment? *Netherlands Journal of International Law* 28:147

Concluding Remarks

Javaid Rehman*

At the beginning of a new millennium, the issue of accommodating national identity within the existing constitutional structures presents a serious global challenge.[1] Crises of national identity are to the fore in many contemporary disputes, and in a number of instances attempts to assert or reinforce ideals of national identity have not only resulted in the breakdown of constitutional order but have also led to serious violations of individual and collective rights. There are tragic cases such as that of Rwanda, Bosnia-Herzegovina, and more immediately that of Kosovo and Chechnya, where the question of identity has been resolved through genocide, or ethnic cleansing of the minority groups. In many other instances, although the existent state structures have been preserved, the issue of national identity nevertheless continues to dictate political and constitutional developments.

The proliferation of the conflicts surrounding national identity and the difficulties in installing effective mechanisms for dispute resolution has highlighted the necessity for reconsideration of existing practices and procedures. The present volume provides a useful analysis of a number of conflicts and is helpful in identifying and articulating new approaches for accommodating competing conceptions of national identity within international and domestic laws. The papers in this book address a range of situations – cases as diverse as that of Bosnia-Herzegovina, Kosovo and the former Yugoslavia, the splintered ethnic communities of Nepal and the indigenous peoples of the Russian Federation and the Western Sahara. A consideration of these cases also highlight the varying demands that are put forward by the minorities in question: secession; devolution; religious or cultural autonomy; equality and non-discrimination are all claims which are used as instruments to augment minority aspirations of national identity.

Notwithstanding the wide diversity and heterogeneity of the cases that are analysed by a set of lawyers with their respective specialisations in domestic constitutional law or general international law, the jurisprudence emergent from an integrated study of the papers is revealing in many respects. While an examination of each of the

---

*   Dr Javaid Rehman, Lecturer in Human Rights and Public Law, University of Leeds, UK.
[1]   For recent surveys, see Minority Rights Group (eds.) (1997). *World Directory of Minorities* (London: Minority Rights Group); Boyle, K. and Sheen, J. (eds.) (1997), *Freedom of Religion and Belief: A World Report* (London: Routledge); Gurr, T. (1993). *Minorities at Risk: A Global View of Ethnopolitical* Conflicts (Washington D.C.: United States Institute of Peace Press); Rehman, J. (2000). *The Weaknesses in the International Protection of Minority Rights* (The Hague: Kluwer Law International).

Stephen Tierney (ed.), Accommodating National Identity: New Approaches in International and Domestic Law, 285–293
© 2000 *Kluwer Law International. Printed in Great Britain.*
First published in the International Journal on Minority and Group Rights, Volume 6 No. 1/2 1999.
This article has been revised for this publication.

papers provides a valuable insight into the complexities inherent in the accommodation of competing national identities within the individual context of a particular dispute, the study as a whole represents the emergence of a number of common underlying values and themes, which will be addressed in turn.

1. INTER-ACTION AND INTER-DEPENDENCE OF DOMESTIC AND INTERNATIONAL LAW

Traditionally international law and domestic law have been treated as distinct, having only an indirect relationship to one another.[2] A significant theme, however, which has emerged from the present volume is the recognition given to the close interaction and interdependence of domestic and international law. An examination of these case studies reinforces the point that the operational framework, and the successes or failures of international human rights law, have to be assessed through the developments at the national level. Thus the perplexing conceptual debate on issues such as the right to self-determination or minority rights in international law is meaningful and of practical significance only when analysed in the domestic constitutional context of a substantive dispute. Conversely, constitutional arrangements with regard to the nature of federalism; devolution; autonomy; secession; incorporation of a bill of rights; the guaranteeing of equality and non-discrimination, are liable to impact upon developments in the sphere of international law. While successful secessionist movements, as in the case of Bosnia or Croatia, led to the creation of new states with independent rights and duties under international law, the establishment of genuine regimes based upon federalism, regional autonomy or devolution may obviate the need for reliance on concepts such as humanitarian intervention to protect the Kurds in Northern-Iraqi 'safe-havens', the Chechen Muslims or the Kosovan-Albanians.[3]

Domestic constitutional arrangements can substantially influence international law – a situation reflected through treaty-based agreements between various Republics of the Russian Federation. Thus the *de jure* prerogatives of the Republics of the Russian Federation include the capacity to conclude treaties and to enter into international relations independent of the Federal government. The emergence of the Russian Federation and the proliferation of treaty-based relationships between the Federation and the Republics has introduced a unique and spectacular element of constitutionalism – a phenomenon representing the unusual intermarriage of constitutional and international law also referred to as 'asymmetrical federalism'.[4] These treaties in adopting a radical approach 'do not even pretend to conform to the norm of the Russian or any other constitutions'.[5] Thus for instance the 1994 treaty

---

[2] For further consideration of this issue see Shaw, M.N. (1997). International Law, (Cambridge: Grotius) 4th edn., 99 – 136; Akehurst, M. (1987). *A Modern Introduction to International Law*, (London: George Allen and Unwin) 6th edn., 43 – 52.

[3] For a succinct analysis of the issues surrounding the legality of humanitarian intervention post-1945 see S. Tierney's chapter 'The Road Back to Hell: The International Response to the Crisis in Kosovo'.

[4] See Bowring, B. 'Ancient Peoples and New Nations in the Russian Federation: Questions of Theory and Practice'.

[5] *Ibid.*

between Russia and Tatarstan in failing to recognise the superiority of federal laws over those of the Republic 'has created a dangerous precedent of exceeding the region's authority above the limits set by the federal constitution, arbitrarily redistributing authority and jurisdiction without regard for consistency with the federal constitution, and delegating certain concessions and benefits to a region which are denied to others'.[6]

Notwithstanding a constitutional recognition of an autonomous status for the Republics under the 1993 Constitution (as the case of Chechnya affirms) in reality the Federation remains a conglomeration of artificial entities that may suffer from further disintegration. There are other examples, however, where the international trends of autonomy and regionalism have actively been incorporated into constitutional frameworks to produce positive results. Protagonists engaged in conflicts surrounding 'national identity' might consider the federalist and autonomist approaches adopted by the Belgian,[7] Spanish,[8] and Italian[9] constitutional arrangements. Many conflicts of 'national identity' have roots in allegations of discrimination and denial of the right to equality. These allegations of discrimination and of inequality represent the core claims of most minority groups including the Irish Catholics, the Scots, and the French Quebecois. Indeed in a number of instances, the manifestations of discrimination take extreme forms; the Bengalis of the former East Pakistan suffered from campaigns of physical extermination and genocide[10] and the Baluchis and Sindhis are having to endure a similar fate in the truncated Pakistan.[11]

Amongst the cases analysed in the present book, several examples can be found which underpin and highlight the close interdependence of domestic and international

---

[6]   Lysenko, V. N. (1996). Distribution of Power: The Experience of the Russian Federation, in *Preventing Deadly Conflict. Strategies and Institutions. Proceedings of a Conference in Moscow*. Carnegie Corporation, at http://www.ccpdc.org/pubs/mosvcow/moscow6.htm, p.3. Cited *ibid*.

[7]   As the constitutional reforms of 1993 have confirmed, Belgium is now a federal state made up of three communities and having four linguistic regions. While cultural and communal matters are within the purview of local community councils, territorial autonomy is established through regional institutions. See the Constitution of Belgium (1993); Fitzmaurice, J. (1996). *The Politics of Belgium: A Unique Federalism* (London: Hurst).

[8]   Article 2 of the Spanish Constitution (1978) recognises and guarantees 'the right to autonomy of the nationalities which make up the Spanish State'. The Law on Regional Autonomy has granted regional governments jurisdiction over a wide range of issues. See Hoffman, R. (1986). 'The New Territorial Structures of Spain: The Autonomous Communities' 55 *Nordic Journal of International Law* 136–141; Hannum, H. (1990). *Autonomy, Sovereignty and Self-Determination: The Accommodation of Conflicting Rights* (Philadelphia: University of Pennsylvania), 263–279.

[9]   See Title V (Articles 114 – 113) of the Constitution of Italy (1948) as amended; see also Alcock, A. (1994): 14–20, "South Tyrol" in Miall, H. (ed.), Minority Rights in Europe: The Scope for a Transnational Regime (London: Pinter).

[10] See International Commission of Jurists, *The Events of East Pakistan 1971* (Geneva) 1972; Mascarenhas, A. *The Rape of Bangladesh,* (Dehli: Vikas Publications) 1971; Salzberg, J. (1973). 'UN Prevention of Human Rights Violations: The Bangladesh Case', 27 *International Organisation*, 115.

[11] Harrison, S. S. (1981). *In Afghanistan's Shadow: Baluch Nationalism and Soviet Temptations* (New York: Carnegie Endowment for International Peace); Baloch, I. (1983). 'The Baluch Question in Pakistan and the Right to Self-Determination' in Zingel, W.-P. et al (eds.), Pakistan in its Fourth Decade (Deutshes Orient-Institut), 188–209; Kennedy, C. H. (1990). 'The Politics of Ethnicity in Sindh' 31 *Asian Survey* (1991) 938; Salim, A. (1990). *Sulagata Howa Sind* (Lahore: Jang Publishers).

law. These include the former Yugoslavia, Northern Ireland and Canada, although perhaps the most striking and illustrative case is that of Western Sahara.[12] Western Sahara is a problematic case and one whose resolution appears difficult.[13] Despite the World Court's emphatic assertion of the existence of the international legal right of self-determination for the people of Western Sahara, it has not been possible thus far to find an appropriate constitutional framework for the application of this right. Whilst all those concerned with the future of Western Sahara agree on the fundamental principle that 'it is for the people [of Western Sahara] to determine the destiny of the territory...'[14] there are substantial disagreements as to identification of the people entitled to participate in a national referendum.[15]

The former Yugoslavia and Northern Ireland are examples of highly volatile conflicts which have readily engaged trans-national actors.[16] The failings in the constitution of the former Yugoslavia to accommodate the competing national identities generated a crisis for international law. The vitality of the organs of the United Nations and regional agencies was tested and strained. More importantly there was the arduous and difficult demand for legitimising secession as a rightful expression of the right to self-determination. In the post-colonial context self-determination is a difficult right to concede especially if a realisation of this right means the fragmentation of existing states. Self-determination is a right that belongs to peoples.[17] While the meaning of the term 'peoples' has remained a matter of controversy, it is clear that minorities or indigenous peoples *per se* cannot be identified as 'peoples' having a right to self-determination.

In the case of the former Yugoslavia, international law reluctantly acknowledged this secessionist expression of self-determination although its application was contradictory and inconsistent. While statehood in the name of self-determination was deemed as rightful and legitimate for Slovenia, Croatia, Bosnia and Macedonia, the same was denied to Kosovo.[18] This failure to resolve the status of Kosovo at the time of the dissolution of the Yugoslavia was to have serious consequences; the increasing repression by the Serbs, matched by the Kosovo-Albanians' determination to gain complete independence led to considerable human suffering and mass displacement of people. The use of military force by NATO allies has not alleviated the suffering of the people of Kosovo. At the same time, the exact constitutional position of Kosovo remains in a limbo.

---

[12] See Castellino, J. National Identity and the International Law of Self-Determination: the Stratification of the Western Saharan 'Self'.

[13] Ibid; see also Shaw, M. N. (1978). 'The Western Sahara Case' *British Year Book of International Law* 49:119; Franck, T. M. (1976). 'The Stealing of the Sahara' *American Journal of International Law* 70: 694.

[14] ICJ Reports 1975, 122; see also Higgins, R. (1983). 'Judge Dillard and Self-Determination' *Virginia Journal of International Law* 23: 387.

[15] Harris, D. (1998). *Cases and Materials on International Law* (London: Sweet and Maxwell) 5th edn., 119.

[16] See D. McGoldrick's chapter and Tierney, S. (1999). "In a State of Flux: Self-Determination and the Collapse of Yugoslavia" *International Journal on Minority and Group Rights* 6: 197.

[17] Thornberry, P. (1991). *Minorities and Human Rights Law* (London: Minority Rights Group) 10; R Higgins 1991. 'General Course on Public International Law', *Recueil des Cours de l'Academie de Droit International,* 170.

[18] See S Tierney's paper supra footnote 3.

The specific dynamics of the Northern Irish conflict, with its two communities portraying identities whose locus is based outside the territory, necessarily involves elements of international law; the Protestant majority owing an allegiance to London and wishing to remain part of the United Kingdom as against the minority Catholics who remain committed to a united Ireland. International law is operative through the Anglo-Irish Agreement (1985), the Downing Street Declaration (1993) and the Multi-Party Peace Agreement (1998). These functions however need to function in conjunction and in harmony with constitutional practices that would guarantee *de facto* equality and non-discrimination and greater recognition of identities and traditions of the peoples of Northern Ireland.

In all the situations alluded to thus far it is significant to note that in the attempts to restore viable constitutional frameworks (where competing national identities could be accommodated) there has been considerable involvement from international organisations and institutions, the revised constitutional arrangements in each instance ensuring a continuous engagement of mechanisms of international law.[19] Thus in the case of Western Sahara, there has been the noticeable influence of the General Assembly, the Security Council and the Organisation of African Unity. Similarly the conflicts emerging from the former Yugoslavia and Northern Ireland have invoked the involvement of international as well as regional agencies.

The Canadian situation, as Oliver in his paper elaborates, has been less volatile in comparison to the former Yugoslavia, Northern Ireland or Western Sahara. Certainly, there have been attempts to install mechanisms for ensuring self-determination through constitutional and legislative mechanisms. However, in the highly significant case of *Reference re Secession of Quebec*, the Canadian Supreme Court was faced squarely with the issue of the constitutional application of the right of self-determination. The Court's refusal to recognise the Quebecois as a 'people' under international law is understandable, as is its determination not to authorise the government of Quebec to effect secession unilaterally. The Court nevertheless had to adopt a methodology of tact and diplomacy and in coming to its judgement mixes considerations of international law with vital constitutional principles such as federalism, rule of law and democracy.[20]

In some of the other situations examined in this volume the interaction between the constitutional position of ethnic minorities and international laws may appear to be less direct but there are specific reasons for this. In a number of instances, as in the cases of Quebec, Scotland and Wales, the conflict of identity has not (at least at the present time) fractured the existing constitutional order. In these instances involvement of international law and international actors has remained curtailed, operating largely behind domestic constitutional actors. In other cases, the ostensible lack of involvement has been a product of authoritarian regimes relying upon the 'state sovereignty principle' in their efforts to deny minorities and indigenous peoples

---

[19] See Thompson, B. "Transcending Territory: Towards an Agreed Northern Ireland" and papers by Professor McGoldrick supra footnote 16 and Stephen Tierney, supra footnote 16.
[20] See Oliver, P. Canada's Two Solicitudes: Constitutional and International Law in Reference re *Secession of Quebec*. For a detailed study of the case see Bayefsky, A.N. (2000). *Self-Determination in International Law: Quebec and Lessons Learned* (The Hague: Kluwer Law International).

fundamental rights guaranteed under international law.[21] The Pakhtuns and Baluchis of Pakistan, the ethnically diverse communities of Nepal and the Roma of Central and Eastern Europe present a few such examples. The ending of the Cold War which revitalised the interest of international law in minorities also contains a hint of promise for many of the groups which have historically suffered from discrimination and deprivation within their domestic constitutional frameworks.[22]

In Pakistan's practices, there is a tradition of discrimination and persecution of ethnic minorities and indigenous peoples. The official constitutional position is that there are no ethnic or linguistic minorities within Pakistan. While incredible, and practically untenable, such a view has been persistently maintained ever since the establishment of the state in August 1947.[23] The Bengalis of East-Pakistan were subjected to discrimination and persecution prior to their successful secessionist campaign in 1971. The case of the Federally Administered Tribal Areas confirms that the approach towards the Pakhtun and Baluchi communities is based as much on an attitude of apathy and disregard as it is on active policies of discrimination. Similar policies of neglect and indifference are evident from a consideration of the plight of the ethnic and linguistic communities of the Kingdom of Nepal.

It can be hypothesised that the commitments of positive discrimination at the international level through ratification of the International Convention on Elimination of All forms of Racial Discrimination would prove instrumental in instigating complementary constitutional practices within Pakistan and Nepal.[24] The Kingdom of Nepal is also a party to the International Covenant on Civil and Political Rights, whilst Pakistan is not.[25] The Roma of Central and Eastern Europe remain a disadvantaged group, economically, socially and politically; the transition – from communism to constitutions representing democracy and civil and political rights – appears not to have accorded adequate consideration to their situation. The extent to which international initiatives (through the work of such agencies as the Organisation on Security and Co-operation in Europe (OSCE) and the Council of Europe) could bring about a change in the position of the Roma remains to be seen.

---

[21] Heavy reliance has been placed upon the domestic jurisdiction clause of the United Nations Charter. Article 2(7) of the Charter provides: 'Nothing contained in the present charter shall authorise the United Nations to intervene in matters which are essentially within the domestic jurisdiction of any State or shall require the members to submit such matters to settlement under the present Charter'. United Nations Charter (1945) UNTS XVI; UKTS 67 (1946); Cmnd 7015.

[22] See Ali, S. 'The Rights of Ethnic Minorities in Pakistan: A Legal Analysis'; Subedi, S.P. 'Constitutional Accommodation of Ethnicity and National Identity in Nepal' and Pogany, I. 'Accommodating an Emergent National Identity: the Roma of Central and Eastern Europe'.

[23] For substantiation on Pakistan's position see the proceedings of Committee on Elimination of All forms of Racial Discrimination which operates under the auspices of the *Convention on the Elimination of All forms of Racial Discrimination* (1965) Pakistan fourth periodic report before the Committee (CERD/C /SR.322 para 3); Pakistan's fifth periodic report (CERD/C/20.Add.15 para 1); Pakistan's fourteenth consolidated report (CERD/C/299/Add.6 para 12); see also Rehman, *supra* footnote 1, 136–140.

[24] See 60 UNTS 195; 77 UKTS (1969); Cmnd 4108; Pakistan ratified the Convention on 21 September 1966. Nepal acceded to the Convention on 30 January 1971.

[25] 999 UNTS 171; UKTS 6 (1977); Cmnd 6702; Nepal acceded to the *International Covenant Civil and Political Rights* on 14 May, 1991. It is also a party to the first Optional Protocol to the Covenant.

2. PRAGMATIC APPROACHES TO ANALYSING CONFLICT AND PRESENTING POSSIBLE SOLUTIONS

There is undoubtedly great value in analysing conflicts of identity through an approach that integrates and combines international law with domestic laws. The advocacy of this coherent and logical approach, however, does not mean a negation of the peculiarities and distinctiveness inherent in each of the situations. As the papers contained in the present volume confirm, every case-study presents a distinct scenario, and being different and detached from the rest, must be examined in the light of its own peculiar socio-political, regional and historical circumstances. It is in fact the case that a wide variety of historical, economic, cultural, sociological and political factors have an important bearing not only on the form and nature of claims that are made by the groups in question but also on the reaction to these demands on the part of the states concerned.[26] The differing visions of identity are matched by a variance in the demands that are put forward: the ethnic Pakhtuns, Baluchis or Sindhis view their identity claims as being determined through federalism and autonomy; in the case of the Scots (or the Welsh) devolution claims may act as an intermediary step towards federalism or even independence.[27] Conflicting positions on the issue of national identity led to the breakdown of Yugoslavia and the failed attempts to install a regime of autonomy for Kosovo beckons the further disintegration of Serbia. Claims put forward by Nepal's diverse ethnic communities, and the Roma population of Central and Eastern Europe are largely emblematic of demands for non-discrimination and *de facto* equality. A study of this book also reveals that conflicts of identity cannot be so easily dissociated from their historical impressions. The modern political geography is a product of historical cycles of colonisation and decolonisation in which many of the weaker nations and communities were wiped out or subdued.[28] Every situation, with its distinct historical background therefore presents a unique scenario; for a successful resolution of any contemporary dispute, its historical origins deserve a comprehensive analysis and understanding.

A pragmatic vision that emerges from a study of this book is that while there is no single set of answers to all the problems and afflictions that are generated through conflicts of national identity, in order to advocate practical mechanisms for conflict resolution existing limitations must not be overlooked. While legal norms and values can have an important bearing, it needs to be appreciated that the relevance of law in conflicts of identity can only be limited. As Professor McGoldrick notes '[m]any lawyers tend to the view that problems can ultimately be resolved by legal solutions. It is undoubtedly true that law and lawyers can have a major role to play. It must be

---

[26] For further elucidation of the point see Hannum supra footnote 8; Rehman, J. (1999). 'The Concept of Autonomy and Minority Rights in Europe' in Cumper, P. and Wheatley, S. (eds.). *Minority Rights in the 'New' Europe* (Hague: Kluwer Law International), 217 – 231.

[27] See also the paper by Professor Munro, "Scottish Devolution: Accommodating a Restless Nation".

[28] See Kuper, L. (1981). *Genocide: Its Political Use in the Twentieth Century* (New Haven and London: Yale University Press); Potter, J. (ed.) (1982). *Genocide and Human Rights: A Global Anthology* (London: University Press of America); Kuper, L. (1985). *The Prevention of Genocide* (New Haven: Yale University Press); Kuper, L. (1982). *International Action Against Genocide* (London: Minority Rights Group).

stressed though that accommodating national identity is often concerned with the most powerful and destructive of social and political factors, rather than with legal ones'.[29] Although Professor McGoldrick's comments are made in the context of the former Yugoslavia, they could authoritatively be applied to the situations in Western Sahara, former USSR and Yugoslavia, Northern Ireland, Canada, Scotland, Nepal and Pakistan.

3. CONCEPTUALISING NATIONAL IDENTITY

One of the crucial themes which emerges from a consideration of the papers in the book relates to the conceptualisation and elucidation of the terms 'nation' or 'national' and 'identity'. The concepts of 'nation', 'nationality' or 'nationhood' have been used in a variety of contexts, often producing conflicting and confusing interpretations. In common with terminologies such as 'minorities', 'peoples' and 'self-determination', these are elusive concepts and legal jurisprudence has been unable to provide a definitive meaning for these phrases. Conceptualisation of national identity, however, cannot be relegated as a preoccupation of the theorists; serious practical consequences ensue from the ways in which ethnic groups, minorities or indigenous peoples perceive notions of nationhood and identity. The lessons to be learnt from the present volume point towards a pragmatic approach in conceptualising values of identity and nationhood. It is difficult to surmise that 'national identity' is a representation of concepts that are absolute and definitive in nature. While the bonding of a 'nation', much like the bonding of a 'people' or a 'minority' could be consequent upon a range of factors—a common language, religion, culture, tradition, ethnic or racial origin, perceptions of identity are based on similar inter-dependent features. As the case of Western Sahara confirms, amidst competing values and claims it can often be impossible to identify a 'nation' having a sole or conclusive identity. Thus, it has so far proved impossible to ascertain the precise identity of the population of Western Sahara. Equally, as the case of the former Yugoslavia and USSR suggests the concept of a nation can be a misnomer; a difficult and dangerous concept that fails to reflect the complex taxonomies of modern state structures.

The existence of a common identity does not necessarily mean the existence of a nation. There are instances where notwithstanding perceptions of a common identity and a common destiny a nation is yet to be formed; the case of the Roma of Central and Eastern Europe provides one such example.[30] In other instances, perceptions of 'national identity' vary depending upon the issue in question or on the composition of the opposing party to the conflict. Thus, the Pakhtuns and the Baluchis have an 'ethnic' identity in their conflict with the State of Pakistan which is dominated by ethnic Punjabis. However the Pakhtuns and Baluchis also portray a 'religious' (Muslim) national identity in the dispute with the Hindu dominated India, and a 'sectarian' *Sunni* identity in the rifts with a *Shia* communities of Iran and Afghanistan.

---

[29] McGoldrick, supra footnote 16.
[30] See the chapter by Professor Pogany.

Similarly, the diversified groups of Nepal while differing in their languages, and ethnic background may be able to form a national identity based around the Hindu religion. In Northern Ireland, in the case of a conflict of 'identities' which one would take precedence – an identity based on political affiliations (Unionist or Republican), or one based on religion (Protestant or Catholic)? Do the Scots or the Welsh necessarily identify themselves with a homogenous Scottish or Welsh national identity, or are there elements of the broader British identity or even a greater overarching European identity? There may be instances when members of one 'nation' have differing and conflicting views over that 'nation's' identity and its future. Thus divergent views about the identity of Quebec and the future of the Quebecois are represented by two francophone leaders, Pierre Trudeau and Réne Lévesque. A theoretical construct of national identity and nationhood, although of significance, nevertheless remains a hazardous task. Whilst scholars such as Tishkov have made attempts to discern theories of national identity and nationalism, they remain wary to such an extent that for them, in the words of Bill Bowring, the term '"nation" does not constitute a scientific category, and ought to be expelled from the discourse of science and politics'.[31] In interpreting Tishkov's sentiment, Bowring notes, 'either all ethnic communities should call themselves nations, if this continues to have any significance whatever in the world of contemporary politics – or none of them should. If none of them do, then politicians and scholars should stop using the term too, and their theory and practice would not suffer . . . Tishkov argues, the abolition of this category would help in the understanding of the nature of human coalitions, their cultural differences and political configurations. Tishkov's slogan is: forget about Nations, in the name of peoples, states and cultures, even if future scholars cast doubt on these last definitions as well.'[32]

Conceptualising 'national identity' is as problematic as making practical recommendations for conflict resolution. While the essays in this book have confirmed that no straight-forward answers can be provided, the contributors have done well to consider and analyse some of the most complex situations in which these issues are made manifest. The ideas and propositions that are advanced also reflect maturity and innovation. At the present time it would be premature to proclaim an impending demise of the state structures upon which both international law and domestic constitutional laws are based. Having said that, it can be predicted with certainty that issues of accommodation of national identity are likely to confront national and international law with increasing vigour. The substantive analysis conducted in this volume and the proposals which emerge from it should be beneficial to constitutional and international lawyers, and should also prove immensely helpful to policy makers, politicians scientists and more generally to thoughtful readers.

---

[31] Bowring, supra footnote 4.
[32] *Ibid.,* Italics provided.

Index